Education
and
Society
in the
New Russia

Education and Society in the New Russia

EDITED BY ANTHONY JONES

M. E. Sharpe

Armonk, New York ▪ London, England

146214

Library of Congress Cataloging-in-Publication Data

Education and society in the new Russia / edited by
Anthony Jones.
p.   cm.
Includes index.
ISBN 1-56324-209-5 (cloth).   ISBN 1-56324-210-9 (pbk.)
1. Education—Russia (Federation)
2. Russia (Federation)—Social conditions.
3. Russia (Federation)—Intellectual life.
I. Jones, Anthony, 1940–
LA839.2.E38   1994
370'.947—dc20
CIP

Printed in the United States of America

The paper used in this publication meets the minimum requirements of
American National Standard for Information Sciences—
Permanence of Paper for Printed Library Materials,
ANSI Z 39.48-1984.

∞

BM (c)   10   9   8   7   6   5   4   3   2   1
BM (p)   10   9   8   7   6   5   4   3   2   1

For Tamara,
who teaches me so much.

Contents

About the Editor and Contributors

ANTHONY JONES is Associate Professor and Chair of Sociology at Northeastern University and a Fellow of the Russian Research Center at Harvard University. His recent publications include *In Search of Pluralism*, edited with Carol Saivetz (Westview Press, 1994); *Ko-ops: The Rebirth of Entrepreneurship in the Soviet Union*, with William Moskoff (Indiana University Press, 1991); editor, *Professions and the State: Expertise and Autonomy in the Soviet Union and Eastern Europe* (Temple University Press, 1991); and *Soviet Social Problems*, edited with Walter Connor and David Powell (Westview Press, 1991). He is the editor of the journal *Russian Education and Society*.

DEBORAH ADELMAN is Assistant Professor of Communications at the College of DuPage. Her first visit to the Soviet Union was in 1978; she has returned frequently since then and has lived in Moscow for two years. She is the author of *The "Children of Perestroika": Moscow Teenagers Talk About Their Lives and the Future* (M.E. Sharpe, 1991), based on interviews conducted with Russian young people while she was a member of the State University of New York/Moscow State University faculty exchange program. On a return visit to Moscow in the summer of 1992, she completed follow-up interviews with the same group—now young adults—which are presented in *The "Children of Perestroika" Come of Age: Young People of Moscow Talk About Life in the New Russia* (M.E. Sharpe, 1994).

LYNNE ATTWOOD received her doctorate in Soviet Studies and Sociology from the Center for Russian and East European Studies, University of Birmingham, England. She is the author of *The New Soviet Man and Woman: Sex Role Socialization in the USSR* and has contributed to a number of other books on Russia and the Soviet Union. She has taught Russian Studies at the University of Texas at Austin and the University of Humberside (England). She is currently Lecturer in Russian Studies in the Department of Russian Studies, University of Manchester.

HARLEY D. BALZER is Associate Professor of Government and Director of the Russian Area Studies Program at Georgetown University. He received his Ph.D. in History from the University of Pennsylvania and has taught at Grinnell College and Boston University. His research interests include Russian and Soviet social history, science and technology, and politics. His most recent publications include *Soviet Science on the Edge of Reform* (Westview Press, 1989) and an edited volume on perestroika, *Five Years That Shook the World* (Westview Press, 1991; revised edition, 1992), which was selected by *Choice* as an outstanding book for 1992.

JULIE V. BROWN is Associate Professor of Sociology at the University of North Carolina at Greensboro. She is the author of a number of articles on health care, responses to mental disabilities, and the medical profession in Russia and the Soviet Union.

NICHOLAS DANILOFF is Director of the School of Journalism at Northeastern University and a fellow of the Russian Research Center at Harvard University. He is the author of *Two Lives, One Russia* and *The Kremlin and the Cosmos* and is a former Moscow correspondent for *U.S. News and World Report*.

JOHN DUNSTAN is Senior Lecturer in Education at the Center for Russian and East European Studies, University of Birmingham, England. He was formerly the Center's Deputy Director. His publications include *Paths to Excellence and the Soviet School* (1978), *V.N. Soroka-Rosinsky, Soviet Teacher, in Fact and Fiction* (1991), and the edited volumes *Soviet Education Under Scrutiny* (1987) and *Soviet Education Under Perestroika* (1992), and many contributions to books and journals.

WILLIAM B. HUSBAND is Associate Professor of History at Oregon State University. He is the author of *Revolution in the Factory: The Birth of the Soviet Textile Industry, 1917–1920* (Oxford, 1990). His articles have appeared in *Slavic Review, Russian Review, World Politics, The Carl Beck Papers*, and elsewhere. He is currently writing a social history of atheism in the former Soviet Union.

MIKHAIL IVANOV is a professor at the Ioffe Institute, Academy of Sciences, St. Petersburg, and chairman of Ioffe Physical Technical High School.

STEPHEN T. KERR is Professor of Education in the College of Education at the University of Washington. He has written on change in Russian educational institutions under conditions of rapid secondary and higher education, on changes in teacher education, and on the use of technology and computers in Soviet and Russian education, and he has guest-edited an issue of *Russian Education and Society* devoted to "The Alternative Educational Press" (vol. 36, no. 1 [January 1994]).

IGOR V. KITAEV is a program specialist at the International Institute for Educational Planning, Paris.

LEV LURIE is a professor at the St. Petersburg Institute of History and dean of Instruction and Faculty at St. Petersburg Classical Gymnasium.

SHEILA M. PUFFER is Assistant Professor at the College of Business Administration, Northeastern University and a fellow at the Russian Research Center, Harvard University. She is a graduate of the Plekhanov Institute of the National Economy in Moscow and received her Ph.D. in business administration from the University of California, Berkeley. Her research, teaching, and consulting are in the areas of human resources and international business, with a focus on the Russian Republic. She has co-authored the book *Behind the Factory Walls: Decision Making in Soviet and U.S. Enterprises* (Harvard Business School Press, 1990) and edited *Managerial Insights from Literature* (PWS-KENT) and *The Russian Management Revolution: Preparing Managers for the Market Economy* (M.E. Sharpe, 1992).

NINA L. RUSINOVA is Senior Researcher at the Institute of Sociology (St. Petersburg Branch) of the Russian Academy of Sciences. She has written numerous articles on social aspects of health care, health policy, and health reform in Russia and the USSR.

JANET G. VAILLANT is Associate Director of Harvard University's Resource Center for Russian, East European, and Central Asian Studies. She was co-director in a two-year study with American and Russian educators involving history and social sciences education and, with John Richards, has authored *From Russia to USSR and Beyond* (1993, reprint).

STEPHEN WEBBER is a Ph.D. candidate at the University of Exeter, England, from which he also received his B.A. in Russian and French languages. He is currently conducting research on reforms of the Russian school system since 1994.

TATIANA WEBBER is a graduate of the Yaroslavl State Pedagogical Institute, Russia, and is currently studying for the M.Phil. degree at the University of Exeter, England. She is conducting research on the teaching of foreign languages in Russia, teaches Russian at Kingshurst City Technology College, Birmingham, and is a Committee member of the UK Study Group on Education in Russia, the Independent States, and Eastern Europe.

MARIE A. WESTBROOK received her Ph.D. in Sociology of Education and Russian Studies from the University of Virginia. She has been a visiting professor at the Ioffe Institute, St. Petersburg, the St. Petersburg Institute for the Training of Master Teachers, and visiting scholar at the Academy of Sciences in Moscow and Armenia. Dr. Westbrook is president of Triangle Development Specialists, an international consulting firm.

Introduction

ANTHONY JONES

After decades of subordination to the goals of the communist regime, educators in Russia now find themselves part of a fundamental social, economic, and political transformation. The difference between now and earlier times, however, is that the central authorities are weak, the path ahead ill-defined, and the finances necessary for the task unavailable. Today, the schools are expected to find their own solutions to educational problems, after being dictated to for the last seventy years. Needless to say, the Russian education system is ill-equipped to deal with the new situation. And yet, if the transformation currently under way is to solve the long-term problems of the nation, the schools must play a major part. It will be in the schools that the knowledge and attitudes necessary for a new society will in part be formed. It is in the schools that the future labor force will be prepared. It is in the schools that future citizens are shaped. In short, the emerging society will be influenced in no small measure by what happens in education.

At the same time, what happens in the schools will be strongly affected by what happens in society. The kinds of tasks that the educational system will undertake, the goals that the curriculum will try to meet, and the resources necessary for functioning will all come mainly from the world outside of the school. Education in Russia already looks different in significant ways than it did during the Soviet period, and its relationship with political authorities has seen profound changes. To an extent not true just a few years ago, education now has a chance to control more of its activities and to reorganize its relationships with other major institutions of society. It is this changing relationship, and the ways in which education and society are influencing each other's development, that are the themes of this book.

While it is convenient to date the beginning of the "new" Russia from the formal dissolution of the USSR in December 1991, it actually predates the collapse of the Soviet Union. During the Gorbachev period (1985–91), the political, economic, and social structure of the society (and the relations of power and exchange that operated between them) underwent such important changes that one could speak of the birth of a new society. Thus, post-Soviet developments are an extension of changes that were already in motion when the USSR finally collapsed. The contributors to this volume have therefore provided the reader with enough information on trends that developed during the period of perestroika to understand what has happened in post-Soviet Russia. In addition, since recent trends need to be seen in historical perspective, we have provided as much background on the Soviet period as space allows. Our main concern, however, is the relationship between education and society in the new Russia, and it is to this that contributors have given most of their attention.

As the reader will see, there is a considerable degree of continuity between Soviet and post-Soviet education, and many of the current trends have their origin in the earlier period. Also, in spite of important changes in educational thinking, the patterns of the past still linger in the minds of many reformers.

To offer some background on the past, and on the legacy of Soviet education in the new Russia, the first chapter outlines some of the organizational, philosophical, and material factors that defined the state of education on the eve of the collapse of the USSR. It is this legacy that educators have been trying to bring into line with the conditions and needs of the new society, and one cannot appreciate their ideas and actions without seeing them in this context. In looking at this struggle, it appears that it is the institutions of higher education (VUZy) that are experiencing the greatest amount of difficulty and stress. The replacement of central economic planning with a nascent market has meant that every aspect of higher education (including admissions policies, the structure of specialties and curriculums, and placement in the economy) requires new approaches. Not least among the difficulties facing VUZy is finding the money to pay for their operating costs. These and other topics are analyzed by Harley Balzer, who notes that one of the most interesting new departures is the growing emphasis on humanistic and pedagogical issues and on serving the needs of those seeking higher education rather than tying VUZy to the needs of economic planners. It is clear that the programs being introduced will result in greater diversity among VUZy, a development that is well under way at the secondary level. As Stephen Kerr demonstrates in his chapter, many new types of schools have been created in Russia, and the greater decentralization of education has provided teachers with the opportunity to put into practice the innovative pedagogical methods that were so hotly debated during the 1980s. Differentiation of educational approaches is also discussed by John Dunstan, whose main focus is on how changes in curriculum are affecting the more gifted children. As he shows, the age-old struggle between those who think education should be "egalitarian" and those who favor "differentiation" according to abilities reemerged with greater intensity as the society began to move in a new direction. A resolution of this conflict will be a long time coming, and the two approaches are likely to remain a source of social and political tension in the coming years.

An important part of the new diversity is the development of private schools, which are now found throughout Russia. The situation of private schools in St. Petersburg is described in the chapter by Marie Westbrook, with Lev Lurie and Mikhail Ivanov. After tentative beginnings, these schools have quickly established themselves as an attractive alternative to public schools. But their very success has raised the question of social fairness and whether the financially better-off should be able to buy special educational advantages for their children. At the same time, these schools are contributing to the rebirth of an independent civil society in Russia and to the pluralism so essential to a resolution of the nation's problems.

The socialization (or "upbringing") function was always an important consideration in Soviet education, since it was central to the Communist Party's program of ideological control. The end of the USSR and the removal of the CPSU from power have drastically altered the ideological responsibilities of the school. As William Husband shows, the hold that professional historians have had over the kind of history that was taught in the schools has been broken. With the development of private publishing, greater teacher control over the curriculum, the emergence of competing interpretations of history, and the growth of independent schools, the imposition of a single historiography on all pupils is no longer possible. The new links between courses in history and the teaching of social studies in Russian schools is analyzed by Janet Vaillant. She shows how complicated it has been even to produce history textbooks that reflect the new reality and describes in detail the ways in which educators are struggling to devise a new social studies curriculum to replace the old courses, whose main function was political indoctrination rather than education.

Changes in professional education are essential to the functioning of Russia's new society, both to instill new ethics of practice and to acquire the skills necessary to deal with new demands. An enormous challenge facing education is that of finding ways to prepare new and prospective managers to survive in a market economy, and Sheila Puffer describes how this challenge is being met. Although the barriers are daunting, the newly emerging business schools that she discusses are exhibiting great energy and imagination in creating what is essentially a new branch of education. In spite of problems such as a lack of adequate finances, the need to train professors, and trying to import mysterious-looking management curriculums from abroad, Puffer shows that there is reason to be optimistic about the long-term development of management education. In the case of medical education, Julie Brown and Nina Rusinova show that current efforts are part of a long-standing concern over the adequacy of preparation of medical personnel. While there are some necessary innovations underway, the medical profession faces such financial and bureaucratic difficulties that major improvements are unlikely in the immediate future. Moreover, the move to a new system of health insurance will complicate attempts to bring medical education closer to international standards.

Journalists, like historians, were kept within narrow ideological boundaries up until the late 1980s, but now they too have a degree of freedom hitherto only dreamed of. The ways in which the journalists' education (and that of their reading public) is changing is described by Nicholas Daniloff. The move to a more democratically based polity and the virtual elimination of censorship have presented working journalists and schools of journalism with new responsibilities. Their degree of success or failure in meeting these responsibilities will almost certainly have an effect on the development of democracy in the coming years.

The fate of current attempts to reform the education of managers, doctors, and journalists depends in large measure on the ability of teachers to carry them out. But who will teach the teachers? And how? Some answers to these questions are provided by Stephen and Tatiana Webber. They note that while there is greater pragmatism in the new programs for teacher education, and certainly more imagination, attempts to do too much too fast may cause the reforms to founder.

Many changes that occur in the schools and universities go unnoticed by the general public, but one that has not escaped attention is the attempt to introduce sex education into the curriculum. Lynne Attwood describes not only the new concern with this topic in Russian schools, but also the historical situation out of which this concern has come. The consequences of this innovation may go well beyond sexuality, since, as Attwood notes,

> Giving people more information about sex and enabling them to use it freely allows them to take greater responsibility for their personal lives. Hence, advocates see sex education as an important step on the path to democratization. Tolerance of different sexual preferences, and accepting that there is not one model of sexual behavior which everyone must follow, is part of the broader concept of pluralism.

Greater frankness about sexuality is just part of the rapidly changing world to which young people in Russia are having to adapt, and insight into the ways in which they are dealing with change is provided by Deborah Adelman. The young people she interviewed reflect the views of many of their contemporaries, a great number of whom see little point in pursuing an education that cannot guarantee an interesting or well-paid job after graduation. The rapid growth of the private economy has distorted not only the career paths and incomes of young people, but their values as well. For many of them, as for their elders, life is increasingly insecure, and the rules for success uncertain or unpleasant. Moreover, they face a job market that is profoundly different from that of previous generations. In the concluding chapter of this volume, Igor Kitaev examines the ways in which the transition to a market economy is influencing the career choices of youth, and the ways in which educational institutions are, or are not, responding to the new needs of their students. As we would expect, in this as in the areas discussed by the other contributors, the past continues to influence strongly the new processes that are being created.

As the political, economic, social, and cultural foundations of the new Russia continue to evolve, we should expect a more organic relationship between education and society to emerge. As in so many areas of life during the Soviet period, programs were devised, decisions were made, and relationships were created not on the basis of the needs and desires of those who carried them out and those they were supposed to serve, but by the bureaucrats and their masters on the basis of unquestionable assumptions about national priorities. One of the reasons why problems accumulated is that the link between the rules people had to follow and their personal or organizational needs was at best weak, and at worst nonexistent. Now that people are able to bargain and to negotiate with each other without the omnipresent influence of the CPSU, relationships and programs can be more pragmatic and more likely to serve the needs of the population. This by no means guarantees a period of enlightenment and justice, any more than it has in other industrial societies. But in the case of education, at least, it is already producing some astonishing changes.

THE SOVIET LEGACY

1

The Educational Legacy of the Soviet Period

ANTHONY JONES

In the two years since the formal end of the USSR, Russian educators have been trying to create an educational system that is more in tune with the needs of a new society. New kinds of schools have sprung up, new curriculums have been developed, and new methods of pedagogy have been put into action. These changes have been made possible by the collapse of the Soviet Union, but they are in many ways a continuation and acceleration of pressures for change that had been building up for a decade or so. However, although the new Russia has been able to draw upon ideas that had been forming for several years, it has also had to contend with the less helpful aspects that have been inherited from the Soviet period.

For more than seventy years, the schools in the USSR were an integral part of the Communist Party's attempts to bend society to its will. The educational system was designed not only to serve the needs of the program of industrialization, but also to enhance the Party's ideological hold over society. This dual function, however, involved tensions and conflicts that were never really resolved and which continue to operate in post-Soviet Russia. The new society now has to work with the philosophical, organizational and social legacy which Soviet society has bequeathed it, and this legacy is severely restricting the ability of the new society to create an educational system more attuned to a changed situation.

The Legacy

In the early period of communist rule, education was innovative and open to experimentation. At the same time, it was left in no doubt that education was expected to serve the revolution and to help the regime in its attempts to create a "New Soviet Man." In the 1930s, however, there was a return to more conventional approaches to learning, including a return to strict discipline in the classroom and a uniform national curriculum. Pedagogy was based upon the assumption that the teacher's task is to pass along prepackaged materials, and the student's task is to memorize these materials. Although there was considerable tinkering with education in the post-Stalin period, by the late 1980s the schools still operated on the same basic philosophy.[1] It is this approach that Russian educational reformers are now trying to replace.

Another cornerstone of the Soviet school was the emphasis on "upbringing"—the notion that the school is responsible for molding the personality of the student. Even though an enormous amount of time and money went into this program, there is little evidence that it has had much effect. It has certainly not created the obedient new Soviet men and women that the regime expected to emerge from the schools, as is evidenced indirectly by the speed with which public and private morality collapsed as the Soviet period ended. That people could be "molded" was the central assumption of all of the reforms of the Soviet period. In reforms in labor education, for example, the goal was always to fit the student's personality to the needs of the economy, rather than to reorganize the way things were done to fit the needs of the individual.[2]

In spite of having a standardized, national curriculum and system of pedagogy, the administrative structure of Soviet education was complex. Beyond the preschool institutions (which catered to about 70 percent of children), there were general secondary schools, schools specializing in particular subjects (such as English language), vocational secondary schools, specialized secondary schools (providing paraprofessional and skilled-trade education), boarding schools, evening schools, and schools for children with special needs (i.e., with mental and physical handicaps). At the level of higher education, there were universities, polytechnics, and specialized institutes, each with evening and extramural programs of study. Integrating and coordinating these levels and types would be a difficult task for any nation, but it was made more complicated by the variety of bodies responsible for running the system, especially at the level of higher education.3 Moreover, a new policy for any given part of the system quickly led to problems at other levels, which was one of the reasons why Soviet education seemed perpetually to be undergoing reform. At the same time, very few of the reforms actually achieved their goals, and most were successfully resisted or circumvented by teachers and administrators.

By 1992, there were 66,679 schools in Russia, with an average of 2.6 meters space per pupil (two-thirds of the official norm), and a total of 1.28 million teachers. A quarter of the schools currently have at least 881 students, and the overloading is such that almost a third of the schools operate two or three shifts a day. About 2 million students are graduating from the ninth grade each year, and only a little over half of them move on to the tenth grade. The expectation is that this situation will worsen as the economy declines, since many more young people will be forced to move to vocational training sooner, or to leave school altogether.[4]

Russia has inherited a system of very large schools as a result of deliberate policy and of the Soviet government's failure to build enough schools. This has meant not only overcrowding and a resort to the shift system but also difficulties for administrators, and so new organization methods and new ways of training managers of educational institutions are needed (Masnyi and Bessarab 1992).

The problems of Russian education are compounded by the continuing organizational complexity and uncertainty. In 1988, the three main bodies responsible for education—the USSR Ministry of Education, the State Committee for Vocational and Technical Education, and the Ministry of Higher and Specialized Secondary Education—were replaced by the State Committee on Public Education, which did not achieve ministry status until 1993. Meanwhile, specific aspects of education (general, vocational, scientific, technological, etc.) were parcelled out to separate organizations, and the Russian Ministry of Education was reformulated. Then, at the end of 1993, proposals were put forward to recentralize educational administration under a single roof. Such constant reorganization only increases the uncertainty that teachers and administrators have to face and makes plans for new educational programs and structures difficult to implement.[5]

Part of the increasing complexity has been the fast development of newer types of schools; from 1990 to 1991, those schools specializing in the in-depth study of certain subjects doubled to a total of 6,698, and the number of preparatory schools and lyceums tripled to about 500.[6] More than a third of a million pupils were enrolled in these "alternative" schools by 1992. Overall, about 40 percent of the special schools emphasized the humanities; 30 percent emphasized physics and math; 20 percent emphasized the natural sciences; 5 percent were oriented toward religion, and another 5 percent serviced a particular nationality or ethnic group.[7]

In principle, access to all levels of the secondary system was available on the basis of choice and to the upper levels on a competitive basis. Since all education was freely provided, there were supposedly no financial or social barriers to the success of any child who had the necessary intelligence and motivation. It had become obvious by the 1950s, however, that social factors had an important effect on educational attainment in the Soviet Union. This practice led to a series of reforms aimed at reducing the effects of social background while maintaining standards in the following two decades.[8] Many of the reforms were also an effort to deal with the fact that in the years following World War II, young people had become ever more disdainful of manual work, aspiring in greater and greater numbers to higher education and the entry to the intelligentsia that this would ensure. Reversing this trend proved beyond the power of officials, while the move toward universal secondary education increased the desire for higher education even more. In spite of what may have been a slight easing of the situation in the decade prior to perestroika, aspirations remained high up to the end of the Soviet period.[9]

Sociological studies of educational attainment from the 1960s onward showed that despite the regime's claim that there was equality of opportunity, the family continued to be an important factor. Not only did the education and occupation of a student's parents have a major effect on progress in school, but many schools came to draw their students from a narrow range of social groups. Vocational schools, in particular, became filled for the most part with children from working-class families, and were used as dumping grounds for troublemakers. It was not until the era of perestroika, however, that the stratified nature of education was openly discussed, but by that time the nation was on the edge of changes that would ultimately make educational inequalities even greater.[10]

In the late 1980s, there was increasing public frankness on the part of officials about the lamentable conditions in most schools. The physical conditions were especially poor: 21 percent of the students were in schools without central heating; 30 percent of the schools had no running water; and 40 percent did not have indoor toilets or an indoor gymnasium.[11] The problems were worst in rural schools, which accounted for about 75 percent of all schools, and about 40 percent of all students.

In 1994, the situation is considerably worse: The deterioration of buildings continues due to the lack of funds; many schools still lack such basic necessities as heating and plumbing; overloaded schools still run up to three shifts a day; the differences between urban and rural schools have worsened; and the differences in quality between one school district and another not only remain but widen as schools have to rely more often on local funding. The rush to find "sponsors" (i.e., individuals or organizations willing to provide money) for schools has led to the creation of so-called "profile" schools, which create specializations to please the sponsors and to serve their needs—for example, providing an enterprise with skilled workers.

During the period of perestroika, education began to be exposed to the same changes that were operating in the wider society. At the same time, there was increasing willingness to discuss the extent to which the problems of the wider society had been influencing what went on in the classroom.[12] Together with their supporters, those educators who had been calling for a new philosophy of education, were able to put the democratization of education on the agenda, and to do so in the name of perestroika. Administrators eventually proclaimed this the goal of the nation's schools, although the precise meaning of "democratization" was never clearly spelled out. The general thrust, however, was that it included more active involvement of students in the conduct of classes, more choice for students in the courses they were taking, a stronger role for teachers in deciding the curriculum, and greater involvement of parents in the activities of the school (Eklof and Dneprov 1993).

The innovation movement's major aim was to make education more student-centered[13] and to develop cooperation between teachers and students, and this inevitably meant more flexibility and creativity in dealing with the differing needs and skills of students than was possible under the existing model. The uniform curriculum of the Soviet period meant that even at the preschool level "the content, methods and forms of education . . . displayed little variety. Educators were forced to work with uniform standards, to rely exclusively upon the calendar age rather than the developmental stage of the child, and to ignore individual distinctions. A tightly regulated curriculum drove all creativity out of the educational process" (Dneprov, Lazarev, and Sobkin 1993, p. 157). While there were some slight variations at other levels, this situation prevailed in Soviet schools in general.

Alongside the move to democratize education, there was a call for greater differentiation of the curriculum, a development that was not without its critics. There was concern among some people that it would weaken the basic curriculum. In particular, science education was seen as losing ground, a situation not adequately redressed by the creation of a new, general course on "natural sciences and technology." Greater local control of education, in the words of one critic, "looks very impressive.

But the state needs a certain standard of general education in those sub-jects whose content is not dependent on national characteristics, geograph-ical location, or other factors. Without a doubt, mathematics, physics, chemistry, biology and information science are just such subjects."[14]

Current Issues

Changes in the educational process have become necessary as a result of the increasing intrusion of social problems into the school. An ever in-creasing number of schools now have to deal with the problems children bring with them from troubled families.[15] This, together with the declining birthrate, prompted a special committee of the Supreme Soviet to draft a law aimed at protecting families. The aim was to extend the legal rights of nontraditional families and to provide material and other assistance to families with children and with special problems. While the financial provisions envisaged were necessary, the parlous state of the economy and state budget will make it impossible to provide the sought-for protection.[16] Just before the election of December 1993, Yeltsin raised the minimum wage to 14,620 rubles a month (a 90 percent increase),[17] but the conse-quence of this (and of the subsequent plans to spend more on social programs and on paying the debts of state-owned businesses) will be increased inflation and therefore an increase in the burden on families.

Schools are also increasingly caught up in the struggle to deal with the growing linkages between poverty, health and crime. A large-scale study, funded by UNICEF and completed in 1993, has found that the health profile of Russian children is similar to that of people in their sixties. By 1993, diphtheria had become a serious problem in at least seventeen re-gions, and specialists expected that at best it would take two to four years to remedy the situation.[18] Because of the crisis in the health-care system, many children have been infected with the HIV virus, and it was not until late in 1992 that the government drew up a program to educate the public about AIDS.[19]

The treatment of children with other health problems is also cause for concern. Children who have psychiatric or psychological problems or who are progressing more slowly than their cohorts are frequently misdiag-nosed and sent to institutions for the mentally retarded, while mistakes are common in diagnosing the conditions of newborns. One study suggests that up to 70 percent of cases are misdiagnosed, subjecting many children to drugs and poor conditions.[20]

Autism, a disorder still not understood in Russia, is not on the list of developmental disorders requiring special treatment or facilities; for the 3,000–4,000 autistic children in Moscow alone there are no teachers or special facilities and no jobs adapted to their needs.[21] For mildly retarded children, there is little alternative to a life in special residential institutions (in which abuse is a serious problem) because there are almost no family-style facilities for them. Almost none of them are able to get a job to support themselves.[22]

In all areas of life, children are being severely affected by the profound changes occurring in Russian society. As one Russian social scientist recently put it, in addition to "child vagrants, indigent children, child criminals, rapists, and murderers," there is now

> purely juvenile organized crime, a purely juvenile black market. And it is not only an asocial environment that is being reproduced. It is the minor offspring of the most well-placed families who are filling these ranks at an intense pace. This is an extremely alarming symptom. It tells us that the protective barrier of culture, the continuity of generations in the family and in society, are breaking down ("The Family Budget" 1993, p. 43).

Moreover, families in recent years have been less and less able to provide for their children's needs. For example, by May 1992 the average per capita real income was only 39 percent of the 1989 level. This has especially affected children, since they are more often found in the poorer parts of the population: "There are 40.1 million children in Russia today, and of these, roughly half are of preschool age; they belong to the poorest strata of the population; the closer one gets to the top, the fewer children there are" (Ibid., pp. 46, 47). Recent estimates of the poverty level in Russia since the Soviet period vary widely from 20 percent to 90 percent of the population, depending on the definition of "necessary minimum" that is used.[23]

One of the legacies of the economic crisis will be an increasing number of children with health problems in the schools. As family income goes down, children's diets worsen, and their parents are less able to take them to clinics and to buy the scarce and increasingly expensive medicines.[24] In addition, child-abandonment and the health hazards of environmental damage are adding to the problem.

The number of homeless children has grown in recent years, a situation reminiscent of the Russian revolutionary and civil war years when social dislocation created huge numbers of children living in the streets. While it is difficult to know the full extent of the problem, estimates of homeless children in St. Petersburg alone range from 10,000 to 20,000. Many of these children (some of them as young as five years old) have set up homes in basements.[25] For many Russians, this is a lost generation, a generation without morality and a source of trouble for others. As the vice-president of the Association of Women Employees of Internal Affairs Agencies has put it, Russia

> now has teenage black marketeers, homeless kids, newspaper sellers and youngsters living in attics and cellars. Moreover, as a specialist I will say that nobody today has any use for these children of the era of perestroika. It used to be that the schools taught them moral and social values. Maybe they didn't do a great job of it, but at least the process went on, and the children knew what was good and what was bad, what was allowed and what was forbidden. Now everything has changed. Hobby clubs and activity sections are closing, and academic and athletic competitions and festivals have faded into oblivion. . . .

She went on to note that many teenagers will now "do anything to escape from poverty. At best they sell newspapers and wash cars; at worst they steal. Property crimes predominate among teenagers, and they are rising catastrophically. We now have ten- and eleven-year-old thieves and fourteen-year-old prostitutes."[26]

Life is also becoming more difficult for children and young people in other ways. In the late 1980s and the early 1990s, life became increasingly arduous for those who were graduating from the secondary schools. For many of the 75 percent or so who did not go on to some kind of postsecondary education, employment became harder to find. The consequence was that more graduates than usual began their working life "in backward plants with harsh working conditions, low pay and no hope of acquiring a good specialty. . . . These kids have brushes with the law five times as often as those who were lucky and found jobs immediately. . . ."[27] The growth of juvenile crime has led to increased pressure being put on the schools to provide intervention and prevention. Methods are being developed to predict which students are likely to go astray (Zavrazhin 1992; Popov 1992), and teachers are expected to provide guidance to children to prevent alcohol and drug abuse (Levin and Levin 1992).

The collapse of the Komsomol and of organizations which provided activities for youth has exposed young people to a wide array of groups, clubs, and meeting places, many of which are antisocial. One of the more troubling developments has been the cooptation of alienated youth by right-wing political groups, who see these youth as shock-troops of the future. The apolitical stance of increasing numbers of youth, and the moral and social collapse which surrounds them, make them vulnerable to the message of extremist political groups. As one reporter put it, "Thousands and thousands of young social outcasts passionately believe in their idols, who are able to give them hours of escape from their longing for a decent human life. And it appears that the right-radicals are gradually taking over their souls—thereby demonstrating the powerlessness of politicians and the government to influence the hordes of alienated youth whose numbers are growing in geometric progression."[28] The rapid growth of new cultures and groups among Russian youth, the so-called "informal groups," has presented a special challenge to teachers, who now have to compete for the attention and attachment of their students with the allure these new groups and ideas provide[29] (Tolstykh 1992).

Young people are also exposed to illicit drugs. By the end of 1992, the drug trade was estimated as at least 100 billion rubles per year. Crime associated with drugs has increased significantly, and the age of those caught up in this goes down each year.[30] Dealing with this problem is even more difficult in Russia than in most other societies, since Russian society is totally unprepared for it. As one observer has put it, "The thing is, the problem of addiction among children and young people requires a single, unified state program that would include, in addition to specifically targeted methods of treatment and rehabilitation, a whole network of specialized psychotherapeutic care and job placement, and solutions to the problems caused by being taken out of one's former environment. We have nothing like that."[31]

This problem, as is true of all the others, will require enormous financial investment if it is to be dealt with. But one of the legacies of the Soviet period is an educational system that needs enormous investment in combination with an economy that is unable to pay for it. In an effort to prevent even greater damage being done to education, the government has tried to maintain education's share of the budget; even so, it still remains at about 5 percent of the state budget, compared to 8 percent in the late 1980s and 11 percent in 1970.[32] By law, it is supposed to be 10 percent, but the situation is even worse than this shortfall would suggest. Thus, the Ministry of Finance does not allocate the amount that it should (for example, in August 1993, only 50 percent of the salary bill was allocated), and the Ministry of Education is running into debt.[33]

Economic troubles are also having a great effect on higher education. Late in 1993, the financial difficulties of the central government led state officials to propose that local governments pay for higher education and that payment by the state would occur only for the education of specialists that were "needed" instead of on the basis of enrollment numbers. Moreover, payment for these specially designated specialties would be on a competitive basis. Apart from financial considerations, this move was prompted by the recognition of government officials that they cannot know how many and what kind of specialists are needed in each region, and that this decision should be left in the hands of local authorities, especially since the system of sending graduates to regional areas upon graduation has been terminated. Also, the plan called for the State Committee on Higher Education to be the sole body responsible for overseeing the nation's need for specialists, instead of the twenty-one different ministries and departments that shared this task as of the end of 1993. While such a move creates severe problems for all institutions of higher education (VUZy), the greatest difficulty in all likelihood will be faced by the teacher-training institutions. Even the First Deputy Minister of Education saw such a move as likely to lead to "the complete disruption of the system of education in the schools. . . the main customer for teachers is the schools, and separating one from the other is not only senseless, it's harmful too."[34] These moves come on the heels of a trend toward having VUZy find ways to pay more of their own operating costs. Many institutions had already entered into contracts to sell their services to industry and to charge these companies for part of the cost of training the hired graduates. Finding new sources of income had by necessity become a preoccupation of most administrators as they searched for ways to replace the dwindling support of the state.[35] The problem, of course, is that businesses could not afford to pick up the slack.

The changes have thrown many VUZy into a state of confusion. Part of the problem is that new organizations have been created with little regard for quality or consequence. Provincial authorities have rushed to upgrade institutes into universities or academies, mainly because the prestige is greater. From September 1992 to the end of 1993, over one hundred such conversions were made. More than half of the institutes converted were former teacher-training institutes. Consequently, some provinces have had to "re-create" teacher-training colleges in order to maintain the supply of new teachers![36] Meanwhile, concern has grown about the lowering of standards. For example, many VUZy have dropped admission exams in areas outside of the chosen specialty (such as language and math!) and have lowered the standards for written language skills.[37]

The old practice of bribing admissions officials has continued in the new Russia and has taken its place alongside charges for tuition. For example, at one Moscow institute in 1992 it apparently cost 30,000 to 50,000 rubles to buy an "A" on the admissions exam. Yearly tuition charges can also be high, from 40,000 rubles a year at the Institute for

International Business Statistics, to $5,000 (in real U.S. dollars!) at one of the divisions of the International University in Moscow.[38] By 1992, it was claimed that almost half of all VUZ students were paying tuition fees of one kind or another.[39]

There is also the legacy of low morale. In the latter part of the 1970s, there was increasing dissatisfaction among VUZ students with their career path (Avis 1987a). It is clear that from the 1960s onward, the system of planned enrollments in specialties, and the difficulty of getting into the program of one's choice or of switching one's major, had resulted in a poor match between desires and skills and a student's educational program. This encouraged a culture of apathy and opportunism and cultivated an educated labor force that was less than enthusiastic about its situation and prospects.

At the other end of the spectrum, preschool education is also experiencing difficulties. After decades during which kindergartens could take care of children for a fairly small fee, most parents now find preschool facilities less available and more expensive, a situation that was brought about by the failure to build enough kindergartens and the current shortage of state funds. At the same time, preschool education has experienced many of the same changes that were set in motion during perestroika, such as localization and regionalization of programs, the encouragement of preschools in the home, and the development of groups of professionals and parents working together to improve the quality of preschool education.

Russian education now finds itself caught up in the national search for a moral foundation for the new society. In the past, Soviet schools were expected to inculcate communist values in their students through an interlocking set of programs, ranging from involvement in such organizations as the Young Pioneers and the Young Communist League to more subtle messages that were an integral part of the curriculum. Political and moral lessons were presented in classes such as language, history, geography, and even (in earlier times) in math and science. The end of the communist regime meant not only an end to these organizations, but also an end to the cult of Lenin and to the myths and legends of Soviet culture. The situation has been further complicated by the fact that the consciousness of young people has been strongly influenced by the national malaise of the last decade of the Brezhnev era. The lampoon figure that Brezhnev became, and the increasingly obvious emptiness of official rhetoric, weakened further the attitude of youth toward authority.[40] The question now facing educators, of course, is what should replace the old, politically based system of morality? What are to be the new sources of moral upbringing, the new values that will provide a guide to appropriate behavior? In part it will come from the culture of the pre-Soviet period (Plekhanov 1992), which includes a return to religion. One of the more astonishing developments at the end of the 1980s was the involvement of the Russian Orthodox Church in the schools. After tentative beginnings, religion has come to be a routine element in many schools, and religious organizations are now even running their own schools.[41] However, the Minister of Education is on record as being an opponent of mandatory classes on religion (save as part of a history course), although local school authorities are free to offer optional courses on religion. His reasoning seems to be that religion is already a source of conflict in the post-Soviet era, and bringing it into the classroom is likely to make matters even worse.[42]

The schools are also faced with the task of having to teach about the values that underlie democracy and having to prepare their young charges for a new kind of citizenship. If democracy is to become firmly embedded in the new Russia, then tolerance and a respect for freedom and the rights of others will have to be established. But, as one mother has put it, "How are educators who themselves do not know what freedom is going to educate free people?" (Begisheva, p. 50). Neither teachers nor students have been prepared for life in a democratic, market-based society. The passivity that was encouraged during the Soviet period has left many young people ill prepared to show initiative or to set their own direction in life, and the standardized methods that teachers had to follow have left them unprepared to deal with the diversity of views and skills that students bring to the classroom (Korotov 1992; Paltyshev 1992).

The move toward a market economy has had an enormous effect on Russian society, including all of those who work or study in the schools and universities. The number of new challenges that this has created for schools grows daily and includes issues such as competing for finances and students; finding ways to generate income instead of relying on the state to pay for everything; preparing students for dramatically altered employment opportunities (including that of unemployment); and ensuring that graduates are prepared for a career in which they will have to retrain constantly. Now rural schools have to prepare their students to be independent farmers instead of state workers, and teachers have to be able to talk to students about new careers as businessmen, social workers, and bankers.[43]

The eventual realization (and acknowledgment) of the extensive ecological disaster created by the USSR on its own territories has led not only to an ecological movement, but also to a demand for education on ecological issues in the schools. As a result, from the late 1980s to the present time, courses on ecology have been introduced at all levels in the system, and existing courses have been redesigned to incorporate ecological ideas.[44]

As schools have become more diverse, the laws governing education have had to change as well. The Law on Education of 1991 tried to take account of the new situation but caused concern in some quarters by providing compulsory education only until the age of fifteen. At the same time, it banned activities by political and religious groups in the public schools and required schools that provided an "inadequate" education to pay for whatever remedial education was necessary. Also, in addition to state and municipal schools, the law gave religious and private schools legal status and even made provision for home education, with the provision that state-set standards of adequacy were followed. Methods of instruction and choice of textbooks were to be left to the schools. Thus, only "the end result [of education] is subject to monitoring by the state. Nothing else! And the checking will be done by the state certification service, which is independent of the bodies that administer the educational system."[45]

Given the scope of the changes taking place, it is not surprising that an air of uncertainty hangs over education. As one observer put it, the "situation in the educational system is indeed difficult right now. For almost the whole year [of 1993], higher schools have been in a state of prestrike readiness due to constant delays in the payment of salaries and stipends. Secondary schools face an impending textbook disaster because of the Russian Ministry of Education's insolvency. The production of school textbooks has been shut down at three of Russia's printing combines, and there is now a backlog of 15 million unprinted textbooks."[46]

Like many workers in industry—including doctors[47]—teachers have become more willing in the post-Soviet period to engage in strikes in order to force the government to address their problems, particularly the problem of low salaries.[48] While several salary increases have been made, the high rate of inflation has meant that teachers are not really much better off in comparative terms than they were before. Since this situation is unlikely to change as long as the economy is weak, public schools will find it more difficult in the years ahead to prevent teachers from leaving their profession. However, teachers in the private sector, since they are not dependent on the state for salary increases, are likely to preserve their current advantage.

Looking to the Future

Just two years or so after the formal end of the USSR there is doubt about the future shape of education, including the question of the extent to which education can be provided free as a right for every child. The draft of the new Russian Constitution had specified free education only for nine years, and the Law on Education does not guarantee access to the final two grades. As Minister of Education Evgenii Tkachenko recently put it, competition for grades ten and eleven "is good; a teenager must understand that knowledge is capital, too, and it must be fought for."[49] The growth of institutions that require students and parents to pay tuition, and the use of competitive admissions at the secondary level, have focused attention on the issue of the inequality of access to education.[50] Indeed, the new educational structure (there are now five types of schools: regular schools; schools offering a choice of instruction in additional subjects; those offering intensive study of elective subjects; schools that prepare students for VUZ entry; and schools with innovative, experimental programs) virtually guarantees a stratified system of education.[51] While educational inequality was present during the Soviet period in the form of "private" schooling for the children of the elite, the barriers were indirect and not overtly financial.

The constant tinkering with education during the Soviet period and the failure of large-scale attempts, such as the 1984 reform, to change education have left many teachers and administrators in the public system skeptical of new programs. This psychological barrier, as well as financial, bureaucratic, and other constraints, will make real improvements difficult to achieve. In microcosm, Russian education is experiencing the same problems as Russian society: it is trying to change too many things at once with inexperienced personnel, no clear-cut goals, a looming financial crisis, and political in-fighting.

The issue of language instruction raises some important questions for the future, since the Russian language has been traditionally the only means by which diverse cultural groups could interact. None of the new nations can ignore Russian entirely, for economic relations between the former republics will continue to exist. Even within Russia itself, however, there is likely to be continual conflict over language as the regions assert their right to some independence from Moscow. Will Russian language need to be taught in the independent states for purposes of trade, creation of a common labor pool, and coexistence? Will there be a need to standardize qualifications between states? And what about the relations between the regions within Russia itself? What will be the fate of minority cultures and languages in the post-Soviet era? Will these minorities have separate or integrated schools? Will there be an attempt to preserve their way of life as an alternative to becoming submerged in a larger, Russian culture?

The Minister of Education has recently expressed his concern about the language issue, saying that there is a need to "get out of the vicious circle in the sphere of nationality-based education. Schools in Russia, which has 120 ethnic groups speaking 76 languages, can award diplomas in only three languages: Russian, Tatar and Bashkir. This approach must be changed by introducing a bilingual system of educational documents in the national regions. To this day, the seeds of present and future conflicts between nationalities lie in the unresolved status of these questions."[52]

The future almost certainly will see a continuing debate over the content of school curriculums. But how will it be decided what cultural, political and social agendas will be pursued in the schools? And who will decide the content? The trend toward more and more local responsibility and control has already led to a tripartite curriculum with federal, regional, and local components.[53]

As the standard of living of teachers continues to decline, it will prove more difficult for them to remain in the state sector or even in the profession. There has been a shortage of teachers for many decades, and it has been very difficult to persuade young people that teaching is a worthwhile career. Given the greater variety of career opportunities in the emerging market economy, getting and keeping good teachers will become a matter of even greater urgency.

Rural schools are likely to continue to have severe problems due to the harshness and poverty of life in most villages, the low educational level of parents, the necessity of working on the farm in times of need, and the lack of equipment and facilities and shortage of teachers in rural areas. Preparing students for a career in teaching is especially difficult in such conditions, and many talented children are not recognized and given the education of which they are capable (Ivanov 1992). The fate of rural schools is unlikely to improve in the coming years, since their problems cannot be solved unless a massive infusion of capital occurs. In the absence of an economic miracle, this is not likely to happen. But if the schools do not improve, the flight of young people from the countryside will not subside—it may even increase. However, if the planned privatization of agriculture is to succeed in its goal of improving the nation's food supply, the villages will need to retain young families and have a better educated, more productive labor force. Improved schools could certainly help achieve these goals.

One of the most difficult problems for the future will be finding the necessary finances. What will schools and VUZy have to do to survive in a market economy? How much will they need to rely on tuition fees, and what are the implications of this for equality of opportunity? To what extent will the state continue to be responsible for paying the education costs for the skilled professionals that will be needed in the next century? The current economic and political crisis already has seriously undermined the position of scientists and academics. Not only has their income fallen further behind, but the prestige that they used to enjoy is ebbing away fast. This poses a threat not only to the nation's scientific and scholarly future, but also to the ability of the schools to prepare future scientists and researchers. Children know that education can no longer guarantee a career, that those with the most education frequently receive very little for their efforts, and that an uncertain future lies ahead. Moreover, some observers see the decline of the intelligentsia as having grave implications for the future of democracy in Russia, since it is the intelligentsia who has done the most to move Russia in a more democratic direction.[54]

There are already serious problems in the realm of science. By late 1993 the budgetary crisis had put the Russian Academy of Sciences "on the brink of a financial disaster that will mean cessation of the activity of the country's prominent research institutions and their fulfillment of commissions for the state."[55] As a consequence, the nation's program of basic research is in jeopardy. This state of affairs will certainly not encourage students to train for a career in science, particularly since the value of a higher education has slipped because of the fast money that can be earned in the private economy.

Unemployment is also affecting the more educated sections of the population as the nation shifts from a state-owned to a mixed economy. The effects are especially noticeable in regions where manufacturing, defense, scientific, educational, and cultural sectors are well developed. Surveys conducted in St. Petersburg and the Yaroslavl' Oblast, for example, have shown that perhaps as many as 75 percent of the unemployed have a higher or a secondary specialized education. Moreover, women are more likely than men to lose their jobs and are more likely to have difficulties finding new employment (Gendler and Gildingersh 1994).

In 1990, the question of a "brain drain" began to be discussed, with attempts to estimate its positive and negative consequences for Soviet development.[56] Since the collapse of the USSR, however, the exodus of highly educated people has accelerated, and the number of those wishing to leave but having no opportunity to do so has also increased. The issue is especially acute in the case of nuclear scientists and engineers, but scientists of all kinds will have dismal career prospects unless the economic decline of Russia is reversed. To try to halt the decline in science, members of the Russian Academy of Sciences held a rally in Moscow in November 1992. The purpose was to draw attention not only to the very low incomes paid to scientists and researchers, but also to the growing number of those who were losing their jobs.[57] Education's task clearly is not made any easier as students become more aware of the problems facing those in the scientific fields.

In the coming years it will be interesting to see what effects the increasing "internationalization" of Russian education will have on society and particularly on the intelligentsia. The recent past has seen greater contact between education in Russia and other societies, representing a change in frequency and also in content. In the Soviet past, contacts were primarily politically motivated and overwhelmingly were with other socialist societies and industrially underdeveloped nations. The goal of such contacts was not to learn from the experiences of others but to export the Soviet way of life and to gain friends for Soviet foreign policies. At best, the results were mixed and probably not worth the cost involved. By the end of the 1970s, relations between foreign students and their hosts worsened, and institutions responded by cutting back on the numbers of foreigners or trying to get rid of them altogether (Il'chenko and Sokol 1992). With society opening up from the late 1980s on, however, it became clear that the Russians needed the knowledge and skills of other nations in order to survive. This led to more contacts between Russian and foreign educators and officials and to a rapid growth in the number of Russians studying abroad. Since the end of the Soviet period, the only barrier that remains is financial, and it is now common to find Russian students in foreign schools and universities and vice versa. This movement has been a crucial part of attempts to import organizational technology and to "professionalize" the intelligentsia (Kapterev 1992). However, while Russian education gains a richer and more diverse array of options through internationalization, there is the added possibility that it will further increase the migration of skilled and educated people to other countries.

Demographic trends will create a more urgent need in the coming years for the educational system to prepare a high quality labor force. Currently, about 29 percent of the population is above working age, and about 77 percent is of nonworking age (children plus retirees).[58] In addition, the birthrate is still falling, and in some areas is considerably lower than the death rate![59] The dwindling number of workers will have to be productive enough not only to pay for the reconstruction of the nation, but also to provide for the needs of an ever-growing nonworking population.

The challenges facing education in the post-Soviet era are enormous.

Teachers, administrators, students, and parents face a world for which they have not been prepared and for which they must make adjustments that would be painful in any society. That they have to do so in such uncertain economic and political conditions makes the challenge even greater. Regardless of how people deal with the situation, however, it is clear that the material, moral, organizational, and cultural problems that the new Russia has inherited from the Soviet period will affect the educational system in the foreseeable future.

Notes

1. For an account of reforms since the death of Stalin, see Matthews 1982.

2. For an account of this and of the failure of earlier reforms, see Jones 1991.

3. For a brief description of the situation prevailing at the end of the Soviet period, see Dneprov 1993. Useful descriptions of the earlier period can be found in Matthews 1982 and Shturman 1988.

4. *Izvestiia*, February 14, 1992.

5. *Izvestiia*, December 24, 1993.

6. *Izvestiia*, February 14, 1992.

7. *Nezavisimaia gazeta*, July 16, 1992.

8. For an account of the forms of inequality and the programs aimed at reducing them, see Jones 1978.

9. For accounts of the relationship between aspirations and achievements, see Jones 1978 and Averichev 1992.

10. The development of new types of schools and later the creation of private schools with tuition fees meant that the older forms of inequality based on political influence and privilege would give way to educational inequality based on income. This development is certain to gain momentum as private education expands further.

11. *Uchitel'skaia gazeta*, February 18, 1988, pp. 1–4.

12. For an account of the ways in which social problems were affecting education, see Jones 1991.

13. This has meant not only a change in the classroom but also the development of new services such as psychological counseling. For a discussion of the changing role of the school psychologist, see Pakhal'ian 1990.

14. *Pravda*, November 17, 1990.

15. The problems that students bring with them from home require that teachers increasingly act as social workers. Otherwise, as Khaikin has noted, mistakes in upbringing in the schools exacerbate the problems children experience in their troubled families (Khaikin 1994).

16. *Izvestiia*, March 18, 1992.

17. *Izvestiia*, December 7, 1993.

18. *Nezavisimaia gazeta*, November 9, 1993, p. 1

19. *Izvestiia*, August 13, 1992.

20. *Komsomol'skaia pravda*, February 1, 1992.

21. *Izvestiia*, February 11, 1992.

22. *Rossiiskaia gazeta*, February 12, 1992.

23. *Izvestiia*, February 20, 1992. Late in 1993, an Academy of Sciences report

divided the population into the richest (4 percent), the middle class (10–15 percent), the ordinary poor (30–35 percent), and the poorest (40–50 percent). *Izvestiia*, September 15, 1993.

24. *Pravda*, October 23, 1991.

25. *Izvestiia*, February 7, 1992.

26. *Pravda*, January 22, 1992. Translated in *Current Digest of the Post-Soviet Press (CDPSP)*, vol. 44, no. 3, p. 29. The privatization of housing has prompted some parents to sell out, take the money for a drinking spree, and abandon their children. *Izvestiia*, September 15, 1993. This situation has given rise to proposals amending the laws on house-ownership to give children some protection. *Izvestiia*, September 17, 1993.

27. *Sovetskaia kul'tura*, November 10, 1990. Translated in *Current Digest of the Soviet Press (CDSP)*, vol. 42, no. 45, p. 26.

28. *Izvestiia*, November 12, 1993. In *CDPSP*, vol. 45, no. 46, 1993, p. 17.

29. For accounts of youth culture, see Riordan 1989.

30. *Megalopolis-Express*, December 16, 1992.

31. *Megalopolis-Express*, December 16, 1992.

32. *Izvestiia*, May 29, 1992; *Uchitel'skaia gazeta*, February 18, 1988.

33. *Nezavisimaia gazeta*, August 31, 1993.

34. *Nezavisimaia gazeta*, December 14, 1993. Translated in *CDPSP*, vol. 45, no. 50, p. 17.

35. For articles discussing this issue, see *Russian Education and Society*, vol. 35, no. 12 (December 1993).

36. *Nezavisimaia gazeta*, December 14, 1993.

37. *Moskovskie novosti*, July 19, 1992.

38. *Moskovskie novosti*, July 19, 1992.

39. *Izvestiia*, June 1, 1992.

40. For an eye-witness account of the life of pupils and students in the 1970s, see Young 1989. Also, see Pearson 1990.

41. For accounts of the attempt to deal with moral issues in the classroom and of the growing influence of religion, see Zhukhovitskii 1993; Stepanian 1993; Shargunov 1993; Anisimova 1993; and Strogetskii and Viazemskii 1993.

42. *Nezavisimaia gazeta*, August 31, 1993.

43. For discussions of the effects of the market on education, see *Russian Education and Society*, vol. 35, nos. 1 and 2 (January and February 1993).

44. Articles on ecological education can be found in *Russian Education and Society*, vol. 31, no. 1 (January 1991). See also Gaidamak and Tiittanen 1992, and Bogdanets and Smirnova 1992.

45. *Izvestiia*, August 6, 1992. Translated in *CDPSP*, vol. 44, no. 31, p. 25.

46. *Izvestiia*, December 24, 1993. Translated in *CDPSP*, vol. 45, no. 51, p. 20.

47. *Kuranty*, no. 82, April 28, 1992.

48. *Nezavisimaia gazeta*, May 8, 1992.

49. *Nezavisimaia gazeta*, August 31, 1993. Translated in *CDPSP*, vol. 45, no. 35, p. 11.

50. *Izvestiia*, December 24, 1993.

51. *Nezavisimaia gazeta*, August 31, 1993.

52. *Nezavisimaia gazeta*, August 31, 1993. Translated in *CDPSP*, vol. 45, no. 35, p. 11.

53. *Nezavisimaia gazeta*, August 31, 1993.

54. *Izvestiia*, April 24, 1992.

55. *Pravda*, December 24, 1993. Translated in *CDPSP*, vol. 45, no. 51, p. 20.
56. *Izvestiia*, April 9, 1990; *Dialog*, no. 5, March 1990.
57. *Izvestiia*, November 2, 1992.
58. *Rossiiskie vesti*, July 7, 1992.
59. For example, in the city of Tula, the death rate is twice that of the birthrate. *Izvestiia*, March 30, 1992. In Russia as a whole, the birthrate declined by 12 percent between 1991 and 1993.

References

Anisimova, R.A. (1993). "The School and Religion: Do They Need One Another?" *Russian Education and Society*, vol. 35, no. 10 (October), pp. 69–77.

Averichev, Iu.P. (1992). "Guiding School Students into the Blue-Collar Occupations." *Russian Education and Society*, vol. 34, no. 3 (March), pp. 26–37.

Avis, George (1987a). "Student Response to Communist Upbringing in Soviet Higher Education." In *The Making of the Soviet Citizen*, edited by George Avis. New York: Croom Helm.

———, ed. (1987b). *The Making of the Soviet Citizen*. New York: Croom Helm.

Begisheva, E. (1992). "A Free Human Being in a Free School." *Russian Education and Society*, vol. 34, no. 4 (April), pp. 50–56.

Bogdanets, T.P. and L.Ia. Smirnova (1992). "The Shaping of Six-Year-Old First-Graders' Ecological Ideas." *Russian Education and Society*, vol. 34, no. 11 (November), pp. 58–61.

Brine, Jenny, Maureen Perrie, and Andrew Sutton, eds. (1980). *Home, School, and Leisure in the Soviet Union*. London: Allen and Unwin.

Dneprov, E.D. (1993). "The Educational System of the Russian Federation." In *Democracy in the Russian School: The Reform Movement in Education Since 1984*, edited by Ben Eklof and Edward Dneprov. Boulder, CO: Westview Press, pp. 221–35.

Dneprov, E.D., V.S. Lazarev, and V.S. Sobkin (1993). "The State of Education in Russia Today." In *Democracy in the Russian School: The Reform Movement in Education Since 1984*, edited by Ben Eklof and Edward Dneprov. Boulder, CO: Westview Press, pp. 148–220.

Eklof, Ben and Edward Dneprov, eds. (1993). *Democracy in the Russian School: The Reform Movement in Education Since 1984*. Boulder, CO: Westview Press.

"The Family Budget and Children's Talents: An Interview with Natal'ia Rimashevskaia" (1993). *Sociological Research*, vol. 32, no. 6 (November-December), pp. 41–48.

Gaidamak, A. and T. Tiittanen (1992). "The Social-Ecological Ideal." *Russian Education and Society*, vol. 34, no. 11 (November), pp. 43–57.

Gendler, Grigorii and Marina Gildingersh (1994). "A Socioeconomic Portrait of the Unemployed in Russia." *RFE/RL Research Report*, vol. 3, no. 3, pp. 28–35.

Geyer, Georgie Anne (1975). *The Young Russians*. Homewood, IL: ETC Publications.

Holmes, Larry (1991). *The Kremlin and the Schoolhouse: Reforming Education in Soviet Russia, 1917–1931*. Bloomington: Indiana University Press.

Il'chenko, V.I., and V.V. Sokol (1992). "International Contacts of the USSR in the Field of Education." *Russian Education and Society*, vol. 34, no. 9 (September), pp. 6–19.

Ivanov, A.F. (1992). "The Rural School: Current State and Prospective Development." *Russian Education and Society*, vol. 34, no. 3 (March), pp. 56–71.

Jacoby, Susan (1975). *Inside Soviet Schools*. New York: Schocken Books.

Jones, Anthony (1978). "Education and Modernization in the USSR." *Social Forces*, December, pp. 522–46.

Jones, Anthony (1991). "Problems in the Schools." In *Soviet Social Problems*, edited by A. Jones, W. Connor, and D. Powell. Boulder, CO: Westview Press, pp. 213–26.

Kapterev, A.I. (1992). "A Model for the Administration of Professionalization." *Russian Education and Society*, vol. 34, no. 9 (September), pp. 33–40.

Khaikin, V.L. (1994). "On the Tasks of Creating the Moscow Center for the Sociopsychological Support of Children and Adolescents." *Russian Education and Society*, vol. 36, no. 3 (March), pp. 14–31.

Korotov, V.M. (1992). "Students' Self-Directed Activity in Class." *Russian Education and Society*, vol. 34, no. 2 (February), pp. 22–33.

Levin, B. and M. Levin (1992). "In Order to Combat Evil . . . We Ask the Teachers." *Russian Education and Society*, vol. 34, no. 12 (December), pp. 41–52.

Matthews, Mervyn (1982). *Education in the Soviet Union: Policies and Institutions Since Stalin*. London: Allen and Unwin.

Masnyi, V.D. and L.V. Bessarab (1992). "Administration and the School Complex." *Russian Education and Society*, vol. 34, no. 1 (January), pp. 6–14.

Muckle, James (1990). *Portrait of a Soviet School Under Glasnost*. New York: St. Martin's Press.

Pakhal'ian, V. (1990). "Rabota psikhologa pri podgotovke i provedenii pedagogicheskogo konsiliuma." *Voprosy psikhologii*, no. 2, pp. 86–90.

Paltyshev, N.N. (1992). "Once More on the Subject of Slow Learners." *Russian Education and Society*, vol. 34, no. 2 (February), pp. 34–41.

Pearson, Landon (1990). *Children of Glasnost: Growing Up Soviet*. Seattle: University of Washington Press.

Plekhanov, A. (1992). "Russian Folk Wisdom About Upbringing." *Russian Education and Society*, vol. 34, no. 4 (April), pp. 57–66.

Popov, V.A. (1992). "The Subject and Tasks of Preventive Pedagogy." *Russian Education and Society*, vol. 34, no. 12 (December), pp. 31–40.

Riordan, Jim, ed. (1989). *Soviet Youth Culture*. Bloomington: Indiana University Press.

Shargunov, Archpriest Aleksandr (1993). "Only Love Can See." *Russian Education and Society*, vol. 35, no. 10 (October), pp. 60–68.

Shturman, Dora (1988). *The Soviet Secondary School*. New York: Routledge.

Stepanian, E. (1993). "Childhood in a World Without Religion." *Russian Education and Society*, vol. 35, no. 10 (October), pp. 48–59.

Strogetskii, V. and E. Viazemskii (1993). "Filling Society's Spiritual Vacuum." *Russian Education and Society*, vol. 35, no. 10 (October), pp. 89–104.

Tolstykh, Aleksandr V. (1992). "The Adolescent in the Informal Group." *Russian Education and Society*, vol. 34, no. 10 (October), pp. 6–72.

Traver, Nancy (1989). *Kife: The Lives and Dreams of Soviet Youth*. New York: St. Martin's Press.

Young, Cathy (1989). *Growing Up in Moscow: Memories of a Soviet Girlhood*. New York: Ticknor and Fields.

Zajda, Joseph (1980). *Education in the USSR*. New York: Pergamon Press.

Zavrazhin, S.A. (1992). "Predicting Deviant Behavior in Students." *Russian Education and Society*, vol. 34, no. 12 (December), pp. 21–30.

Zhukhovitskii, L. (1993). "An Atheist's Prayer." *Russian Education and Society*, vol. 35, no. 10 (October), pp. 38–47.

NEW STRUCTURES, NEW CURRICULUMS

2

Plans to Reform Russian Higher Education

Harley D. Balzer

Well before the demise of the USSR, some analysts sought to demonstrate that, far from being totalitarian monoliths impervious to social influences, Soviet institutions were deeply affected by characteristics of the society. For example, the misguided debate over the "militarization" of Soviet society generally ignored the reciprocal influences of social problems on the military (Odom 1976; Balzer 1985). With the frenzy of revelations and self-criticism accompanying perestroika, Western specialists joined their Soviet colleagues in providing an unprecedented chronicle of the difficulties besetting the society (Jones et al. 1991). For a few years, it was enough merely to demonstrate that the "USSR has warts, too," to generate newspaper headlines. But the days of such easy shots were numbered. Now analysts, and the Russians themselves, must move on to the much more demanding task of chronicling the complex interrelationship between institutions and society.

I have argued elsewhere that education in any industrial society is intimately bound up with the entire social system (Balzer 1991). In the USSR, this interrelationship meant that the repeated efforts at social engineering through education were strongly influenced by societal forces, frequently producing results different from those intended by Soviet planners.

The education system in Russia and the rest of the former Soviet Union is now in the midst of changes even more sweeping than those envisioned during perestroika. The only parallel may be the revolution in education carried out in the 1920s and early 1930s; but even those changes affected only a small portion of the population. All that may be stated with certainty at this stage is that the new system(s) will be more diverse and much harder to monitor than was the highly centralized Soviet system. How long it will take for this diversity to provide a positive pay-off in terms of educational attainment and economic performance is decidedly an open question. Thus far, there have been a few small reasons for optimism alongside a daunting array of difficulties and unanswered questions.

This chapter will consist of three sections. First, we shall briefly summarize the changes in higher education during perestroika. These reforms have been recounted in some detail elsewhere (Balzer 1987; 1989; 1991; Kerr 1991), so their treatment here will be limited to a review of a few basic principles. Second, we will examine the most recent programs for reform of higher education in Russia. While all such projects are subject to revision, these programs represent the most complete statement of recent thinking about higher education. We will conclude with some comments about the likely impact of the reforms and their broader societal implications.

The most recent cycle of Russian higher education reform began in 1986, following the announcement of initiatives to "restructure" secondary education. Despite the greater involvement of Gorbachev reformers in preparing the higher education reform program, which raised hopes that it might surpass achievements in general education, change was painfully slow. While a few leading VUZy (*vysshye uchebnye zavedeniia*, or higher educational institutions) led by innovative administrators implemented interesting experimental programs, most institutions of higher education remained under the control of conservative rectors. The higher education administration was slow to act in encouraging substantial change.

The education reforms, like all of the early initiatives encompassed in perestroika, were a response to unfavorable economic and demographic trends. Top officials focused on improving economic performance and making better use of available physical and human resources in a so-called intensive mode of development. Many educators seized on the reforms as an opportunity to advance more purely scholastic and even humanistic concerns, but these agendas were secondary to the economic and labor-force needs driving Gorbachev's initial program.

The basic principles of higher education reform articulated in 1986–87 included improving quality, in large measure by raising standards and eliminating weak students and institutions; adopting new, more carefully targeted admissions arrangements, including special arrangements for veterans and workers; introducing more accountability into the system of planning admissions and placing graduates; instituting revised and individualized curricula, with increased emphasis on student participation in scientific research; emphasizing "continuous" education, with retraining and recertification every five years; and devoting additional resources to education, to be provided mainly by the ministries and enterprises employing graduates of the VUZy. The reform was to achieve greater independence and diversity within a context of more rational use of scarce human and material resources.[1]

After 1988, most of the reform initiatives by the USSR government were bogged down in political struggles over economic reform and sovereignty. In many areas, such as education, this opened the way for initiatives at the local and republic levels. One might even speculate that education reformers working at lower levels of the system had the luxury of proposing truly radical approaches, knowing that with the old USSR bureaucracy in place there was little chance of these measures being implemented. Between August and December 1991, this situation changed drastically. Russian Republic education officials found themselves fully in control of their system, with their only strategic plans being in the documents prepared by the reformers.

State Programs for Higher Education in the Russian Republic

The most complete outline of Russian Republic plans for higher education reform is presented in two pamphlets issued by the RSFSR State Committee for Science and Higher Schools (*Gosudarstvennyi komitet po nauke i vysshemu obrazovaniiu* [GKNVSh]) (GKNVSh 1991a; 1991b). While these materials were prepared specifically for the Russian Republic, they are similar to the programs developed in Estonia and the other Baltic republics.[2] The power vacuum in central authority following the failed August 1991 coup led to increased importance for Russian Republic institutions. Even though these plans were adopted while the USSR still existed, the higher education programs were the work of individuals who continue to have responsibility for education in the Russian Federation. They have been refined but not superseded by several subsequent official documents (Komitet 1992a; 1992b).

The Russian State Program begins with a harsh critique of defects in the existing system. It is worth noting which problems the authors emphasize. It directs its major concerns and criticisms at the "social," "economic," and "administrative and financial" shortcomings of the Soviet education system. In a marked departure from Soviet practice, the social issues are treated first. The number 1 social issue it discusses is unsatisfied demand for higher education: "Every year the need for continued education is not met for some 400,000 citizens of Russia who present their documents at VUZy on the territory of the RSFSR, including almost 100,000 who successfully pass the entrance examinations" (GKNVSh 1991a, p. 3). It also points out that the need for more educational opportunity is heightened by the absence of an adequate system for independent study (*externat*).

A second major topic of criticism involves "personality." The authors of the program assert that "in the majority of VUZy the conditions necessary for the multisided development of personality (*lichnost'*) do not exist." The obstacles to personal development include both material conditions and the tendency to treat students as "passive objects." The familiar criticism of narrow specialization is articulated, but it is interesting to note that narrow specialization is criticized not for practical limitations on the capabilities of specialists, but rather for fostering a lack of broad culture and humanism—again invoking the need for well-rounded education focusing on the complete person.

A final social shortcoming concerns more traditional technocratic issues. The "gigantic system of training and raising qualifications of specialists meets overall demands by 25 percent and satisfies *only 1 percent* of the demand for retraining in new directions of science and technology" (*sic*; my emphasis). This is closer to traditional rhetoric, and was probably included to satisfy the industrial ministries. The statistics do not necessarily reflect actual conditions.

The "economic" defects cited in the program encompass a well-known array of problems, including an inadequately educated labor force (with an average of 9.8 years of formal schooling, compared to fourteen years in the United States and other "developed" nations); poor relations between the "economic mechanism" and higher schools, based on centralized ordering and placement of specialists by ministries that bear no responsibility for the consequences; the lack of an adequate system for projecting personnel needs;[3] an excessively uniform approach to training specialists; lack of adequate incentives; obstacles to the most promising forms of integrating higher education with Academy of Sciences institutes and industrial research; and the divorce of Russian higher schools from the world systems of higher education and division of labor.

The administrative and financing difficulties cited in the program are even more familiar: the difficulty of elaborating a unified state program when higher schools are subordinate to twenty-eight diverse ministries and departments; bureaucratic limitations on the initiative of VUZ faculty;

miserly financing, which has resulted in a pathetically inadequate infrastructure and poorly equipped schools; and abysmal levels of support for retraining and continuing education.

The litany of these familiar shortcomings is worth reviewing for the tone and context of their presentation. Unlike the critique by Egor Ligachev in 1988, which emphasized a utilitarian (economic) rationale for reform, the emphases of the 1991 Russian Republic plan are on humanism and personality. The Russian State Program represents a "human capital" approach in the best sense of that term—that investing in people by maximizing their opportunities for general education will ultimately pay off for all of society. But the goal of maximizing each individual's potential is tempered by a serious dose of economic reality.

The humanistic and "personality" focus of the higher education reform program also emerges clearly from its listing of consequences that might be expected if the prevailing "ineffective" system of higher education were permitted to remain unchanged. These include losing the possibility of democratic development due to inadequate legal, economic, and political education; a growing crisis among young people resulting from their defenselessness in a market economic system; the nation's concomitant inability to compete effectively in the global economy; and Russians' loss of connection to their rich humanitarian culture.

In addition to avoiding these adverse consequences, Russia's new system of higher education is designed to achieve five quite general goals:

1. "Offer each citizen of the republic the maximum opportunity for intellectual, cultural and moral development; for obtaining higher education and qualifications corresponding to their abilities and knowledge."
2. Provide opportunities for improving knowledge and retraining.
3. Meet the social demand for specialists.
4. Guarantee the breadth and quality of education necessary for (occupational) mobility and "social defense" under market conditions.
5. Reach a new stage in the development of education, science, and culture.

In its initial formulation, the program was to be realized in three stages. But the language used to describe these stages did not inspire much confidence that it had been carefully worked out.

1. 1991–92: "The final result of this stage [will be] reform of the existing system of higher education, formation of the new system and the mechanism of its operation."

2. 1993–95: Completion and stabilization of the new system, practical implementation of its mechanism, and the beginning of integration into the international system.
3. 1996–2005: Augmenting the potential and quality of the system, and fully integrating it into the international system of education and employment.

The basic determinants of the choice of means, forms, and methods for realizing the program will be: decentralization and democracy (*samorazvitie*); quality; diversity; a unified system of uninterrupted education;[4] attention to the needs of various regions and republics (effectiveness); and equality of opportunity. The new system will eventually eliminate the distinction between higher and specialized secondary education in favor of a multilevel system of higher education. The provision of *external* opportunities would make higher education accessible to everyone regardless of age.

In a major departure from the Soviet approach, the Russian Republic plan proposes a decentralized educational administration, with authority vested in local, regional, and republic bodies. The goal is to decentralize the process of decision making and regulation, "introducing the international standards of UNESCO for reporting and for comparative evaluation of VUZ activity."

The VUZ is to be a juridical entity with an official seal (very important in Central Europe with its respect for notarized paper), its own financial assets and property, and its own statutes. VUZy may determine their own admissions plans, the specialties to be taught, their structures, and the content of educational programs based on "the provision of quality education and the requirements of agreements with sponsors" (*zakazchiki*). All internal administration, financing, staffing, and other decisions are to be the prerogative of the VUZ. Each VUZ may allocate funds from sources other than the state budget, including for salaries and stipends, but salaries and stipends may not be below the level of those paid from the state budget (cf. Kossov and Kniazev 1991).

Internal administration at each VUZ will be overseen by a rector appointed by the GKNVSh on the recommendation of the institutions' academic council. The GKNVSh has responsibility for defining overall strategy, for coordinating the activity of all educational and scientific institutions regardless of departmental affiliation, for overseeing state budget financing, for representing Russian higher schools in international organizations, and for organizing a system to evaluate the quality of all types of activity of VUZy and scientific organizations.

Regional development strategies and labor resources, along with the determination of regional priority directions in science, are to be the responsibility of regional centers of science and higher education. Participation in these centers will be voluntary, and may include representatives of VUZy, scientific institutions, regional soviets, councils of factory directors, and social and professional organizations.

The ultimate goal of the reformers is a flexible system of preparing specialists in accordance with the changing character of the Russian economy and labor market. Evaluating and forecasting personnel needs will be an important part of the committees' job. According to 1991 projections, the share of specialists in economics, management, jurisprudence, sociology, psychology, biotechnology, informatics, and microelectronics was to be increased to between 60 and 70 percent of graduates. (Currently, less than 40 percent of students study in these specialties in Russia.) The share of full-time students ("day" as opposed to evening and correspondence) should be increased to between 70 percent and 90 percent. (Currently about 42 percent of VUZ students in Russia study in part-time programs.)

A basic principle of the Russian higher education program is that "higher education must be accessible to everyone, in accordance with their possibilities and talents." The government will expand the system of higher education at the level of fundamental humanitarian general-professional preparation (basic higher education), to include a greater number of persons, and it must maintain state standards for the quality of this education. The entire framework is predicated on a widespread system of short-term (one- to two-month) special courses providing on-the-job training for people with basic higher education. The implication is that specialists will refresh their knowledge and learn about new developments periodically throughout their careers.

The reorganized higher education system is to consist of four levels, or stages, with broad access to the first level and competitive procedures for those wishing to study at more advanced levels. The first stage will last two years, and graduates will receive a certificate of "incomplete higher education," conferring the right to continue their studies in any VUZ of a compatible profile.

The second level, "basic higher education," will provide professional training in one of the areas of science, technology, or culture, based on their foundation in "incomplete higher education." The course will be two years for those with incomplete higher education, and four years for those with secondary education. Graduates will receive a diploma and a baccalaureate degree. The diploma will permit them to work in any position requiring that type of higher education, and/or to continue their education at the third level.

A portion of those completing basic higher education will be selected by competition for admission to the third stage, "complete" or "specialized" higher education, based on a professional, educational, and scientific research program in the area of future professional activity. The length of the program will be determined by each VUZ in consultation with sponsors (*zakazchiki*), but will not be less than two years. Most third-level programs will include a period of internship (*stazhirovka*), normally at the future place of employment. Those completing the third level of higher education will receive a diploma certifying their status as specialists with complete higher education. Those performing the requisite scientific research may be awarded the degree of *magistr*.

The fourth level of higher education—graduate study—is designed to prepare scientific and professorial cadres. Competitively selected students will participate in a three-year program of study and research, which leads to the degree of *kandidat*. There is some ambiguity in the documents regarding this fourth level. It is comparable to the existing *aspirantura* level, which leads to both *kandidat* and doctoral degrees. In some places, mention is made of *doktorantura* programs; in others, the *kandidat* degree is discussed. Obviously, these details have not been worked out.

Resolving the issue of advanced degrees will be particularly difficult due to the large number of credentialed specialists who have a very direct interest in any changes that are implemented. Will the existing *kandidat* degree retain its status? Under conditions of more flexible funding and a genuine labor market, will credentials retain their significance? There will be an immediate need for professional organizations to fill the vacuum created by the dismantling of state control over accreditation.

It is possible that the degree of *doktor nauk* will become less and less important. There will be little demand for this credential in a market system, and what demand does remain can be satisfied by the rank of "professor" (Torchinskii 1991). As the nation strives for participation in the international system of education and degree equivalence, there is likely to be even more pressure from the tens of thousands of candidates of science to consider their degrees as equivalent to American Ph.Ds.

The new multilevel system was introduced on a voluntary basis as of September 1, 1992, and is to function parallel to the existing system. Adoption of the new system is left to the discretion of each VUZ, and may be implemented wholesale or in part. Individual divisions, faculties, or departments may adopt the new system at their discretion. This would seem to be an invitation to chaos, as students studying according to different programs may be attending the same schools and in some cases might be in the same classrooms.

Some of the more specific goals for the period up to 2005 include:

- 1991–93: Shift to a new system of admissions and graduations based on population growth and social-demographic projections, raising the potential contingent of students and the overall educational level of the population (statistics are in Tables 2.1 and 2.2).
- 1995–2000: Change the structure of admissions and graduations in accord with population growth and new job openings so that the system meets 75 percent of the demand for the first level of higher education and 90 percent of the demand for education in information and services.
- 2000–2005: Raise the training of specialists at the second and third levels of higher education to the level prevailing in developed countries.

During 1992, the GKNVSh was supposed to work out an administrative system and develop criteria for evaluating quality; elaborate republic and territorial systems; and begin the process of accrediting VUZy. Accreditation was to be conducted with the participation of scholars from the Academy of Sciences, creative unions, and engineering and other professional societies (Akimov et al. 1991; Saltychev et al. 1991). Needless to say, the breakup of the USSR forced changes in these timetables. In many regions, accreditation was carried out during 1992–93 with the assistance of local education communities.

The central task of the reform is to improve the quality of training for specialists, eventually bringing it into accord with world levels. The VUZ student body will be constituted on the basis of a new system of guidance (*proforientatsii*). Graduates will be permitted to choose their places of work and may negotiate contracts with enterprises, organizations, and other sponsoring institutions.

International contacts are to be increased, and serious efforts will be made to meet world standards, particularly those of UNESCO. Special attention will be given to the UNESCO indicators of performance quality, and the GKNVSh will seek international cooperation on establishing degree equivalency.

The reform programs recognize that one of the major barriers to development in VUZy is the appallingly weak material base at most of these institutions (GKNVSh 1991a, Appendix III). In the future, VUZy may be

Table 2.1

Projected Admissions to Higher Education, RSFSR (in thousands)

	Base year[a] (1990)	1995	2000	2005
Total admissions to higher education	1,415	1,510	1,900	2,240
Admissions to first level	813	870	1,100	1,100
Fulltime	523	610	710	740
Evening and correspondence	290	260	390	360
Admissions to second level	—	470	600	850
Fulltime	—	280	420	600
Evening and correspondence	—	190	180	255
Admissions to third level	602	165	200	290
Fulltime	366	150	180	260
Evening and correspondence	236	16	20	30

Source: Gosudarstvennaia programma razvitiia vysshego obrazovaniia v RSFSR (Moscow: 1991), p. 21. Columns may not add due to rounding of totals.

[a] "Base year" data represent admissions to RSFSR higher and specialized secondary institutions.

financed by the state budget, regional government, ministries and enterprises, as well as by private contributions. All VUZ income and all monies contributed to VUZy will be free from taxation. VUZy will have the right to conduct commercial activity in the areas of education, science, production, and culture, both within Russia and abroad, and may maintain bank accounts in Russia and other states.

The GKNVSh developed grandiose plans to create a unified republic, regional, and VUZ system of guidance, selection, and enrollment based on early evaluation and support of gifted young people. In 1991–93 a republic system of identifying talented young people and getting them into special forms of study in priority disciplines was to be formulated and introduced. This has now been superseded.

Reflecting the emphasis on broad, humanistic education, the State Committee accorded universities a special role in the new system of higher education. Universities will emphasize preparation of specialists with academic degrees (baccalaureate, *magistr*); training of pedagogical cadres for all levels of education, in the first instance in fundamental

Table 2.2

Projected Graduations from Higher Education, RSFSR (in thousands)

	Base year[a] (1990)	1995	2000	2005
Total number of specialists graduated	1,073	1,055	1,190	1,400
Graduates from first level	640	610	710	710
Fulltime	407	425	440	490
Evening and correspondence	233	185	270	215
Graduations from second level	—	330	355	510
Fulltime	—	200	250	360
Evening and correspondence	—	130	110	155
Graduations from third level	433	116	125	180
Fulltime	238	104	110	160
Evening and correspondence	195	12	13	18

Source: Gosudarstvennaia programma razvitiia vysshego obrazovaniia v RSFSR (Moscow: 1991), p. 21. Columns may not add due to rounding of totals.

[a]"Base year" data represent admissions to RSFSR higher and specialized secondary institutions.

natural science and humanities disciplines. The status of Russian universities has been explicitly defined, and this is facilitating the creation of new types of universities (technical, humanities, etc.). Universities are supposed to receive priority financing.[5]

The reform programs propose a new system of postgraduate education (*poslediplomnoe obrazovanie*). By 1995, professors and instructors in all important disciplines are to be retrained, and, by the year 2000, retraining should extend to the entire VUZ teaching staff. By the end of the century, admissions of candidates to doctoral programs should increase by six times; in the system of retraining and raising qualifications, enrollments would rise by a factor of seven.

Reformers proposed creating a legal basis for a new system of doctoral study (*doktorantura*). They envisioned training doctoral students at all leading universities and VUZy, and, beginning in 1991, at least 10 percent of doctoral students were to be trained abroad.

Some of the most intriguing and utopian proposals concern creating a VUZ-based system of science in Russia. The reform plan includes quite specific provisions regarding scientific research, which would make VUZy the key institutions not only in training but also in scientific research and development. According to the proposals, the Russian Republic would shift to a competitive contract system for the financing of scientific work. The state reformers further proposed combining academic, branch, and VUZ scientific structures on the basis of those in universities and leading VUZy. VUZy would become the major centers of scientific research, with priority financing from the state budget. The scientific and educational processes thereby would be unified, raising the level of training and involving VUZ teachers and students in the research process.

Among the changes proposed to achieve a reorganization of science education and development were: formulating a new organizational structure that will combine higher schools of the university type with academic institutions and branch scientific research institutes; actively using market mechanisms to increase competition among scientific collectives; introducing alternative forms of research and development that would assist in the development of small innovational firms and other new forms of scientific-and-technical activity; and raising state budget financing of scientific research at higher schools by three times by 1995 and by four to five times by the year 2000.

The proposals also include legal and tax incentives for inventions, stimulating the education system to help enhance the climate for innovation. Scientific organizations will be self-governing. Fundamental research will be supported by a system of grants administered by the Russian Science Fund. Efforts will be supported to finance parallel (competing) lines of research. Advantageous conditions are to be created for alternative small innovational firms, for the Centers of Scientific-Technical Creativity for Youth (TsNTTMs), for cooperatives, and for other small, flexible initiatives.

Five concrete measures are proposed to foster innovation:

1. The immediate reallocation of funds for financing research, putting up to 80 percent of the resources at the disposal of group programs.
2. The creation of a commercial bank to finance scientific-technical development.
3. The creation of a fund under the GKNVSh RSFSR for financing fundamental and exploratory scientific research.
4. The working out of a schema for establishing technology parks and technopolises in the RSFSR (by 1995 no fewer than twelve technology parks and technopolises should be in operation).
5. In cooperation with the ministries, the creation of a system for forecasting and evaluating the main directions of science and a system for concrete and competitive financing of R&D.

The plan promised a major program of material support for and improvement of education and scientific research and development, designed to match the level of the best Western institutions. New equipment was to be procured at a cost of 23.1 billion rubles by 1995 and 32.3 billion by the year 2000.

In a bow to economic reality, two possible variants of funding were proposed in the 1991 programs. One envisioned bringing all 495 Russian VUZy up to the 1990 Western level by some time between 1995 and 2000. The second variant would have provided major support for the hundred strongest VUZy, ensuring a nucleus of high quality institutions. Given resource stringency, the more modest proposal will likely be more than enough of a challenge, particularly since a number of the specialized secondary schools (technicums) are being incorporated in the system of higher education as first-level institutions or as part of new technical universities. When I inquired about the status of these proposals in meetings at the reorganized State Committee for Higher Education in 1992 and 1993, I was told that the question is "in a fog."

Officially, the programs worked out in 1989–91 and published in 1991 still represent the intentions of Russian higher education administrators. But the administrative system itself has changed, and emendations are inevitable. Most important, the effort to combine the administration of science and education in a single agency did not work. The Ministry of Science, Higher Education and Technology Policy, headed by Boris Saltykov, was reorganized in spring 1993. Vladimir Kinelev, who had made no secret of his dissatisfaction at presiding over a "mere" State Committee for Higher Schools within Saltykov's ministry, became chairman of the new State Committee for Higher Education with the rank of minister. This rearrangement will diminish the likelihood of rapid integration of scientific research and development with higher education. At the same time, it may have some positive effect, allowing higher education officials to focus more on educational matters rather than campaigns for independent ministerial status. At the end of 1993, the Russian government was discussing a proposal for a single ministry responsible for all types of education.

Evaluating the Prospects

The latest Russian higher education reform program retains a number of the principles articulated during perestroika, while departing significantly from others. The most important departure underlying all the new proposals is a humanistic and pedagogical motivation, in place of the previous priorities of demographics, economics, and labor-force concerns. For the

Table 2.3

Competition to Enter Selected VUZy, Summer 1991

VUZ or Group of VUZy	No. of Applications	Planned No. of Places	Applicants per Opening
<u>VUZy GKNVSh RSFSR</u>			
Rostov University	2,606	1,175	2.2
Leningrad Engineering-Economics Institute	1,325	375	3.5
Iaroslavl' University	1,470	560	2.6
Moscow Humanities University (former Historical Archives Institute)	2,100	340	6.2
Pedagogical VUZy in City of Shui	1,000	500	2.0
VUZy of RSFSR Education Ministry	46,500	18,000	2.5
VUZy of Uzbek SSR Education Ministry	42,324	18,500	2.3
VUZy of Agriculture Ministry (11)	14,823	5,800	2.5
VUZy of USSR Ministry of Transportation[a]	17,796	8,475	2.1
VUZy of Ukrainian Ministry of Higher Education	111,372	52,325	2.1
VUZy of USSR Ministry of Culture	4,880	440	11.09
Leningrad VUZy (40)	68,116	25,584	2.6
MGIMO	1,870	390	4.8

Source: Poisk, no. 32 (118) 2–8 August, 1991, p. 6.
[a]Data for 10 of 14 institutions

first time since the USSR's first five-year plan, the major emphasis in Russian education is on maximizing human potential rather than meeting specific economic and personnel needs.

Emphasis on human potential is reflected in the proposed increase in the number of students to be admitted to higher education. In place of Soviet attempts to plan admissions, the new system is designed to be much more sensitive to student demand—and indications are that the demand for higher education remains high (Balzer 1989, pp. 20–28; Lenshin 1993, p. 10; see also Table 2.3). Under the command-administrative system, there was an artificial labor shortage in the Soviet economy, making time spent in education a serious problem for the planners. During the transition to a market economy, the most serious labor force problem is likely to be unemployment, and we should expect young people to react as they do in other market societies during tough economic times—by seeking to delay their entry into the labor force through enrollment in advanced education. These economic pressures, along with strong intelligentsia traditions favoring education, will at least partly compensate for a perceived decline in the prestige and economic utility of higher education.

An increased demand for education does not preclude a major shift in students' choices of specialties. The USSR trained a massive and indeed superfluous number of engineers. A far smaller number of engineers should be trained in the future, and they will need a much broader curriculum emphasizing economic and social factors in production. Many of the engineering and technical specialists trained in the Soviet period will be replaced by students of business, marketing, economics, public relations, and other disciplines related to a market economy and service sector. (A degree in engineering often provided social mobility for children of families with no higher education. Children of parents with a higher education were more likely to choose a nonengineering specialty.)

The emphasis on quality in the 1986–87 USSR higher education reforms included implicit threats to reduce the number of students and to close weak VUZy. While it was possible to eliminate some of the "deadwood" from the student body, it proved extremely difficult to close institutions (Balzer 1992). Under the new conditions of increased local control, the number of institutions claiming the status of VUZy is increasing. (More than fifty new VUZy were created in the two years following the August 1991 coup, including many private institutions that might eventually qualify for government support.) Opportunities to convert strong specialized secondary schools to first-level VUZy will encourage the process, as will the option of including technicums in new specialized universities.[6] Leaving admissions to the discretion of individual VUZy will almost certainly result in an increase in the number of students, at least initially.

Despite changes in emphasis in the Russian higher education reform program, a number of themes have been retained from the era of perestroika. Education is to be uninterrupted, with retraining programs available throughout an individual's working life. Individualized programs of study are to replace the rigidly stipulated curricula that were common in Soviet VUZy. Resources are to be increased, with some of the funds coming from the state budget, but much attention will be given to eliciting contributions from the private sector. A growing proportion of students are to study either as stipendiaries of their place of work, or under contract arrangements that oblige them to work for their sponsor following graduation.

The sponsorship arrangements can be made to sound like a form of indentured servitude, differing little from the now-discredited system of *raspredelenie*. However, a few enterprises have taken the enlightened view that the entire society benefits from improved education, and that if some of the students they support eventually work for them, that is enough of a return.[7]

The Russian Republic program for higher education not only envisions VUZy playing a greater role in scientific education and encouraging student involvement in research-and-development activity, but it also envisions the VUZy and particularly the universities becoming major centers of scientific research. Little was done to realize these aspirations in the short period during which science and higher education were combined under a single minister. Movement toward a university-based science system is likely to be even more difficult with separate administrative domains.

The economic crisis affecting all public institutions has had a devastating impact on both education and science in Russia. While economic stringency might provide an impetus for reform, with economic necessity forcing changes that policy choices alone might not achieve, this has not been the result. Rather, virtually every institutional actor has taken the stance that the economic crisis requires devoting all their attention to basic survival, and that it could be disastrous to experiment at a time of such financial peril. The result is likely to be that any chance for planned, rational reductions in the R&D system will be missed. The inevitable weeding out will occur on a haphazard basis, with luck and connections playing at least as great a role as judgments of merit and priority.

Some observers, including many in the West, have assumed that some type of commercial solution to the economic difficulties can be found. VUZy in Russia and other areas have begun to experiment with tuition fees. But foreign students, who were numerous when the USSR provided free tuition and paid stipends for purposes of propaganda, prestige, and "Communist internationalism," have not proved to be willing consumers—especially at a time when the quality of life in Russia is perceived to be declining. There have been experiments with charging tuition for students who score less than outstanding grades on VUZ entrance exams, particularly in such popular specialties as foreign languages. This has provoked concerns about quality that would sound familiar to many

American college administrators. But thus far, those able to pay VUZ tuition constitute a small portion of students, and their payments amount to a tiny fraction of the institutions' budgets (Analytical Center 1992; Lenshin 1993).

Another source of revenue might come from the sale of the products of research conducted at VUZy. But here, too, the problems are enormous. Production by students at educational institutions is notoriously uneconomical—though the provision of tax exemptions in some cases makes it attractive, and in other cases encourages varieties of subterfuge. It is difficult to overestimate the problems stemming from economic illiteracy and from the lack of management skills and other kinds of market-related knowledge and training.

Commercializing the products of VUZ research through invention and innovation represents a more promising long-term strategy, and again one that has been adopted by many American universities. Specialists long argued that the major obstacles to applying technical processes developed in the USSR were structural and systemic. If the economic problems can be overcome and the systemic inhibitions and irrationalities can be reduced, the crucial need will be for entrepreneurial skills, as many of the scientific and technical people are already qualified to handle the creative aspects of innovation—indeed, their complaint has long been that no one needed their innovations in a socialist system (Fedorov 1990). These new skills may be the sort that can be acquired only in the marketplace, but the basis for them constitutes the core of economics and business programs. To the extent that Russian VUZy, and especially technical VUZy, now intend to broaden their approach to education, including economic and sociological components in virtually every specialty, the schools could make a significant contribution to unblocking the innovational and technical development processes.[8]

But first the schools must survive. Education has been a clear priority of the Yeltsin government—Yeltsin's first decree following his election was on education, promising VUZ faculty salaries at a level double that of the average wage. However, the resources to fulfill the promises have not been available. (This has been repeated several times, most recently in promises of assistance before the April 1993 referendum, followed by renewed concern for structural economic stability and inflation after the votes were counted.) Budgets have decreased in real terms over the past two years, and the trend is likely to continue for at least another year.

Along with economic woes, the VUZy are experiencing a loss of prestige. Graduate study is no longer avidly sought, and the number of students enrolling in graduate programs has dropped by a factor of more than two. Many of these individuals might have been potential members of the "scientific proletariat," but the reductions are so great as to make some fear that science will cease to be a feasible career option. Much of the contract research once financed by industry is no longer being funded, and few students now have opportunities to participate in scientific work.

Even some of the initial success stories in higher education are turning out to be built on shaky foundations. Western-style economics and business programs enjoyed a major boom for several years, but now many are finding that Western business programs and market economics do not really prepare individuals to function in conditions of *biznes po-russkii*.

Any judgment of the current situation must inevitably be contradictory. During periods of massive change, winners and losers appear with stunning rapidity. For the first time since the late 1920s, the creative potential of the population may now be given free rein. Few expect miracles, but it is not unreasonable to expect positive results within the next decade. However, these positive results are likely to be seen only at a limited number of institutions, particularly in the elite VUZy that have already been involved in experiments and reforms. During the transition it will be important to remember that all nations have a range of higher educational institutions. The Russian problem has been twofold: The human and intellectual contributions from the best VUZy were poorly used; and the drop-off below the level of the elite institutions was quite steep. If the elite institutions are given the conditions to make a larger contribution, the longer-term impact might be an economy that could better support a broader range of schools.

The magnitude of the changes in Russia also constitutes a challenge to the West. Despite all its shortcomings, the education system in Russia has been a unique and valuable resource. Its destruction would represent a serious loss, and not only to Russia. If the education (and science) system is allowed to atrophy, recreating it later will cost many times what would be required to preserve it now. But serious Western help will depend on Russia itself producing a rational program to confront the crisis, and such an approach is not yet in evidence.

Notes

1. Draft guidelines for the reform of general education were published in the central press on January 4, 1984. Following three months of public discussion, a revised version was published on April 14, 1984. "Basic Directions," for the restructuring of higher and specialized and secondary education, appeared in the central press on June 1, 1986. There was again a public discussion, but the issues proved difficult

to resolve. The Politburo approved the Basic Directions "in principle" on August 28, 1986, but instructed the Ministry of Higher and Specialized Secondary Education to continue working on the legislation. On January 6, 1987, the Politburo again referred the project back to their specialists for additional work. In February, Mr. Gorbachev acknowledged that there were sharp differences of opinion about the reform. On March 21, 1987, the central press published a revised version of the Basic Directions, followed by five major decrees implementing portions of the reform (March 25–29, 1987). Despite, or more likely because of, the prolonged deliberations, these documents were less specific than the general education reform materials.

The combining of the two reforms and their extension was first articulated at the Central Committee Plenum of February 17–19, 1988. See Egor Ligachev's speech at the Plenum, *Komsomol'skaia pravda*, February 18, 1988; and the decree of the Central Committee, "O khode perestroiki srednei i vysshei shkoly i zadachakh partii po ee osushchestvleniiu," *Sovetskaia Rossiia*, February 20, 1988.

2. The Estonian plans for higher-education reform were outlined to a delegation from the U.S. National Science Foundation during meetings in Tallinn on June 5–7, 1991. These plans envision universities becoming the major agencies of scientific research; a system with at least two "choke points" to separate out practitioners from researchers; and an American-style system of higher degrees (M.A. and Ph.D.).

3. According to 1991 data, 50 percent of specialists with higher education did not work in their specialty, and 20 percent were employed in positions not requiring higher education.

4. The use of the words "diversity" and "unified" here do not represent a contradiction. In the Russian context, "unified" does not mean standardized, but rather refers to a system in which each level of education may lead to the next higher level—a system where no type of school represents a "dead end" precluding further study. The issue is particularly sensitive in the history of Russian pedagogy, due to the tsarist government's effort to maintain two separate systems of education, one for the nobility and one for the lower classes. "Liberal" Russian educators consistently fought for a "unified" school system that would allow all qualified students the opportunity to attain a higher education.

5. Priority in financing universities may help explain the current rush among VUZy to redefine themselves as universities. Iurii Afanas'ev's Historical Archives Institute has become the "Humanities University;" the Bauman Moscow Higher Technical School is now a "technical university;" and several pedagogical institutes have dubbed themselves "pedagogical universities." In St. Petersburg, eleven of the forty-three VUZy are now officially universities, certified by a regional committee of higher school personnel. The trend is likely to continue if universities manage to consolidate their privileged place in the new system.

6. The experience in the years following the 1917 revolutions, when local authorities sought to establish their "own" VUZy despite the forbidding economic conditions, may well be repeated. See Sheila Fitzpatrick, *Education and Social Mobility in the Soviet Union, 1921–1934* (Cambridge University Press, 1979), pp. 48–49.

7. This was the view articulated to a delegation from the U.S. National Science Foundation during a visit to the Leningrad NPO for Scientific Instruments in June 1991.

8. For comments on the potential VUZ contributions to innovation see V. Ezhkov, "O mekhanismakh podderzhki i prodvizheniia naukoemkikh inovatsii," *Alma mater*, no. 2 (February 1991), pp. 17–23, which focuses on creating a better climate to attract venture capital; and V. Poliakov, "V poiskakh mekhanisma obucheniia innovatsiiam," *Alma mater*, no. 3 (March 1991), pp. 10–12, where the author stresses the role of

46 HARLEY D. BALZER

consulting arrangements as a way to break out of the vicious circle of poor education and poor industrial performance.

Bibliography

Akimov, Iu, A. Kushel', and V. Meshalkin (1991). "Attestatsiia i akkreditatsiia vuzov," *Vestnik vysshei shkoly,* no. 4 (April), pp. 11–14.
Analytical Center (1992). *Nauka Rossii segodnia i zavtra. Sostoianie otechestvennoi nauki i prognoz ee razvitiia na 1993 god.* Moscow: December, issue 2.
Balzer, Harley D. (1985). *Effects of Soviet Education Reform on the Military.* McLean, VA: SAIC.
————.(1987). "The Soviet Scientific-Technical Revolution: Education of Cadres." In Craig Sinclair, ed., *The Status of Civil Science.* Dordrecht: Martinus Nijhoff.
————. (1989). *Soviet Science on the Edge of Reform.* Boulder, CO: Westview Press.
————. (1991). "From Hypercentralization to Diversity: Continuing Efforts to Restructure Soviet Education." *Technology in Society,* vol. 13, nos. 1/2, pp. 123–50.
————. (1992). "Educating Scientific-Technical Revolutionaries? Continuing Efforts to Restructure Soviet Higher Education." In John Dunstan, ed., *Soviet Education Under Perestroika.* London: Routledge.
Fedorov, V.P. (1990). "Ne v kadrakh delo!" *EKO,* no. 6 (192).
GKNVSh RSFSR. (1991a). *Gosudarstvennaia programma razvitiia vysshego obrazovaniia v RSFSR* (Proekt).
————. (1991b). *Vremennoe polozhenie o mnogourovennevoi sisteme vysshego obrazovaniia v RSFSR* (Proekt).
Jones, Anthony, Walter D. Connor, and David E. Powell, eds. (1991). *Soviet Social Problems.* Boulder, CO: Westview Press.
Kerr, Stephen (1991). "Debate and Controversy in Soviet Higher Education Reform: Reinventing a System." In J. Dunstan, ed., *Soviet Education Under Perestroika.* London: Routledge.
Komitet po vysshei shkole (1992a). *Vysshee obrazovanie v rossiiskoi federatsii: vremia peremen.* Moscow: Logos.
————. (1992b). *Nauchnaia pogramma "universitety Rossii."* Moscow: Ministerstvo nauki, vysshei shkoly i tekhnicheskoi politiki Rossiiskoi federatsii.
————. (1992c). *Programma konversii nauchno-tekhnicheskogo potentsiala vuzov.* Moscow: Ministerstvo nauki, vysshei shkoly i tekhnicheskoi politiki Rossiiskoi federatsii.
Kossov, B. and E. Kniazev (1991). "Eshche raz o kontseptsii obrazovaniia." *Alma mater,* no. 4 (April).
Lenshin, Valery (1993). "Higher Education in Russia Under the Pressure of Reform," unpublished paper presented at the seminar "Science and Technology With A Human Face." Cambridge: Massachusetts Institute of Technology, April.
Ministerstvo nauki, vysshei shkoly i tekhnicheskoi politiki Rossiiskoi federatsii, Nauchno-issledovatel'skii institut vysshego obrazovaniia [NIIVO] (1992). *Obrazovanie v Rossii. Spravochnik.* Moscow: NIIVO.
Odom, William E. (1976). "The 'Militarization' of Soviet Society." *Problems of Communism,* vol. 25, September-October.
Saltychev, A., Iu. Akimov, and E. Burykin (1990). "Itogi attestatsii," *Vestnik vysshei shkoly,* no. 1 (January), pp. 52–53.
Torchinskii, M. (1991). "Uchenye stepeni bez dissertatsii." *EKO,* no. 4.

3

Diversification in Russian Education

STEPHEN T. KERR

A few years ago, a chapter with a title such as this would have been recognized instantly as an oxymoron by those interested in the fate of schools, students, and education in what was then the USSR. If there was one thing that the highly centralized system of that country prized, it was uniformity—uniformity in textbooks, teaching practices, syllabi, methods of preparing teachers, ways of assessing students, and patterns of school organization. Outcomes, too, were to be uniform—so many students prepared for roles in industry, so many for manual labor on farms, and a few to move on to universities and other specialized careers. While there was in fact considerable diversity within the system, most of it was not of the sort that Soviet educational planners wanted to underscore. There were, for example, special schools that catered exclusively to the elite, and segregated schools for the handicapped and retarded that kept them effectively out of public view; there were also huge, but largely unacknowledged, differences between rural and urban schools. The projected and desired image was one of a system in which minimal, planned diversity contributed to the overall purpose of the Soviet state in creating an "all-around, harmoniously developed personality."

The advent of Mikhail Gorbachev, the promulgation of perestroika and its associated reforms, and the eventual breakup of Communist Party power, brought a dizzying series of changes in this tightly controlled educational world. For our purposes here, we can think of these developments as divided roughly into three periods: the first reform efforts generally followed the old Soviet model of centrally dictated changes required of all schools and teachers, but at the same time allowed more experimentation around the fringes than had been permitted previously; next, as the era of perestroika continued, old centers of power and influence began to decay, and new ones arose—sometimes briefly—to take their place; finally, before and after the collapse of the USSR at the end of 1991, changes of a more far-reaching nature began to be proposed for the system of schools in Russia.

The first of these phases has been adequately discussed elsewhere, so we will not dwell on it extensively here. The second phase has also been described, although less thoroughly, and so some aspects of it warrant our attention here. The final stage is unfolding as this book is in preparation, so we can provide only outlines of what the future may bring. In each of these periods, diversification was encouraged differently, took place to different degrees, and had different consequences. The conclusion will draw together these threads, and will suggest what future may await Russian education.

Background: The Last Soviet Reforms

In 1985, Soviet schools made up a large and inert institution. While many recognized that there was a need for change, and while there had been a number of reforms promulgated over the preceding years to encourage this system to function more efficiently for the economy and for social order, few substantive changes had taken place over the previous two decades in the ways that teachers taught or students learned. Much of the discussion about educational change in the late Soviet period before perestroika (1975–85) revolved around an issue central to the economic health of the socialist state: How could students be steered into manual jobs at a time when population growth in European Russia was static, when inefficient Soviet factories needed more laborers, and when higher education was increasingly available? In the context set by this critical issue, matters of pedagogy, of the psychological nurture of students, all took second place; the question of changing the underlying assumptions on which the system of schooling rested was still not raised at all in official forums.

Then came glasnost and perestroika. These changes brought a new environment for discussion of educational issues that was at once troubling and exhilarating for those who worked within the Soviet system of schooling. Some changes instituted after 1985 were simply more thoroughgoing instances of shifts that had already been proposed or tried before. But others were significantly new, representing sharp breaks with earlier practice and structure. In the former category were the attempts to revivify the Academy of Pedagogical Sciences, to restructure the series of government ministries and committees that oversee the educational system, and to restructure the curriculum. On a more fundamental level, there was now the possibility for alternative voices to be raised and for independent groups of various kinds to emerge; these new possibilities did not come to fruition immediately. Educators, perhaps even more than most groups in Soviet society, had been selected and trained to be loyal servants of the state, and so invitations to partake of newly available freedoms were not quickly or eagerly accepted.

The chronicle of change in Soviet education after 1985 is a relatively long one, and parts of it have been documented elsewhere (Dunstan 1987; Balzer 1985; Kerr 1989, 1990, 1992a, 1992b; Szekely 1986). In brief, the attempts of the education bureaucracy to improve the efficiency of the system through a set of reforms in 1984–85 (in general education) and 1986–87 (in higher education) provided only partial improvements. A new grade level was added to the general school, providing eleven years of education for a secondary school graduate instead of ten. Schools were charged to develop relationships with factories, farms, and other enterprises that would both introduce students more directly to the world of work, and also, it was hoped, overcome the notorious inefficiency of the educational system in preparing and placing its graduates by providing direct transition to employment following graduation. A new subject, fundamentals of computer science, was also added (principally in the hope of giving students some inkling of what might happen in the USSR if Soviet industry ever began to use enough computers to make a difference). In higher education, the economic rationale was also predominant: institutions of higher education (VUZy) were to work jointly with factories to prepare specialists, and faculty were to take more time actually to work in industry and therefore presumably do a better job of instructing their students with current procedures and needs in mind. Rectors and administrators, as well as faculty, gained some new rights to determine curriculum and procedures for evaluating faculty at the local level (Dobson 1987; Dunstan 1992; Kerr 1988, 1992a).

The official structures changed slowly. In 1989, the ministries and committees that had formerly guided all aspects of the educational system were reorganized and replaced with a single State Committee on Public Education. While few substantive alterations took place in the period immediately following this shift, there were a number of interesting events connected with it, including a National Congress of Education Workers in December of 1988 which gave some hint of the changes to come.

Gennadii Yagodin, the chairman of the new committee, was a typical Gorbachev-era figure—too radical in his vision of the future for many moderates and conservatives, too slow-moving and unsupportive of serious change for the radical reformers.

One bastion of conservatism that had a continued effect on the entire Soviet educational establishment was the Academy of Pedagogical Sciences (APN). Through its research and development activities, which included such things as developing all texts and supplemental materials used in the school system, the Academy exercised a nearly invisible but profound influence over all aspects of the educational system. Since the Academy, the ministries, the Party, and the trade union controlled all the journals through which teachers might express themselves, there was little opportunity for truly independent thought to emerge from among the normally passive ranks of the nearly two million teachers who worked in the nation's schools. Although a committee was established in the summer of 1988 to consider what changes might be made in the Academy, and a new process for selecting members was proposed and adopted, little seemed to change. The names of those proposed as candidates or full members during 1989 included a few well-known and respected pedagogues, but many more provincial hacks and unproductive scholars. Indeed, some of the best-known figures of the nascent education reform movement were either conspicuous in their absence, or were voted down in the balloting in favor of lesser-known figures. (Some measure of the persistence of the pedagogical elite may be seen in the names proposed for candidates or full membership in APN for 1989 and 1990. The 1989 list contained 375 names and the 1990 list, 303 names; 173 names appeared on both lists.)

Changes in curriculum also came slowly or not at all. The much discussed addition of computer science to the curriculum in 1985 was purportedly an attempt by Gorbachev to show "there is something new in education," but the move backfired when providing the needed hardware and software proved an impossible task for the hard-pressed Soviet computer industry (Kerr 1991). Arranging the mandated experiences with industry also became increasingly difficult as firms struggled to support themselves under the new "self-financing" economic conditions imposed by the central government. Factories, which had formerly regarded the training and orientation of young workers as an unproductive but unavoidable and not especially costly part of their mission, now had good financial reason not to cooperate. Too, the addition of the extra grade level was accomplished slowly, and there was much consternation about the inabil-

ity of six-year-olds to sit quietly in the prescribed Soviet fashion through a
long day of classes.

Signs of Diversity, 1987–91: The Movement and Its Aftermath

The most interesting indicator of change on the Soviet educational scene
in the post-1985 era was the rise of diversity outside the official governmental structure. This development included such phenomena as the appearance of a national network of "Eureka" clubs (or discussing and
modeling alternative pedagogical styles and theories) from about 1986;
the founding of the independent Creative Teachers Union during 1988;
and the increasing attention given to about a dozen so-called innovators in
education. If there is a single person to be credited with the early and
forceful emergence of this movement, it is Vladimir Fedorovich Matveev,
editor of *Uchitel'skaia gazeta* (Teachers Gazette) from 1984 until early
1989. Matveev, who died in October 1989 must surely rank among educators as one of the unsung heroes of perestroika. His uncompromising
integrity in the face of corruption and muddle-headed bureaucracy would
have made him an outstanding figure in any society; that he managed to
do what he did in the early Gorbachev period is indeed almost unimaginable. That he eventually suffered for what he did, even in the heady days
of 1988–89, provides an indicator of what must still lurk in the backs of
the minds of many Soviet citizens bent on challenging the institutions of
their society to change.

Matveev started out as a journalist specializing in children's and educational issues. He worked first for *Komsomol'skaia pravda*, then for
Murzilka, a children's magazine that might well have remained a backwa-
ter were it not for Matveev's insistence on finding excellent authors who
would write for children. When he came to *Uchitel'skaia gazeta* in 1984,
he was in his early fifties and had little direct experience in education. He
did, however, immediately identify and encourage a remarkable team of
writers and teachers to join him on the journal. Quickly identified as
"Matveev's team," they began to produce a remarkable series of articles,
features, and serial publications that focused public attention on the problems of education in new ways. School directors who ventured to try
something new suddenly found themselves in the spotlight rather than cut
off from public attention. Teachers with talent or a different way of working with children found their ideas and approaches welcomed. Those who
thought that parents had been too long ignored by the system found themselves with a platform for their views.

At a series of conferences of the teacher-innovators starting in 1985, Matveev encouraged and publicized the very different ways of working that these educators had developed, and soon there appeared (again, with his firm support and expert coaching) a network of clubs, most under the name "Eureka," to discuss, extend, and test the ideas the innovators had developed. By the summer of 1988, these clubs had formed themselves into the Creative Union of Teachers, a group that was independent of the official educators' trade union and committed to diversity and the exploration of alternatives. Several open conferences for the presentation of alternative models were held during 1987 and 1988, leading to a final round of demonstrations for six "featured" models. Aleksandr Adamskii, a physics teacher from Moscow, Simon Soloveichik, a correspondent and writer whose views encouraged parental involvement and increased care for children, and Oleg Gazman, a follower of V.A. Sukhomlinskii and a specialist in "upbringing" work, were all key figures in the movement at this stage.

The Union held its first congress in the spring of 1989, and accounts suggest it was a lively and well-attended affair. After this event, however, it slipped into a long period of anonymity. Several factors probably explain this. First, there was the continuing hostility to the movement on the part of the educational establishment; the Academy of Pedagogical Sciences took the lead in this regard. Those who worked at APN's institutes and labs made no secret of their scorn for the "impostors" and "self-advertisers" who claimed to speak for pedagogical science. Also, the Union had great difficulty simply in getting itself organized. While many of its members were enthusiasts, they were enthusiasts for pedagogy, not for organization or management. The bickering and internal feuding that immediately seemed to seize the Union is evident in many accounts of meetings during the period from 1989 to 1991. Nor did the Union ever manage to publish a regular newspaper—two issues of *Peremena* appeared in 1989 and 1990, and there was apparently a great demand for such a paper, but the intricacies of editing, printing, and distribution, combined with the usual difficulties in assuring a regular supply of newsprint, doomed the venture (material under the rubric of "Peremena" and edited by Aleksandr Adamskii appeared during 1991 in *Demokraticheskaia Rossiia*). A further factor in the decline of what once appeared a hopeful sign in the Soviet pedagogical firmament, was the departure of several of the key innovators (especially Adamskii, later V.F. Shatalov and S.N. Lysenkova) to form their own consulting groups, or to engage in other activities (Sh. Amonashvili went to the Supreme Soviet; Eduard Dneprov went to the Center for Pedagogical

Innovations, and then to the RSFSR Ministry of Education; and Soloveichik went to *Novoe vremia*).

But more than anything else, it was the change in leadership at *Uchitel'skaia gazeta* that caused the downfall of the movement for greater teacher control in the Soviet educational system. Matveev was nothing if not a controversial figure; his constant attacks on the Party and on its heavy-handed approach to schools and education won him no friends in the CPSU education bureaucracy. Likewise, he managed to alienate rather completely those in the Academy of Pedagogical Sciences whom he felt were merely hacks and poseurs and not real scholars and educators. Finally, and probably most unforgivably, he took on CPSU Secretary Egor Ligachev himself. For refusing to abide by a direct order from Ligachev that he not publish disparaging material about Ligachev's performance as a CPSU functionary during his time in a provincial capital, Matveev was simply removed from his position as editor of *Uchitel'skaia gazeta*. Indeed, so great was the ire of the secretary that there was serious doubt for a while that the paper itself would even survive. It did, but only after becoming an organ of the CPSU with a party hack as editor (Gennadii Seleznev, who went on in the spring of 1991 to head *Pravda*, apparently successfully since he was reconfirmed there as editor after the coup). Matveev, disillusioned and sick (perhaps from a cancer contracted during a required "sabbatical" to edit a rural teachers' paper in Belarus during 1986), died in October 1989. (Some materials on Matveev's life and work may be found in Matveeva 1992; see also Kerr 1994.)

In Matveev's absence, the movement he had created grew increasingly splintered. As noted above, the Creative Union found it difficult to operate without sufficient management expertise and commitment from its creators. But some of these, notably Aleksandr Adamskii, found new allies among teachers and schools willing to branch out and experiment under the new conditions of freedom and uncertainty that the pedagogical glasnost of the late 1980s had created. Adamskii's own intellectual progeny, the "Eureka" clubs, had come together to form the Union, but they also retained in large part their original independent form, and thus provided a set of local bases for further renewal of educational organizations. Adamskii capitalized on their willingness to try new approaches by creating a consulting group to provide seminars and advice to schools and regions wanting such services. In addition to working with a number of city regional education departments, he formed particularly close ties with several innovative schools that were already well known throughout the country for their outspoken and talented directors. These included, among others, Aleksandr Tubel'skii at School 734 in Moscow (the School of Self-Definition), Tat'iana Kovaleva who started a private school in Tomsk, and Isak Frumin, who directed a laboratory school in conjunction with Krasnoiarsk University in that city.

The success of Adamskii and company seemed to give heart to others among the innovators of the mid-1980s. Lysenkova and Shatalov started their own consulting services, and others engaged in increasingly public debate about a wide variety of educational policies, not merely teaching methods. The Creative Union, in the meantime, seemed to degenerate into a typically Soviet institution—an increasingly bureaucratic and rule-bound structure, to be milked regularly by its leaders for perks and privileges. By early 1991, the activities of the Union's leaders (particularly Yaroslav Beregovoi and Vladimir Daineko, but several others as well) were once again on the pages of *Uchitel'skaia gazeta*, but this time in a very negative light. There were accounts of nepotism, misuse of funds, and intellectual bankruptcy (Kvartskhava 1991).

Coverage of the Creative Union and other alternative groups increased in *Uchitel'skaia gazeta* during 1991, especially after Seleznev moved to the editorship of *Pravda* in April. His successor, Petr Polozhevets, while following basically the same line and adhering to CPSU policies, seemed somewhat more open to admitting that there were other educational forces at work in Soviet society, and therefore began once again to recognize the legacy of Matveev (publishing, for example, a long account of the *Matveevskie chteniia* (Matveev lectures) that took place on the former editor's birthday in June). Polozhevets also attracted some younger journalists (such as Ivan Bogachev, a talented writer on economics and education) to work for the paper, and asserted that its pages were to be "open to all." While the generally lackluster style of the paper continued, there were at least occasional flickers of controversy and dissent visible on its pages.

The events of the second congress of the Creative Union, however, demonstrate how difficult real progress in education is these days in the former USSR. Staged in the Crimea in October 1991, the meeting quickly degenerated into a shouting match among rival factions, each claiming to speak for "real teachers." There were tussles for the microphone, long arguments over procedural matters, and disputes as to both form and substance. Most of the original founders of the Union (Adamskii, Gazman, Tubel'skii, and so on) suggested that its presence was no longer as critical as when it was created. With Dneprov sitting in the position of RSFSR Minister of Education, the Academy and the federal educational bureaucracies in increasing disarray, and the official pressure for reform coming more and more from those who, once outsiders, were now in positions of real power, there seemed little reason for a strong alternative with an elaborate administrative structure and rules for governance. Others, apparently attracted to the Union because of what it might materially offer as a vedomstvo (administrative department), were incensed that anyone should want to do away with "their own child," and therefore worked for its continuation and increased support. While there was agreement at the end of the meeting to have a small organizing committee to consider alternatives for further action, the prospects for significant action out of the Creative Union appeared dim (Borisova, Nikolaev, and Trukhacheva 1991; Riurikov 1991; "Igra" 1991). As noted below, however, several of the Union's founders have moved into new areas of activity that may carry forward its program in more effective ways than its structure allowed.

Power to the Disenfranchised: The Rise of Eduard Dneprov

In retrospect, it will probably be clear that no other event so shaped the future of education in the former USSR as Eduard Dmitrievich Dneprov's appointment as the minister of education of the RSFSR in June 1990. While the action at first appeared merely to be part of a rather thorough house cleaning of the ministry that Dneprov himself characterized as a "nest of the Black Hundreds," it gradually became clear over the ensuing year that what Dneprov had in mind was something quite new.

Dneprov's own background as a historian gave him a unique perspective on the problem of bringing diversity to Russian education. His own previous work had been largely focused on the schools of the Russian Empire immediately prior to the Russian Revolution of 1917, with particular attention to the condition of peasant and village schools. In 1988, when he took on the job of directing the work of VNIK-Shkola (*Vremennyi nauchno-issledovatel'skii kollektiv-Shkola*, the Ad Hoc Scientific-Research Collective on the School), he was viewed as something of an outsider among the academicians in the Academy of Pedagogical Sciences for his outspoken and critical views of much current pedagogical practice. VNIK quickly established itself as a group that would tolerate no compromise with what most of its members regarded as the obvious faults of the status quo. Instead, over the next two years, there appeared under VNIK's imprimatur a remarkable series of documents and proposals calling for a fundamental recasting of the Soviet system of education. While many of these papers were roundly ignored by the educational establishment as they were published, they soon came to have a second and more vigorous life after Dneprov became minister of education. Many of his former colleagues in VNIK, as well as many of the ideas they had generated, found new homes in the RSFSR Education Ministry.

The details of Dneprov's vision came into sharp relief in a document that he and his team published in January 1991: *Russian education in a period of transition: A program of stabilization and development* (Dneprov et al. 1991). It contains many proposals for and indications of new policy directions. Some of the ideas that are especially relevant to the question of diversification within the educational system include arrangements for teacher preparation; differentiation of the system of schools and educational institutions (including provisions for nongovernmental and private schools); the provision of new kinds of textbooks and other instructional materials; and new emphasis on the education of national minorities. What follows is drawn largely from that document, as well as from conversations with Dneprov and other officials (Vladimir Sobkin, Viktor Bolotov, Oleg Gazman, Elena Lenskaia, Vladimir Novichkov, and others) in the RSFSR Ministry of Education.

Diversifying Teacher Education

The reformers in the Russian Ministry of Education clearly have no illusions about the problems they face in reconstructing teacher education. Among teachers, 73 percent see schools as being in a "state of crisis"; 37 percent find themselves in "regular conflict" with at least some students, and 60 percent feel that "the family has abdicated its responsibility for raising children"; some 37 percent accuse other teachers of "apathy and carelessness" toward their colleagues (Dneprov et al. 1991, p. 27). Of the teachers taking courses through in-service institutes, 93.9 percent were unhappy with what they were offered and thought that these courses did little to stimulate creative approaches to their work (Ibid., p. 46).

Dealing with these problems, and educating teachers able to think for themselves, will require the organization of local instructional-research pedagogical complexes. These organizations will be based either at institutes or the lower pedagogical academies (*uchilishche*), but they may also include schools and businesses. (Some of the language of the document here is remarkably similar to that in the proposals in the United States for the development of professional development schools.) The outflow of "the best and the brightest" teachers will be somewhat compensated for by recruiting part-time teachers from the ranks of industry, scientific institutes, and universities (Ibid., pp. 175–76 [again, the solution calls to mind the many suggestions in the United States to provide alternative access routes to teaching for midcareer professionals]).

The thinking and pedagogical approaches of student teachers are to be diversified by exposing them to a variety of teaching models and encouraging them to make real pedagogical choices, rather than (as of old) having them adhere to a single "approved" model. Some specific changes in the preservice teacher education curriculum are closely tied to Soviet work in developmental psychology, particularly the work of L.S. Vygotsky and his followers (e.g., V.V. Davydov and his "activity approach"). As Viktor Bolotov, head of teacher preparation for the Russian Republic, recently put it, the teacher must "know what should change in your student and be able to create the conditions for this change" (Bolotov 1991, p. 1). Another model, the so-called dialogue of cultures, is based on the work of Vladimir Bibler. It postulates that children's thinking should retrace the developmental course of European civilization, beginning with the Greeks. Other approaches include Aleksandr Tubel'skii's school of self-determination, a kind of Soviet effort at site-based management (teachers, administrators, parents, and students join in setting the general direction for the school; students have freedom of choice in many activities, but the educational staff try to create options so attractive that students will voluntarily choose a desirable course of action [Tubel'skii 1989]). Approaches that focus on the "whole child," such as those of Carl Rogers and Rudolf Steiner (the Waldorf School) are also very popular and will get strong exposure in the pedagogical curricula of Russian teacher education institutions.

Diversifying the Structure of Schools and Educational Institutions

Russia is currently wrestling with the privatization of the educational sector. The new Russian Law on Education explicitly provides for the existence of nongovernmental educational institutions; several new organizations for those interested in private education have been formed, including the Russian Association of Nongovernmental Education (RANGO, or *Rossiiskaia assotsiatsiia negosudarstvennogo obrazovania* [Rezoliutsiia 1991]) and the Association of Directors of Experimental Schools and Centers. Private schools have begun to appear, with particular emphases and foci that vary from the entrepreneurial (business and management academies being a special favorite at the moment) to the religious (there are now schools with distinctively Orthodox and Jewish curricula). In addition, an increasing number of public schools are finding ways to make themselves distinctive—by designing special curriculums (often very similar to that of the former special schools [*spetsshkoly*]), returning to the classical studies common in the lycées and gymnasia of the early twentieth century, finding some other distinctive niche (such as the recently organized School of Slavic Cultures in Moscow), and by setting up increasingly selective entrance criteria.

While some educators clearly revel in the new freedom to create pedagogical alternatives, many (among both conservatives and reformers) seem quite troubled by the suggestion that private schools may "cream" the best students and teachers, leaving the regular public schools to deal with an increasingly fractious and alienated student body. The question of whether or not private schools should continue to receive government support has become the touchstone of this issue and, while the initial legal position of the ministry is that such aid should not go to schools in the private sphere, arguments continue, and there seems as yet no clear-cut resolution to this debate.

Another aspect of the effort to diversify education is the appearance of a large number of independent organizations, consulting services, and other interest groups. Some of these are organized principally as not-for-profit educational support operations, while others clearly hope to turn a profit. A survey of these suggests they fall into roughly five categories. First are the traditional pedagogical societies and societies that are focused on the work of an individual or on a school of pedagogical thought (the Pedagogical Society of the RSFSR, the Russian Anton Makarenko Association, the Comenius and Korszak Societies, and so on). These have found new life as the old restrictions have been loosened and their members enabled to be able to discuss and travel more freely; their roles, however, have not changed radically. Second, there are new groups focused around teachers' interests—the Moscow History Teachers Club, the Association of Informatics Teachers, the "Soviet Teacher" and "Torch" projects (the latter organized by *Uchitel'skaia gazeta* apparently as a counterweight to the Creative Union), and the New Pedagogical Technologies Association of Educators and Psychologists. While some of these groups are organizing their own interesting projects, most focus on the needs and interests of particular subsets of the educational community.

A third set of groups includes those organized by the new pedagogical entrepreneurs. Some of these people see education as a vehicle for direct economic gain (for instance, the Soviet-American Management Institute, established to provide courses on American business management techniques, or the Center for System Research and Educational Technology, created to provide programming services in exchange for computer hardware); others offer pedagogical services to the more independent school administrators, and hope thereby gradually to change the educational system (for example, the Creative Pedagogy group formed by the Center for Pedagogical Innovations and the Creative Union of Teachers, and cooperatives formed by notable teacher-innovators such as Shatalov and Lysenkova). Fourth are groups that include those united by common interests in creating and preserving a place in the educational system (for example, the several groups formed around private schooling such as RANGO and the International System of Alternative Educational Systems). Finally, there is a fifth set of parent and community groups, including such new entities as the Parent-Student-Teacher Research Association, the Association of School Councils, and the Association for the Pedagogical Support of Parents.

It is difficult to say what lasting effect these many new independent groups will have on education in Russia. Clearly, many of them were merely adventitious responses to a changing situation, attempts to carve an economic or political niche for their founders in a time of chaos and confusion. Many of the entrepreneurial groups are probably in this category, as are some of the new teacher-focused groups. Others (including the traditional pedagogical societies and groups formed around teachers' instructional interests, some of the community groups, and the interest groups with a focus on encouraging diversity through privatization) are likely to remain, especially if they are given priority status (as has been suggested by Russian Education Minister Dneprov) in the new trade union for teachers.

Diversification in Curricula and Materials

Curricula and educational materials are also to become more diverse, and it is increasingly possible to create them at the local level. But while this is now legally permissible, developing and distributing such materials in practice has proven to be enormously difficult. In part, the difficulty is material and financial: The ministry's report indicates only tiny press runs of new textbooks (e.g., 12,000 copies of physics texts, 9,850 of biology) were produced in the mid-1980s, leading to enormous unfilled demand (22 percent of all secondary teachers in specific subject fields—about 150,000 for each field—indicated a desire to use new texts [Dneprov et al., p. 36]). Some help is now coming from new publishing ventures with European partners, but the need is obviously still great. Shortages of paper, primitive printing technology, lack of computers for design and layout, and the absence of a well-developed system for ordering and distributing texts remain difficult obstacles.

Perhaps more serious than the financial hurdles are the psychological and institutional ones. In a system that has for years handed down new curricula and teachers' materials from the center, and where the very notions of curriculum design and instructional development—common in the West—are difficult to translate for an audience of educators, the idea that teachers can create the content of education either individually or at the level of the school is indeed novel. A number of projects sponsored by the Ministry of Education and various Western groups to try to overcome these barriers are now underway, but they have a long road to travel.

The success of these efforts has yet to be tested, but it is clear that the Russian Ministry of Education is working toward a fundamental reconceptualization of how materials and curricula are put in place. Connections have been established with a number of European groups, including IMTEC (International Movement Toward Educational Change), and with such experimental centers in the United States as the Chicago schools and the site-based management trials in Dade County, Florida. Given the almost unimaginable problems that the ministry faces in the printing and dissemination of materials, it is not surprising that one of its top priorities has been to establish working linkages with Western publishers so as to translate and disseminate basic works on pedagogy for both preservice and in-service teacher preparation.[1]

Diversification to Meet the Needs of National Minorities

Dneprov's charter for the Russian Ministry of Education, *Russian Education in a Period of Transition*, provides what is perhaps the first clear look at the dimensions of ethnic minorities in the Russian Republic—a catalog of groups and their relative student populations, together with a detailed listing of which languages are actually used for instruction and the length of time a student may study using them. In most cases, a non-Russian language is used only the first few years of schooling. These data also point out the huge administrative problems that face the ministry if it tries to provide a more truly bilingual curriculum, since many of the language groups are both tiny and isolated.

The data in Table 3.1 suggest that the position of the Soviet government over many years—that national minority groups were recognized and well provided for within the educational system—was overstated. If true bilingualism in education is intended to make available a full range of educational services in a student's native language over the full course of his or her educational career, then there are only three groups in Russia that meet this criterion: the Bashkirs, the Tatars, and the Georgians. Nine other groups, with student linguistic populations ranging from just over 3,000 (Kazakhs; this excludes fifty-six Estonians) to more than 145,000 (Chuvash) have instruction in their native languages available for more than two grades but fewer than eleven; the group with the longest grade-level coverage is the Yakuts, with nine grades. Some ten other groups, with populations ranging from just over 2,300 (Tabasarans) to over 84,000 (Ossetians), have instruction available for only one or two years. For the largest number of minority groups, some forty-three in all, only instruction about their native languages is available.

The classification proposed by the ministry for these language groups and their schools is instructive: a five-way distinction is proposed, based partly on nationality and partly on levels of economic development.

1. Languages of "autonomous" groups with a "mature" base (Russians, Bashkirs, etc.)
2. Languages of groups spread across several territories (Greeks, Gypsies, Nogai, etc.)
3. "Independent" groups "which can count on the support of their historic homelands" (Koreans and Germans)
4. Languages of peoples of other republics (Ukrainians, Georgians, Estonians, etc.)
5. Languages of small northern peoples—groups which are "not capable of independent development"

The way in which a nation treats its least powerful citizens may be taken as an indicator of its general level of concern about social welfare issues. If this is so, we must seriously wonder what will happen to the "small-numbered peoples" of the Russian Far North. This is a part of the country where levels of economic development are far behind those in other areas and whose educational position, as the Ministry suggests, "can be characterized as catastrophic" (Ibid., p. 147). Diversification of the educational system here will require a different kind of approach; simply saying to these long-oppressed groups, "Now figure out your own educational system," will not work.

Table 3.1

Language Instruction in the National Schools of the Russian Republic
(1989–1990)

Native Language	Instruction in the Language (grades)	Instruction about the Language (grades)	Number of Students (1989–90)
Abazin	—	1–11	13,520
Avar	1–2	1–11	76,452
Adygei	—	1–11	10,366
Azeri	1–2	1–11	4,209
Altai	1–3	1–11	11,269
Armenian	—	1–4	5,124
Balkar	—	1–11	7,900
Bashkir	1–11	1–11	81,451
Buriat	1–3	1–11	119,485
Veps	—[a]	1–2[b]	89
Georgian	1–11	1–11	389
Dargin	1–2[a]	1–11	43,220
Dolgan	—	1–2	246
Hebrew-Yiddish	—[a]	1–2	63
Itel'men	—[a]	1–2	49
Ingush	—	1–2	34,590
Kabardin	—	1–11	46,794
Kazakh	1–7	1–11	3,399
Kalmyk	1–2	1–11	23,193
Karachaev	—	1–11	13,520
Karelian	—[a]	1	571
Ket	—[a]	1–2	131
Komi-zyrian	—	1–11	22,369
Komi-permiak	—	1–8	6,413
Korean	—[a]	1–2	254
Koriak	—	1–4	616
Crimean-Tatar	—[a]	1–2	92
Kumyk	1–2	1–11	32,003
Lak	1–2	1–11	6,760
Lezgin	1–2	1–11	30,982
Lithuanian	—	1–4	20
Marii	1–4	1–11[c]	33,169
Mordovian	1–4	1–11[c]	24,771
Mansi	—	1–4	261
Nanai	—	1–4	449
German	—	1–11	11,960
Nenets	—	1–7	5,157
Norwegian	—[a]	1–2	480
Nivkh	—	1–3[d]	460
Nogai	1–2	1–11	5,206

Table 3.1 (continued)

Ossetian	1–2	1–11	84,835
Russian	1–11	1–11	18,881,183
Saam	—	1–2	34
Sel'kup	—[a]	1–2	1,784
Tatar	1–11	1–11	551,511
Tabasaran	1–2	1–11	2,332
Tat	—[a]	1–2	15
Tofalar	—[a]	1	35
Tuvinian	1–7	1–11	64,947
Turkmen	—[a]	1–11	62
Udegei	—[a]	1–2	250
Udmurt	—	1–11	43,408
Finnish	—	1–11	3,410
Khanty	—	1–4[e]	629
Khakas	—	1–11	6,669
Chuvash	1–4	1–11	145,804
Chechen	—	1–11	162,664
Cherkes	—	1–11	4,680
Chukot	—	1–7	4,355
Shor	—[a]	1	63
Estonian	1–7	1–11	56
Even	—	1–4	1,433
Evenki	—	1–8	1,492
Eskimo	—	1–4	258
Iukagir	—	1–2	84
Iakut	1–9	1–11	46,250

Source: Dneprov, Lazarev, and Sobkin (1991). *Russian education in a period of transition: A program of stabilization and development*, pp. 56–58.

[a] Instruction in these languages introduced in the past 10 years
[b] Veps: Instruction about the language on an oral basis
[c] Marii and Mordovian: "Instruction about" two literary languages
[d] Nivkh: "Instruction about" two dialects
[e] Khanty: "Instruction about" three dialects

What is being done to deal with these particular nationality issues is interesting and cause for hope: the Institute on National Problems of Education was created during 1991 (under the direction of Mikhail N. Kuz'min, a respected historian and scholar of ethnicity); materials for still-nonliterate peoples are being prepared; new national content is being included in teacher-training programs and in-service institutes; and two new journals dealing with national issues have appeared—*Life of Nationalities* and *Arctic Journal for Children and Youth*. Later steps are to include fuller efforts to create true national syllabi for these groups, the founding of local gymnasia and lycées to assure better educational standards, and the creation of national–regional centers to provide general support. The eventual hope is that each of the majority of these groups will be able to pursue its own development independently, with the smaller groups developing in a stable (but probably still dependent) fashion.

At least some efforts are being made to provide the same kinds of affirmative action programs for these groups that have existed in the United States for the past twenty years or so: A recent Ministry of Education decree announced that places would be reserved in pedagogical institutes and other institutions of higher education, institutions that are under the ministry's control for members of the Far North minority groups. Whether members of the groups will take advantage of these new opportunities, and whether the existence of such programs will generate the same kinds of dissatisfaction and protest that have been witnessed in the United States, remain to be seen.

The Routinization of Diversity: Developments in 1992

To say that the postcoup era in Soviet and Russian education has been eventful would be an understatement. Changes during this period include increasing diversification among educational institutions, the groups serving them, the educational press, and the centers of power actively seeking a voice on the nation's educational scene. Reviewed briefly here are the growing numbers of private schools and lycées, the arguments surrounding their funding, and the appearance of competing associations to provide a voice for them; the fate of *Uchitel'skaia gazeta* and the emergence of a new paper to serve teachers, *Pervoe sentiabria*; the genesis and growth of several organizations to provide in-service and other advanced training for teachers; the growing devolution of power from the Ministry of Education to levels further down the administrative pyramid; and the gradual fractioning of forces in the Academy of Pedagogical Sciences (now the Russian Academy of Education).

Private Lycees and Experimental Schools

Vasilii Davydov, vice president of the Russian Academy of Education, recently estimated that there are more than 500 private schools now operating in Russia (Davydov 1993). Developments in late 1991 and early 1992 gave some idea of the scope of interest in creating new types of independent schools. Meetings held at the Ministry of Education and at the offices of *Uchitel'skaia gazeta* during this time drew more than a hundred participants from all parts of the country. While some of these schools were actually in operation, more were still in the planning stages, and their directors and managers seemed hungry for information and advice. Unfortunately, according to at least one participant in the meetings, the principal organizer, Vladimir Zhukov, seemed unable to break out of past models, and insisted on delivering long speeches at the opening meetings. Several of those attending reportedly walked out in disgust. The meetings sponsored by *Uchitel'skaia gazeta*, however, did lead to the creation of an association that now seems to sport a full complement of officers and titles.

Competing with RANGO for the attention of those interested in new forms in education will be the Association of Directors of Experimental Schools and Centers, led by Aleksandr Tubel'skii. Tubel'skii's own Moscow School No. 734, the School of Self-Definition, has garnered considerable attention over the past several years, and the new group seems to have drawn in many creative thinkers, including Isak Frumin of Krasnoiarsk and Tat'iana Kovaleva of Tomsk, as well as Adamskii, Anatolii Kasprzhak, and Elena Khiltunen of Moscow, Viacheslav Lozing of Kemerovo, Sergei Nekrasov of Krasnodar, Nikolai Guzik of Odessa, and Sergei Vetrov, rector of the Ukrainian Open University. The group seems more open than RANGO and is committed to modeling their systems through open seminars and festivals.[2]

The Pedagogical Press

At the beginning of 1992, *Uchitel'skaia gazeta* announced to its readers that it had available only enough capital to publish perhaps eighteen issues instead of the fifty-two planned for the year. Financial aid provided by Boris M. Bim-Bad's Russian Open University enabled the beleaguered weekly to limp forward, publishing a regular insert with material for teachers prepared by the university's staff. Nonetheless, there seemed to be a large group of teachers still searching for a publication more attuned to their daily needs, more like Matveev's paper.

In the summer of 1992, Bim-Bad—acting in concert with former *Uchitel'skaia gazeta* correspondents Soloveichik, Adamskii, and T.I. Matveeva (the widow of the newspaper's former editor)—decided to found a new paper for teachers. Under the title *Pervoe sentiabria* (September First), the first issue arrived in time for the start of the new academic year, and was issued in a press run of 50,000 copies. The new thrice-weekly paper seemed to find an audience quickly among teachers. Estimates suggested that it might quickly surpass *Uchitel'skaia gazeta* in total readership. Part of the reason for this may be the fact that it contains not merely news for teachers in the manner of the former Uchitel'skaia gazeta, but rather is intended to be a working resource for the teacher's daily life: the paper comes accompanied by several supplements each week which focus on the teaching of separate subjects (chemistry, physics, history, English [American English!], and children's health). In a society starved for new ideas on pedagogy, new textual materials are very attractive (much of the initial content of the supplements seemed to be reprinted texts and teachers' materials). The paper's focus on the needs of teachers is seen in its subtitle, "The Teacher of Teachers" and in the encouraging aphorism running under the masthead on each issue, "You are a brilliant teacher; you have wonderful pupils." The latter, which Simon Soloveichik admits is designed to counter the mood of despair among teachers, may be the best indicator of the current state of mind in Russia's schools.

Other new pedagogical publications served to increase the variety of opinion circulating in the marketplace of pedagogical ideas. The popularly oriented publication *Magistr i*, on psychology and education, seemed aimed at the readership of *Narodnoe obrazovanie*. The ill-fated *Pedagogicheskii vestnik*, published by the Soviet Association of Researchers–Educators, which enjoyed a brief flurry of popularity in 1990–91, seemed almost to have disappeared from popular attention by 1992.

Clearly, the financial obstacles to publishing a regular paper under current conditions will deter many would-be press entrepreneurs. But the thirst for new ideas continues, and the demand for new pedagogically oriented publications suggests the importance of the printed word in a society and an occupation so long restricted in what was available.

In-service Training for Teachers

Teachers have continued to demand new approaches to in-service training, new ways of discovering and implementing new methods and techniques in the classrooms. Several consulting organizations have appeared to address their needs. Perhaps best known has been Aleksandr Adamskii's Eureka Center for Socio-Pedagogical Design (also known as the Eureka Open University). Serving teachers through seminar workshops around the country, Adamskii's group has provided several hundred seminars since 1987. Some of these are national in scope and are designed to attract primarily city and regional educational administrators, as well as teachers who have already made preliminary changes in their own work. Additional seminars are offered at the district and city levels and call for perhaps a somewhat lesser degree of commitment on the part of teachers. The seminars are partly informational, with different pedagogical and administrative models presented and discussed, but also partly transformational, with participants effectively isolated for a period of several days and subjected to an overload of new ideas and images of how education might be carried out. There is also a strong emphasis on theoretically grounded models, such as the Vygotsky–Davydov School of Development, the Biblerian Dialogue of Cultures model, the resurrected School of Tolstoy, the imported Waldorf school, and occasional glances in the direction of Maria Montessori and Carl Rogers. Eureka's prospects appear bright, but it is difficult to tell whether the transformative method it uses will continue to find favor in lean times.

Other in-service groups have used different approaches. One that is especially popular is the so-called game method popularized as a consciousness-raising technique in the late 1980s. A principal proponent has been Petr Shchedrovitskii, son of the well-known psychologist of the same name. His School of Cultural Policy treats education as an essential part (but only a part) of the social and economic development of a region. Students now study with Shchedrovitskii and his colleagues and work with them to put on seminars and stage large-scale simulations in various parts of the country.

Perhaps most successful so far among the new educational entrepreneurs has been Boris Bim-Bad's Russian Open University (ROU). The essential quality here has been organizational and managerial skill combined with a flair for marketing. The new university boasts an enrollment of some 17,000 students, almost all studying in the evenings in faculties with formerly unfamiliar titles: "Andragogy," "Waldorf Pedagogy," "Business and Management," and the "Higher Christian-Orthodox School." Styled after the British and other foreign open universities, ROU may be the first Russian institution to ask students on its application form to list the types of books they have in their personal libraries (Rossiiskii 1991). Keeping the university afloat is a steady influx of dollars from contacts (and contracts) with a number of American institutions, which send their students to Moscow for intensive language and cultural courses. ROU has an appeal for teachers, but as it is organized in traditional fashion with courses and exams, over the long run it may do less to reshape teachers' perceptions of what is possible than the previous two operations.

The fate of the other numerous consulting organizations that were formed in the late 1980s is difficult to predict. Many will doubtless disappear in the economic whirlwinds now sweeping the Russian landscape. Some, like Tvorcheskaia Pedagogika, the commercial arm of the former Creative Union of Teachers and Dneprov's Center for Pedagogical Innovations, may survive because of their connections and their image among teachers. Others, such as Viacheslav Pogrebenskii's new psychological consulting firm, seem poised to recast teacher in-service training along newer, less traditional lines.

The Rise of Local Control

The program developed by Eduard Dneprov provided for the increasing devolution of financial control of the schools' budgets to lower levels (oblast, region, or city), with the ministry playing more the role of guide and helper than of controller. Indeed, the overall leadership of the educational system changed in late 1992 as Dneprov moved from his position as minister of education to the post of advisor to President Yeltsin on educational issues. Dneprov's replacement, Evgenii Tkachenko, pledged to follow the program designed by his predecessor. These changes, completely unimaginable in the previously centralized Soviet system of education, is now slowly coming into being, though not without some difficulties for those involved. As anyone familiar with budgeting and accountability in the United States is aware, local control is both a blessing and a curse—a blessing because it permits local change and experimentation on a scale unknown elsewhere in the world, but also a curse because it can lead to disaster either financially (which occasionally happens) or pedagogically (which happens more frequently, as school superintendents and principals make hesitant decisions, order and use mass-produced texts, or stick with tried-and-true though unimaginative methods).

In Russia, there was simply no groundwork done before decisions about financial matters were forced down onto the local level. The results do not appear to have been universally good. The general absence of abilities to deal with local budgeting, to negotiate with teacher unions, to define the roles of the city and district education heads, to determine what kinds of training and retraining teachers should receive, and, in rural areas, to cope with the continuing impoverishment of life generally—all hinder the possibilities for change. As Eureka and other in-service providers offer training to local and regional school heads, these needed skills may begin to emerge, but at the moment there are vast problems connected with the new freedoms.

Competitors to the Academy

The problems associated with changing the USSR Academy of Pedagogical Sciences into the Russian Academy of Education are many and have been dealt with elsewhere. What is interesting with regard to the creation of additional diversity in education within the Russian Federation is the appearance, at least briefly, of competing structures, such as the Moscow Academy for the Development of Education. This group, which appeared at the beginning of 1992 and published a series of articles outlining its platform in *Uchitel'skaia gazeta*, brought together some serious figures in Russian psychology and education, including Vitalii Rubtsov, a protegé of Davydov, and Iurii Gromyko, one of the founders of the game approach. While their attempt to redefine the terms under which the Academy works may have been partly motivated by self-interest (several were eventually named as members to the Russian Academy of Education), the effort at least demonstrated that there was no cow too sacred for the reformers to take on under the new, post-Soviet conditions (Moskovskaia 1992).

Stable Diversity through Disorder: Cautions and Prospects

Cautions

Clearly, there is much conflict and confusion within the Russian educational system at the moment: Formerly subservient education offices at the oblast, regional, and city levels are asserting control, as are the newly emergent ministries of education in the autonomous republics and regions. The federal structures that for so long determined what would happen throughout the Soviet empire—the State Committee and its predecessor ministries, the Academy of Pedagogical Sciences, the CPSU—are in disarray, and many (the Academy and the CPSU) will not likely return; new groups and organizations assert their existence daily (usually accompanied by pleas for financial support). Communication continues to be a problem, as supplies of paper and typographic facilities remain rare. Through it all, teachers and administrators desperately seek ways to acquire new approaches and the means for putting them into practice.

Perhaps most critical is the hard task of nurturing democratic habits of thought and action. There is still a hesitancy to trust processes that have never been strong parts of the Russian cultural tradition, and so open debate, respect for opponents' positions, and the ability to judge a person on merit do not come easily. What to do if one loses an intellectual or social struggle poses a particular problem for educators. There are also the details of democratic life in schools and institutions: Who is to have what powers? How can decisions be made without involving everyone all of the time? How can rights and responsibilities be described and communicated in a way that all will accept? How much democracy in school organization and decision making (in matters affecting curriculum and instruction, for example) is it reasonable to try to effect? What rights are there for private schools to go their own way, and what responsibility does the federal or republic government have to assure comparability of educational experience and equality of opportunity? Working with educators in the former USSR today frequently gives one the feeling that one is watching the writing of the educational equivalent of the eighteenth-century American Federalist Papers, but without the benefit of knowing how the values being expressed will be played out over the subsequent two hundred years of history.

Additional barriers to increasing diversity are mostly administrative and bureaucratic: the uncertainty surrounding the new Law on Education regulating what can and cannot happen in schools at the level of cities and regions; and the general fears accompanying the high rate of inflation and the difficulty in predicting how much will be available for schools in the near future. In some cases, attempts to adopt popular Western models have been undertaken too rapidly: the appearance of many cooperative ventures involving the teaching of business and management skills; some similar attempts by Western entrepreneurs to "sell" local Russian authorities on a particular plan or program; and the adoption of voucher systems and radical free-market economics as solutions to educational problems.

Prospects

There are signs of hope. Diversity among schools and pedagogical approaches is no longer seen as heretical; educators of a reformist bent have been encouraged by the coup and its aftermath and feel charged to pursue their programs more strongly than before. More teachers seem attracted to public life, and more intellectuals and scientists (who a few years ago would have shunned any contact with the schools) are becoming involved through school councils, classroom teaching, and writing.

Significantly, the heritage of Russian education seems to come more and more often to the fore as a basis on which new approaches can be built. In Adamskii's Eureka, for example, there is a strong tendency for teachers to gravitate to those models with a distinctive Russian stamp—the models of Vygotsky, Tolstoy, and Bibler seem genuinely new, but at the same time are in some ways familiar. Whether this theoretical purposiveness can remain and spread on a wider plane will be interesting to see, for lack of theoretical substance has long been a weakness in Western in-service training for both teachers and administrators. It may be that the Russian genius for theory will find an outlet as teachers are prepared and retrained for work in the new schools of Russia.

As Russian schools become more diverse, there are a great many questions that Western researchers can pursue. Answers to these will be useful, not merely as description, but as a means to help in the further development of education in Russia. If diversity in education is valued not as an end in itself, but rather as a precondition for the creation of a more fully democratic and civil society, then we must pay attention to a number of issues.

How Much and What Kinds of Diversity?

The growth in diversity needs to be cataloged and examined. What groups are strong and have reasonable prospects? How will they work to express the interests of their constituents, and how will they respond to the need for some kind of common coordination? What kinds of new pedagogical approaches will be tried, and to what effect? What will be the role of national minorities, how much independence will they be given, and how much central coordination will continue to be exerted? How will private education develop, and what is reasonable to expect from a private-school sector that has no traditions? How will the issues of equity be handled? Perhaps most interestingly from an American perspective, do diversity and choice really lead to improved quality in educational outcomes? And how should those outcomes be defined, anyway?

Whither Vocational Education?

The relationships between education and the economy also need to be watched. Historically, educators in Europe and the USSR have paid more attention to issues of vocational education and the movement of students into productive roles in the economy than have Americans. Will the chaotic current state of the Soviet economy permit schools and firms to interact? Will the approach of the early 1980s—to link schools and firms—be abandoned, reshaped, or completely rethought? What kinds of skills will vocational tracks stress, and how will these be tied into the changing nature of the workplace? What, to mirror an emphasis of Soviet sociological studies in the early 1970s, will be the balance between unrestrained vocational choice and the needs of the economy?

Schools and Democratic Society

The role of the schools in creating a democratic society should also be studied. Clearly, there are difficulties here. The conservatism of the teacher corps is well documented, and the schools have not been called upon in recent years to exercise dynamic leadership in recreating society in a new image. Nonetheless, there are things that could be done. The writing of new texts in history and economics, and even on such topics as family relations, will bear watching to see if democratic values are incorporated. Likewise, the practices of teachers and administrators with respect to democratic processes within schools and classrooms should be observed. Are schools really providing a model for what a democracy needs to be? (American educators might rightly protest that we ourselves are not paragons in this matter).

Schools and Communities

The relationships between schools and parents and schools and communities also bear close watching. Previously, many parents reported having to deal with the psychological problems of their children, problems stemming from the ways that they were treated in schools. Teachers and directors once felt well insulated and able to ignore the demands of communities (if such demands were ever voiced); now, there is a new sense that the public cannot be ignored and that educators must in some ways be accountable. What forms will that accountability take? Will school councils evolve to express community interests? What forms of governance will appear, and what will be the balance there among the interests of parents, teachers, and officials? Will local control develop to such an extent that truly individual local curricula and practices will result?

Education and the National Agenda

Finally, and most important, what place will education come to have on the national agenda? In the West, governments have become accustomed to giving lip service to educational questions, with little real action in policy, financing, or public decision making ("America–2000" and the

New American Schools Development Corporation are good examples of this in the United States). While public volunteerism and "new thinking" may be important, they are not likely to go far without strong leadership from some quarter to keep public attention focused on real educational issues rather than on red herrings. What will those forces be in Russia? What will be the issues that the new post-Soviet society will choose to advance in the field of education? And, for those who want to go beyond study to action, what can be done to help?

Notes

1. V. Sobkin, personal communication, April 6, 1991.
2. T.M. Kovaleva, personal communication, October 1992.

References

Balzer, H. (1985). "Is Less More? Soviet Science in the Gorbachev Era." *Issues in Science and Technology, 1*(4), pp. 29–46.

Borisova, L., Nikolaev, V., and Trukhacheva, A. (1991). "Soiuz umer. Da zdravstvuet soiuz!" (The union is dead. Long live the union!) *Uchitel'skaia gazeta*, no. 41 (8–15 October), p. 1.

Davydov, V. (1993). "The Transformation of Russian Schools." Paper presented at the Annual Meeting of the American Educational Research Association, Atlanta, Georgia, April.

Dneprov, E.D., Lazarev, V.S., and Sobkin, V.S. (Eds.) (1991). *Rossiiskoe obrazovanie v perekhodnom periode: Programma stabilizatsii i razvitiia* (Russian education in the period of transition: A program of stabilization and development). Moscow: RSFSR Ministry of Education.

Dobson, Richard B. (1987, July–August). "Objectives of the Current Restructuring of Soviet Higher and Specialized Secondary Education." *Soviet Education, 29*(9–10), pp. 5–25.

Dunstan, John. (Ed.) (1987). *Soviet Education under Scrutiny*. Glasgow: Jordanhill College Publications.

Dunstan, J. (Ed.) (1992). *Soviet Education under Perestroika*. London: Routledge.

"Igra v s''ezd, ili 'parlamentskii kretinizm' " (Playing at a congress, or "parliamentary cretinism"). (1991). *Uchitel'skaia gazeta*, no. 43 (22–29 October), p. 3.

Kerr, S.T. (1988). "The Soviet Reform of Higher Education." *The Review of Higher Education, 11*(3), pp. 215–46.

——— (1989). "Reform in Soviet and American Education: Parallels and Contrasts." *Phi Delta Kappan, 71*(1), pp. 19–28.

——— (1990). "Will 'Glasnost' Lead to 'Perestroika'? Directions for Educational Reform in the USSR." *Educational Researcher, 19*(7), pp. 26–31.

——— (1991). "Educational Reform and Technological Change: Computer Literacy in the Soviet Union." *Comparative Education Review, 35*(2), pp. 222–54.

——— (1992a). "Debate and Controversy in Soviet Higher Education Reform: Reinventing a System." In J. Dunstan (Ed.), *Soviet Education under Perestroika*. London: Routledge, pp. 146–63.

——— (1992b). "USSR." In P.W. Cookson, Jr., A.R. Sadovnik, and S.F. Semel

(Eds.), *International Handbook of Educational Reform*. Westport, CT: Greenwood Press, pp. 473–93.

——— (Ed.) (1994). "The Alternative Pedagogical Press." (Thematic issue of) *Russian Education and Society*, vol. 36, no. 1 (January).

Kvartskhava, V. (1991). "Seichas, kak poltorasta let tomu nazad, streliaet zlo v dobro" (Now, as 150 years ago, evil is firing upon good). *Uchitel'skaia gazeta*, no. 28 (July 9–16), p. 3.

Matveeva, T. (Ed.) (1992). *Vladimir Fedorovich Matveev*. Moscow: Russian Open University.

"Moskovskaia akademiia razvitiia obrazovaniia" (The Moscow Academy for the Development of Education). (1992). *Uchitel'skaia gazeta*, no. 9 (3 March), pp. 10, 15.

"Rezoliutsiia II Vsesoiuznoi vstrechi (konferentsii) organizatorov chastnykh shkol" (Resolution of the II All-Union meeting [conference] of organizers of private schools). (1991). *Uchitel'skaia gazeta*, no. 42 (15–22 October), p. 1.

Riurikov, Iu. (1991). "Pedagogicheskaia revoliutsiia: Kliuch kliuchei." (A pedagogical revolution: The key of keys). *Uchitel'skaia gazeta*, no. 41 (8–15 October), p. 3.

Rossiiskii otkrytyi universitet. Prospekt, 1991–1992 (Russian Open University. Prospectus, 1991–1992). (1991). Moscow: Russian Open University.

Szekely, B. (1986). "The New Soviet Educational Reform." *Comparative Education Review, 30*(3), pp. 321–43.

4

Clever Children and Curriculum Reform

The Progress of Differentiation in Soviet and Russian State Schooling

JOHN DUNSTAN

Introduction

In this chapter we shall consider change in the structure of Soviet and Russian general schooling with particular regard to its curriculum over the period since 1984–85.[1] "Clever children" come into the title partly to indicate a thematic continuity with the writer's earlier work (Dunstan 1978; 1988) and partly because individual abilities have been a focal point of public attention in recent times. Abilities, especially above-average ones, tend to be highlighted when it becomes a priority to make the most of individual potential in different ways. Thus another frequent key word has been differentiation, by which we mean the development of special structural forms for particular purposes.

Back in 1986, there was much talk of social justice, in the name of which Mikhail S. Gorbachev at the Twenty-seventh Party Congress called for equality of access to education. Equalization—the reduction of differences in life-chances and in the means of furthering them—conventionally plays a countervailing role to differentiation. They are both imperatives as well as processes. Of course, in tribute to "political correctness" if nothing else, the fostering of differences in career opportunities cannot be allowed by its advocates to be seen as a repudiation of social justice. Although differentiation (unless "positive") tends to relegate social justice to the back burner, it presents itself as the necessary means to the same eventual end: by the creation of wealth, all shall benefit. Indeed, not only in theory but also in their practical outcomes, the two imperatives are not always mutually exclusive.[2] More often, however, they are in a state of conflict, and unless confrontation is for some reason desirable, policy makers have to devise ways of regulating the conflict or effecting a truce. In Soviet secondary general education policy, after some eight turbulent years in the late 1950s and 1960s, a rather superficial compromise was reached in the form of elective studies, which catered for special talents without prejudice to the basic curriculum.

As we look at Soviet and Russian education over the last few years, certain questions press themselves upon us. What has become of the old *modus vivendi* between the two imperatives? If differentiation is again in vogue, how far can this be attributed to the conventional reasons? How evenly is it manifested across the spectrum of the schools? How seriously are talents and abilities being taken? How far have moves to reform the curriculum for their advancement been constrained or frustrated, and why? To what extent has the imperative of equalization survived? And given the fundamental changes in the political order of the former Soviet Union, how much are these educational changes due to new causes and how much are they rooted in the past? As we seek some answers to these questions, we shall trace the principal developments in curriculum differentiation over our appointed period, first in general terms from official and unofficial public pronouncements and documents, and second with regard to ordinary or "mass" schools, old-style special schools, and more recent alternative forms of educating the young within the state sector.

Curriculum Differentiation: Debates and Developments

From the 1984 Reform to the 1988 Plenum

There had been some discussion of curriculum differentiation immediately before and during the draft stage of the 1984 reform guidelines, but the final document was brief on this to the point of neglect: in the new grades 8 (with entry at age thirteen) through 11, students would be given the opportunity for in-depth study of particular subjects of their choice within three groups—physics and mathematics, chemistry and biology, and social sciences and humanities—"with the help of electives," whatever that might mean ("Osnovnye napravleniia" 1984, p. 303). There was no mention of special schools and classes, which suggests that their future role was as yet undecided. The lack of real interest in provision for special abilities and talents on the part of the country's rulers had become fairly obvious as the 1970s unfolded. The top educational goal of the decade had been ten-year general schooling for all.

Special schools and classes were nevertheless soon to receive a degree of attention from the USSR Ministry of Education, initially in consequence of the 1984 reform's vocational thrust for general schooling. Arrangements for labor training were spelled out in new model curricula and regulations for language schools and other schools and classes that provided in-depth study of particular subjects (Dunstan 1988, pp. 49–51).[3] But probably the most interesting feature of these ordinances was the enhancement of the position of the other schools and classes, inasmuch as their senior-stage special curricula were extended downward by two years to begin in the new grade 8, thus becoming four-year courses. So by August 1985, the actual date of ministerial approval of the new curricula, those scientists and educationists who had been pressing for the further differentiation of the school structure saw their persistence rewarded. This was surely not unconnected with the inauguration of perestroika at the Communist Party's Central Committee plenum in April of that year. Yet in February 1986, the Twenty-seventh Party Congress was to criticize the speed and depth of perestroika in the schools.

The five-year research plan of the Academy of Pedagogical Sciences, approved in March 1986, reflected the new mood in a hesitantly evolutionary fashion. It confined itself to reinforcing the principle of the elective as the normal means of differentiating the curriculum in the ordinary school. Up-to-date syllabi and back-up materials were to be created for electives in all subjects. For schools with in-depth study, a new curriculum was to be drawn up for 1989, "providing for the differentiation of teaching according to pupils' abilities" ("Plan-zakaz" 1986, p. 18). Except for a minority of its membership, the Academy was to prove a force for restraint and caution in the process of educational restructuring, which it nonetheless found itself required to lead with ideas and literature.

It is not surprising that a movement advocating radical educational change should emerge at this time. The impetus for it was supplied by the teachers' newspaper *Uchitel'skaia gazeta* under its editor Vladimir Matveev. In October 1986 the paper convened the first of a number of meetings of innovative Soviet educators and published their first manifesto, "Pedagogy of Cooperation." As the title suggests, it called for a fundamentally new relationship among teachers, children, and parents and an unshackling of content and method to usher in a more personal approach to teaching and learning. It stated that children should be given a choice of tasks and encouraged to go beyond the syllabus, but the innovators' overall aim was to discover how to educate *all* children, eliminating both selection and dropping out. The manifesto presented a fairly obvious challenge to the Academy of Pedagogical Sciences. Silent at first, they subsequently adopted an attitude of damning with faint praise. This was in the context of a heated debate, not confined to the educational newspaper but led by it ("Pedagogika sotrudnichestva" 1986; Suddaby 1988, pp. 3–7). The paper was also instrumental in setting up Eureka Clubs of Creative Pedagogy, intended in the first instance for teachers but not restricted to them.

We note, then, that the sort of differentiation espoused by the teacher-innovators and their supporters did not extend to selective schooling. In this respect they embraced an ideological fundamentalism which their adversaries (or some of them) in the Academy had been obliged to jettison. The Ministry of Education, however, seems to have felt able to approve quite a broad spectrum of ways and means for developing individual abilities and interests; at least its chief inspectors expressed their support of the pedagogy of cooperation (Suddaby 1988, pp. 3–4).[4]

As for the public, views were mixed. Ordinary people were quite receptive to any innovational proposals that persuaded them that the quality of their children's education in ordinary schools would be enhanced. Teachers reacted according to their position along the conservative-radical spectrum. While there remained an inbred tendency at least to pay lip service to Party and government policy, the light of glasnost was gradually dawning. Encouraging people to have their say emboldened not only the radicals, for whom things were still moving too slowly, but also those conservatives who were starting to feel the ground shifting beneath their feet, and others again who wanted change but objected to the unleashing of hitherto restrained policies and practices that they had long regarded as seriously flawed.

An illustration of the situation is provided by the fairly brief (but quite intense) debate on the question of special schools early in 1987. This seems to have been sparked off by the Politburo's release of the new draft Statute on the Secondary General School for public discussion. In the light of Party concern about the slowness of perestroika in the schools and the recent contribution of the innovators to educational debate, the document sounds incredibly traditionalist and cliché-ridden. It did, however, clarify certain questions of differentiation that had been left vague or unmentioned in the 1984 reform guidelines. Electives in grades 7 through 11 were said quite specifically to be the channel for pupils to deepen their knowledge in particular subject areas—that is, they had more than the auxiliary function which might previously have been inferred— and technology was added to the three named subject groups for in-depth study. The teacher had to concern herself with the "development of pupils' cognitive interests and abilities," but nothing else was said about differentiation of the curricular menu to this end, apart from a brief allusion to labor training. Unlike the guidelines, the draft statute also referred to "schools and classes with in-depth study of particular subjects, branches of knowledge and kinds of art and sport." This was in the context of child welfare provision, which would seem odd but for its precedent in the 1985 Legislative Principles ("Update" 1986, p. 31; "Ustav" 1987). The relevant regulatory documents issued by the Ministry during 1986[5] had received next to no publicity. Now that openness was meant to be the order of the day, can this rather bizarre listing of facilities for special talents under the rubric of child welfare have been a continued, if increasingly inept, attempt to ward off criticism?

If so, it did not succeed. Focusing on language schools, sections of the press asserted something long suspected but never openly stated: such schools had previously been off limits to investigative journalism. But now it all came out.[6] Criticism centered on the elitist nature of these schools, which tended to be urban and located in districts heavily populated by intellectuals, and whose pupils, consequently were predominately the children of intellectuals. Worse still, numbers of these pupils were forced upon principals with regard not to their abilities, but to their influential parents' addresses. This meant that the schools were unable fully to perform their ascribed function of training skilled linguists, but often excelled in their inadvertent role of turning out spoiled brats to bask in privilege.

Naturally, people wrote in to the press to deny the charges as well as to substantiate them. Suggested remedies varied from complete closing of the language schools—inappropriate because the economy needed good linguists—to vast expansion—impractical because of the expense and the shortage of suitable teachers. The most feasible solution, though not without cost, was to bring forward the age for starting the language from grade 4 to grade 1 in every such school, admitting children exclusively from the school's microdistrict (designated catchment area), and to begin the in-depth teaching somewhere in the middle-school stage. The catchment principle, it was suggested, should also be applied to schools with in-depth teaching of other subjects.

The journalist who had spearheaded the campaign in *Moskovskaia pravda* to introduce social justice into the special schools mentioned that the educational leadership was contemplating a large-scale experiment on just these lines (Muladzhanov 1987). Three days later, the ministry issued its first model curriculum for in-depth language study for grades 7 through 11 ("O shkolakh" 1987, p. 17). In August, experimental curricula for ordinary schools were published, duly providing for foreign-language study from the first grade ("O novom" 1987). The order of 28 September approving the accompanying statute on schools with in-depth language study went further, instructing the Union's republic ministries to convert the old-style schools "teaching a number of subjects in a foreign language" into establishments of this new type ("Ob utverzhdenii" 1988, p. 4). Schools with in-depth mathematics teaching, for example, were generally regarded by the public as more academically serious and therefore more acceptable than traditional schools specializing in a language, so the Ministry's strategy was evidently to try to make language schools analogous to them, thereby moving toward democratization. The old charge levied in the West that greater equality of opportunity means greater opportunity to become unequal does not appear to have been addressed in these debates; to move from rank inequality to a modicum of equality of opportunity was one step enough for them.

Meanwhile, in April 1987, Gorbachev had declared in a speech to the Twentieth Komsomol Congress that the school reform was slipping, spinning like the wheels of a car stuck in the snow. It now became clear to the ministry that the ordinary Soviet school needed something a good deal more revolutionary to transform it than guidelines predating the era of perestroika, let alone a statute churning out rancid platitudes. In July, the ministry issued a set of "theses" reviewing recent discussions on restructuring the schools and inviting constructive comment. Paying tribute to the innovators, it said:

> Perestroika is a radical change in looking at the student. Not in words but in deeds we must recognize the pupil not only as the object but also as the subject of pedagogical activity, realistically incorporating in the educational process the fundamental principle of socialism "from each according to his abilities" and at the same time endeavoring to provide for each the maximal conditions for all-round harmonious development on the basis of differentiation of teaching. . . . ("Perestroiku shkoly" 1987).

Among much else, this new-line document stated that work was going forward on regulations and experimental curricula that would introduce differentiated teaching at an earlier age and in accordance with pupils' abilities, interests, and potential. A variant would provide for compulsory-choice courses (*kursy po vyboru*).[7] The ministry had established the Methodological Council for the Diffusion of Advanced Pedagogical Experience, which had already examined and approved the work of innovators I.P. Volkov, S.N. Lysenkova, E.N. Il'in and V.F. Shatalov, and had recommended that the Academy of Pedagogical Sciences—which it criticized for its laggardly ways—set up a laboratory in Donetsk to develop Shatalov's system ("Perestroiku shkoly" 1987). In February 1988, Shatalov himself was to be appointed to head this laboratory.

As already noted, in August 1987 the new experimental curricula were published. A commentary listing five principles then followed. The first of these principles addressed provision for differentiated teaching: "Given that a general education which is the same for all children does not guarantee sufficiently intensive development of their abilities and aptitudes in a particular sphere of knowledge," up to 25 percent of lesson time might be organized as compulsory-choice subjects and electives. The other four principles provided for an increase in the humanities orientation, a reduction of subjects by integration, a reduction of study load, and electives, clubs, and student organizations in the second half of the day. The curricula themselves, presented Soviet-style as a snapshot of an eleven-year school's lessons over a single week, did not in fact achieve a significant diminution of workload, but two of the variants included the novel feature of six and nine weekly periods allocated to compulsory-choice courses in, respectively, the tenth and eleventh grades. These courses were intended for in-depth study of two or three subjects and were to be determined by the education authorities in consultation with the schools, whereas the schools were solely responsible for electives. The plan was for the new curricula to be discussed at the forthcoming All-Union Education Workers' Congress—itself already postponed once and to be postponed again—and then to be completed and tried out for four or five years. "In effect, we are talking about the school curriculum of the year 2000" ("O novom" 1987). Or so they thought.

Though soon to be permanently eclipsed by events and to be passed over unobserved by commentators, the 1987 theses and curricula deserve a place in the history of Soviet education. For the first time at ministerial level since the 1920s, it had been proposed that differentiation by compulsory choice might be a regular feature of the ordinary Soviet school. But for those who sought profound change, this was no more than a modest start. Some of them felt that the system remained hamstrung by the unrealizable requirement of a common level of knowledge, abilities, and skills for all, and especially by the insistence on mastering the "fundamentals of the sciences." They also thought the range of compulsory-choice courses should not be restricted to academic subjects. Various other kinds of differentiation were put forward. One was that every child should be able to study every subject at either a "normal" or in-depth level, respectively a little easier or more difficult than current syllabi, while electives could bring them to a third, "enhanced" level. Researchers had successfully tried this out in Russian schools (Gorchev 1988). On the surface, at least, this sounds like the "streaming" that occurred experimentally in the Soviet Union in the late 1960s (Dunstan 1978, pp. 202–3). Another suggestion was differentiation by time, with a basic primary course of four years, to complete which some pupils might take three years or five (Gorchev 1988). The practical problems that this degree of diversity would raise if attempted on a mass scale received less scrutiny. To do the original innovators justice, it should be stressed that in their third manifesto they strongly opposed separating children by general ability, mainly because of the undesirable social attitudes that this would engender or perpetuate (Amonashvili et al. 1989, pp. 71–72).

In February 1988, while such arguments were going on, the Central Committee of the Communist Party held a plenum at which education came top of the agenda. That was so unusual as to have been significant even if they had stuck to the old platitudes. But this time the gap between proclaimed and actual levels of student achievement led to a clear repudiation of the 1984 reform and (among much else) to a call for schools to have the right to be creative and choose their own methods of teaching and upbringing, as well as for the creation of various models of schools. "In short, it is essential to focus *the main attention on the development of the students' individual abilities*" (Ligachev 1989, pp. 20–21; emphasis in the original). Details, it was said, should be left to the experts. The innovators, particularly their minority in the Academy of Pedagogical Sciences, and like-minded people at the Ministry of Education and elsewhere, must have found this at the time immensely encouraging, but also not a little piquant, coming as it did from the lips of the Central Committee's conservatively disposed secretary, Egor K. Ligachev.

From the 1988 Plenum to the 1989 Curriculum

As the Party was now calling the new tune, even the traditionalists in the Academy had to join, if somewhat ungracefully, in the dance. The choreographer was Gosobrazovanie, the new State Committee for Education formed in March from the three former education ministries; and public presentations continued to be organized by *Uchitel'skaia gazeta*. The dance was now led by a new group founded in June and known at first as *VNIK Bazovaia shkola* (Provisional Research Group on the Basic School).[8] It was headed by the reformer Professor Eduard Dneprov, later to become the Russian minister of education. In August, it supplied the basis for the State Committee's Draft Regulations on the Secondary General School ("Polozhenie" 1988) and issued its Conception of Secondary General Education ("Kontseptsiia" 1988a). Two days later, the Academy countered with its Conception of Secondary General Education as Basic in the Unified System of Permanent Education ("Kontseptsiia" 1988b). Again we must confine our discussion to what these widely ranging documents said about our theme; a broader view is available elsewhere (Muckle 1990, pp. 76–81). VNIK saw the school in three stages: primary, main, and senior. As early as the primary level, elements of differentiated teaching would be introduced to take account of children's aptitudes and abilities, initially in physical, aesthetic, and labor education and later in the native and foreign languages, mathematics, and "technical creativity." The children would start school at the age of six or seven, and the primary stage would last three or four years, depending on the individual pupil's abilities.

In the main school, 20 to 25 percent of study time would go to supplementary subjects chosen in accordance with aptitudes and interests, the time for these increasing as pupils progressed. The development of pupils' aptitudes and abilities would also be served by electives, multilateral teaching (i.e., with programs at varying levels of difficulty), and extracurricular activities. At the senior stage, differentiation would be of such breadth and profundity that it would amount to a new approach. It would permit maximum development of the pupils' abilities and occupational self-determination. The school could offer one or several subject groups— humanities; physics and mathematics; chemistry and biology; economics; technical subjects; agriculture; the arts; and so on—with labor training organized accordingly. The compulsory subjects, occupying a minor part of the time, would form integrated courses focused on man's interaction with the environment; this would eliminate the negative centrifugal tendencies of differentiated teaching. Evening and correspondence schools would become departments of senior-stage schools, providing students with a first or further "profile" or specialism at this level ("Kontseptsiia" 1988a).

The Academy's rival conception was a curious hybrid. Where it could, it followed the State Committee's draft regulations, for example in setting the period of compulsory schooling at nine years (instead of the existing eleven); and its preamble defined the five buzzwords of the day: integration, humanization, differentiation, individualization, and democratization. But old ways died hard: it tended to be much more cut and dried than the VNIK document, and it sometimes revealed familiar categories of thinking: "communist upbringing," "the dialectical-materialist worldview," and "ideological conviction." (The draft regulations had indeed mentioned "formation of a communist worldview" among the objectives of the Soviet school, but had linked it with "humanistic values" and "new thinking.") The number of compulsory subjects, according to the Academy, should be reduced from twenty-two to fourteen or fifteen, integrating some or creating electives. This document also stated that handicapped and gifted children alike needed special diagnostic help. Otherwise, differentiation at the primary stage would simply give the children a choice of objects to draw, poems to learn, and topics to write about.

Under the Academy scheme, differentiation in grades 5 through 9 would take the form of electives, mainly to prepare students for their choice of occupation. To facilitate this and to take account of conditions within the republics, the timetable allocation for subjects determined at the USSR level would be reduced by 25 to 30 percent. At the senior stage, literature, history, art (or world culture), social studies, mathematics and information science, and physical education would remain compulsory, along with an integrated natural-science course for humanities students. In addition, two or three subjects would be studied in the selected profile in special classes, with related labor activity. As an alternative to this, students could transfer to special schools or into technical or vocational education, as was already possible, or opt for nonspecialized studies from syllabi similar to the existing ones ("Kontseptsiia" 1988b).

Although both conceptions are sometimes less than specific about what they mean, it is clear that the VNIK view of differentiation was much broader and much more oriented to the individual than that of the Academy, which now seemed to be thinking along the lines of the experimental curricula of 1987. The majority Academy attitude to the innovators is epitomized in a long section on the process of education that manages to avoid mentioning them until the very last breath!

A prominent member of the innovators' movement has described the period 1986–88 as its heyday (Adamskii 1992, p. 2). As their fourth manifesto, "Let's Go into the New School" (Amonashvili et al. 1988), implies, they had great hopes of the much-deferred All-Union Education Workers' Congress, which finally took place in December 1988. But it turned out to be a talkshop and not much else, and the reputedly progressive Gennadii Yagodin, chairman of the State Committee, gave them little comfort. The most striking feature of the Congress was the intensity of conservative feeling.[9] It became depressingly clear to the innovators that, despite the Party's apparent espousal of their cause only months earlier, they had many opponents—not only in the Academy of Pedagogical Sciences but, worse still, among the rank and file of teachers. Their gloom was compounded by the sacking of Vladimir Matveev as editor-in-chief of *Uchitel'skaia gazeta*, reputedly "at the hands of E. Ligachev," no less. Many had seen Matveev as the real leader of the renewal movement (Adamskii 1992, p. 2). No longer was any great harvest of the new thinking an immediate prospect in the schools. Yet seeds had been sown and would germinate and grow to the extent that the capricious climate permitted.

Thus, stressing the role of differentiated teaching and learning in the development of children's creative potential, the Congress, together with the February 1988 plenum, nevertheless provided some impetus for the formulation of a state program on the education of gifted children. The matter was considered by the collegium of the Academy in April 1989. Reviewing the experience of special schools, olympiads, and the like, the collegium's resolution regretted the uncoordinated character of past research and the lack of longitudinal studies on the former students of such schools. Among other things, it resolved to draw up a research program on the discovery, diagnosis, and development of talented young people; to establish a center for creative giftedness; to hold a competition for the best diagnostic and teaching/learning materials; to publicize the existing experiences with individual syllabi for gifted youngsters and facilities provided for them by leading universities and to encourage other universities to do likewise (for example, by opening humanities and natural sciences boarding schools in Rostov, Voronezh, Irkutsk, and republic capitals). With the resolution, it issued a description of the aims and objectives of the proposed center, and a draft Conception on Gifted Children as the theoretical underpinning for future work ("O pervoocherednykh merakh" 1989).

July 1989 saw the issuing of the Provisional Regulations on the Secondary General School. While curbing some of the excesses in the draft of August 1988, and affirming the role of the education authorities in certain matters, it remains an overall forward-looking ordinance. Both the 1988 and 1989 versions refer repeatedly to the development of individual abilities, aptitudes, and interests, which is envisaged as taking place within the ordinary general school and in general schools of different types. Thus the legitimacy of special-profile schools is reaffirmed. True, the earlier provision for electives at the primary stage in physical, aesthetic, labor, and foreign-language education is deleted. The 1989 regulations retain the innovation of compulsory-choice subjects to develop aptitudes and abilities from the middle stage (first proposed in the 1987 theses, and to be taken in addition to the more familiar electives and extracurricular activities) and also permit multilateral programs. They add references to the USSR State Committee for Education, which would specify the basic compulsory subjects and, with the republic ministries, draw up the core of the multilateral syllabi. The general school is obligatory to grade 9. At the senior stage (grades 10 and 11), "broad and deep" differentiation is required, with the continuation of compulsory-choice subjects, and the school council is given the option of introducing one or more specialisms out of the most extensive list yet: "general, humanities, physics and mathematics, chemistry and biology, technical subjects, agriculture, economics and others" ("Polozhenie" 1988; "Vremennoe polozhenie" 1989).

The last major educational event squarely under the old regime was the issue of the "Baseline Curriculum for the Secondary General School" later in 1989. This curriculum represented the practical working-out of the regulations and expressed more graphically still the trend toward national and local differentiation. It differed drastically from its predecessors in being divided into three sections (*komponenty*) labelled according to the level at which decisions on content were to be made: Union and republic; republic; and school. The USSR State Committee and the ministry of each republic were to determine jointly the content of studies in Russian language, mathematics and information science, natural science (including geography), social science (including history), and, at the senior stage, USSR peoples' literature. Each republic ministry and its regional authorities were to determine the content of studies in national language and literature, foreign language, republic history and geography, music, art, labor training, and physical education with military training. These two sections of the curriculum each constituted just over 41 percent of the whole. The move away from the centralized curricula of the past, making only relatively minor concessions to nationality interests, is apparent.

When, however, we look at section three, representing the school level of curriculum decisions, and comprising 17 percent of the overall content and one-third of the senior-stage content, the extent of the change strikes us much more. Even at the primary level, two lessons a week were earmarked for possible remedial work or interest-based activities (not far, conceptually, from the electives mentioned in the State Committee's draft regulations). At the five-year middle stage, four periods a week were available for electives and supplementary studies, rising to six periods in each of the two senior grades. So far, these allocations were at the exclusive disposal of the school. They could be used for whole-class activities, group teaching, or even individual tutorials; they could be adapted to achievement at the remedial levels; they could provide local applications of general subject syllabi. At the senior stage, the students might even work on individual programs. In addition to electives and supplementary studies, two weekly periods in grades 8 and 9 (top of the middle stage) and six in the two senior years were allotted to compulsory-choice courses giving a broad learning experience from grade 8, and to specialized studies (*profil'noe obuchenie*) from grade 10. The republic was to take the lead in listing each of these and supplying syllabi and backup materials for them. The school council was to select from the lists according to student demand and staff availability. Compulsory-choice courses were meant to help develop interests, independence, and creative activity. Specialized studies were intended to introduce vocational training in a group of subjects "in which the student has shown stable interests and abilities" ("O bazisnom" 1989; "Ob utverzhdenii" 1990, pp. 17–20; Shadrikov 1990). The reader should particularly note that, after the RSFSR Declaration of Sovereignty in June 1990 and the demise of the USSR late in 1991, this curriculum was essentially retained by the Russian Federation under its progressive education minister, Eduard Dneprov, appointed in July 1990.

From the 1989 Curriculum to the 1992 Law

By the spring of 1990, there was said to be a wide consensus favoring differentiated schools, although some teachers were still objecting. Perhaps it was because of this that the Conception of Differentiation of Teaching in the Secondary General School, prepared by the Institute of Curriculum and Method (renamed Secondary General Education) and presented to the presidium of the Academy of Pedagogical Sciences in April (Vendrovskaia 1992, p. 93), made little impact in the press.[10] To clear the ground methodologically, the 1990 conception distinguished between internal and external differentiation as means of individualization.

External differentiation envisioned the creation of stable student groups, whereas internal differentiation did not. Internal differentiation covered, first, the "differentiated approach," a familiar notion since the 1960s that simply heeded individual characteristics; and, second multilateral differentiation, permitting mastery of the common curriculum at various levels above the basic minimum. Either case might entail flexible grouping, differentiated assignments, and a variable tempo. External differentiation might be either elective—with free-choice subjects with or without a fixed core and extracurricular forms—or selective, involving specialized classes and courses of in-depth study. While free-choice electives and in-depth courses were already familiar, the new conception stated that specialized classes at the senior stage should be considerably expanded; in-depth and specialized classes should not basically differ from ordinary ones in content, but requirements as to assimilation and performance should go further. It had been decided, said the commentators, that the Soviet school should provide in-depth study for four years from grade 8, or three years from grade 9 (though reference to the latter is not to be found in the documents we have cited). Because fifteen years was the most favorable age for starting selective differentiation, the baseline curriculum provided for it (presumably, by specialized studies) from grade 10, but unfortunately only for two years. Until the school system could institute a third senior-stage year, the commentators were able to recommend selective differentiation merely for lycées and gymnasia and the like (Monakhov et al. 1992, pp. 48–49, 56). This conception is of historical interest since it focused on probably the first ever Soviet effort to present a broad-spectrum classificational system for curriculum differentiation.[11] Apart from its suggestion of a third senior year, however, it reads like a slightly fuzzy résumé of recent thinking on the subject. Visually it must have been intended as a blueprint; aurally it was no more than a new setting of an already familiar tune.

For the USSR Academy of Pedagogical Sciences, the 1990 conception was almost a swan-song. During 1991, Soviet education ceased to be a subject for debate or a field for development and innovation, although the notion lived on in the minds and practices of numerous educators. For the rest of our period we shall have to confine our discussion mostly to the largest player—Russia.

At an All-Russian Teachers' Conference in March 1991, the RSFSR Ministry of Education presented its Program of Stabilization and Development for the period of transition to the market economy. This was a substantial volume to which Minister Dneprov had put his name along with his chief consultants, V.S. Lazarev (administration) and V.S. Sobkin (sociology). It represented the fruits of the labors of a working party of some two dozen members, only two of whom were listed with Academy of Pedagogical Sciences affiliations (Dneprov et al. 1991, p. 5). Successive sections provided a critical analysis of the state of education, considered its future within the framework of socioeconomic change, outlined ministerial policy for stabilization and development, and, finally, set out a specific action program with dates. The entire document is of interest, but space restricts us to our principal theme of differentiation.[12]

In the past, the report said, only the higher administrative organs of the state had been able to determine types of educational institutions and to change curriculum and method, a state of affairs which was unfavorable to innovation. The school had been oriented not to the individual's development but to a general "averaging out" (Ibid., 1991, p. 14). The existing network could be characterized as "weakly differentiated," for recently new types of establishments such as gymnasia and lycées had emerged. Such a development was positive, expanding the possibilities for young people to satisfy their educational needs; thus it was all the more regrettable that contemporary conditions were not conducive to the creation of an alternative, nonstate educational network. The report said that the curriculum must provide for multilateral teaching of various subjects and for different curricular decisions to be made at federal, regional, and school levels (this was very much the State Committee scheme of fifteen months earlier, adapted now to a sovereign Russian setting). Differentiation was seen primarily in terms of the broad opportunity for pupils to choose the groups of subjects in which they wished to specialize; in-depth study (though still important) and completely new subjects or electives were second and third priorities (Ibid., pp. 32–34). This would significantly heighten demands on the school, especially at the senior stage which was set to become much more the preserve of those aspiring to higher education, and at a time when teachers in quest of better pay would be moving into the private sector or out of education altogether (Ibid., pp. 39–40).

The second half of the report became increasingly precise about the ministry's aims and objectives. Starting with the primary stage, it said, schools must be made more aware of innovation, focusing on the development of cognitive abilities (Ibid., p. 194). New rural primary schools were to prepare pupils for specific types of secondary schooling, such as lycées and agricultural schools (Dneprov 1991). The main secondary stage called for more pupil choice, with multilateral syllabi and individually directed teaching (Dneprov et al. 1991, p. 194). On completion of this stage, students continuing to the senior stage must have the opportunity to choose their school (Dneprov 1991). At the senior stage, there was to be free selection of subject orientations—for example, humanities, psychology and pedagogy, or natural science—and of individual subjects (except for a common core), plus a range of variational curricula and textbooks, certain new subjects, and intensive courses in the field of business studies (Dneprov et al. 1991, p. 195). Over the following two years, newly oriented syllabi and teaching materials were to be made available over half of the RSFSR, while variational curricula, syllabi, and textbooks would be introduced into about one-third of the schools (Ibid.; Dneprov 1991). Examples of the last-mentioned were *Comparative Politics, Biology and Principles of Agriculture,* and *History of the Peoples of the RSFSR.* Among many other things, courses for in-depth language classes and electives on religious topics were also provided for (Dneprov et al. 1991, pp. 260–62).

Our final set of documents is comprised of various texts of Russia's Law on Education. The first draft (I) appeared in July 1991; a revised version (II), apparently many drafts later, came out in January 1992, and no longer referred to the RSFSR but to the Russian Federation; and the final text (III), with a decree on its implementation, was signed on 10 July 1992 ("Zakon ... Proekt" 1991; "Zakon ... Proekt" 1992; "Zakon" 1992). Comparing these versions in depth in an attempt to discern the development of policy is unlikely to be productive, and is apt to lead to the wrong conclusions. What then can be said about them with reasonable certainty? There is an unsurprising move away from the phraseology of the old regime and its modes of thinking. Describing general education, the first version gives all citizens "equal opportunities for the due receipt and continuation of their education in accordance with every person's calling, interests and abilities, and with reference to societal requirements" (Art. 14.1). The second version drops that last phrase. The final text appears to omit the whole statement; perhaps by then it was felt to be self-evident. Under the heading "General Propositions," all three versions speak of special grants for persons possessing "exceptional" (I, Art. 5.6) or "outstanding" (II, Art. 5.6; III, Art. 5.7) abilities; but the final version goes significantly further, saying that the state helps such citizens to receive "elite education."[13] There is a precedent for this in Version II: "The organs of state power and administration may set up educational establishments of an elite type for specially gifted children, adolescents and young people" (Art. 36.10). Version III repeats this "social guarantee" but replaces "specially gifted" with the phrase "[those] who have displayed outstanding abilities" (Art. 50.13), making the criteria somewhat more objective.

All three texts assert a pupil's right to choose his or her individual curriculum (or words to that effect), but the last two anchor this within the framework of state educational standards (I, Art. 37.2; II, Art. 36.2; III, Art. 50.2). They all also affirm the right to receive supplementary educational services. The two later versions are slightly more expansive on this than the first one. Briefly, such services are to be paid for by the clients, presumably by the pupil's family or possibly his or her future employer; they go beyond the state standards for the type of institution; and they may include specialized courses (profiling), in-depth study, and coaching (I, Arts. 14.9 and 35; II, Arts. 14.5 and 34; III, Arts. 14.6 and 45.1). Finally, the successive drafts legitimize nonstate educational institutions (I, Art. 11.2; II, Art. 11.2; III, Art. 12.3), although only the first refers specifically to gymnasia and lycées (Art. 11.8). Overall, while these documents do not give such matters as differentiation and outstanding abilities, or new means of provision for them, as high a profile as one might have expected from the pedagogical literature, they are now firmly enshrined in the law, and the old ambivalence has gone with the old regime.

Curriculum Differentiation in State Schools

Let us now undertake a brief review of the schools, to discern how much things were changing and how effectively policy was being implemented. The only kind of formal or external differentiation—that is, differentiation involving fixed groups—in the vast majority of ordinary schools was in optional classes, or electives. Catering in 1973 to 54 percent of pupils in the eligible age groups (Kashin 1976, p. 30)—the top four years from grade 7, then with the entry at 13 years—and 91.5 percent in the early 1980s (Monakhov and Orlov 1986, p. 31), elective classes are said to have reached their peak of popularity during that period. Subsequently, however, their quality declined along with the general morale in the education system, and interest in them slackened (Vendrovskaia 1992, pp. 92–3). This fall-off must have been considerable; in 1991, Dneprov's team reported that in Russia electives were favored by only 5.6 percent of senior pupils, which made them the least popular classes (Dneprov et al. 1991, p. 34). From this, we might infer that the decision to leave the content of electives up to the schools helped to undermine various experimental curricula derived in 1990–91 from the State Committee's "Baseline Curriculum" of 1989; but because very few schools adopted these curricula anyway (Ibid.), they cannot have made much difference.

It is quite true that there has been very little talk of electives in either the popular or the academic educational press in recent years. Exceptions include a detailed account of experimentation in two districts of Belarus, where electives were linked with specialized classes (Ogurtsov 1992, p. 65). A much more radical scheme, which still accommodated the State Committee curriculum, was reported from Ukraine. It involved differentiated teaching from the first year of school, with tests being administered to assign the children to standard classes (about 65 percent), accelerated classes (15 percent), or "classes with enhanced individual attention" (CEIA) for the 20 percent or so lagging behind their age-norm. Those in accelerated classes finished the primary course a year earlier than the average pupil, and at the middle stage proceeded to intensive study of a chosen group of subjects in the form of electives. At the senior stage, there was to be division into three cycles: humanities, natural sciences, and technical subjects. Interestingly, although the schools advised parents on the most suitable type of class for their child, the parents had the right to choose. It was claimed that this removed mistrust and tension. Accelerated classes were said to change significantly parents' attitudes toward their role in preparing children for school. The aim of the experiment was high achievement by all pupils, irrespective of their class, but there was an admitted problem in the subject specialists' lack of training for CEIA classes higher up the ladder (Gil'bukh et al. 1991, pp. 15–22).

It is inadvisable to dwell further on experimentation in the ordinary state sector, lest the wrong impression be given: rank-and-file schools in Russia, at least (and we must accept the minister's word), have not changed much overall. The picture is somewhat different, however, when we consider well-established variants in mass secondary general education, such as schools with in-depth teaching of certain subjects. Following the 1966 decree legitimizing them, these classes (excluding language schools) numbered 1,804 across the USSR by 1971, or 1.2 percent of ten- or eleven-year schools (Dunstan 1978, pp. 159, 172). During the 1970s, their total apparently reached some 5,000, only to decline to 2,513 by the early 1980s (Vendrovskaia 1992, p. 90).[14] By 1988, however, with the encouragement of perestroika, they had risen again to just over 4,000 (including also classes in languages, music, and sport), though Ligachev (1989, p. 21) called this "just a drop in the bucket." There has certainly been growth in Russia and Belarus in recent years. Dneprov's team reported a considerable expansion in specialized schools and classes in the RSFSR over the preceding quinquennium: the 1990 figure was 3,116 schools, 6.6 percent of the total, representing 15.7 percent of urban schools and 1.8 percent of rural ones and involving 9.9 percent of pupils in grades 5 through 11. In-depth studies were sought by three times as many pupils (Dneprov et al. 1991, pp. 39–40). Some would achieve their dream: in 1991 there were 6,698 such schools (Prelovskaia 1992), while early in 1993 a total of 7,398 was reported ("Panorama" 1993). Belarus had 222 schools with in-depth teaching in 1986 and 1,226 by 1989 (Ogurtsov 1992, p. 61).[15]

That very rarefied sector of general education, boarding schools for academically or otherwise gifted children, though little in the news of late, has been affected in another way. Presumably in keeping with the policy to increase efficiency in the teaching of specialisms, academic boarding schools in Moscow, Leningrad, Novosibirsk, and Krasnoiarsk were fully transferred to universities beginning in 1988. Several sports boarding schools were handed over to the State Committee for Physical Education and Sport, which turned them into Schools of Olympic Reserves (Dneprov et al. 1991, p. 75). There are also what might be described as experimental halfway houses between academic boarding schools and schools with in-depth study: specialized schools that have developed more advanced forms of sponsorship. For instance, Schools No. 542 and No. 1170 in Moscow, both specializing in physics and mathematics at the senior stage, were reported to have formed part of an experimental teaching complex at Moscow Institute of Physics and Engineering (MIFI). The institute gave the schools free use of buildings and equipment, paid for maintenance costs, selected the pupils, and set the semiannual exams ("Vnimaniiu rabotnikov" 1990, pp. 26–27). By early 1991, 198 of Russia's schools were attached to higher educational establishments (Dneprov et al. 1991, p. 32).

Finally, we take a look at alternative education within the state system. "Alternative schools" basically means schools differing from the traditional authoritarian ones (Adamskii 1992, p. 2). Formerly, they were synonymous with private schools (Sutherland 1992, p. 26), but their status has become much more diversified (Vaganova 1991).[16] Early in 1992, they numbered more than 500 in Russia, nine in ten being former secondary schools, with over 333,000 pupils; the same source mentions more than one hundred nonstate secondary schools, with 7,000 students (Baiduzhii 1992). Here we confine our discussion to examples of those gymnasia and lycées with state backing.

In the spring of 1989, following talks with interested school directors, a decision was taken to create three gymnasia and three lycées from six Moscow schools: a State Committee order of 18 July provided the legal basis for the move. The new schools remained under the aegis of the district education authority. Gymnasia, based at schools, were intended to provide broad general education from the age of six or seven, with in-depth studies from grade 7 or 9, while lycées, independent of ordinary schools, admitted their students beginning at grade 8 and focused more explicitly on the discovery and promotion of giftedness. Each type of school was free to develop its own curriculum. Both had competitive entry; E.S. Topaler, a prime mover in all this, even announced on televi-sion that his school's telephones would be disconnected during the com-petition, thus neatly sidestepping the pressure that powerful parents traditionally exerted on school administrators at such times (Louis 1989; Nikonov 1990; "Vnimaniiu rabotnikov" 1990, pp. 31–32). Gymnasia and lycées have since mushroomed; early in 1991 the RSFSR had 177 of them, all but four in urban areas (Dneprov et al. 1991, p. 40); two years later, they numbered five hundred ("Panorama" 1993). Schools in Mos-cow could achieve alternative status with the City Education Committee, but would not be under its authority, as it had no funds for them (Vaganova 1991).

This brings us to the major problem confronting differentiated teach-ing in state schools: it costs money. To be sure, conservative and ill-prepared teachers are another big obstacle. Yet it is the parlous financial state of Russian education, exacerbated by the liberalization of prices, which strikes us most forcibly. Witness the ex-minister's contribution to the first issue of a new teachers' newspaper. He devotes it to the impossibility of meeting the provisions on teachers' pay in Yeltsin's Decree No. 1 of July 1991, On Urgent Measures to Develop Education in the RSFSR (to bring their salaries up to the nationwide industrial average from 1 January 1992). Given the stringent budgetary cuts, spending on everything but pay, student stipends, meals, and heat-ing and lighting has been blocked (Dneprov 1992). In such a situation, there are clearly no funds for expensive extras, let alone in-service training and teaching aids. True, state schools are allowed to charge fees for supplementary studies, and understandably this opportunity is being increasingly exploited. Yet as a commentator bluntly remarks, "This is a very dubious solution of their financial problems, even if they do offer yoga or marketing" (Baiduzhii 1992). The alternative is to accept parental "donations" (presumably, fees by another name) or to seek out wealthy sponsors. Thus School No. 1043 in Moscow, which was to be the base of the Children's International Complex pursuing technical and managerial creativity, is sponsored by a South Korean firm and pays its staff partly in foreign currency (Chernyi 1991). But this school is light-years away from the rank and file.

Conclusions: Egalitarians and Differentiators Revisited

The feud between egalitarians and differentiators (Dunstan 1978, pp. 248–51) has continued, though with drastically redrawn battle lines and much blurring of positions, while elective studies have become too attenuated to exert their compromise function any longer. Many of the old arguments regarding special provisions for high achievers have resurfaced. On the negative side, arguments may be "societal-hostile"[17] when a commitment to the pursuit of actual equality (however unrealistic) provokes charges of elitism; or "individual-hostile" when fears are expressed about the strain to which the child will be exposed or the feasibility of early selection (Gil'bukh et al. 1991, p. 22; Frumin 1992, p. 29). From what has been said above, it will be no surprise that arguments in support of differentiation have become more frequent and more confident. "Societal-supportive" views—those that see education as investment to serve the "national interest" most effectively—have gained enormous weight with the transition to the market economy (Dneprov et al. 1991, pp. 138–39, 195), for the market principle demands real choices according to abilities (Kravchina and Rudik 1992, pp. 72–73). This is, of course, a fundamentally new factor favoring differentiation.

Such views enjoy an alliance with the "individual-supportive" stance which was the epitome of the innovators' movement and a major formative force in subsequent policy making: individual differences are vital and require a flexible approach; talents must be sought out and encouraged; all need help to realize their potentials (Gil'bukh et al. 1991; Monakhov 1992, p. 40). These views have sometimes been expressed in terms of stringent criticism of the old school (e.g., Gorchev 1988). There are, however, signs of dissension from within the supporters' camp, for market forces rigorously applied—as in proposals to make state schools fee-paying—would adversely affect youngsters who are financially (and perhaps intellectually) worse off. Some advocates of differentiation are apt to forget about the imperative need to help all children.

Talents and abilities have been taken very seriously indeed since the later 1980s, but there is a palpable gap between policy and practice. Although in-depth studies have developed in state schools, no more than two in three of Russian pupils who are actively interested had access to them in 1991. For the most part, schools have been very slow to adopt experimental curricula (Dneprov et al. 1991, p. 34; Roganovskii 1991, p. 41). Yet although it is easy to accuse teachers of conservatism, it is difficult not to empathize with them, underpaid as they are in their understaffed and underresourced schools and sick at heart from hope deferred. Lack of funding has undoubtedly been the main constraint on real curriculum change. It is also demoralizing to work in a sector treated with contempt by many people because of its past associations and what they see as its present state of dereliction.

This contempt for the Soviet curriculum is relevant to the redrawing of the battle lines between the differentiators and the egalitarians. The latter have lost massive ground, almost to the point of becoming marginalized. They have been immensely weakened by the identification of their beliefs and practices with the tenets of a defeated ideology. Unlike in 1958–73, recent individual-hostile criticism of differentiation by ability has studiously avoided the subject of the fostering of undesirable character traits. The July 1992 law has relegated the word *vospitanie* (upbringing), from its once all-embracing sense to the status of being only a component of *obrazovanie* (education) and secondary to *obuchenie* (instruction); it is for many tarred irrevocably with the Communist brush. The innovators have tried to depoliticize the notion and put it forward as part of "developmental education." But to write off the egalitarians as yesterday's men and women, who think in outmoded categories and occasionally preach an outworn creed, simply will not do. Here also some differentiation is needed!

For there are "new egalitarians" who, paradoxically perhaps, see equalization as the achievement of maximum differentiation to suit all children. In fact, they might just as well be called "radical differentiators," engaging in a new conflict with those who favor selective differentiation for a fortunate minority but expressing their position in unfamiliar terms. One of their most articulate representatives, Isak Frumin, the principal of an experimental school, shall have the last word, for there has been little mention of this in our foregoing discussion. He is referring to early selection: "To this end we are destroying various pedagogical structures, maybe poor and inferior, but oriented to the universality and real accessibility of education. But the most dangerous thing is this: the best ideology of our teachers, their humanistic ideals, are being eaten away, corroded as it were" (Frumin 1992). He alludes to the early Soviet heritage of Tolstoy and Ushinskii; teachers used to see themselves as missionaries, but now they have to be marketeers. Children whose parents can pay or render services are selected, and increasingly at age six. Beneath the new forms of differentiation lies a reluctance to awaken the potential that slumbers in every child. "By all means," he sardonically concludes, "if some people want them, let there be private schools, gymnasia and lycées, sorting children out and rejecting them like defective goods (otbrakovyvaiushchie). But the priority for education must be the development of various types of mass schools, including a new model of school which will support the 'cooks' children' " (Ibid., p. 29).[18] With that priority the innovators would heartily agree, and I believe that it would still strike more than a few chords at the Russian Ministry of Education. But as of now, it looks like a long time coming.

Notes

1. Grateful thanks for supplying some of the references used in this chapter go to my Birmingham colleagues, Mike Berry, Julian Cooper, and Bob Davies; and also to Jim Riordan (University of Surrey) and Stephen and Tanya Webber (formerly University of Exeter).

2. These matters are discussed more fully in Dunstan 1987b, pp. 32–35 and 60–61.

3. The truly dedicated can track down the details in *Biulleten' normativnykh aktov Ministerstva prosveshcheniia SSSR* (1986), no. 2, pp. 14–21 (curricula), and no. 5, pp. 42–44 (regulations, except language schools); (1987), no. 6, pp. 42–44 (regulations for boarding schools with oriental languages), and no. 7, pp. 17–18 (mainly, curriculum for schools with in-depth language teaching from grade 7); (1988) no. 1, pp. 4–6 (regulations for language schools). For a selection of the curricula, see "New Model Curricula" (1988), pp. 29–31.

4. More research is needed on the stance of the USSR Ministry of Education and its successor State Committee toward innovation during the 1980s. As Sutherland (1992, p. 16), points out, their attitude was not always consistent.

5. See Note 3.

6. For full documentation see Dunstan 1988, pp. 52–59. There had been a slightly earlier exposé of a special music school in Tashkent (Mylnikova 1986).

7. This translation is evident from the context. Later, *obiazatel'nyi* (compulsory) would be added, to remove any doubt.

8. Some new terms present translation difficulties. Despite the odd sound to English ears, I have used "basic" for *bazovyi* (*bazovoe obrazovanie*: "basic education"). *Osnovnaia shkola* (or *osnovnaia stupen'*) as the middle component of the *bazovaia shkola* is translated as "main school" (or "main stage"). Kuebart (1991b, p. 18) suggests *untere Sekundarstufe* (lower secondary stage). This undoubtedly adds clarity, but perhaps diminishes the notion of adequacy which *osnovnaia* is intended to convey here. (Confusingly, the term *osnovnaia shkola* has occasionally been found to mean the primary plus the middle stages.) For *bazisnyi*, I have borrowed the inspired "baseline" from *Soviet Education*; thus *bazisnyi uchebnyi plan* becomes "baseline curriculum."

9. For a fascinating series of reports from the Congress, see the 25 January 1989 issue of *Current Digest of the Soviet Press*, vol. 40, no. 52, pp. 1–7.

10. I have been unable to locate a text of this, but Monakhov et al. (1992) appear to be presenting an exposition of it.

11. Several years ago I myself attempted something similar, but oriented to varying attitudes toward diverse forms of differentiation in the Soviet general education system: Dunstan 1978, pp. 248–51 (classification system of forms); 1983 (analysis of data on attitudes); 1987a (classification system of attitudes).

12. For a brief and reliable introduction to the whole report, see Kuebart 1991a.

13. To translate *elitarnogo* here, I am using the noun adjectivally, in a sociologically neutral sense; it is difficult in English to rid "elitist" of its pejorative overtones. In present-day Russian, *elitarnyi* seems to be used both pejoratively and nonpejoratively.

14. It is not clear whether the figures given by Vendrovskaia include language classes. Over the period she cites, they were not usually regarded as analogous to in-depth studies. On the other hand, she is writing at a time when this perception has officially changed.

15. These figures may well include state-supported gymnasia and lycées, considered below.

16. According to Dneprov, schools were classified in four categories, depending on the degree of participating bodies' involvement: state, state–public, public–state, and private (Vaganova 1991).

17. I am using the categories set out and explained more fully in Dunstan 1987a, pp. 50–52.

18. "Cooks' children" is an allusion to a notorious education ministry circular of 1887: in effect, only children suitably provided for at home should be admitted to schools (gymnasia!) preparing pupils for university, while the children of cooks, for example, should keep to their station in life (Alston 1969, p. 128).

References

Adamskii, A. (1992). "Gde uchit' detei?" *Ogonek*, no. 20–21, pp. 1–3.

Alston, P.L. (1969). *Education and the State in Tsarist Russia*. Stanford, CA: Stanford University Press.

Amonashvili, Sh. et al. (1988). "Voidem v novuiu shkolu." *Uchitel'skaia gazeta*, 18 October.

———. (1989). "The Methodology of Reform." *Soviet Education*, vol. 31, no. 7, pp. 44–77.

Baiduzhii, A. (1992). "Streliat' i molit'sia." *Nezavisimaia gazeta*, 16 July.

Chernyi, S.G. (1991). "Kto na noven'kogo?" *Uchitel'skaia gazeta*, no. 2 (8–15 January), p. 3.

Dneprov, E.D. (1991). "U nas est' dva goda . . . " *Uchitel'skaia gazeta*, no. 15 (9–16 April), p. 4.

———. (1992). "Obrazovanie i obshchestvo." *Pervoe sentiabria*, no. 1 (1 September), p. 1.

Dneprov, E.D. et al., Ed. (1991). *Rossiiskoe obrazovanie v perekhodnyi period: Programma stabilizatsii i razvitiia*. Moscow: Ministerstvo obrazovaniia RSFSR.

Dunstan, J. (1978). *Paths to Excellence and the Soviet School*. Windsor, Berks.: NFER Publishing.

———. (1983). "Attitudes to Provision for Gifted Children: The Case of the USSR." In B.M. Shore et al., Ed., *Face to Face with Giftedness*. New York: Trillium Press, pp. 290–307.

———. (1987a). "Attitudes to Provision for Gifted Children." *Education and Society*, vol. 5, no. 1/2, pp. 49–54.

———. (1987b). "Equalisation and Differentiation in the Soviet School 1958–1985: A Curriculum Approach." In J. Dunstan, Ed., *Soviet Education under Scrutiny*. Glasgow: Jordanhill College Publications, pp. 32–69.

————. (1988). "Gifted Youngsters and Special Schools." In J. Riordan, Ed., *Soviet Education: The Gifted and the Handicapped*. London and New York: Routledge, pp. 29–69.

Frumin, I. (1992). "Kukharkiny deti." *Ogonek*, no. 24/26, pp. 28–29.

Gil'bukh, Iu. et al. (1991). "Kak ne ubit' talant?" *Narodnoe obrazovanie*, no. 4, pp. 15–22.

Gorchev, A. (1988). "Pust' begut vse vmeste?" *Uchitel'skaia gazeta*, 16 January.

Kashin, M.P. (1976). "Ob itogakh perekhoda sovetskoi shkoly na novoe soderzhanie obshchego obrazovaniia." *Sovetskaia pedagogika*, no. 3, pp. 24–32.

"Kontseptsiia obshchego srednego obrazovaniia" (1988a). *Uchitel'skaia gazeta*, 23 August.

"Kontseptsiia obshchego srednego obrazovaniia kak bazovogo v edinoi sisteme nepreryvnogo obrazovaniia" (1988b). *Uchitel'skaia gazeta*, 25 August.

Kravchina, N. and Rudik, A. (1992). "Shkola v usloviiakh rynochnoi ekonomiki." *Ekonomika Ukrainy*, no. 2, pp. 72–75.

Kuebart, F. (1991a). "Bildungspolitik zwischen zentralen Koordination und Bildungshoheit der Republiken: Das Stabilisierungs- und Entwicklungsprogramm für das Bildungswesen der RSFSR." *Halbjahresbericht zur Bildungspolitik und pädagogischen Entwicklung in der UdSSR, der Republik Polen, der CSFR und der Volksrepublik China*, no. 1, pp. 7–12.

————. (1991b). "Der Entwurf eines Bildungsgesetzes für die Russische Föderation." *Halbjahresbericht zur Bildungspolitik und pädagogischen Entwicklung in der UdSSR, der Republik Polen, der CSFR und der Volksrepublik China*, no. 2, pp. 11–25.

Ligachev, E.K. (1989). "On the Course of Restructuring the Secondary and Higher Education System and the Party's Tasks in Carrying It Out." *Soviet Education*, vol. 31, no. 4, pp. 6–67.

Louis, J. (1989). "A Fresh Start That Echoes Tsarist Times." *The Times Educational Supplement*, 14 July, p. 13.

Monakhov, V.M. (1992). "Tendencies in the Development of the Content of General Secondary Education." *Russian Education and Society*, vol. 34, no. 1, pp. 32–44.

Monakhov, V.M. and Orlov, V.A. (1986). "Uglublennoe izuchenie otdel'nykh predmetov." *Sovetskaia pedagogika*, no. 9, pp. 31–33.

Monakhov, V.M. et al. (1992). "Differentiation of Instruction in Secondary School." *Russian Education and Society*, vol. 34, no. 1, pp. 45–59.

Muckle, J. (1990). *Portrait of a Soviet School under Glasnost*. Basingstoke and London: Macmillan.

Muladzhanov, Sh. (1987). "Eshche raz o spetsshkolakh." *Moskovskaia pravda*, 10 March.

Mylnikova, G. (1986). "Fal'shivaia nota." *Sobesednik*, no. 38, p. 10.

"New Model Curricula for Language Schools and Selected Other Schools Specialising in Particular Subjects" (1988). *Soviet Education Study Bulletin*, vol. 6, no. 1, pp. 28–31.

Nikonov, I. (1990). "Zdravstvui, gimnaziia!" *Uchitel'skaia gazeta*, no. 18 (April), p. 4.

"O bazisnom uchebnom plane" (1989). *Uchitel'skaia gazeta*, 28 December.

"O novom eksperimental'nom uchebnom plane" (1987). *Uchitel'skaia gazeta*, 22 August.

"O pervoocherednykh merakh po vyiavleniiu i vospitaniiu osobo odarennykh uchashchikhsia" (1989). *Biulleten' Gosudarstvennogo komiteta SSSR po narodnomu obrazovaniiu. Seriia: Doshkol'noe vospitanie i obshchee srednee ob-*

razovanie, no. 9, pp. 9–19.

"O shkolakh (klassakh) s uglublennym izucheniem inostrannogo iazyka" (1987). *Biulleten' normativnykh aktov Ministerstva prosveshcheniia SSSR*, no. 7, pp. 17–18.

"Ob utverzhdenii gosudarstvennogo bazisnogo uchebnogo plana srednei obshcheobrazovatel'noi shkoly" (1990). *Biulleten' Gosudarstvennogo komiteta SSSR po narodnomu obrazovaniiu. Seriia: Doshkol'noe vospitanie i obshchee srednee obrazovanie*, no. 1, pp. 17–23.

"Ob utverzhdenii polozheniia ob obshcheobrazovatel'nykh shkolakh s uglublennym izucheniem inostrannogo iazyka" (1988). *Biulleten' normativkykh aktov Ministerstva prosveshcheniia SSSR*, no. 1, pp. 4–6.

Ogurtsov, N.G. (1992). "Differentiated Instruction in Belorussian Schools." *Russian Education and Society*, vol. 34, no. 1, pp. 60–72.

"Osnovnye napravleniia reformy obshcheobrazovatel'noi i professional'noi shkoly" (1984). *Vedomosti Verkhovnogo Soveta SSSR*, vol. 47, no. 16, pp. 298–320.

"Panorama" (1993). *Poisk*, no. 8 (19–25 February), p. 2.

"Pedagogika sotrudnichestva" (1986). *Uchitel'skaia gazeta*, 18 October, p. 2.

"Perestroiku shkoly—na uroven' sovremennykh trebovanii" (1987). *Uchitel'skaia gazeta*, 14 July.

"Plan-zakaz Ministerstva prosveshcheniia SSSR Akademii pedagogicheskikh nauk SSSR na razrabotku problem sovershenstvovaniia obucheniia i vospitaniia podrastaiushchego pokoleniia v 1986–1990 godakh" (1986). *Biulleten' normativnykh aktov Ministerstva prosveshcheniia SSSR*, no. 7, pp. 16–37.

"Polozhenie o srednei obshcheobrazovatel'noi shkole. Proekt" (1988). *Uchitel'skaia gazeta*, 16 August.

Prelovskaia, I. (1992). "Renewal in Order to Survive." *Current Digest of the Post-Soviet Press*, vol. 44, no. 7, p. 26.

Roganovskii, N. (1991). "Differentsirovannoe obuchenie—kak ego osushchestvit'?" *Narodnoe obrazovanie*, no. 3, pp. 41–43.

Shadrikov, V.D. ([1990]). "Problems of the State Basis Plan Development for General Education School." Undated, unpaginated paper presented to Symposium on National Curricula, Institute of Education and USSR Academy of Pedagogical Sciences, London, May.

Suddaby, A. (1988). "V.F. Shatalov and the Makarenko Tradition in Soviet Education Today." *Soviet Education Study Bulletin*, vol. 6, no. 1, pp. 1–11.

Sutherland, J. (1992). "Perestroika in the Soviet General School: From Innovation to Independence?" In J. Dunstan, Ed., *Soviet Education under Perestroika*. London and New York: Routledge, pp. 14–29.

"Update of Legislative Principles on Public Education" (1986). *Soviet Education Study Bulletin*, vol. 4, no. 1, pp. 29–31.

"Ustav srednei obshcheobrazovatel'noi shkoly. Proekt" (1987). *Uchitel'skaia gazeta*, 31 January, pp. 2–3.

Vaganova, N. (1991). "Sem' raz otmer' ... ." *Uchitel'skaia gazeta*, no. 2, 8–15 January, p. 3.

Vendrovskaia, R.B. (1992). "Lessons of Differentiated Instruction." *Russian Education and Society*, vol. 34, no. 1, pp. 73–94.

"Vnimaniiu rabotnikov narodnogo obrazovaniia i vsekh, interesuiushchikhsia novymi vidami uchebnykh zavedenii!" (1990). *Biulleten' Gosudarstvennogo komiteta SSSR po narodnomu obrazovaniiu. Seriia: Doshkol'noe vospitanie i obshchee srednee obrazovanie*, no. 12, pp. 25–32.

"Vremennoe polozhenie o srednei obshcheobrazovatel'noi shkole SSSR (primernoe)" (1989). *Uchitel'skaia gazeta*, 16 August.

"Zakon Rossiiskoi Federatsii ob obrazovanii" (1992). *Uchitel'skaia gazeta*, no. 28 (4 August), pp. 10–15.

"Zakon Rossiiskoi Federatsii ob obrazovanii. Proekt" (1992). *Uchitel'skaia gazeta*, no. 2 (14 January), pp. 11–13.

"Zakon Rossiiskoi Sovetskoi Federativnoi Sotsialisticheskoi Respubliki ob obrazovanii. Proekt" (1991). *Uchitel'skaia gazeta*, no. 29 (16–23 July), pp. 2, 5.

5

The Independent Schools of St. Petersburg

Diversification of Schooling in Postcommunist Russia

*MARIE A. WESTBROOK WITH
LEV LURIE AND MIKHAIL IVANOV*

In recent months there has been much speculation regarding the impact of the demise of Communist rule on Russian schooling. If Russia elects to follow the example of other East European nations, the role of independent schools will be paramount in proposals for education reform. Even before the all too familiar events of August 1991, amidst grave economic hardship and social uncertainty, a handful of individuals had successfully launched a number of "independent" schools as a basis for improving the quality of education and promoting social change. Although it is much too soon to establish a measurement of their effectiveness or longevity, their presence may be evidence of an emerging pattern of individual and group influence on social organizations such as schools that will be crucial to the restoration of civic and economic life in Russia.

In an apparent move toward diversification of Russian schools, the January 1992 draft legislation on education for the Russian Federation includes a provision for the development of nonstate (*negosudarstvennye*), for-pay (*platnye*), and commercial (*kommercheskie*) schools. Although this might appear to be legislation designed to initiate social change, the social process of change in reality had taken the lead over the legal process. There is evidence of the successful development of independent schools as early as

1987. What is most compelling about these schools is their potential role not only in the diversification of the Russian school system, but also—and in direct contrast to their function in the Soviet period—in promoting a value system that is representative of the social aspirations, economic expectations, and cultural needs of the Russian people.

Given the rapid pace of economic decline and the competing social forces of restructuring, self-protection, and dismantling clearly evident in contemporary Russia, any attempt to delineate the future prospects for independent schools is at best speculation. Our goal in this chapter, therefore, is to provide the reader with a sense of the origin of independent schools; an understanding of the social and educational issues these schools hope to address; the values that unite or differentiate the new independent schools from existing schools; and the potential benefit and conflict created by this first step toward diversification of Russian schooling.

Independent schools, by their very nature, are a response to the perceived inadequacies of the social system that require the development of alternate mechanisms for the transmission of knowledge and culture. In Russia, these schools evolved not only because of the loosening of political and social boundaries during early perestroika, but also as a response to the social and political conditions that contributed to a climate of social alienation within schools, to limited access to special schools, and caused concern over the efficacy of Soviet schools. In order to understand the context of schooling that advocates of independent schools wish to change, it is necessary to examine the educational issues raised during perestroika and the past strategies for school reform.

School Reform During Perestroika

Since the 1980s, a common assessment of the Soviet educational system is that it existed in a state of crisis. What is unusual about the early stages of this crisis is the public and unobstructed manner in which discussion took place. In the mid-1980s, the promotion of a politically motivated plan for education reform along with a remarkably unusual tolerance for glasnost, or openness, brought the ever-present struggle for power from the inner workings of the Party apparatus into the public arena. The outcome of the nationwide discussion of conditions inside Soviet schools "literally smashed the myth of well being" (Anisin 1987, p. 11). The educational sores of Soviet society were freely displayed and discussed in a multitude of public arenas. What became apparent was the existence of a school system laboring under a rigid, multilevel bureaucracy known more for inertia than change, and faced with a number of difficulties reminiscent of those in developing nations.

In a series of articles and speeches, Soviet teachers and academicians joined more liberal educational leaders in describing conditions inside Soviet schools which had never before received public recognition. Their appraisal, as reported in publications such as *Izvestiia*, *Pravda*, and *Literaturnaia gazeta*, provided a long list of shortcomings. These included inadequate heating, sewerage, and water supply in 50 percent of the schools; overcrowding that required 25 percent of students to attend school in split shifts; limited access to kindergartens (Yagodin 1988, p. 15); serious health and nutritional deficiencies in school-age children (Anisin 1987, p. 11); a chronic shortage of teachers[1] (Yagodin 1989, p.1); the absence of modern textbooks and teaching resources (Shcherbakov 1987, p. 30); the elimination of parental participation or influence in the schools;[2] and a decline in the proportion of funds allocated to the general (nonspecialized) schools (Shukshunov 1990, p. 33).

In a joint survey of teachers' attitudes conducted by the Academy of Pedagogical Science (APN) and the University of Sheffield, 72.6 percent of Soviet teachers interviewed agreed that the school system was in a severe crisis and in need of fundamental reorganization (Gershunsky and Pullin 1990, p. 310). When asked to evaluate the "most negative aspects of teaching," 97 percent of the respondents listed the "bureaucratic character of educational management," 59 percent cited "parental indifference to the upbringing of their children," 50 percent cited "education's low prestige," and roughly 45 percent cited both the "absence of good textbooks" and the "absence of a link between school programs and life demands" (Gershunsky and Pullin 1990, p. 311). What emerges is a vision of teachers strangled by red tape and frustrated by demands to provide "quality education" with limited economic and educational resources, meager social recognition, and limited community support.

Teachers were not alone in their concern for the severity of the crisis in Soviet education. Residents of sixty-six cities and thirty-four towns and villages cited the "low level of education and culture of the upcoming generation" as a problem which must be "tackled without delay" (Sogomonov and Tolstykh 1990, p. 60). In recognition of the gap between the direction of Gorbachev-era educational reforms and historical reality, the typical Soviet school was described as "often a dreary place: a decrepit building with few books, outdated equipment, alienated students, bored teachers, and an authoritarian administration" (Kerr 1990, p. 27). Although rather harsh in its appraisal of general schools, this assessment represented a more universally shared feeling of an ever-increasing problem with the efficacy of the Soviet system of education.

The product of this much publicized discussion of the crisis in education was an onslaught of reform proposals which threatened literally to smother the school system with conflicting diagnoses, leaving teachers, students, and parents adrift in a plethora of reform documents from above. Some of the strategies under consideration included decentralization of school administration; the development of school councils comprised of parents, industry representatives, teachers, and students who would be responsible for school governance; the modernization of instruction and curriculum; reorganization of the Academy of Pedagogical Sciences; the development of co-op schools; an emphasis on education for gifted students; and an increase in state expenditures for schools.[3]

Problems of Social Access

Concern for the efficacy of schools was not the only problem to be faced during perestroika. Inequality of access to specialized schooling was recognized in the mid-1970s and prompted the president of the Academy of Pedagogical Science to call for the evaluation of special language schools for elements of "social selection reminiscent of bourgeois notions and practices" (Dunstan 1978, p. 100). More recently, special language schools have been described as providing education for the "children of the elite and the especially talented" (Kerr 1990, p. 27), as "known to cater to the more privileged families" (Dunstan 1978, p. 92; see also Matthews 1982, pp. 24–37), and as providing a significant advantage for entry into VUZy or higher education institutions (Jones 1991, p. 224). Although there is some disagreement as to whether limited access was a "deliberate piece of social engineering"[4] or an unintended consequence of academic specialization, the characterization of special schools as limited-access schools is routinely accepted.

In the Soviet system of education, the issue of access became excessively exacerbated due to a predominately low level of educational preparation in the general school and the high percentage of special language school graduates who went on to higher education.5 The academic aspirations of general school graduates were hampered by both limited opportunities for entrance into higher education institutions and severe deficiencies in the quality of education provided them.

In November 1990, economist Igor Kirillov reported that of the 2.2 million applicants to higher education institutes, less than 25 percent were admitted as full-time students. The prospects for admission were even worse for applicants rural school (Kirillov 1990, p. 26).

Problems of Social Alienation

During perestroika, the issues of access and efficacy received considerable attention in public debate. One issue that has yet to receive public recognition is now clearly evident in the emerging sociological studies of school life (Westbrook 1993). Soviet schooling was, for the most part, a dehumanizing experience for students, teachers, and (if we consider the emotional cost of maintaining divided loyalties) some directors as well. In testimony to the legacy of the Soviet philosophy of man as an instrument of the state, Russian students describe the experience of school as, variously "directed at the destruction of school pupils' individuality," "a nightmare," and "boring and common"; and they blame the difficulties in their schools on the low level of teaching, on overcrowding, and on poor relations between teachers and students. Teachers find fault in the disinterest of students, in the rigidity of school rules, in overcrowding, and in poor relations between directors and teachers.[6] What both groups seem to be describing is a complete disintegration of the school system's functional ability to operate as a mechanism for schooling (learning).

Looking at this from a sociological viewpoint, we begin to detect what may be the fatal flaw of Soviet schooling. Soviet schools, in keeping with the philosophy of the Soviet state, were designed and rewarded for their ability to function as political and narrowly defined educational institutions, but not as social institutions. The institutional function of schooling is at the very least to provide a context of community which invites participation, promotes identity formation, and ascribes duties and rewards based on role differentiation.

In this regard, the Soviet system was designed to fail. The process of determining rewards and responsibilities was self-defeating. Creative thinking was suspect, compliance was rewarded, meaningful participation was thwarted, and identity formation was based on an ideology that over time completely lost credibility.

The failure of the school system to recognize social needs (and even more, its failure to represent those needs, often described as a "gap between school and life") created a climate of social alienation in which meaningful participation by parents, teachers, and students was essentially eliminated. The failure of the system to reform itself, and the low level of social participation in schools, characterized the education systems of societies in other East European nations as well (Croghan and Croghan 1980, pp. 179–84).

Initial Evidence of Diversification

While the public debate held the attention of most educators, a small group of individuals worked to promote both social and educational reform by establishing new schools or modifying existing schools. Although small in number, these new schools could have fundamentally altered the nature of Soviet education by providing provocative alternatives to traditional Soviet schooling.[7] Within the current context of the Russian educational system, such schools are often referred to as gymnasium (*gimnaziia*), lycée (*litsei*), or academy (*akademia*) schools. The Russian Ministry of Education classifies them according to the focus or direction of their academic program as humanities (*gumanitarnyi*), natural science (*estestvenno-nauchnyi*), national (*natsional'nyi*), religious (*religioznyi*), elementary (*nachal'nyi*), and medical (*lechebnyi*) schools.[8]

Any distinction between these schools and existing secondary institutions is still unclear. It is possible, however, to begin to develop a classificational system based on certain distinctive characteristics. For matters of clarification, these schools can be divided into two categories: the new gymnasium and the independent gymnasium.

New gymnasium aptly describes those secondary-level schools which exist within the traditional education system and which experiment with slight modifications of such internal elements as curriculum, teaching methods, parent and student involvement, and dress codes; but they leave pre-existing funding and regulatory relationships with the ministry and regional departments of education intact. In contrast, *independent gymnasium* refers to a secondary-level school which exists outside the traditional framework in that it has been established by independent parties (teachers, scientists, parents, institutes). These schools receive limited funding from the Ministry of Education; have limited regulatory relationships with the ministry and regional departments of education (sufficient only to receive official sanction and accreditation); and independently determine such matters as teacher selection, curriculum, teaching methods, instructional resources, and location of facilities.

School No. 566: Ioffe Physical Technical High School

School No. 566, a secondary-level mathematics school, serves as an example of an independent gymnasium with no direct financial or regulatory ties to the Ministry of Education. Due largely to the efforts of liberal scientists who recognized the importance of early academic preparation for the study of science and the need to reduce the negative impact of the "departmental principle,"[9] members of the educational division of the Ioffe Institute developed, over a period of years, a proposal for the development of a secondary mathematics school. The curriculum of this school emphasizes the training of young scientists in the areas of advanced physical mathematics and engineering.[10]

School Admission

Admission to School No. 566 is based on a series of oral and written examinations. An initial written examination is given to all applicants and includes ten to fifteen problems designed to test for mathematical ability, analytical skills, and comprehension. Seventy-five candidates are selected from the first exam, roughly forty of whom will receive admission to the school without further examination. Of the thirty-five remaining candidates, twenty-five are invited to participate in the next level of evaluation which includes participation in a classroom physics exercise, small group discussion activities (all of which are observed by members of the school council), and individual interviews. Following a rather lengthy and exhaustive process of elimination, the school council decides, by consensus, which candidates will be admitted.

As of fall 1992, the student body consisted of 180 students ranging in age from thirteen to seventeen years, covering the eighth through the eleventh grades. Students are able to seek entry at the eighth grade and pursue a four-year course of study, or they may enter at the tenth grade and complete a two-year course. The admission statistics of the last few years show that between 250 and 300 students competed for admission to the fifty available seats for the entering class. The desirability of admission to School No. 566 can be attributed to the apparent success of its graduates, who have been able to secure admission to VUZy, to publish articles in research journals, and in some cases to continue their studies at foreign universities. In addition, the expectation of an academically rigorous program, the availability of laboratory facilities for use in research projects, and sponsorship by the Ioffe Institute of Physics and Technological Science, all greatly enhance the prospects for the continued efficacy of this school.[11]

The importance of economic support should not be underestimated. Given the continual need for updating and expanding educational services in modern society, and the presence of a global revolution in educational technology and computing, Russia's inability to increase funding for public education takes on added significance.

Faculty

Another strengthening factor of the academic program is the emphasis placed on the qualification of the faculty. As of fall 1990, 18 percent of the faculty held candidate degrees (approximately equivalent to a Ph.D.) and 20 percent were senior scholars in science, engineering, physics, biology, psychology, and art. Governance of the school is carried out through a school council composed of the chairs of the Physical Technical Department of Ioffe Physical Technical University, leading scientists of the Ioffe Institute, and students' parents. The council determines such matters as the number and level of final examinations, election of the school director, and review of applicants for teaching vacancies.

School No. 610: St. Petersburg Classical Gymnasium

Our second example of an independent gymnasium is of School No. 610. In the fall of 1989, an adjunct faculty member of School Number 30 met with a group of tutors, past graduates of the Department of Classical Languages of Leningrad State University, and interested parents. Their goal was to design an alternative educational program along the lines of the classical gymnasium, with emphasis on the study of classical and modern languages, mathematics, history, and Russian literature. Other subjects such as music and art would be offered as electives in special evening classes. The result of their work was School No. 610, the St. Petersburg Classical Gymnasium (SPCG).

Admission

Admission to SPCG is based on the results of entrance examinations which consist of twenty questions (ten written and ten oral) covering analytical skills, geography, world history, and ancient culture. Scores are computed on a scale of zero to two with a maximum composite score of forty. The results of the test are made public, and faculty are willing to meet with the parents of nonadmitted students to go over examination results. In this case, the availability of definitive evidence for the nonadmission of a candidate represents a significant departure from past Soviet practice under which "evaluation and grading of [exam] results is at best a subjective process" (Hecht 1982, p. 113).

In August 1989, 352 students competed for the fifty available openings. Under an agreement with the administrative staff of School No. 30, space for two classes of seventh-grade students was allocated within the existing building. The first test of the students' academic achievement occurred during the Leningrad Mathematics Olympics. Students from the SPCG won one-third of all awards for their respective age groups. As the public knowledge of the school grew, applications for admissions increased. By the second academic year, there were 650 applicants.

By fall 1991, the gymnasium had 168 students in six classes—two of the sixth grade (age ten-eleven), two seventh-grade classes (age 12–13), and two eighth-grade classes (age 13–14). Class size is limited to twenty-eight students. By fall 1994, those students who are at present in the eighth grade will have matriculated to the eleventh grade, effectively establishing the full integration of a four-year course of study.

Faculty

Most members of the faculty involved in teaching and administrative activities were involved in the early stages of the philosophical and institutional development of SPCG. Between 40 and 50 percent of the instructional faculty hold candidate degrees, and close to 50 percent are associated with local scholarly institutes such as the St. Petersburg Institute of History. However, not all faculty possess previous experience in secondary-level teaching.

Financing and Problems

Funding from independent sources continues to be crucial to the durability of independent gymnasiums. During the academic year 1989–1990, SPCG received 70,000 rubles from the Variant Engineering Cooperative of the Komsomol, 10,000 rubles from an organization known as the Soviet Cultural Foundation, and 6,000 rubles from the Cooperative of Leningrad Tutors. Efforts have also been made to establish contacts with Western organizations in an attempt to locate sources of support. The success of these external funding arrangements is at present uncertain.[12]

For students and parents in St. Petersburg, SPCG appears to be a popular and intriguing alternative to traditional (Soviet) schools, but the attitudes of officials are mixed. Detractors fall into two categories: those who are overtly antagonistic to independent schooling, and those who resist by omission in their inability or unwillingness to exert sufficient effort to offer assistance when needed. A good example of resistance by omission is the response of local officials to requests for assistance in obtaining a new facility to house the school. During the 1990 school year, the SPCG moved from its shared quarters in School No. 30 to three rooms in the local Palace of Pioneers. This facility, mostly vacant during the daytime hours, proved suitable until the spring of 1990, when the school was asked to vacate because of concern that the building would not withstand the wear and tear of continuous daytime use. Essentially left without a building, school representatives approached local officials for assistance. According to those officials, there were no available vacant buildings that were suitable for school use. School directors then located ten unoccupied buildings, including many Khrushchev-era school–factory facilities. When they asked for permission to move to one of these, they found themselves caught in a power struggle between the newly elected president of the Leningrad Commission for Popular Education (M. Bashmakov) and the remaining members of the old educational establishment, and were informed that a "building could not be located." It was only after a direct order from the Leningrad City Soviet that a building was found (Panchenko 1991, p. 2).

Difficulties such as these are but one of the tensions that exist between groups with different perspectives on educational reform and social change. Views in support of and in opposition to experimentation or differentiation in Soviet education are well known. N. Shakhmaev, a corresponding member of the Academy of Pedagogy, recently stated that "under the banner of democratization, the State Committee has essentially abandoned the principle of a uniform school system. . . . Differentiation is a mistake that could have unpredictable consequences" (Shakhmaev 1990, p. 26). Another education official, I. Prelovskaia, has written in a more positive vein, that "students are now free to choose their own philosophical positions and intellectual interests, which is a real consequence of the changes in our society's life" (Prelovskaia 1990, p. 1).

How Independent Schools Differ From Normal Soviet Schools

It would be difficult today to describe a normal Russian school. Although in some schools, the external trappings of the Soviet culture of education remain, the level of independent activity in even the most renitent of the Soviet-legacy schools speaks of a style of decision making, independent program development, and experimentation with pedagogy[13] that may herald the abandonment of the unified school as well as substantial change in the culture of Russia's schools.

Thus there is a degree of agreement between the independent and former Soviet-legacy schools. Of prime concern to educators in both types of schools is the ability to provide quality education to Russian youth. The mechanisms may differ, but on the issue of efficacy, the intent is the same. The issue of access is yet to be resolved, however, and this may prove to be a dividing point as educators in both independent and state schools face difficult decisions regarding access to a high-quality education.

Another unexpected point of concurrence is in the general disregard and disinterest in government-designed education reform. School directors in both state and independent schools show a remarkable degree of autonomy in decisions on the restructuring of school activities and policies. Since August 1991, in the absence of concrete educational policy, it is conceivable that the future framework for Russian education is being defined by the activities and behaviors within schools, and that a model is thus being created to which centrally defined policy must now adapt.[14]

Impact of Independent Schools

Because of the perceived social benefit of diversified schooling, the direction of education policy in Russia (as in other East European nations [Glenn 1991] is moving in the direction of a dual system of education, incorporating state and nonstate schools.[15] Independent schools can be socially useful if they continue to promote social relations within schools that reduce the legacy of alienation; if they develop programs that respond to educational needs and social aspirations of the community; and if they provide employment for displaced but highly skilled intellectual workers. In addition, the potential role of independent schools as contributors to the effectiveness of state schools must also be recognized. Independent schools can provide successfully tried ideas, teaching methods, and alternative philosophies and mechanisms of schooling. This has already occurred in Poland, where it is noted that "well functioning non-state schools have a positive influence upon the nearby state schools" (Glenn 1991, p. 57). The concept of a dual system of education has emerged also in other East European nations. Preliminary data reveal the relative importance of independent schools in education policy, indicated by their inclusion in draft legislation in Bulgaria, Czechoslovakia, Germany, Hungary, and Poland (Glenn 1991, p. 57).

Public Attitudes Toward Privatization

The population's view on the role of independent schools is not well defined. In Russia, the issue of privatization in itself raises much anxiety over the prospects of increased social class distinctions if proper equalizing measures are not implemented (Kerr 1990, p. 26; Jones 1991, p. 224). Such difficulties could be avoided if both school policy and official sanctions follow along the lines of the German system, which forbids independent schools to charge excessive fees and are required to "reserve places for pupils whose parents cannot pay fees at all . . . to prevent an unconstitutional separation of pupils on the basis of social class" (Glenn 1991, p. 59).

The issue of access to specialized schools (now the new or independent gymnasiums) returns once again as a pivotal concern. School policy as practiced by teachers and directors, even more than educational policy as defined by the state, becomes instrumental in deciding whether historical patterns of selectivity and privilege diminish or are reinforced.

Conclusion

Diversification is clearly a new dimension in Russian society, and it comes at a time when the Russian education system is entering a period of unparalleled difficulty. The raft of issues raised during the public discussion of the crisis in education remains unresolved. The legacy of Communist Party control of education policy and practice leaves in its wake an education bureaucracy essentially without credibility, a population with limited experience in participatory decision making, a fragmented system of schools, limited economic and instructional resources, and the absence of ideological or philosophical consensus.

Steps that have been taken so far to develop legislation in support of alternative schooling, and to define the mechanism for the legal sanction of independent schools, can promote structural diversity. Decentralization of decision making and a shift in the locus of authority from state to regional government are also structural changes. The context for substantive change in such matters as the transmission of knowledge, socialization, and moral and social development is as yet undefined.

One of the fatal flaws of the Soviet system was its failure to promote social institutions designed to represent the aspirations and meet the needs of the population. As a result, people in Russia are now having to build civil society one step at a time, one institution at a time. The school is inescapably and necessarily a part of this social transformation.

Notes

We are indebted to Academician Zhores Alferov and Academician Boris C. Gershunsky for their technical support and intellectual contribution to this study and to Dr. Leo Hecht for his careful review of an earlier draft. Research for this article was supported in part by grants from the Social Science Research Council and the International Research and Exchange Board (IREX), with funds provided by the National Endowment for the Humanities, the United States Information Agency, and U.S. Department of State. None of these organizations is responsible for the views expressed.

1. Changes in policies concerning privatization have led to an increase in the development of joint ventures which offer lucrative employment to bilingual workers, further reducing the ranks of qualified foreign-language teachers. Emergency programs are now in place to retrain unemployed workers as teachers of English for the school system.

2. Although there were some recent attempts to include parents as members of school councils, it is clear that the current economic conditions prevent most parents from participating in school activities.

3. For viewpoints in support of decentralization, see Shukshunov (1990), p. 3, and Anisin (1987), p. 11. For contrasting views in support of continued centralization, see Shakhmaev (1990), p. 3, and Baronenko (1989), p. 4. For viewpoints in support of increased access and choice for parents and students, see Prelovskaia (1990), p. 1, and Kerkadze (1987), p. 2. A discussion of the prospects for cooperative schools can be found in Kreidlin (1987). In a survey conducted by the All-Union Center of the Study of Public Opinion, 53 percent of the respondents saw cooperative schools as "not necessary," 27 percent saw them as "necessary," and 20 percent found it "difficult to say" (Avdeenko et al. 1990 p. 15). For viewpoints in support of gymnasiums and lycées, see Prelovskaia (1990), p. 29.

4. In Dunstan's study of foreign-language schools he recognizes the existence of controlled access but attributes it more to the "inadvertent outcome" of a market-based labor policy (Dunstan 1978, p. 101). In contrast, Burg asserts that the foreign-language schools were principally for the "scions of the Soviet aristocracy" (Burg 1960, p. 120).

5. This trend was evident as early as 1968, when studies showed that 65.7 percent of language-school graduates in a sample group entered VUZy in comparison with 25 percent of graduates from all full-time secondary schools. In some cases, language schools reported an admission rate to VUZy of more than 80 percent (Miroliubov 1970, pp. 48–49).

6. These comments, and the assessment of student and teacher attitudes, come from interviews conducted in St. Petersburg from February 1992 through May 1992. For a more complete discussion, see Westbrook 1993.

7. In a March 1991 presentation to the Kennan Institute, Dimitrii Panchenko estimated that there were eight independent schools in St. Petersburg. I would classify six of these schools as "new gymnasiums" and two as "independent gymnasiums."

8. Figures available for March 1992 show registrations of new schools in Moscow: eleven humanities schools, one natural science school, three national schools, four religious schools, six elementary schools, and one medical school. Interview with Boris Gershunskii, "Obrazovanie i budushchee" (Education and the Future), March 25, 1992.

9. The departmental principle refers to the separation of industry-affiliated re-

search institutes, the Academy of Sciences, and higher education institutions from each other, contributing to what the vice chairman of the (former) USSR State Committee on Public Education described as a compartmentalization which results in scholars and scientists working in isolation from one another. (Shukshunov 1990, p. 11).

10. The curriculum in School No. 566 includes weekly lessons in mathematics (eight hours), physics (four–six hours), computer science (four–six hours), English (five hours), Russian history (two–four hours), literature (two–four hours), chemistry (two–four hours), biology (two–four hours), physical training (two–four hours), and astronomy (one–two hours).

11. School No. 566 receives all of its funds from the Ioffe Institute. Although the contribution in 1991 represented less than one percent of the total operating budget, the presence of adequate funds cannot be ignored as a significant factor in the early success of this mathematics school. Under current economic conditions, the impact of economic reform has reduced the budgetary abilities of the main source for Ioffe funds, the Academy of Sciences, which in turn has had a significant impact on School No. 566. If unresolved, cosponsorship by other institutes or agencies will be required.

12. In September 1992, the Soviet Cultural Foundation became the St. Petersburg Cultural Foundation and continued its financial commitment to School No. 610. There was also some success in locating external funds through the Sorus Foundation in the United States; and a donation of 150,000 rubles came from two St. Petersburg cooperatives.

13. Some examples of experimentation within normal and specialized state schools in St. Petersburg include reduction of class size, grouping students based on ability, charging special fees for advanced classes or for entry into smaller classes, and in some cases the division of the school into two programs which could be described as for gifted and general-track pupils.

14. A review of education legislation passed by the Supreme Soviet on May 22, 1992, supports this assumption. Overall, beyond accreditation and compliance with curriculum standards schools, public or private, are, for the time being, left to determine their philosophical, instructional, administrative, and economic affairs independently. See "Zakon Rossiiskoi Federatsii ob Obrazovanii" (The Law of the Russian Federation on Education), *Rossiiskaia gazeta*, 31 July 1992. p. 3.

15. During interviews conducted in March and April of 1992 at the Russian Ministry of Education and at the Academy of Sciences, it was confirmed that the direction of education policy within Yeltsin's government is clearly in support of the concept of independent (nonstate) schools. It should be noted, however, that serious criticism has been expressed within the Academy of Sciences concerning the perceived abandonment of the unified school system under this policy.

References

Anisin, N. (1987). "According to the Old Schedule." *Pravda*, 16 October, p. 2. In *Current Digest of the Soviet Press (CDSP* hereafter) 39, no. 34, p. 11.

Avdeenko, T., Grazhdankin, A., Rutgaizer, V. and Shpil'ko, S. (1990). "The Attitude of the Population toward the Development of Cooperatives." In *Soviet Sociology*, vol. 29, no. 5, pp. 10–19.

Baronenko, A. (1989). "The Mission of the Teacher and Instructor is Noble and Responsible." *Uchitelskaia gazeta*, 24 December, p. 3. In *CDSP* 50, no. 52, p. 4.

Burg, D. (1960). "Notes on Foreign Language Teaching in the USSR." In G. Bereday and J. Penner, eds., *The Politics of Soviet Education*. New York: Praeger Publishers, pp. 117–31.

Croghan, M. and Croghan, P. (1980). *Ideological Training in Communist Education: A Case Study of Romania*. Washington, DC: University Press of America.

Dunstan, J. (1978). *Paths to Excellence and the Soviet Schools*. Oxford, England: NFER Publishing.

Glenn, C. (1991). "Educational Reform in Eastern Europe." Quincy, MA: Office of Educational Research and Improvement Programs.

Gershunsky, S. and Pullin, R. (1990). "Current Dilemmas for Soviet Secondary Education: an Anglo-Soviet Analysis." In *Comparative Education*, vol. 26, no. 2. pp. 305–18.

Hecht, L. (1982). *The USSR Today: Facts and Interpretations*. Springfield, VA: Scholastic Publishing.

Jones, A. (1991). "Problems in the Schools." In Jones, A., Connor, W., and Powell, D., eds., *Soviet Social Problems*. Boulder, CO: Westview Press.

Kerkadze, E. (1988). "What Should Schools Be Like?" *Izvestiia*, 28 December, p. 2. In *CDSP* 39, no. 51, p. 24.

Kerr, S. (1990). "Will Glasnost Lead to Perestroika?" In *Educational Researcher*, vol. 19, no. 7, pp. 26–31.

Kreidlin, G. (1987). "We Want to Open a School on a Cooperative Basis." *Literaturnaia gazeta*, 15 July, p. 10. In *CDSP* 39, no. 38, p. 20.

Kirillov, I. (1990). "No Ticket to the Future." *Sovetskaia kul'tura*, 10 November, p. 5. In *CDSP* 42, no. 45, p. 26.

Matthews, M. (1982). *Education in the Soviet Union: Policies and Institutions since Stalin*. Winchester, MA: George Allen & Unwin Ltd.

Miroliubov, A. (1970). "The Russian Way: How Successful Is It?" *Times Educational Supplement*, 20 February, pp. 48–49.

Panchenko, D. (1991). "New Forms of Schooling in the USSR." Washington, DC: Presentation to the Kennen Institute, 21 March.

Prelovskaia, I. (1990). "Education Ministers Speak on Changes in the Administration of Higher and Secondary Education." *Izvestiia*, 25 October, p. 1. In *CDSP* 42, no. 43, p. 32.

Sogomonov, A. and Tolstykh, A. (1990). "About Our Concerns." In *Soviet Sociology*, vol. 29, no. 3, pp. 56–62.

Shakhmaev, N. (1990). "A Blank Space on the Graduation Certificate." *Pravda*, 17 November, p. 3. In *CDSP* 42, no. 47, p. 26.

Shcherbakov, S. (1987). "Private Schools at the Center of Our Attention." *Pravda*, 15 December, p. 3. In *CDSP* 39, no. 50, p. 30.

Shukshunov, V. (1990). "Otherwise We'll Become Intellectually Impoverished." *Pravda*, 28 August, p. 3. In *CDSP* 42, no. 35, p. 33.

Westbrook. M. (1993). "Changing Schools: Student Perceptions of Independent Schools and School Reform in Post-Soviet Russia, St. Petersburg, Russia (1992)." Ph.D. dissertation, University of Virginia.

Yagodin, G. (1988). "Speech to Comrades." *Pravda*, 2 July, p. 9. In *CDSP* 40, no. 34, p. 15.

———. (1989). "Toward Humanization and Democratization, Toward A New Quality of Education." *Pravda*, 21 December, p. 3. In *CDSP* 40, no. 52, p. 1.

6

History Education and Historiography in Soviet and Post-Soviet Russia

WILLIAM B. HUSBAND

> *The school in the period of perestroika has found itself in an extraordinarily complicated situation. A huge torrent of information has come down not only on teachers, but also on students. This information is in no way systematized, [and] it does not correspond to textbook material and books on methods.*
>
> —N.I. Voshchinnikov
> history teacher, Moscow School No. 32

> *The humanitarian science of history is a means for teaching elevated human qualities. . . . A new spirit in the teaching of history is more important to me than the distribution of hours among courses, methods of inquiry and the organization of work with textbooks. . . . What is needed is a transition from the journalistic sneak attack on history to its deeper comprehension on the basis of new approaches.*
>
> —A.B. Sokolov
> Candidate of Historical Science

It should generate scant surprise that establishing a practicable relationship between secondary-school history education and scholarly historiography has proven elusive in post-1985 Russia. Indeed, determining the function and content of history education gives rise to frequent contention, not only in societies in transition, but wherever schools exist.

Works as diverse as George Orwell's *1984*, Peter Novick's *That Noble Dream*, and Robert Darnton's *The Kiss of Lamourette* have all observed how historical lessons can be patterned to support a predetermined point of view. Those who seek to shape a given social environment often try to fashion an educational curriculum that legitimates their own version of historical truth.

Professional historiography by no means plays a universally central role in formulating the representation of the past that public education teaches the young. In the West, scholarly agendas and state-of-the-art historical research are usually far from paramount in this process. Revisionist and serious conventional scholarship almost always run well ahead of textbook and classroom presentations below the university level. Thus, although scholarly interpretations eventually do inform secondary-school history education, at least indirectly, by the time they penetrate the classroom they are commonly diluted, used selectively, and sometimes adapted to purposes other than those intended by their originators.

In Russia, the relationship among scholarship, history education, and society has developed differently. There the idea that history is a repository of lessons enjoys unusually widespread acceptance. Long before the Communist régime rewrote the past for its own purposes, the pre-revolutionary intelligentsia laid particular emphasis on the didactic potential of historical experience. History-as-metaphor was a dominant device in the music, painting, journalism, and especially *belles lettres* of the nineteenth century, and by the end of the tsarist period Russian scholars enjoyed full standing in the international historical community. Even extensive falsification during the Soviet period did not eradicate this preoccupation with history.

Such statements require clarification. On the one hand, there can be no denying that the state-sanctioned version of the nation's past enjoyed at least partial acceptance, especially on subjects such as the nature of the country's role in World War II, where there existed a sustained predisposition toward belief. Yet over time, the manifold contradictions between the overarching message of the official story and existing social memory became evident even to school children. Certainly not later than the mid-1950s a significant majority of Russians rejected privately and in privileged conversations historical interpretations they could not comfortably challenge publicly. By the 1980s, such skepticism was virtually universal.

Yet however much Soviet citizens doubted the *content* of the received historical message, the idea that history had the capacity to teach important lessons retained a significant constituency. Large numbers of those who did not identify extensively with the general aims of the Soviet state still accepted historical rationales for promoting positive social values. At the same time but in a different vein, the effort by isolated individuals to preserve society's historical memory became itself an important mode of political dissent. One might even speculate, on the basis of the character and scope of recent historical debates in the former USSR, whether extensive falsification during the Soviet period strengthened rather than weakened the conviction in society that historical knowledge is directly applicable to contemporary experience.

No analysis of current attempts to reinvigorate the study of the past in Russia, therefore, can underestimate the legacy of falsification. In the 1930s, Joseph Stalin promoted an extensively adulterated version of history, encapsulated in the *History of the Communist Party of the Soviet Union (Bolsheviks): Short Course*. Published in 1938, this *Short Course* established a basic canon from which no representation of the past could deviate significantly. In so doing, it eliminated meaningful distinctions between the substance of professional historiography and secondary education, since both had to conform to the same basic source. Even after its repudiation following Stalin's death, the *Short Course* retained significant influence over Soviet research and education in history. During these post-Stalin years, orthodox and revisionist historians carried on protracted battles over the limits of acceptable interpretation, although they placed decidedly less emphasis on accommodating methodological diversity. While these conflicts were being waged, it was the nonrevisionist scholars who continued to dominate textbook preparation, a fact that guaranteed that the school version of the past would reflect the most orthodox of extant interpretations, characterized by critics as little different from the *Short Course*.

When Mikhail Gorbachev's policies of openness forced a serious reconsideration of the nation's past in the late 1980s, therefore, society's collective memory and the long-term legacy of Stalinist falsification came into ineluctable conflict. At stake were nothing less than the credibility of the régime and the viability of its reform program. Initially, however, professional historians and secondary-school educators were slow to respond to the new opportunities for frank discussion. Tainted by their long association with now-discredited versions of the past, neither group displayed the ability or inclination to seize the initiative. As many observers have noted, the artistic community and the general public, not historians and educators, fueled the unprecedented historical revelations and discussions that startled Soviet society in 1987–88. For their part, historians had produced no corpus of previously unpublishable work now begging for general release; and, rather than generating new programs, educational administrators turned for inspiration to school reforms already in motion. Thus, in 1987, Soviet society began a mass exercise in historical cathar-sis—in the national press, in public lectures and discussions, and in high politics—that first generated revelations on Stalinism, then moved rapidly through the full range of party and revolutionary history, and soon opened all topics of the Russian and non-Russian past. Over time, some artistic and journalistic revelation remained responsible and rigorous; other examples drifted into sensationalism, the selective use of evidence, and false-hood. Nothing in these proceedings, however, promoted confidence in existing scholarship and public education.

There was no uniform response from professional scholars. Rather than transforming it, this far-reaching public reassessment further divided the community of historians. Initially, scholars generally debated a new pro-fessional agenda and ethos rather than producing specific reinterpreta-tions. Only slowly did revisionists begin to challenge conservatives, who were often well enough entrenched in important institutions to defend themselves effectively. In secondary education, the impact was more im-mediate. The wholesale discrediting of official history in the mass press and in public forums made necessary a thorough reconsideration of curric-ula and textbooks. Students increasingly challenged lessons that con-tradicted recent revelations; classroom teachers began to express frustration over their lack of control of lesson content; examinations were canceled for want of credible teaching materials. Thus, by 1988, there began a process that continues to the present moment: a halting search for new interpretations among historians and a comprehensive reassessment of curricula and textbooks in secondary education.

But disproving falsifications, although a non-negotiable first step, falls well short of establishing a consensus on an acceptable framework for historical discourse in scholarship, the schools, or lay discussions. In the years that followed the intensive scrutiny of history that took place in 1987–88, several important factors changed. First, the discussion of his-tory in the public sphere quantitatively and qualitatively declined. Histori-cal disclosures continue—especially where the culpability of the former Soviet government and Communist Party can be demonstrated—but with-out the former sense of immediacy. In Russia, an infatuation with topics of the tsarist past has significantly displaced post-1917 history as the center of public interest. Second, as other chapters in this volume convinc-ingly demonstrate, the teaching of history by no means dominates the

agenda on the future of Russian education. Solutions to other, more fundamental issues may well have to precede any ultimate redrafting of the
history curriculum. Third, the nation's political and economic ills continue
to dissipate human and material resources crucial to a timely resolution of
the problem. Most specifically, the contraction of resources undermines
all proposed correctives to the critical shortages of scholarly and educational materials.

Yet despite recent setbacks, professional historians and secondary educators give no indication that they intend to abdicate their traditional roles,
even though they will certainly be subject in the future to greater public
accountability for what is taught. In reality, any long-term translation of
the refuted version of post-1917 Russian history into an effectual mode
will almost certainly have to include a key role for scholars as well as for
secondary-school educators. The nonprofessionals who participated in the
invalidation of official Soviet history have demonstrated little propensity
for the less glamorous work of detailed revision. Equally to the point, in
the absence of any single repository of truth analogous to the *Short
Course*, and without the production and distribution of reliable new classroom materials, history teachers in secondary schools must increasingly
rely on professional scholarship as a source of the prodigious amounts of
basic information they lack. Reformist teachers themselves made this
point in 1987 when they demanded greater support from the scholarly
community. Since then, leading professional history journals have responded by making secondary-school teaching a higher priority.

This state of affairs presents both opportunities and problems. For professional historians, scholarship is now able to inform, rather than follow,
the presentations of textbooks, since a basic canon does not now dictate
any one interpretation. This reverses the condition that existed when the
Short Course prevailed and, as the experience of the recent past illustrates,
can lead both to more penetrating inquiry and to the fragmentation of the
historical discipline. To be fair, it would be extremely unrealistic to expect
this process to have produced a significant mass of studies from which sophisticated new generalizations can be derived in the short time since 1985.

Secondary-school teachers face different prospects. Even as they strive
for greater control over the general curriculum and their classrooms, they
increase their dependence on professional historians for what they teach.
Such dependence is in one sense not new; as already noted, orthodox
professional historians dominated post-Stalin textbook preparation. The
current state of the relationship, however, includes an important modification. Because teachers presently exercise greater latitude in shaping the

content of lessons, they need reliable information from which to construct the more critical versions of the past that some of them desire to teach. And lack of access to credible historical materials—the unavailability of journals and books—has emerged as one of the teachers' foremost complaints during the reform process. Hence, they are dependent on a body of scholarship which, although superior to former history scholarship, is itself in flux. Education and professional scholarship are therefore inextricably linked, but in pursuit of goals that are decidedly different from previous ones.

In my opinion, uncertainty over the content of history education at the secondary-school level in Russia will not be resolved before professional historians gain a new sense of scholarly direction. Writ large, contemporary choices appear to be between the emergence of a new orthodoxy, or of continuing intellectual and methodological diversity. Current conditions augur badly for a new orthodoxy, and there are far more indications that much will depend on the accommodation of diversity. But despite recent activism by both educational reformers and historical revisionists, and countless declarations of allegiance to pluralism, there is little to indicate that such accommodation has anywhere become a leading priority.

With these considerations in mind, let us turn our attention to the broad issues linking professional historiography, education, and society: rebuilding credibility, establishing a new framework for historical discourse, and redefining professional and intellectual relationships. Information is drawn mainly from the leading historical journals, and to some extent from the mass press. The conclusions offered should be seen as tentative, especially since recent experience has amply demonstrated the potential for Russian reality to defy expectations.

New Opportunities and the Persistence of Orthodoxy

The opportunities to reevaluate history and education which Gorbachev's accession to power created did not immediately produce widespread challenges to established conventions. The reticence of historians is understandable. As demonstrated by the well-known Burdzhalov Affair of the mid-1950s and the fate of outspoken but less publicized figures thereafter, losers in intradisciplinary battles could expect serious professional penalties (Burdzhalov 1987, pp. ix-xvii). Thus, a reference by Gorbachev to the need for an historically informed public in his initial address as leader in March 1985 (*Materialy* 1985a, p. 11) was far from sufficient to inspire mass action. Practiced in preemptive obedience, and sensitive to the gap between *pro forma* calls for reform and actual practice in the past, most professional historians initially exhibited more caution than enthusiasm.

The experience of Iurii Afanas'ev suggested that circumspection was indeed the most prudent course. At the time a section head in the Institute of World History and member of the editorial board of the Party's main theoretical journal *Kommunist*, Afanas'ev published an article in September 1985, "The Past and Ourselves," which advocated reconsidering the prevailing representation of history in order to face the future more effectively. Although reserved in comparison to his later denunciations of falsification, Afanas'ev was forceful by the standards of the moment in his choice of topics: the importance of collective memory; history as the product of the present; the dangers of remaining silent and of idealizing the past; the need to tolerate a broader range of methodologies, including those from the West; and criticism of various professional institutions for their poor anticipation of and response to current historical issues (Afanas'ev 1985, pp. 105–16). As the initial major assault on official history, "The Past and Ourselves" was bold, and one year later Afanas'ev was out of a job,[1] ostensibly the victim of staff reductions (Murakara 1987a, p. 448).

Other scholars spoke more guardedly, largely by couching their words as responses to Party initiatives. In this regard, the October 1985 Plenum of the Central Committee and the Twenty-seventh Communist Party Congress of February–March 1986 broadened the possibilities for attacking the schematicism that characterized existing political and Party history. Although generally presented as a revitalizion of history in order to raise social consciousness and, by extension, economic productivity, Party discussions tacitly recognized the need for a more honest assessment of social questions, the previous neglect of which had made possible the crude equation of the nation's past with Party high politics (*Materialy* 1985b, pp. 8–14; 1986, pp. 28, 44, 48–49). This development enabled the small number of professional historians who responded publicly to justify their words with references to recent Party pronouncements, even as their ideas began to test existing limits. Several advocated reintegrating the so-called human factor into history. This phrase became shorthand for denouncing the omission of social forces from existing historical accounts, which by implication represented a leading basis of falsification. In 1986, *Voprosy istorii KPSS* (Questions of History of the CPSU), formerly a staid Party journal, emerged as a forum for frank attacks on hackneyed, faceless, and clichéd views of history (El'baum 1986, pp. 45–48; Koltsov 1986, p. 33; "Pervye uroki" 1986, pp. 3–8; Egorov 1986, pp. 7, 16). And in August 1986, *Kommunist* criticized what it referred to as scholasticism and dogmatism and advocated the incorporation of more sociological scholarship into history as a way to energize human issues ("O zhurnale 'Kommunist,' " 1986, pp. 3–6).

Those who spoke for secondary education were more noncommittal. *Prepodavanie istorii v shkole* (Teaching History in the School), published by the USSR Ministry of Education, featured articles that managed to praise the current climate of reform without actually advocating changes in the *status quo*. For example, a summary assessment of the year 1985, co-authored by the chief editor of the university and secondary-school history textbooks on the Soviet period then in use, expressed support for Party initiatives, but without referring specifically to the need to revise existing versions of history (Kukushkin and Nenarokov 1986, pp. 10–15). A representative article on the implications for public education of the directives of the Twenty-seventh Congress buried mention of past short-falls and the importance of the human factor under a celebration of the role of the classroom teacher in the implementation of Party resolutions. It proposed alterations of methods, but skirted the more contentious issue of the content of lessons ("Ob izuchenni" 1986, pp. 2–6). Another discussion of the Twenty-seventh Congress and the teaching of history began with the issues of reform and the human factor, but soon degenerated into a patriotic paean (Koloskov 1986, pp. 13–15). Additional contributions either were so vaguely expressed that their true intent could not readily be discerned (Klokova and Batsyn 1986, pp. 19–23) or celebrated examples of the "old" history as "new" ("Novyi uchebnik" 1986, pp. 41–45).

In light of these early trends, it is difficult to exaggerate the importance of the acceleration of developments in 1987–88. On the level of national attention, Gorbachev's now famous call at the beginning of 1987 for the removal of "blank spaces" from Soviet history set into motion an outpouring of long suppressed emotions and questions, beginning with those from the artistic community. The mass press and public meetings emerged by the spring of 1987 as additional forums in this discussion first of Stalinism and then of all post-1917 history. The momentum of these extensive attacks on falsification—and the story is too well documented to require recapitulation here—continued throughout 1988 (Davies 1989; Wheatcroft 1987a, pp. 85–132; 1987b, pp. 57–114; Von Hagen 1988, pp. 1–8). Above all, it was the accusations and revelations made in these public venues that transformed private skepticism into a full public loss of credulity for the state-sanctioned version of history.

Secondary-school history education felt the reverberations immediately. In 1987, editor Vladimir F. Matveev opened the pages of the national newspaper for secondary-school teachers, *Uchitel'skaia gazeta* (Teachers' Gazette), to genuine debate, and the tone of criticisms printed there turned more strident by 1988. The paper included criticisms of falsified history and of the Stalinist legacy in education, but devoted its main effort to promoting changes—the dissolution of the Academy of Pedagogical Sciences, for example—that would remove impediments to greater flexibility. At the same time, independent organizations of classroom teachers called Eureka Clubs began holding regional conferences, which led to the formation of a national Creative Union of Teachers in 1989. The autonomous Provisional Research Collective–School (*VNIK-Shkola*), which also formed in 1988, publicly supported fundamentally different approaches in the classroom: encouraging critical thinking and differences of opinion; reducing the influence of Marxism–Leninism; reintroducing prerevolutionary culture; and allowing classroom teachers to select their preferred syllabi and texts from a range of offerings ("Kontseptsiia" 1990, pp. 18–24). By year's end, a Congress of Workers in Public Education convened in Moscow, the principal result of which was to publicize the existence of a general crisis in education and of low morale among classroom teachers. Throughout these developments, newspapers continued daily to expose the wisdom of textbooks as falsehood. Traditional instruction in history became impossible, and the Ministry of Education canceled the secondary-school final examinations scheduled for June 1988 (Kerr 1990, pp. 26–31; Muckle 1990, pp. 74–76; Husband 1991b, pp. 9–10). As one critic noted at the time, existing secondary-school history had failed in any higher purpose because it concentrated on the transfer of information rather than on the teaching of historical thinking. Ironically, such a concentration on program over approach faltered to the extent that most secondary-school graduates entered the universities not only unfamiliar with the rudiments of critical analysis, but also with basic facts about the past (Lerner 1987, pp. 120–23).

The cumulative effect, however, fell far short of a rapid and decisive victory for educational reformers. An energetic mandate from the usually cautious Politburo member Egor Ligachev in January 1988, to revitalize the social sciences, certainly did not decide the issue ("Priblizhat' " 1988, pp. 1–2). Nor did a consensus take shape when Ligachev expanded his views at the February 1988 Plenum of the Central Committee. On that occasion, he left no possibility for misunderstanding when he denounced as insufficient the pre-1985 school reforms that nonreformist educators were now using as a rationale to slow the pace of change, and he called for alterations in content as well as methods in all academic and technical education. While he did not endorse those who would demolish the educational system as it then existed, he saw the need for new approaches as so pressing that he could not support those who called only for gradualism (*Materialy* 1988, pp. 10–14). Ligachev's initiatives produced little demonstrable effect: as in society at large (Davies 1989, pp. 141–46), those who favored the retention of existing orthodoxies in the school effectively defended their positions. Consequently, Western observers in Soviet secondary schools at this time reported that marked changes were in progress, but saw little evidence of the coordination of efforts even on the local level (Muckle 1990, pp. 96–102; Shukman 1990, p. 15). The opening of school in autumn 1988 allowed teachers so inclined to employ diverse approaches and materials in teaching history. Revisionism, however, did not sweep away formerly sacrosanct versions. Indeed, the best anecdotal evidence indicates that, when testing resumed in 1989, correct answers most often reflected the "old" history.

Thus, although the climate for the discussion of broad issues in society at large became more permissive, historical scholars and educators moved slowly when they approached specifics. For example, the recently energized *Voprosy istorii KPSS* featured an extended debate on historical periodization that began in the second half of 1987 with an exchange of articles and letters, and other journals featured the topic prominently as well. Since Stalinist falsification distorted the periodization of Party history in a way that enhanced Stalin's role (for example, by citing the year he entered the Central Committee as the definitive beginning of the Party), the topic was by no means neutral. But on the other hand, these criticisms presented the Stalinist version chiefly as a deviation from a Leninist framework, an approach that simply favored another teleology. An even greater focus in journals was discussion of the health of the profession itself, which in general provided strident criticism of the lack of professional vitality but said little about concrete new approaches (Riabov 1987, p. 4; Tikhvinskii 1987, p. 4; Emchenko 1987, pp. 97–100). Professional conferences at this time, regardless of their ostensible purpose, uniformly fell into discussions of the state of the profession. As one representative gathering at the Central Committee's Institute of Marxism–Leninism demonstrated, these produced a facile consensus against "dogmatism" and "bureaucratism" but no agreement on blame, correctives, or even whether too much emphasis was perhaps being placed on topics such as Stalinism, to the neglect of other important subjects (Khmara and Davydov 1988, pp. 128–34). Indeed, when extensive changes in the editorial board of the prestigious *Voprosy istorii* (Questions of History) occurred at the beginning of 1988, the new chief editor (A.A. Iskenderov) pointedly noted the need to move beyond conversation to actual work (Iskenderov 1988, p. 4).

Several central issues made progress in the teaching of history difficult. First, with educational reform now proceeding with the imprimatur of the Party, opposition to change began to follow more circuitous paths, at least in print. Calls for a less structured program of training teachers in order to prepare them for the greater independence now extant in the classrooms, for example, were buried in a plethora of clichés (Furaev et al. 1988, pp. 170–76). At the same time, an apparent endorsement for revising the history curriculum praised more of the "old" history than it criticized, and repeatedly shifted the focus away from central issues of content to tangential ones (Koloskov 1988, pp. 8–14). Second, the initiatives among classroom teachers aimed at setting up national organizations were accompanied by overtures for greater direct control at the classroom level. Frustrated at having been included as targets of criticism for teaching the "old" interpretation, history teachers were determined not to repeat the experience. They even rejected a more truthful version of history dictated from above in favor of greater control in shaping their own lesson content (Husband 1991a, pp. 471–76).

But the third factor, the production of reliable new histories, proved to be the one that most complicated the relationship between scholarship and secondary education. On the one hand, teachers before 1985 had had little reliable information at their disposal. Aside from the current edition of a uniform national textbook on the Soviet period, distributed in press runs of four million, teachers lacked materials. In remote localities, they complained that even prominent Party publications such as *Kommunist* did not arrive regularly, while scholarly works and professional journals were almost never seen. Therefore, a significant number expressed concern that, despite their desire to present history truthfully, they did not know what to say in class under the conditions of greater freedom. Others added that the poor quality of the existing textbooks favored the teachers who strove to retain dogmatism in the classroom (Pronina 1988, p. 181).

Obviously, this could not be resolved until new texts, collateral materials, and curricula were produced. The process of creating these resources began with the cancellation of the 1988 examinations and continues to the present day, but material shortages, the reluctance of historians to work on textbooks in the current climate of contention, and the general uncertainty about the future of public education in Russia undermine it. Ironically, however, one Moscow teacher—undoubtedly representative of many—

identified yet another facet of the problem when she complained that perestroika had also unleashed a "huge torrent of information on teachers and students . . . [that] is in no way systematized and does not correspond to textbook materials and books on methods" (Voshchinnikova 1988, p. 184). Thus, there may be a paucity of materials, but there is no shortage of new historical developments to digest. The principal corrective to this absence of classroom materials amidst a flood of new historical disclosures was for professional historians and journals to provide greater assistance to secondary-school teachers. As a first step, *Voprosy istorii* added a special section, "In Aid of the Teacher of History," to its pages in late 1988 ("Tochnee informirovat' " 1988, pp. 183–84; Pronina 1988, pp. 179–81).

As the events of 1985–88 demonstrate, the relationship between scholars and secondary-school educators was strained but unbreakable. Indicative of this was a letter from a teacher in Novosibirsk who chided scholars that journalistic publications such as *Ogonek* (Light) rather than the professional journals *Novaia i noveishaia istoriia* (New and Contemporary History) and *Voprosy istorii* had led the way in the discussion of controversial topics such as Stalinism (Kuz'min 1988, p. 189). A comment by the late V.Z. Drobizhev[2] at a discussion on history organized by *Kommunist* may have best summarized the key difference between research scholars and classroom operatives: "While staff members of an institute in the Academy can put the question . . . on the back burner, we as teachers can't do this: we have to prepare in the next year for a new teaching program" ("Osnovnye etapy" 1987, p. 73).

The Beginning of History

As we have seen, from 1989 to the present, the study of history in Russia has been characterized more by an inundation of information than by the emergence of any identifiable sense of direction. Expectations of timely solutions to the issues raised in 1985–88, including those affecting the content of the history curriculum, have not been met. Instead, opportunities for open discussion have produced more complaints and suggestions than concrete proposals. This should be expected, however, in view of the rigidity of the former Soviet system. If anything, the current fragmentation of opinion should be most reasonably viewed as an inevitable stage in the process of redressing the Soviet past, especially since Russia lacks any long-term experience in participatory politics. Complicating the already delicate chemistry of this matter is the fact that the deteriorating national economy now significantly overshadows the reform of education as a major issue. Therefore, whereas the 1985–88 phase of reconciling society's collective memory with history education focused on addressing specific falsifications, the subsequent period witnessed the emergence of multiple agendas, some of which concentrate on but a single issue or sectarian concern. Among these are changes in national educational strategies and their relation to secondary-school teachers' activities; the continued rewriting of Russian history in the press and its effect on scholarship and secondary-school history education; and the connection of these developments to a social and ideological conflict that is the beginning of history in post-Soviet Russia.

At the national level, reformism left no area of academics unaffected. A signal of change came in November 1988, when a change in methods of funding research projects accompanied news of important changes in personnel in the presidium of the prestigious Soviet Academy of Sciences. Subsequently, unprecedented public discussions of scholarly institutions and higher education become common, including pleas from academic officials for increased funding of universities and research institutes; proposals to end centralized academic control and to increase institutional autonomy; fears of stagnation in research programs; attempts to alter university admissions procedures and to introduce tuition; public declarations of disaffection among university students and professors; and even pointed observations of the absence of university students from visible participation in the opposition to the August 1991 putsch.[3]

Parallel but not directly linked to these developments in higher education was the continuation of teachers' attempts to expand their own power within secondary education, with mixed results. In this respect, the December 1988 Congress of Workers in Public Education was a watershed. Teachers—typified at the time, for example, by the faculty of Moscow School No. 848—were unified in their belief that the overcrowding and underfunding of schools impeded effective instruction, as well as in their conviction that transferring more rights to the individual school was the best antidote (Izmailov 1989, pp. 39–42). This rough consensus, however, did not translate into the implementation of well-coordinated correctives. It is true that in June 1990 Eduard D. Dneprov, head of the Provisional Research Collective-School (reorganized as the Center for Pedagogical Innovation [*Tsentr pedagogicheskikh innovatsii*]), became RSFSR Minister of Education, a position he used to advocate, among other changes, revising the system of teacher training. But other developments were less promising. It would be difficult to find a greater disappointment than the much anticipated Second Congress of the Creative Union of Teachers, held in Odessa in October 1991. Instead of forging an expected consensus and organizational base, the congress was plagued by contention and confusion. A large number of participants considered the gathering a failure ("Igra" 1991, p. 3; "Razvod" 1991, p. 4), and the Creative Union subsequently lost momentum.

The vicissitudes of the post-1988 period are illustrated by the fate of *Uchitel'skaia gazeta*. Following months of rumors that the paper would be closed, the assertive Matveev was replaced as editor at the beginning of 1989, and shortly thereafter the Party made *Uchitel'skaia gazeta* an organ of the Central Committee. Publication was reduced from three issues per week to one, and the press run fell from 1.7 million copies to 520,000.[4] In the process, the paper's editorial personality changed. Although *Uchitel'skaia gazeta* still incorporated articles and letters on reform and restructuring, the sense of confident urgency that was the hallmark under Matveev was gone, as if reformist platitudes had replaced pre-glasnost formulas. Early in 1991, Petr Polovzhevets became chief editor and tried to revive what he called "the Matveev spirit," but this did not succeed completely. From early 1990 to the time of the August 1991 putsch, the paper greatly expanded its human interest dimension at the expense of concrete discussion.

As a result of the events of August 1991, *Uchitel'skaia gazeta* changed again. The editorial board took pride in the fact that the putsch committee had included *Uchitel'skaia gazeta* among the newspapers ordered to cease publication. Two days after the collapse of the putsch, therefore, the board repudiated its Party affiliation and registered as an independent publication; the Party organization at the paper voted to dissolve itself the same day. These developments resulted in the paper returning to its role as a forum for all views, but it did not foster a sustained focus on specific issues. On the contrary, it became characterized by its publication of frank but seemingly disconnected articles that appeared to represent sectarian interests, without considering coordination beyond the level of superficial discussion. In reality, part of this generalized format may have been rooted in the financial troubles common to all Russian publications; by the end of 1991, *Uchitel'skaia gazeta* went so far as to place its subscription appeals on the front page. In 1992, the paper continued to provide a forum for diverse topics, including new topics that ranged from religion (Gunding 1992, p. 14; "Nuzhen li shkol'nikam" 1992, p. 3) to whether a teacher-of-the-year competition was actually necessary ("Nuzhen li konkurs" 1992, p. 2).

During this period, the topic of reinvigorating instruction in history all but disappeared. With few exceptions (Myskin 1991, p. 4), the small number of articles on curriculum change fell into the sphere of generality rather than generalization (Bibler 1992, p. 4). Typical of the post–putsch coverage in *Uchitel'skaia gazeta* was an interview with N. Ermoliaeva, deputy head of the Administration of General Secondary Education of the State Committee for Public Education. Ermoliaeva only repeated what was already known: that prominent historians were declining to participate in textbook preparation; that alternative texts were still in various stages of preparation; and that the wisdom of adherence to a single text was under fire. A more recent article from D. Zuev, director of the main publishing house for academic texts, concentrated extensively on the financial problems of producing new textbooks and neglected any serious discussion of substantive reinterpretation (Zuev 1992, p. 5).

To a great extent, this fragmentation of focus in *Uchitel'skaia gazeta* only reflected what was occurring in the national press and in scholarship. By 1989, historical revelations lost much of their potential to shock. Examples of history that would have caused a sensation only a short time earlier now appeared across the spectrum of periodical publications. Although these were diverse and virtually no proscribed topics remained, there seemed to be an infatuation with the history of religion and the prerevolutionary past and with demonstrating the legal and moral bankruptcy of the Communist Party and Soviet state. Hence, the discussion of history had moved beyond the simple disclosure of suppressed information, although frequently in the direction of selective use of historical evidence and in support of a specific political or social agenda.

The new development was that diversity in scholarship began to replicate the diversity in the broader public discussions. Although professional publications had lagged behind lay history before 1988, they began to compensate thereafter. By 1989, virtually any issue of a major historical journal contained material that would have been controversial and noteworthy a year earlier. Examples could be produced endlessly, but worthy of mention are the definitive reemergence of Leon Trotsky as a topic of public discussion and articles on subjects such as the origins of Christianity in Russia (Nikon 1990, pp. 36–53) and Stalin's intimidating 1931 letter to the journal *Proletarskaia revoliutsiia* (Proletarian Revolution) (Babichenko 1990, pp. 94–108). Scholarly meetings also addressed the shortcomings criticized by earlier repudiations of the "old" history. Round tables examined topics such as the newly significant link between history and journalism ("Otechestvennaia istoriia" 1990, pp. 176–90), the possibilities for reforming the social sciences (Kushinov 1990, pp. 134–37), and whether religion should be taught in the schools ("Kruglyi stol" 1990a, pp. 9–21; 1990b, pp. 8–14). New methodologies also began to receive special attention. For example, a conference of young historians interested in oral history was held (Kondrashin 1990, pp. 220–22), and journals began to devote specific attention to methodology in their reviews of works of Western social history, that is, those concentrating on the so-called human factor.[5]

The short-term effect on history education was nevertheless indirect. One preliminary step came from the Institute of History of the Academy of Sciences, where a group of historians generally identified with the revisionist camp co-authored a new "scholarly popular" history to fill in the "blank spaces" of post-1917 history. Beginning with its first issue for 1990, *Istoriia SSSR* (History of the USSR) published in serial form condensed versions of chapters of this work in a special section entitled "For Lecturers and Students" (*V pomoshch' prepodavateliam i studentam*). *Voporosy istorii KPSS* regularly included a similar section entitled "Toward the Restructuring of Instruction in the Social Sciences" (*K perestroike prepodavaniiam obshchvestvennykh nauk*). And when the new journal of political history *Kentavr* (Centaur) debuted in the last quarter of 1991, it too devoted space to questions of teaching. These publications could offer only partial solutions, however, since the principal intended audience of the journal sections was higher and not secondary education, although secondary-school teachers, obviously, could also benefit.

Secondary-school history education nevertheless continued to stumble. One conference for teachers cosponsored by *Voprosy istorii KPSS* addressed a number of the principal complaints of the time. Above all was the question of the reliability of information under the new conditions of pluralism. As the conference observer noted, secondary-school teachers were being bombarded with too much dubious data from television, radio, books, and periodicals. A significant part of such history, he added, was now slanted toward particular interests, and a new but equally reprehensible subjectivism was replacing the schematicism of the Stalinist *Short Course*. In addition, in spite of attempts by scholars to publish interim materials to fill the gaps (especially in social history), professional journals simply could not satisfy all the teachers' needs (Egor'ev 1991, p. 159). In practical terms, the publication of a series of unsatisfactory secondary-school history textbooks failed to resolve the situation (Husband 1991a, pp. 476–79), and participants at conferences and individual contributors to journals repeatedly displayed a greater propensity to identify problems than to reach compromises on them ("Zasedanie sektsii" 1989, pp. 3–66; "Kontseptsiia" 1989, pp. 76–90; Aleksashkina 1991, pp. 121–33). As one observer noted, the initial euphoria of perestroika had been followed by a pluralism that turned into sharp ideological contention (Sokolov 1991, pp. 250–52). Since 1988, the process of recasting the version of the past that society presents to secondary-school students has become inextricably entwined with broader social and ideological conflicts. This is the beginning of history in post-Soviet Russia.

In Place of a Conclusion

This chapter offers no specific predictions. The link between history education and historiography, which is frequently strained even in countries with long traditions of participatory politics and democratic discussion, faces special obstacles in post-Soviet Russia. Buffeted among a legacy of falsification, the growing pains of intellectual pluralism, and a national economic and social crisis that diverts energy and resources from educational reform, history education and historiography currently pursue different objectives more often than they coincide. The influence that professional historians formerly exercised over the representation of the nation's past to young people was too deeply rooted in the hegemony of falsification to have survived the developments of recent years. In addition, secondary-school teachers' vigorous demands for greater control of their own sphere make the imposition of any single new truth unlikely. Finally, attempts to produce textbooks and teaching materials privately, and to establish alternative schools, guarantee for the present the continuation of a pluralistic dimension in Russian secondary education.

Yet despite the forces pulling secondary-school history education and professional historiography away from one another, the two spheres are also connected in new and important ways. As teachers themselves recognized early in the reform process, professional historians are still the chief available resource for filling in "blank spaces," and as the final section of this chapter has shown, scholars have been responding seriously (if sometimes indirectly) to the needs of secondary education since the beginning of 1989. Moreover, secondary-school teachers and professional historians share important mutual concerns. Neither group has displayed any intention to accept a permanently reduced professional role, and both show an interest in integrating into their work a stronger element of the nation's social history—the so-called human factor. In this process, both are in the early stages of working out methodologies that are more rigorous, permanent, and ordered than is the format of journalistic disclosure. In the end, perfect coordination between these spheres is neither probable nor, one might argue, desirable; it is certainly a rarity outside of Russia. But contemporary evidence suggests that the current disarray in the content of secondary-school history education in post-Soviet Russia will not be resolved before historiography works through its current fragmentation to a new sense of professional direction.

Notes

1. Afanas′ev's setback was temporary, and he has once again become an important actor in both the academic and social spheres. In December 1986, he was appointed rector of the Moscow State Institute of Historian-Archivists and, in the following months, wrote frequent denunciations of historical falsifications in the mass press. In 1988, his election to the Congress of People's Deputies launched a political career as an intractable democrat that continues to the present. He currently heads the Russian State Humanities University.

2. Drobizhev at the time chaired the Department of the History of the USSR in the Soviet Period at the Moscow State Institute of Historian-Archivists. A central figure in the development of Soviet historiography since the early 1960s, he previously taught at Moscow State University, as distinct from working in a research institute. Consequently, he was clearly a member of the scholarly community, but—as his reputation as a popular classroom teacher attests—he had grounds for greater empathy with secondary-school teachers than Institute members with no teaching responsibilities. The less pressured tone of professional debates to which Drobizhev refers is evident in the key articles reprinted in translation in "*Glasnost′* and Soviet Historians" (1988). *Soviet Studies in History*, vol. 27, no. 1.

3. While a full discussion lies outside the scope of this essay, Susannah Massey and Alexander Tomasz Massey provide useful coverage in *The Chronicle of Higher Education*. Relevant references for 1990 include: 23 May, p. A36; 25 July, pp. A31–32; 19 September, pp. A45–46; 24 October, pp. A35–36. For 1991 see: 13 March, pp. A1, A38; 17 April, pp. A41–42; 15 May, pp. A35–36; 22 May, pp. A33–34; 29 May, pp. A33–34; 12 June, pp. A31–32; 17 July, pp. A29–30; 24 July, p. A29; 14 August, pp. A1, A30; 4 September, pp. A1, A54–57; 11 September, pp. A43–44.

4. The new conditions of publication seriously hampered the Creative Union of Teachers because, lacking its own resources, it relied on *Uchitel′skaia gazeta* as its principal conduit of information, especially with outlying regions. Also, since the Union's central council saw the influence of what the paper now calls "well-known Central Committee muzzles" in the dismissal of Matveev (who died in 1989), the Union decided to boycott the paper. Only when Polovzhevets became chief editor was there a reconciliation, and on 19 August 1991 (following the putsch committee's announcement of a six-month ban on public meetings) Polovzhevets joined the Union's central council in defying the ban.

5. For examples, see the review of: D. Ransel,"Mothers of Misery," *Voprosy istorii*, no. 9 (1990), pp. 178–80; H. Kuromiya, "Stalin's Industrial Revolution," *Istoriia SSSR*, no. 5 (1991), pp. 207–10; D. Koenker and W. Rosenberg, "Strikes and Revolution in Russia, 1917," *Voprosy istorii*, no.11 (1991), pp. 222–24.

References

Afanas'ev, Iu. (1985). "Proshloe i my." *Kommunist*, no. 14. pp. 105–16.

Aleksashkina, L.N. (1991). "K kontseptsii shkol'nogo kursa noveishei istorii." *Prepodavanie istorii v shkole*, no. 1, pp. 121–33.

Babichenko, L.G. (1990). "Pis'mo Stalina v 'proletarskuiu revoliutsiiu' i ego posledstviia." *Voprosy istorii KPSS*, no. 6, pp. 94–108.

Bibler, V. (1992). "Shkola dialoga kul'tur." *Uchitel'skaia gazeta*, 7 January, p. 4.

Burdzhalov, E.N. (1987). *Russia's Second Revolution: The February 1917 Uprising in Petrograd*. Trans. and ed. by D.J. Raleigh. Bloomington and Indianapolis: Indiana University Press.

Davies, R.W. (1989). *Soviet History in the Gorbachev Revolution*. Bloomington and Indianapolis: Indiana University Press.

Egor'ev, A.A. (1991). "Zhurnal i shkol'nyi uchitel'." *Voprosy istorii KPSS*, no. 1, p. 159.

Egorov, A.G. (1986). "XXVII s''ezda KPSS i voprosy Marksistko-Leninskoi metodologii." *Voprosy istorii KPSS*, no. 12, pp. 3–26.

El'baum, B.D. (1986). "Na perelomnom etape." *Voprosy istorii KPSS*, no. 8. pp. 45–51.

Emchenko, E.B. (1987). "Rasshirennyi plenum nauchnogo soveta po istoriografii i istochnikovedeniiu." *Voprosy istorii*, no. 11, pp. 97–101.

Furaev, V.K., A.A. Anikeev and A.I. Borozniak (1988). "Perestroika prepodavaniia novoi i noveishei istorii v pedagogicheskikh institutakh: Problemy i poiski." *Novaia i noveishaia istoriia*, no. 1, pp. 170–76.

Gunding, D. (1992). "Vse li religii vedut k bogu?" *Uchitel'skaia gazeta*, 21 January, p. 14.

Husband, W.B. (1991a). "Secondary School History Texts in the USSR: Revising the Soviet Past, 1985–1989." *Russian Review*, vol. 50, no. 4, pp. 458–80.

———. (1991b). "Administrative Perestroika and Rewriting History: The Dilemma of Glasnost in Soviet Education." *Journal of Educational Administration*, vol. 29, no. 4, pp.7–16.

"Igra v s''ezd, ili 'parlamentskii kretinizm' " (1991). *Uchitel'skaia gazeta*, no. 43 (22–29 October), p. 3.

Il'ina, I.N. (1987). " 'Kruglyi stol' o vospitanii molodozhei istoriei." *Voprosy istorii*, no. 9, pp. 157–58.

Iskenderov, A.A. (1988). "Perestroika i zadachi zhurnala 'Voprosy istorii.' " *Voprosy istorii*, no. 2, pp. 3–10.

Izmailov, R. (1989). "Shkola: zaboty i trevogi." *Agitator*, no. 3, pp. 39–42.

Kerr, Stephen T. (1990). "Will Glasnost Lead to Perestroika? Directions of Educational Reform in the USSR." *Educational Researcher*, October, pp. 26–31.

Khmara, N.I. and V.P. Davydov (1988). "O sushchnosti mekhanizma tormozheniia. *Voprosy istorii KPSS*, no. 1, pp. 128–34.

Klokova, G.V. and V.K. Batsyn (1986). "O novoi programme po istorii." *Prepodavanie istorii v shkole*. no. 5. pp. 19–23.

Koloskov, A.G. (1986). "XXVII s''ezd KPSS i prepodavanie istorii." *Prepodavanie istorii v shkole*, no. 5, pp. 13–19.

Koloskov, A.G. (1988). "Razvitie shkol'nogo istoricheskogo obrazovaniia v SSSR." *Prepodavanie istorii v shkole*, no. 2, pp. 8–14.

Koltsov, P.S. (1986). "Kontseptsiia uskoreniia i nekotorye problemy izucheniia istoricheskogo opyta KPSS." *Voprosy istorii KPSS*, no. 9, pp. 32–44.

Kondrashin, V.V. (1990). "Konferentsiia molodykh istorikov po problemam ustnoi istorii." *Istoriia SSSR*, no. 5, pp. 220–22.

"Kontseptsiia istoricheskogo obrazovaniia v srednei shkole" (1989). *Prepodavanie istorii v shkole*, no. 6, pp. 76–90.

"Kontseptsiia obshchego srednogo obrazovaniia kak bazovogo v edinoi sisteme nepreryvnogo obrazovaniia" (1990). *Narodnoe obrazovanie*, no. 7, pp. 16–24.

" 'Kruglyi stol' na temu: 'Nuzhno li prepodavanie istorii religii v shkole?' " (1990a). *Prepodavanie istorii v shkole*, no. 5, pp. 9–21.

———. (1990b). *Prepodavanie istorii v shkole*, no. 6, pp. 8–14.

Kukushkin, Iu. S. and A.P. Nenarokov (1986). "God 1985-i." *Prepodavanie istorii v shkole*, no. 2, pp. 10–15.

Kushinov, V.A. (1990). "Politicheskaia istoriia v Moskovskom universitete." *Voprosy istorii KPSS*, no. 9, pp. 134–37.

Kuz'min, G. (1988). "Gde vy, uchenye-istoriki?" *Voprosy istorii*, no. 10, p. 189.

Lerner, I.Ia. (1987). "Obuchenie istorii v shkole i vysshee istoricheskoe obrazovanie." *Voprosy istorii*, no. 9, pp. 120–26.

Materialy vneocherednogo plenuma tsentral'nogo komiteta KPSS: 11 Marta 1985 goda (1985a). Moscow: Politizdat.

Materialy plenuma tsentral'nogo komiteta KPSS: 15 Oktiabria 1985 goda (1985b). Moscow: Politizdat.

Materialy XXVII s''ezda kommunisticheskoi partii Sovetskogo Soiuza (1986). Moscow: Politizdat.

Materialy plenuma tsentral'nogo komiteta KPSS: 17–28 Fevralia 1988 goda (1988). Moscow: Politizdat.

Muckle, J. (1990). *Portrait of a Soviet School under Glasnost*. New York: St. Martin's Press.

Murakara, D. (1987a). "Recovering the Buried Stalin Years." *The Nation*, 24 October, pp. 447–51.

———. (1987b). "A New Revolution in Consiousness." *The Nation*, 31 October, pp. 486–90.

Myskin, V. (1991). "Laboratorno-prakticheskaia rabota na uroke istorii." *Uchitel'skaia gazeta*, 12–19 November, p. 4.

Nikon (1990). "Nachalo khristianstva v rusi." *Voprosy istorii*, no. 6, pp. 36–53.

"Novyi uchebnik po istorii SSSR dlia IX klassa" (1986). *Prepodavanie istorii v shkole*, no. 6, pp. 41–46.

"Nuzhen li konkurs 'Uchitel' goda?' " (1992). *Uchitel'skaia gazeta*, 26 May, p. 2.

"Nuzhen li shkol'nikam zakon Bozhii?" (1992). *Uchitel'skaia gazeta*, 17 March, p. 3.

"O zhurnale 'Kommunist': Postavlenie TsK KPSS" (1986). *Kommunist*, no. 12, pp. 3–10.

"Ob izuchenii materialov XXVII s''ezda KPSS v uchebnykh predmetakh obshcheobrazovatel'noi shkoly" (1986). *Prepodavanie istorii v shkole*, no. 4, pp. 2–10.

"Osnovnye etapy razvitiia sovetskogo obshchestva. 'Kruglyi stol' zhurnala 'Kommunist' " (1987). *Kommunist*, no. 12, pp. 66–79.

"Otechestvennaia istoriia v sovremennoi publitsistike" (1990). *Istoriia SSSR*, no. 1, pp. 176–90.

"Pervye uroki i neotlozhenye zadachi perestroiki" (1986). *Voprosy istorii KPSS*, no. 10, pp. 3–19.

"Priblizhat' reformu srednei i vysshei shkoly k politike perestroiki" (1988). *Biulleten' Ministerstva vysshego i srednogo spetsial'nogo obrazovaniia SSSR*, no. 3, pp. 1–2.

Pronina, G.V. (1988). "Obsuzhdenie raboty zhurnala." *Voprosy istorii*, no. 8, pp. 179–181.

"Razvod po-sovetski" (1991). *Uchitel'skaia gazeta*, 22–29 October, p. 4.

Riabov, V.V. (1987). "Strategiia uskoreniia i voprosy perestroiki obshchestvennykh nauk." *Voprosy istorii KPSS*, no. 3, pp. 3–19.

Shukman, H. (1990). "Lenin or Alexander?" *The Times Higher Education Supplement*, 3 February, p. 15.

Sokolov, A.B. (1991). "Raskreposhchenie istorii." *Voprosy istorii*, no. 9–10, pp. 250–52.

Tikhvinskii, S.L. (1987). "Ianvarskii (1987g). Plenum TsK KPSS i istoricheskaia nauka." *Voprosy istorii*, no. 6, pp. 3–113.

"Tochnee informirovat' o noveishikh issledovaniiakh" (1988). *Voprosy istorii*, no. 5, pp. 183–84.

"Ubezhdennost'—opora perestoroiki: vstrecha v TsK KPSS" (1987). *Kommunist*, no. 4, p. 24.

Von Hagen, M. (1988). "History and Politics under Gorbachev: Professional Autonomy and Democratization." *The Harriman Institute Forum*, vol. 1, no. 11, pp. 1–8.

Voshchinnikova, N.I. (1988). "Uchitelia zhdut pomoshchi." *Voprosy istorii*, no. 5, p. 184.

Wheatcroft, S. (1987a). "Unleashing the Energy of History, Mentioning the Unmentionable and Restructuring Soviet Historical Awareness: Moscow 1987." *Australian Slavonic and East European Studies*, vol. 1, no. 1, pp. 85–132.

———. (1987b). "Steadying the Energy of History and Probing the Limits of *Glasnost'*: Moscow July to December 1987." *Australian Slavonic and East European Studies*, vol. 1, no. 2, pp. 57–114.

"Zasedanie sektsii 'prepodavanie istorii i obshchestvennykh nauk' Vsesoiuznogo s''ezda rabotnikov narodnogo obrazovaniia, 21 dekabria 1988 g. Stenograficheskii otchet" (1989). *Prepodavanie istorii v shkole*, no. 3, pp. 3–66.

Zuev, D. (1992). "Trudnaia sud'ba uchebnikov." *Uchitel'skaia gazeta*, 14 April, p. 5.

7

Reform in History and Social Studies Education in Russian Secondary Schools

JANET G. VAILLANT

History and social studies education is a delicate and controversial matter in all countries. One need go no further than the current dispute over traditional American values and multicultural education in the United States for evidence that the teaching of these subjects arouses strong emotions. All countries try to offer children a view of the national past that supports the belief that theirs is a good society and its present power structure justified and relatively fair. The history taught in schools is therefore shaped to consolidate current values and suggest directions for the future. Nowhere was this more true than in the Soviet Union.

With the advent of Gorbachev's policy of perestroika and its accompanying openness about the past, the need for a new understanding of Soviet history became pressing. Journalists took the lead in revealing the dark side of the Soviet experience, but soon most professional historians and even the political establishment agreed that a more honest version of the Soviet past would support the efforts of society to reform itself. By the end of the 1980s, the discussion had broadened to include social studies education as well. The controversies over history teaching during the 1980s have been chronicled in some detail, as have the accompanying declarations of professional educators about their goals and what needs to be done (Davies 1989; Husband 1991). Indeed, plans and model programs are relatively easy to trace in scholarly journals and the press. It is far more difficult to assess what is really happening in most schools. Because most teachers, in Russia and elsewhere, rely heavily on materials created by others, the extent to which new materials have been created and widely distributed can serve as an indirect indicator of change in the ways different subjects are presented to school children.

In the former Soviet Union, history carried a particularly heavy burden. It was expected not only to teach patriotism, but also to present an ideologically determined, monolithic view of the past. The social sciences as such were not taught at all at the secondary-school level between 1934 and 1962: there was no need to teach any but the sole approved "social science," Marxism–Leninism. This theory provided a strict notion of causality in history. The result was a treatment of the past, even by professional historians, designed to illustrate preconceived abstract ideas, bequeathed by Marx, that would support the legitimacy of the Communist Party.

The Soviet Union's professional historians faced explicit limitations on what questions could be asked and what answers could be found. Insofar as history was considered a science, there was a single truth. Once found, it was enshrined in the official school texts. Therefore, the gap between the writings of professional historians and what was taught in Soviet schools was far narrower than in most countries. Each textbook was written by a committee of professional historians, worked over by professional pedagogues, approved by the Communist Party, and finally sent off for publication and distribution. This process took up to five years. For each grade, there was a single textbook that was translated into multiple languages and used throughout the vast Union. Teachers had guides that told them what, when, and how to teach, so that on each day the same class was to be taught in the same way throughout the country.[1] Pupils were to record, memorize, and reiterate word for word what they read in their books and were told by their teachers. Exams tested their ability to reproduce what they had learned and often required that the very words of the text be repeated to oral examiners.

The Stalinist legacy in history teaching went deeper than simply requiring the learning of a set of facts and their interpretation. It included a Stalinist pedagogy that was vividly described in *Uchitel'skaia gazeta* in the summer of 1988. This pedagogy was designed to teach pupils that the individual counted for little except insofar as he belonged to a vast powerful state. A huge hierarchical educational bureaucracy was created as part of the command-administrative system to train teachers to carry out orders. It told teachers exactly what and how to teach and punished those who deviated from the prescribed program. Teachers in turn exercised absolute authority over their pupils. They became little Stalins in the classroom, threatening pupils who made "mistakes," that is, failed to remember and repeat exactly what the teacher had told them. The teacher's job was to train children to be passive and follow orders. Thus, a culture of the school was created to mirror and reinforce that of the society at large. Official murderings stopped when Stalin died, but the mentality created by fear and this social training remained within the population at large. Teachers were no exception. They continued to depend on their authoritarian habits of instruction and to discourage students from asking questions (Radzikhovskii 1988a).

The pedagogy of Brezhnev's time was somewhat different. In Stalin's time, many teachers had truly believed what they taught but, by Brezhnev's time, many realized that the system was suspect. The Brezhnevite pedagogy was, as Radzikhovskii wrote, like a "spiritual AIDS," breeding cynicism in young people. Teachers continued to teach a history that scholars knew to be false, to expatiate upon Marxism–Leninism, an ideology in which many did not believe, and to prepare pupils for exams on which they would be rewarded for not telling the truth. The school became a place lacking connection with what pupils knew from their own experience. Pupils learned to be cynical as well as passive, and to hold their elders in contempt for repeating lies (Radzikhovskii 1988b).

It is precisely these characteristics of Soviet education that many educational reformers would like to change. The challenges that have faced history and social studies teachers and those responsible for writing new teaching materials reflect in microcosm those facing the country at large. The first step toward reform was to stop the lying and to produce a new, more factually correct version of the country's past. The next step was to deal with the legacy of an extremely centralized hierarchical and authoritarian style of administration, as well as with the internalized attitudes and habits of behavior that it had created in teachers, textbook writers, and school organizations.

By the end of the 1980s, leading politicians, scholars, and the central educational establishment—including the State Committee on Public Education, the Academy of Pedagogical Sciences, and the Russian Ministry of Education—had developed what might be called a negative consensus about the state of history and social studies teaching. In 1988, a high-level commission presided over by Gennadii A. Yagodin, then chairman of the State Committee on Public Education of the USSR, proposed that the entire system of history and social science education be examined (Prokhorov 1989, p. 6). Professional educators jumped forward to condemn what existed and presented a long list of "oughts," or plans for the future (Zubkov 1989, pp. 180-85; Husband 1991, pp. 466-71). Existing textbooks were criticized for containing half-truths and omitting unpleasant facts about the past, notably about Stalin and his crimes. All were to be rewritten; the need for new textbooks on the Soviet period was a top priority ("Obsuzhdenie" 1990, pp. 188-91). Gradually, the criticism broadened to suggest that textbooks were excessively abstract and schematic, that they needed to include more information about religion, cultural life, and the role of the individual, and teach students about the role of choice in history. By implication, the narrowly Marxist interpretation of history, not only false facts, were to be corrected. Some pedagogical experts began to argue that the support of perestroika also required new methods of teaching. They demanded materials that would encourage pupils to be more active and independent, that would allow them to work with primary sources, and that would require them to discuss and defend their points of view in class, thereby strengthening their abilities to think for themselves. The new textbooks should present, for example, multiple points of view so that pupils could develop a capacity for critical thinking (Aleksashkina 1988; Klukova 1989, pp. 52-56). There should also be several books that covered the material at each grade level so that teachers could choose the book they wanted to use.[2] The challenge was daunting: to create new textbooks that had new content and would also break the hold of Stalinist and Brezhnevite pedagogy in the classroom. School materials would have to help old teachers work in new ways.

By the end of the decade, many educators were planning sweeping reforms. They believed, as had Soviet educators in the 1920s, that children could and should be shaped by their schooling in definite ways. While the historians worried about the content of the new history books, others began to speak of the need to teach values that transcended Marxism. They wanted to contribute to the reform and renewal of their society by teaching what they called humanitarian or universal values. Whereas in the past, Stalinist and Brezhnevite pedagogy had created schools that were congruent with the larger society, now reformers wanted to create a new climate in the schools that would be congruent with their vision of the society of the future. They wanted "to teach humanitarian and democratic values" and help form the new socially active person "with a feeling of responsibility for the fate of the fatherland and the world" (Klukova 1989, p. 52). The traditional Soviet and Russian notion that education has a dual function—*izuchenie* (the training of the mind), and *vospitanie* (upbringing)—remained. History teachers were, in short, urged to serve the more general goals of perestroika.

While these general discussions were taking place among educational bureaucrats, pedagogues, and politicians, and the journals and newspapers were full of "new facts," the history teachers in the classroom were left pretty much to their own devices. The names of the organizations responsible for providing new textbooks had changed, institutes had been reorganized, textbook writers' contracts and deadlines had come and gone, but there were still no new texts available for teachers to use in their classrooms. There were no photocopy machines or paper upon which to copy the new essays and historical documents appearing in the journals, and there were few opportunities to discuss with colleagues or anyone else how to achieve these ambitious new goals being thrust upon them. For the 1990–91 school year, the only textbooks on the shelves of most schools were those that had remained essentially unchanged since the Brezhnev era; these in turn had been written by collectives of authors that had been put in place in the late 1950s and had shaped their unchanging outlines in the early 1960s (Dneprov et al. 1991, p. 37; Vaillant 1992; Nikiforova 1990, p. 2). Teachers could choose to use them or not, but had nothing to take their place. Some read aloud from press articles; others told the story of history as they understood it themselves; and a few found old prerevolutionary history textbooks and used them (although as one such teacher sheepishly admitted, "We know a lot more about Mesopotamia today than we did in 1906").[3] One journal for teachers obligingly published excerpts from a prerevolutionary textbook. ("Iz uchebnika" 1991, pp. 70–94) Many teachers simply used the traditional textbooks as if nothing had changed, textbooks that reminded pupils that the collapse of capitalism was imminent and that the Soviet Union was well on the path to building communism (Smirnitskii 1991, pp. 4–5).

The consensus about what needed to be done proved fragile, however, when it came to writing the actual textbooks. Those responsible for producing them understandably hesitated to do so when each day brought new revelations about the past. The situation was summed up accurately in the common joke that the past was changing faster than the present. It was clear that the flood of new information appearing in the press, coupled with press delays, would make any history textbook outdated before it could appear. New problems kept arising that had to be resolved. For example, the textbooks for the history of the Soviet Union had focused almost entirely on Russian history. In keeping with the general policy of decentralization of educational decision making, some began to argue that Soviet history should be integrated into world history, and each republic left to teach its own history as it chose. ("Kruglyi stol" 1990, pp. 7-30) After the collapse of the Soviet Union in 1991, this debate was replaced by concern over presenting the national histories of the peoples of the RSFSR. Add to this ongoing debates about basic historiographical problems, a dearth of author-historians able to present history in fresh and interesting ways, a desperate paper shortage, and continued confusion not only about the content of individual courses but also about which courses should be taught (and even the number of obligatory years of secondary education), and it would be a rare and adventurous person who would volunteer the time and energy necessary to develop these new materials (Ermolaeva 1991, p. 3; Smirnov and Bobkov 1991, p. 5). Books commissioned with 1989 deadlines were still unavailable in 1992 (Viazemskii 1992). The need for new textbooks for the traditional history courses, especially for the final two years of secondary school when pupils studied the Soviet period, was urgent. Not until 1990 did this need begin to be met.

By the fall of 1992, there were several types of new materials available to teachers of history: slightly modified versions of the textbooks for traditional history courses, a generation of so-called transitional texts published in large editions by the state textbook publisher, Prosveshchenie; new materials published by groups such as educational institutes which had broken Prosveshchenie's monopoly on textbook publishing; and articles in periodicals such as *Uchitel'skaia gazeta* and *Prepodavanie istorii v shkole* targeted specifically for secondary-school history teachers. New facts and interpretations published in several books of essays and a wide variety of professional and general periodicals were also available to teachers.

New Textbooks on Russian/Soviet History

The first new history textbook on the Soviet period went to press at Prosveshchenie in December 1988 in an edition of 3,306,000. It was a free-standing booklet by Iu.S. Borisov that covered the period from 1921 to 1941 and contained a note to the effect that it should be used in place of chapters 12 and 13 in the regular textbook by Iu.I. Korablev et al. that covered the period from the turn of the century to 1941 and had been published earlier that year (Borisov 1989). Three months later, the next printing of the Korablev text, 3,110,000 copies, included these sections as well as new sections on culture and religion in the 1920s and on the struggle for power within the Party in the 1920s that included a discussion of Trotsky's role (Korablev et al. 1989, pp. 280-91). The rest of the text was basically unchanged ("Obsuzhdenie" 1990, pp. 188–91).

Borisov's new version of the prewar period included a lengthened, admiring section on the era of the New Economic Policy (NEP) subtitled "The Development of the Soviet Economy and Democracy (1921-27)." It also provided a general criticism of Stalin, explaining that thousands of people were arrested at the time of collectivization, that a command-administrative system was introduced which deformed the revolution and transformed people into mere cogs in a vast machine of state. As an explanation for Stalin's rise to power, Borisov wrote that structural causes and a lack of experience with democracy in Russia created a situation such that, in the struggle between the old forms of government and the new ones which had come into being with the October Revolution and NEP, the old proved victorious. His language was quite traditional and formulaic; for example, "the dissonance between the objective demands of socialist construction and the capabilities of the political leadership to satisfy them competently . . ." (Korablev et al. 1989, pp. 328–29). Borisov's Lenin was still a hero who had foreseen the possibility of such a development but had been powerless to stop it. References to authoritative statements by Marx and Lenin continued to be numerous. Revised and unrevised sections of the text contradicted themselves, if not directly then by implication. In general, Borisov chose a careful path in his revisions, recalling that the 1920s and 1930s were a time of real enthusiasm for the building of socialism but also, for the first time in a school book, providing names and dates for the Stalinist repressions of leading figures, and some detail about hitherto taboo subjects such as the Molotov–Ribbentrop Pact (Ibid., p. 345).

In its conclusion, the Korablev text emphasized that the heroic labor of the workers under the leadership of the Party accomplished great changes in all spheres of social life, but that all of them carried the mark of deformation. Social democracy and glasnost (the words used in the text to characterize the 1920s) were destroyed and social legality broken. In answer to the question of how these contradictions had developed, the authors conclude in their final sentences that the choice for socialism in 1917 was a firm choice, and that the turn to NEP showed how flexible and effective the policies of the builders of socialism might be when they studied the interests of the widest masses of the people. Clearly, the new sections, written at the end of 1988 and the beginning of 1989, represented a step forward in trying to explain some of the complications of Soviet history more clearly and truthfully. At the same time, it was a history textbook written with current political needs in mind. However, its overall approach, its general conception, and its stale, abstract language remained unchanged (Korablev et al 1986; 1989). It was by its own account a transitional text. The new generation of history books were yet to be written, and a nationwide competition was announced at the end of 1988 for authors to create them.

A comparison of two texts published in 1989 is instructive regarding the dilemma then facing history teachers. A text on modern history, authored by a collective led by V.K. Furaev, *Noveishaia istoriia (1939–1988)*, was published by Prosveshchenie in an edition of 2,834,000 copies, the same year that saw the appearance of Korablev's revised text. The Korablev text provides some detail on the provisions of the Molotov—Ribbentrop Pact, including a comment that the agreement to divide Poland "contradicted the norms of international law" (Korablev et al. 1989, p. 345). Furaev's text explains that "reactionary capitalist circles" hoped that Hitler would attack the Soviet Union, thus destroying Communism and weakening Germany. The Soviet Union then had no choice but to sign a nonaggression and neutrality pact with Germany in order to preserve its independence (Furaev et al. 1989, pp. 7–9). Although both books were "new," (and the only ones on their respective subjects available), the Furaev text not only depended on Marxist categories of analysis, as the Korablev text continued to do, but also used the old accusatory language. Where the two overlapped, they contradicted each other. It is interesting to note that Furaev, the leader of the collective that has been responsible for the modern world history course for decades, was also responsible for the new textbook for this course announced by Prosveshchenie in 1992 (Viazemskii 1992, p. 205).

A second large-edition (1,246,000 copies) textbook on this period for grade 10, also dubbed a transitional text, appeared in time for the 1992–93 school year. Its authors, L.H. Zharova and I.A. Mishina, were researchers at the Pedagogical Institute in Kherson, not from leading Moscow or Petersburg institutes. The book covered the same period and virtually the same topics in the same order as the earlier textbook on the history of the USSR for grade 10. Now it was no longer a history of the USSR, however, but a history of "the Fatherland" (Zharova and Mishina 1992). The Soviet Union, of course, was no more, and yet the authors dared not call their book a history of Russia. The new textbook left open the question as to whose fatherland it described, that of Russians everywhere, that of all the peoples of the RSFSR, or that of some other group.

In their introduction, the authors spell out their general view of history in a somewhat confused and confusing way. They announce that they recognize the laws (*pravo*) of the class approach to human existence, but

they want to give priority to general human values as they analyze historical events. They state that they want to show pupils that there were mo-
ments of historical choice. They also state that they want to place special
emphasis on the path of Russian development in its relationship to the
paths of Asian and European development. In describing their pedagogical
approach, Zharova and Mishina promise to present the points of view of
different personages at turning points in history and urge pupils to try to
understand these difficult points of view. Pupils are also urged to be
active in discussions and not to fear "wrong answers" nor to assume
there is one right answer. What is important is to reflect on historical
problems (Ibid., p. 5).

To some extent, these goals are reflected in their text. In their discussion of the end of NEP, for example, the authors point out that there were
alternative choices open to the Party leaders, but then hasten to add that
the alternatives not chosen were unacceptable: The continuation of NEP
would have led to unemployment, the growth of poverty, the development
of capitalist elements, and the sharpening of class contradictions; people
would have said, "What did we fight for?" Had the Party decided to
adhere to true socialist methods at this time, it might have taken decades
for industrialization to occur. The creation of the command-administrative
system was the lesser evil (Ibid., pp. 270–80). Here Zharova and Mishina
are teaching a lesson for the 1990s, but their lesson about the turn away
from NEP differs from the lesson suggested by Borisov in his discussion
of the same period, evidence once again of the tendency to interpret history in terms of the author's view of present needs. Zharova and Mishina
introduce the term "totalitarianism" in the discussion of the cult of personality (Ibid., p. 295). Explanations for this phenomenon include sociological and cultural (as well as political and historical) factors, such as the
habits developed during the early period of Bolshevik power and the Civil
War. In a question on this subject, students are asked, "What features of
the Asian means of production appeared in all spheres of Soviet society in
the 1930s?" Stalin is blamed for crimes not identified in earlier texts, such
as originating the problems among the nationalities by such policies as the
collectivization of the Chechen (Ibid., p. 298). The authors conclude with
a lesson: Command-administrative methods led to totalitarianism which
was built on the "marginalized strata of society" and made possible by
"the low level of education and culture." The 1930s are described as a
contradictory time, one of mass enthusiasm among the Soviet people and
a no less massive repression. In both the internal and external arena, they
conclude, Soviet policies often "boomeranged" (Ibid., p. 333).

What distinguishes this textbook from the work of Borisov and Korablev on the Soviet period is less the historical "facts" it presents (although by 1992 it was possible to include information still taboo in 1989) than the authors' move away from the seamless presentation of an inevitable march of history in keeping with Marxist dogma. The book states that there were alternatives during the Soviet period, even if the text then presents and justifies the choices made as "forced." In general, the writing is more direct, with less of the old Marxist jargon. Excerpts from primary sources are provided, including Trotsky's warning that "the Party organization replaces the Party, the Central Committee replaces the Party and finally the dictator replaces the Central Committee with himself" (Ibid., p. 292). Questions to pupils no longer stress factual knowledge alone, but ask "why" as well as "what," and ask for personal views. In short, this textbook tries (not altogether successfully) to move beyond simply presenting more accurate facts to breaking away from a traditionally Marxist scheme and interpretation. It also takes steps to meet some of the pedagogical goals set for the new textbooks in the discussions of the late 1980s.

There has also been a new book written for grade 11, the final year of secondary school, on the period from 1941 to the present. It was published in 1990 in an edition of 2,905,000 to replace the textbook written by a group led by Iu.S. Kukushkin who, followed by the other members of his authors' collective, categorically refused to undertake the necessary revisions of his textbook. The new textbook, under the direction of V.P. Ostrovskii, follows closely the outline of the old. Facts are corrected, and new political scores are settled (for example with Brezhnev, who is here blamed for ecological problems in Kazakhstan [Ostrovskii et al. 1990, p. 24]). In the introduction, pupils are told that the authors cannot tell the whole truth because the whole truth is not yet clear. The authors also remind students that it is up to us "whether we courageously take the path to a democratized, humanized, and constructive society" (Ibid., p. 4).

Ostrovskii's text moves beyond simply correcting facts to suggest some interpretations that do not follow the Marxist scheme. It suggests that there were alternative choices (at Stalin's death, for example) and provides more complicated lessons than did earlier texts: the "good" Khrushchev triumphed over his opponents, but by calling in Zhukov and the military, he used Stalinist methods (Ibid., pp. 120–22). It includes thought-provoking questions and short excerpts from primary sources, although these are given more as illustrations than as material for students to analyze. As it approaches the present, however, the text becomes more formulaic, relying on Gorbachevian language and phrases. Pupils are told that in the period from the Nineteenth Party Conference to the meeting of the People's Deputies in early 1989, Soviet society experienced a "return to the moral sources of our national culture." The book ends dramatically, as the authors declare that the country has entered into a new stage of its history "devoted to realizing the principles called forth by October: peace to the people, land to the peasants, factories to the workers, all power to the soviets." This text succeeds in filling some "blank spots" and restoring many individuals and events to history, but it follows the traditional conception of the period with a heavy emphasis on the war years and on economic and political developments.

These official books have been supplemented by small-edition texts published by new authors. The first in a three-book series by a single historian, Igor Doliutskii, was published in 1989 under the sponsorship of the Moscow City Committee for Public Education and the Moscow Institute for the Continuing Education of Teachers, thus effectively breaking the monopoly on school-book publishing long held by Prosveshchenie (Doliutskii 1989). A comparison of its treatment of the period 1920-41 with the treatment of that period in the two more widely distributed Prosveshchenie textbooks serves to illustrate what the more conventional books were not doing, both with respect to content and their support for the new pedagogy.

Doliutskii's text is written in a direct language that provides a refreshing change from the abstract and bureaucratic language of all the large-edition textbooks. He takes up additional subjects, returning new groups of people to history. The section "How They Lived in the 1920s," for example, provides information about the popular diet and the life of ordinary people (Ibid., p. 63). The text has footnotes, which are absent in the other textbooks, thus suggesting a bit about the author's method of historical scholarship as well as providing information. Doliutskii offers differing views of contemporaries in their own words, placing debates such as the one over education in contexts that allow pupils to see that the issues are important and enduring ones (Ibid., p. 72ff). Historical choices are presented as complex, so that the lesson for pupils is less oversimplified than it is in traditional textbooks. While sometimes a bit disorganized and breathless, this textbook conveys the sense of excitement as well as the difficulties of the early days of Soviet power. It tries to help pupils to understand the past in its own terms. Unfortunately, Doliutskii's books were printed in a small and diminishing edition, from 20,000 for the first of the series to 3,000 for the last. As "unofficial materials," they were not bought by schools. Those teachers wishing to use them had to purchase them with their own money, if they could find them at all.[4]

New Approaches and Materials for Teaching History

The rethinking of what should be taught about the past has taken on a new dimension as historian-writers have moved on from filling in the blank spots in history to trying to conceptualize history in a less Marxist fashion and turning their attention to new styles of teaching. There have been proposals for a variety of new courses that could be constructed from the ground up, which might make it easier to break out of the structure imposed on history teaching by the old Marxist–Leninist ideology. A number of these courses have been outlined in *Uchitel'skaia gazeta*. Some are quite narrow in scope, focusing on the Bible, the history of religion, mythology and folklore, or local history (Kop'eva and Brodskii 1992, pp. 11-12; Gotovtsev 1992, p. 21; Avdeev and Bugrov 1992, p. 7). Others propose a new way of teaching the traditional final year (grade 11) history course, World War II to the present (Panteleev and Shepetov 1991, p. 26). A few are trying to reconceptualize the whole history curriculum. One such proposed plan is heavily influenced by Marxism (Levit 1992, pp. 6-7), while another (put together by two scholars in St. Petersburg) offers an integrated curriculum for grades 8 through 11, and states explicitly that it is not based on a Marxist conception of history (Smirnov and Bobkov 1991).

The authors of the proposed non-Marxist curriculum, S.V. Smirnov and D.V. Bobkov, argue that Russian history must be taught in the context of world history and also as a part of European civilization (not, as Zharova and Mishina suggested, as the history of a country influenced by both Europe and Asia). Their view of the law of history is that civilizations naturally rise, mature, and fall, and that throughout world history the territory integrated into a single civilization has gradually expanded until, in the twentieth century, a single, interdependent civilization is coming into being (Smirnov and Bobkov 1991, p. 5). The goal of their history course is to show the unique qualities of each civilization and to illustrate for students the contradictory nature of the historical process and the ambiguity of the notion of progress. They have produced a course outline for a four-year sequence that organizes the material more or less chronologically for each year of study and also by culture area. For example, units on Ancient Rome, Byzantium, the Arabs in the Middle Ages, and Europe in the Middle Ages are presented in that order. In a sense, they employ elements of both the world history and world cultures approaches. This curriculum was being taught in one St. Petersburg school in the 1992–93 school year, as well as in one or more schools in Moscow, Samara, Derzhinsk, Tiumen, and Lugansk (Ukraine). Teachers volunteering to teach it attended special summer seminars and received additional help during the school year from the authors of the project.[5]

A flood of new material for teaching history has been created by a variety of new groups and institutes, but little of it has been published in sufficiently large press runs for it to be widely used. The Independent Institute for the Development of Education, under the leadership of Aleksandr Abramov, for example, had more than a hundred textbooks and scholarly books ready for publication by the summer of 1992, including books of readings on Russian history and innovative textbooks such as a "problem book" on early Russian history by S.G. Smirnov.[6] Abramov's institute, like so many others, was searching for financial support from a Western partner to publish these materials, which were ready for press. To compensate in part for publication delays and the likelihood that they would be unable to make large printings of their books, Abramov's institute, with the support of Boris Bim-Bad's Russian Open University, made arrangements to publish outlines for courses and other usable materials in a regularly printed special section of *Uchitel'skaia gazeta* called "Express-Textbook." Another journal, *Prepodavanie istorii v shkole*, has also published projects for new courses put together by scholars from the central institutes, as well as documents and articles on Russian history and long selections from prerevolutionary history texts. Placement of articles in these and other journals is an interim solution to the difficulties caused by the economic problems that make regular large-scale publishing at a price that teachers can afford impossible. These same economic pressures have forced even these journals to reduce the size and frequency of their press runs.

Finally, several new, small commercial publishing houses have sprung up to publish teaching materials. There, too, creative work was ready for press but as yet unpublished in the summer of 1992. Some of this material was extremely imaginative, such as a curriculum unit on the home front during World War II, rich in photographic illustration and excerpts from memoirs and contemporary newspapers put together by two curators at the Museum of the Revolution in Moscow (Klukova and Prokhorova 1992).

By the 1992–93 school year, multiple proposals for new courses had been published for discussion, variants which provided new models not only for what should be taught but also for how teaching should be done.

Most of their authors continued to find "lessons" in the past to press upon students, an approach that threatened to lead to a new type of selectivity and oversimplification. Critics began to warn against romanticizing the tsarist period and introducing a new dogma as tendentious as the old (Golovatenko 1991, pp. 121–31; Komarova 1991, p. 5; Muromtseva et al. 1991, pp. 148–57). Now, however, there were different textbooks with different lessons to teach. Schools had the right to make choices in what they offered, and a wide variety of materials and a bewildering array of subjects and themes were set out before them. Most of the new materials, however, remained unpublished except in very small press runs for local use or as articles in teachers' serial publications. The fact remained that only Prosveshchenie had the capacity to publish history materials in sufficiently large editions to make them widely accessible. These remained relatively conservative in approach, providing new facts to be sure, but following the patterns and interpretations established in the traditional history textbooks of the Soviet era. For example, a new reader for the period 1917–30, which was published by Prosveshchenie in 300,000 copies in 1990, can only be described as a continuation of the old approach in tone, language, and interpretation (Shchagin et al. 1990). Most teachers, therefore, had little choice—and many, little inclination—but to continue to teach their traditional courses and base them on the books available from Prosveshchenie.

New Courses in Social Studies

Public high-level discussions about the need for change in teaching social studies also grew heated in the late 1980s. In 1988, when Yagodin proposed a thorough reevaluation of social studies education, there were three social studies courses taught in the Russian comprehensive secondary schools, "Ethics and the Psychology of Family Life" taught one day per week in grade 9, "Principles of Soviet State and Law" (an optional course that was heavily Marxist in its orientation but still widely taught as recently as 1990-91) once per week in grade 9, and a social studies course for grade 11. Republics had the option of adding social studies courses as needed (USSR State Committee 1990, pp. 10-11). Model exam questions provided for the grade 11 social studies course for the 1989-90 academic year indicate that the students were tested on Marxist dogma. Students were to be asked to discuss "socialism as the first phase of communist formation . . . the dialectic as the science of general social connections and development" and similar old chestnuts (Yagodin 1989, p. 5.).

In his 1988 recommendation, Yagodin further proposed that an integrated system of history and social sciences education be developed for secondary schools in the form of a four-year course, to be called "Man and Society." This course was to support perestroika by contributing to "the humanization of education and upbringing [and by] strengthening the formation of democratic qualities in the citizens, and their ability to live within the parameters of a 'law-governed state.'" It was further intended to do away with "dogmatism and formalism in education" (Prokhorov 1989, pp. 7–8). Some objections were voiced to this idea in 1988-89, specifically against the elimination of the course on scientific communism and the reduced attention to the history of the Communist Party. It was agreed that further discussion with specialists was needed before any final decision could be made.

Little more than a year later, in April 1990, Yagodin announced that the new course, "Man and Society," was to be introduced into all general secondary schools, that is, grades 8 through 11, for students from thirteen through seventeen years of age. It was to consist of two parts of 136 class hours each and replace the three former social studies courses. The second part of the course was also to be taught in the secondary professional-technical colleges (uchilishche). A separate course, "The Foundations of Social Science," was to be introduced into the secondary specialized schools (tekhnikumy) by the 1990-91 academic year or "as fast as the programs and materials could be prepared." Yagodin's order further declared that this course was to be "organically linked" to the teaching of history (though not to replace it), and that schools could choose whether to offer additional related courses. Details about the programs, the preparation of teachers, and the creation of materials were left to the republics (Yagodin 1990, pp. 3–6). This order reflected the continuing tension between the tradition of central control and the new policy of decentralization, which was the more complicated because it was the center, not the provinces, that was pushing for educational reforms. On the one hand, the central educational authority declared that specified new social studies courses were obligatory in secondary schools. On the other, the same document granted to the schools themselves the right to introduce changes in their programs of social science education, "taking into account local needs," and to develop their own forms of examination.

The goals for "Man and Society" were ambitious. The course was to address the vospitanie (upbringing or moral education) issue directly by presenting those themes "which have fundamental significance for forming in pupils the values of a humanistic world view" (Meshcheriakov

1990, p. l). Some emphasized that it should help to form "socialist values." It was also to create "a complete picture of social life on the basis of integrating knowledge from philosophy, political economy, social-political theory, ethics, psychology, social psychology, sociology, political science and jurisprudence" (APN 1990, p. 3). The basic premise of this course appeared to run directly counter to the basic premise of all previous Soviet social science education, namely that Marxism-Leninism offered a sufficient and scientific understanding of the relations of man to the surrounding world.

A number of different institutions worked further to develop programs for this course, including the familiar Academy of Pedagogical Sciences in Moscow, the Department of Social Studies of the State Committee on Education, the All-Union Center for the Sciences of Man of the Soviet Academy of Sciences, and a group supported by the Ukrainian Ministry of Education. In Leningrad (now St. Petersburg), both the city and the regional institutes for the continuing education for teachers developed versions, as did the Herzen Pedagogical University. All followed a general guideline, according to which the section for grades 8 and 9 would first discuss man and his surroundings, drawing on material from biology, geography, and psychology to consider the relations of the individual to nature, other people, family, the "working collective," the state, and to oneself. In grades 10 and 11, personality, morality, and law would be studied. The first part of the section for grades 10 and 11 was to be devoted to civilization, man, and progress, and the second part to the contemporary world and its problems.

Several proposals for the course were published for purposes of discussion in 1990. Virtually all of them declared that their goal was to contribute to the humanization of education, but many depended heavily on Marxist language. One proposed to organize the new course according to the "theory of dialectical materialism" (Lazebnikova 1990, p. 26); another spoke of the means of production, social formations, and social revolutions (Artsishevskii 1990, p. 33ff). A conference to discuss these preliminary proposals was held in October 1990 (Bogolomov 1991, pp. 6–7). The leading variants were published in *Prepodavanie historii v shkole* in May 1991. One of these was by a group from the Academy of Pedagogical Sciences headed by L.N. Bogoliubov that included A.Iu. Lazebnikova, and a second by a group affiliated with the State Committee on Education's main department for the teaching of social sciences under the direction of V.I. Kuptsov. The Bogoliubov-Lazebnikova proposal was strongly Marxist in its first schematic versions, but changed somewhat in response to criticisms and the evolving intellectual climate (Bogoliubov et al. 1991; Bogoliubov 1992a, p. 9). There were occasional complaints that the more creative and non-Marxist proposals for this course were opposed by the central educational hierarchy, but authors continued to work and schools to experiment (Zinchenko 1992, p. 11). By 1990-91, trials for the last year of the course were run in a number of cities under the sponsorship of a wide variety of groups. They involved combinations of teachers, instructors at pedagogical institutes, universities, and institutes for the continuing education of teachers. Their task was particularly challenging because it was impossible simply to follow texts worked out for university students as they had so often done in the past: there was no university model to follow.[7]

By the fall of 1992, when teachers of grade 11 in Moscow were expected to replace the old social science course with the final part of "Man and Society," the only text that was available in quantity (50,000) was Bogoliubov and Lazebnikova's *The Bases of Contemporary Civilization*. This text was supplemented by a series of short pamphlets for teachers published in an edition of 10,000 copies on specific themes to be discussed (Ivanova and Sokolov 1992; Lazebnikova 1992; Bogoliubov 1992b).

The Bases of Contemporary Civilization begins with an outline of the problems facing contemporary society, of which ecological challenges are described as among the greatest (Bogoliubov and Labeznikova 1992). It then presents a brief discussion of the important philosophers of the past, devoting about as many pages (eight) to the discussion of all those preceding Marx as it does to Marx alone, and follows with a brief discussion of the characteristics of the development of civilization from ancient times to the present. The second part of the book is called "Contemporary Society: The Integrated and Interlinked World." It focuses on the position of Russian society in the contemporary world, and the social, political, cultural, and spiritual characteristics of the twentieth century. Topics include political pluralism, the law-governed state, and parliamentary democracy, as well as the role of religion and the impact of the information revolution on the contemporary world. The text tells pupils that there are several points of view on many issues. Of Marx, it is written that there are various views about the contemporary value of his ideas, that it is important to remember the historical context in which he developed his theories, and that it is up to the pupil to decide whether his analysis of society is useful or not (Ibid., pp. 14–15). In evaluating the role of religion, pupils are told that whatever they may think of the role of the church and religion today, and however hard it may be for them to understand the passions religion has aroused in the past, events in history such as the Crusades cannot be understood without taking the fact of religious passion seriously (Ibid., p. 69). In its final sections, the text describes the various types of economic models possible in the contemporary world, devoting a rather long section to explaining how a market economy works and suggesting that there are a number of economic and social models that might be chosen by contemporary societies (Ibid., pp. 120–25). Questions at the end of each section ask students to explain general concepts, to evaluate the arguments of various scholars, and about their own opinions.

The program proposed by V.I. Kuptsov's group, which was a contender for adoption by Moscow schools in the fall of 1992, had not yet appeared in print at the time the course was scheduled to begin. It differed from Bogoliubov's in being considerably more abstract, philosophical, and intellectually demanding. Its teaching materials urged teachers to introduce discussion questions such as, "What is history?" "What is morality?" "Are there laws of history?" "What is the role of force?" Other topics for discussion included the value of various economic models, the role of law in society, whether or not Stalin's dictatorship was a "chance" phenomenon, and, finally, the relative merits of proposals by contemporary "westernizers" and "slavophiles" (Kuptsov et al. 1991, pp. 126–38). Although no textbook was yet available for pupils, a series of thirty-two-page pamphlets written by leading scholars to coincide with the issues to be covered in the course were issued in an edition of 5,000 copies by Znanie publishers in 1991. They were designed for teachers who might choose to follow the Kuptsov program, and for faculty at pedagogical and other institutes who would work with these teachers. Titles of these pamphlets included "Society and Morality," "Problems of Economic Development," "Economic Development in the Twentieth Century," "The Development of Science," "Relations of Religion and Sciences," "Religion and Mythology in the Contemporary World," "Religion in History," and "The Regularities [zakonomernost'] of Historical Development." As these titles imply, the sophistication of the course is high. The introductory pamphlet, written by Kuptsov himself, reflects on Russia's costly isolation from social thought and world culture as a result of insistence on a single view. He concludes that a "renewal of our society is impossible without a significant rise in the educational and cultural level of our people" (Kuptsov 1991b, p. 29). A textbook was promised for "the near future."

The Kuptsov outline and its accompanying materials move further from Marxism and the traditional approach to contemporary history than does the work of Bogoliubov. One pamphlet, on the role of religion and myth in contemporary life, for example, explores the role of myth in modern life and points out that science alone can not solve contemporary problems (Garadzha 1991, p. 10). Nonetheless, like the Bogoliubov materials, these too abound in hortatory remarks: "Man is now at a crossroads where choice is not only possible but obligatory"; "moral duty often demands that a person speak up against social opinion" (Sherdakov 1991, pp. 1, 7). On the other hand, the course and its materials are extraordinarily difficult and abstract, and the material to be covered so extensive, that it is not surprising that most Moscow schools chose the Bogoliubov model for their courses for the 1992–93 school year.[8]

In St. Petersburg, a number of different groups were piloting or teaching courses that met the "Man and Society" requirement by the fall of 1992 (Eliasberg 1992). At the end of the 1991 school year, pupils in a number of St. Petersburg schools were asked if they would like to take a variant of the final-year section of the course which had been worked out by the St. Petersburg City Institute for the Continuing Education of Teachers and the Institute for Adult Education. Several schools had a complement of pupils who did want the new course. Each of these schools then selected a history teacher to work with the creators of the course, which was introduced in the 1992–93 academic year.[9]

To some extent, the very idea of creating a single unified course, which would answer all questions about man and create a new humanistic outlook, is a perpetuation of the traditional Soviet notion that schools must provide pupils with a comprehensive world view. These new courses are explicitly intended to form a point of view compatible with the "new political thinking" (Stepanov 1990, pp. 120–21). Indeed, Bogoliubov himself has acknowledged that he has attempted to provide a new ideology for high school pupils (Bogoliubov 1992b).[10] On the other hand, virtually all versions of the course urge pupils to examine their own relationship to the world around them and to develop their own opinions. This approach contrasts sharply with that of the past, when pupils were presented a monolithic class-based interpretation of history and required to memorize a single set of facts. The new approach also turns pupils' attention to the individual and to small groups, and introduces a wide variety of views ranging from those of the ancient Greek and Roman philosophers to contemporary psychology and natural science. This is a radical departure from the old approach. The course does seem to meet some of its goals. A study of pupils in grade 8 who had studied in a 1990–91 trial of the Bogoliubov syllabus in St. Petersburg in found that 83 percent believed the course had helped them to gain self-knowledge. Fifty-four percent mentioned its practicality; 63 percent found it interesting, and 32 percent wished the number of hours devoted to it to be expanded (Eliasberg and Baranov 1991, p. 145).

It remains unclear whether this ambitious new course, "Man and Society," will be successfully introduced into Russian secondary schools in anything approaching its present form, and whether or not one version of it will prevail over the others. Although the course has been mandated, there are as yet neither textbooks for it nor teachers trained to teach it. Some doubt that such a large-scale integrated course will ever prove practicable.[11] The resolution of this situation will depend in part on the extent to which the school curriculum will be left to regional or local control, either explicitly or implicitly as a result of the examination system. In theory, the fall of 1992 saw the introduction of at least one year of this four-year course in all general secondary schools and all secondary professional-technical schools in Russia. In fact, there were only 50,000 textbooks available for the entire country. Pilot programs were under way in several cities. In theory, schools had a choice as to how to fulfill this requirement. In practice, most teachers had no access to student materials for the course, and no training in either the content or the new teaching style said to be appropriate for it.

Conclusion

The teaching of history and social studies in secondary schools was particularly vulnerable to politically inspired distortion during the Soviet period. For that reason, and because political officials and scholars as well as school reformers continued to believe these subjects to be key vehicles of political socialization, the creation of new teaching materials in these fields was made a top priority in the late 1980s. This was a time of inspirational words and ringing resolutions accompanied by scholarly procrastination. The historians traditionally responsible for creating new textbooks were slow to get started on their work. Not until the 1990s did the long-promised transitional textbooks begin to appear, and they were, for the most part, factual updates that followed the patterns of the texts they were to replace.

Arguments have continued over the degree to which there should be all-Union—or, since 1991, all-Republic—requirements for every school. Nonetheless, in sharp contrast to the long Soviet experience, new authorial collectives, schools, and local institutes have begun to develop and promote new programs for history and the social sciences. Even school children and their parents take part in deciding what they would like to learn. The result has been an explosion of new ideas in the areas of history and social studies. The central monopoly on writing and publishing school materials that had existed throughout the Soviet period has been broken. A market for teaching materials has not developed, however, largely as a result of the general economic crisis which has left both schools and potential publishers unable to support one. Economic difficulties have prevented even Prosveshchenie from meeting the demand for new books.[12]

The ideological legacy of the Soviet past has served to keep the teaching of history and social studies in a prominent place on the political and social agenda. New programs continue to be worked out systematically, to be taken seriously by top scholars, and to be thoughtfully produced by individuals working at institutes of history and pedagogy. Programs are tested in schools, reworked, and improved.

This same legacy has a darker side. Most of the teachers and specialists who chose to work in the fields of history or social studies prior to the glasnost era were people who were willing to make the compromises that ideological conformity required. Experienced textbook writers have found it difficult or impossible to break away from ideologically based history with its rigid interpretations and stilted, bureaucratic language. They cannot change the habits that enabled them to make successful careers under Soviet conditions. History teachers and those now recruited to teach social studies have spent their professional lives teaching Marxist history in authoritarian classrooms. Approximately 50 percent of all teachers have been in the classroom for fifteen years or more (Dneprov et al. 1991, p. 43). They cannot be expected to become sources of creativity overnight. Even if innovative teaching materials are created that provide multiple perspectives and encourage critical thinking, they cannot do the job alone. Even those teachers who would like to change their methods and break away from a Stalinist pedagogy do not know how. Most of the in-service education programs they attend are taught by faculties who themselves do not know how to lead discussions or listen to their students. How are the pedagogical universities and institutes to staff the new departments of social science or humanitarian education that they have been directed to establish, much less find faculty who know how to create a democratic, participatory classroom? There are new groups which would like to fill this gap, but they lack the kind of financial support that would enable large numbers of teachers to benefit from their work (Kerr 1991, pp. 341–44). There are also many educators who remain skeptical as to whether or not, or at what age, pupils should be encouraged to develop their own ideas (Punskii 1991, p. 133).

Much of the optimism of the late 1980s is gone, replaced by more sober assessments about what is practical and possible. In education as elsewhere, economic realities have crippled projects that might have given the reformers more credibility. Teachers are told to teach new courses for which there are no materials. They are urged to introduce new styles of teaching which they have never experienced themselves and for which they are not now offered training. In some ways, the apparent proliferation of new materials and experiments has been deceptive, because in the condition of scarcity, only the most powerful institutes and best-known authors have been able to find ways to publish and distribute their work widely. Economic pressures may yet limit the effectiveness of these experiments, as it may prove more efficient to publish many copies of a single book and to train teachers to teach the same course than to support an array of alternatives. Practical considerations such as these can be expected to influence what is available to most teachers in the near future. Most teachers and schools have had to continue to rely on the books produced by Prosveshchenie, in 1992 the only press yet capable of producing books in large press runs. These textbooks remain the most reliable guide to what is being taught in Russian history classrooms (Dneprov et al. 1991, pp. 36–38).

There have been some signal accomplishments. History textbooks have been published in revised versions that provide a more factually accurate account of the Soviet period. There has also been a conscious effort, not always successful, to break the grip of Marxist-Leninist ideology on history and social studies and to present a wide variety of views consistent with world scholarship and humanistic values. Attempts have been made, again not always successful, to present materials that will promote a new, less authoritarian pedagogy. New writers, institutes, and enterprising schools and teachers have come forward to write and teach new, experimental courses. No longer does the government and a single publisher exercise a monopoly over all available teaching materials.

In the teaching of social studies, the situation is particularly complex. There are no models for the courses that have been mandated for secondary schools. Disarray among Academy and university scholars in these disciplines suggests that there will be no guidance from that quarter in the near future (Kudriavtsev 1992, pp. 46–54). This vacuum has attracted a number of creative proposals from a wide variety of groups who see an opportunity to present an entirely new value system to Russian young people. They have not waited for the professional and political hierarchy to work out a curriculum that will be passed to them from on high. Confusion at the top and the decentralization of responsibility for curriculum have enabled others to take the initiative. This is a development full of significance for the future.

What remains to be seen is whether the Ministry of Education or the political leadership will reassert and enforce central control over the curriculum. Economic as well as political considerations will play a role here. Should the center try to do so, social sciences and history education may experience a long transitional period until a consensus on what should be taught can be reestablished. Such a consensus does not now exist. Should the principle of choice for schools persist, however, different issues will emerge: the relative power and preeminence of different schools of thought; the availability of resources to support the development; the publishing and distribution of new materials; the ingenuity with which teachers can be retrained; and, most important of all, the direction chosen by Russian society as a whole. Genuine debates over the nature and virtues of democracy, over what is valuable in the heritage of world philosophy and what may be of continuing value in Marxism, and, above all over Russia's place in the world between East and West—its cultural distinctiveness and future—are already visible in the materials now proposed for school children. Similar debates preoccupy Russian society as a whole. Discussions about the past have long served both to influence and reflect the social and political weather in Russia. History and social studies lessons in schools will help to direct those discussions for the next generation and so, in their way, contribute to the construction of Russia's identity and goals for the future.

Notes

I would like to thank Galina V. Klukova who introduced me to the arcane world of Soviet education and has helped me to interpret what I have found there, and the National Endowment for the Humanities whose support for a Joint Russian-American seminar for history teachers provided much of the impetus for this article.

1. As recently as December 1991, I observed the same subject being taught in the same week in the history classes of four different schools, three in Moscow and one in Novgorod. To my considerable surprise, considering glasnost, three of the teachers presented the material in virtually the same way, with the same sketch put on the blackboard and the same examples used by each teacher to supplement the text.

2. V.K. Batsyn, (1989). Personal communication to the author, Moscow.

3. Panchenko, D. (1991). Personal communication to the author, Cambridge, MA, April. Panchenko teaches ancient history at a gymnasium in St. Petersburg.

4. Leshchiner, V.R. (1991). Personal communication to the author, Moscow, December. Several of Doliutskii's books were republished in Moscow in late 1992.

5. Bobkov, D.V. (1992). Personal communication to the author, St. Petersburg, July.

6. Abramov, A.M. (1992), Personal communication to the author, Moscow, July.

7. Bogoliubov, V.N. (1992). Personal communication to the author, Moscow, July.

8. Golovatenko, A.Iu. (1992). Personal communication to the author, Moscow, July. Golovatenko was then the deputy director of *Prepodavanie istorii v shkole.* Zakharova, E.M. (1992). Personal communication to the author, Moscow, July. Zakharova was then the head of the history department of the Moscow Institute for the Continuing Education of Teachers and author of teachers' guides including *Poznavatel_'nie zadaniia po kursa istorii SSSR,* Moscow: Moscow City Committee for Public Education and Moscow City Institute for the Continuing Education of Teachers, 1990. Two textbooks for this course, by Bogoliubov and Lazebnikova, were published by Prosveshchenie, in late 1992 and 1993. Some of the Kuptsov material was published in 1993. Mark Johnson (1993), personal communication to the author, December.

9. Vershlovskii, S.G. (1993). Personal communication to the author, January 14.

10. Bogoliubov, V.N. (1992). Personal communication to the author, Moscow, July.

11. Golovatenko, A.Iu. (1992). Personal communication to the author, Moscow, July. Abramov, A.M. (1992). Personal communication to the author, Moscow, July.

12. Even the rather conservative but factually updated books of Prosveshchenie were not readily available to many schools for the 1992–93 year because press runs had had to be curtailed and prices raised beyond what schools could afford. In its list for potential buyers published in February 1992, Prosveshchenie listed only two new history books, the Zakharova and Mishina text, *Istoriia otechestva,* and a new text on prerevolutionary history that was promised for 1993. Even Prosveshchenie's most optimistic future publishing plans presented at a meeting of the Ministry of Education contained nothing else on the period since World War II except for a "new" world history text to be prepared under the auspices of the leading author of the old, Furaev. Despite this limited choice, D. Zuev, the head of Prosveshchenie, reminded *Uchitel'skaia gazeta* readers in September of 1992 that they must order books immediately for the 1993–94 academic year and that they should begin preparing orders for 1994–95 (Izdatel'stvo Prosveshchenie 1992, p. 14; Viazemskii 1992, p. 205; Trushin 1992, p. 2; Ovchinnikova 1992, p. 3). The implication is that there will be nothing new for 1994–95.

Bibliography

Abramov, A.M. (1992a). Introduction to Series Express-Textbook, *Uchitel'skaia gazeta,* no. 15, p.12.

———. (1992b). "Obrazovanie v politike i politika v obrazovanii," *Uchitel'skaia gazeta,* no. 19, pp. 11, 14.

Akademiia pedagogicheskikh nauk SSSR (APN) (1990). Nauchno-issledovatel'skii institut soderzhaniia i metodov obucheniia, "Poiasnitel'naia zapiska," in *Pro-*

gramma kursa, "chelovek i obshchestvo" srednikh spetsial'nikh i srednikh professional'no-teknicheskikh uchebnikh zavedenii. Moscow, pp. 3–5.

Aleksashkina, L.N. (1988). *Samostoiatel'naia rabota shkol'nikov pri izuchenii noveishei istorii (kniga dlia uchitelia).* Moscow: Prosveshchenie.

Artsishevskii, P.A. (1990). "Primernaia programma kursa 'chelovek i obshchestvo,' " in *Varianti tipovikh programm po kursu, "chelovek i obshchestvo."* Moscow: State Committee of the USSR on Popular Education, Main Department for the Teaching of the Social Sciences, pp. 11–42.

Avdeev, A.G. and A.V. Bugrov (1992). "Istoriia preobrazhenskovo i okrestnostei," *Uchitel'skaia gazeta,* no. 5, p. 7.

Bogoliubov, L.N. (1992a). "Trudnii put' k dialogu," *Uchitel'skaia gazeta,* no. 10–11, p. 9.

———. (1992b). *Osnovy sovremennoi tsivilizatsii, didakticheskie materiali k temam, "sovremennii etap mirovogo tsivilizatsionnogo razvitiia i nashe obshchestvo," ekonomicheskoe razvitie sovremennoi tsivilizatsii.* Moscow: Nauchno-metodicheskoe ob''edinenie "Tvorcheskaia pedagogika": "Novaia shkola."

Bogoliubov, L.N., and A.Iu. Lazebnikova (1992). *Osnovy sovremennoi tsivilizatsii,* Part 4, "Chelovek i obshchestvo." Moscow: Biuro Dendi.

Bogoliubov, L.N. et al. (1991). "Tematicheskoi planirovanie kursa, 'chelovek i obshchestvo', " *Prepodavanie istorii v shkole,* no. 5, pp. 116–25.

Bogomolov, V.N. (1991). "Konferentsiia v Lutske," *Prepodavanie istorii v shkole,* no. 2, pp. 3–5.

Borisov, Iu.S. (1989). *Istoriia SSSP, materiali k ychebniki dlia deviatoga klassa srednei shkoli* (History of the USSR, materials for a textbook for the ninth class). Moscow: Prosveshchenie. (Class 9 was renumbered class 10 in the 1989–90 school year when the school entrance age was lowered.)

Davies, R.W. (1989). *Soviet History in the Gorbachev Revolution.* Bloomington and Indianapolis: Indiana University Press.

Dneprov, E.D., V.S. Lazerev, and V.S. Sobkin. (1991). *Rossiiskoi obrazovanie v perekhodnii period: programma stabilizatsii i razvitiia* (Russian education in a transitional period: A program of stabilization and development). Moscow: Ministry of Education, RSFSR.

Doliutskii, I.I. (1989). *Materiali k izucheniiu istorii SSSR, IX klass (1921–41 gg.).* Moscow: Moscow City Committee for Public Education and Moscow City Institute for Improving Qualifications of Teachers.

——— (1991a). *Materiali k izucheniiu istorii SSSR (Rossiia v nachale XXB).* Moscow: Moscow City Committee for Public Education and Moscow City Institute for Improving Qualifications of Teachers.

——— (1991b). *Materiali k izucheniiu istorii SSSR, XX vek (Rossiskaia revolutsiia).* Moscow: Moscow City Committee for Public Education and Moscow City Institute for Improving Qualifications of Teachers.

Dunstan, John (ed.) (1992). *Soviet Education Under Perestroika.* London: Routledge.

Eliasberg, N.I. (1992). *Gumanisticheskie tsennosti evropeiskikh tsivilizatsii i problemiobshcheobrazovatel'noi shkoli.* St. Petersburg: Committee on Education of the mayor of St. Petersburg, St. Petersburg State University of the Pedagogical Craft (Masterstva).

Eliasberg, N.I. and P.A. Baranov (1991). "Pis'mo k redaktsiiu, O programmakh kursa 'chelovek i obshchestvo,' " *Prepodavanie istorii v shkole,* no. 5, pp. 144–46.

Ermolaeva, N.A. (1991). "Khotia tirazhi upali," Interview, *Uchitel'skaia gazeta,* no. 34–35, p. 3.

Furaev, V.K., S.S. Volk, L.E. Kertman, G.V. Levin, A.Ia. Manusevich, E.I. Popova, and R.P. Stetskevich (1989). *Noveishaia istoriia (1939–1988), uchebnik dlia 11 klassa srednei shkoli.* Moscow: Prosveshchenie.

Garadzha, V.I. (1991). *Religiia i mifologiia v sovremennom mire.* Moscow: Znanie.

Golovatenko, A.Iu. (1991). "Deideologizatsiia prepodavaniia ili obnovlenie dogm?" *Prepodavanie istorii v shkole,* no. 2, pp. 121–31.

—— (1992). "Iz istorii sotsialisticheskikh uravnitel'nikh vozzrenii," *Prepodavanie istorii v shkole,* no. 1–2, pp. 49–61.

Gotovtsev, G. (1992). "Volshebnii istochnik," *Uchitel'skaia gazeta,* no. 3, p. 21.

Husband, William B. (1991). "Secondary School History Texts in the USSR: Revising the Soviet Past, 1985–1989," *Russian Review,* vol. 50, pp. 458–80.

Ivanova, L.F. and I.E. Sokolov (1992). *Osnovy sovremennoi tsivilizatsii, didaticheskie materiali k teme "tsivilizatsii proshlogo."* Moscow: Nauchno-metodicheskoe ob''edinenie "Tvorcheskaia pedagogika": "Novaia shkola."

"Izdatelst'vo Prosveshchenie," (1992). *Uchitel'skaia gazeta,* no. 6, p. 14.

"Iz uchebnika novoi istoriia professora P. Vippera" (From Professor Vipper's textbook of modern history) (1991). *Prepodavanie istorii v shkole,* no. 5, pp. 50–77.

Kerr, Stephen T. (1991). "Beyond Dogma: Teacher Education in the USSR," *Journal of Teacher Education,* vol. 42, no. 5, pp. 332–49.

Klukova, G.V. (1989). "Predlozheniia po perestroike shkol'nogo istoriicheskogo obrazovaniia," *Prepodavanie istorii v shkole,* no. 4, pp. 52–56.

Klukova, T. and I. Prokhovova (1992). "Tyl, okupatsiia, soprotivlenie, 1941–1945," unpublished manuscript.

Komarova, E. (1991). "Novie uchebniki: proshedshee: sviato ili prokliato," *Uchitel'skaia gazeta,* no. 39, p. 5.

Kop'eva, E.S. and N.A. Brodskii (1992). "Bibliia kak vidaiushchiisia pamiatnik mirovoi kulturi," *Uchitel'skaia gazeta,* no. 23, pp. 11–12.

Korablev, I.Iu., Iu.S. Kukushkin, I.A. Fedosov, and V.P. Sherstobitov (1986). *Istoriia SSSR, ychebnik dlia deviatoga klassa* (History of the USSR, textbook for the ninth class). Moscow: Prosveshchenie.

Korablev, Iu.I., I.A. Fedosov, and Iu.S. Borisov (1989). *Istoriia SSSR, uchebnik dlia desiatoga klassa* (History of the USSR for the tenth class). Moscow: Prosveshchenie (Class 9 was renumbered as class 10 when the school entrance age was lowered for the 1989–90 school year.)

Kruglyi stol (1990). "Istoricheskaia nauka i shkol'noe istoricheskoi obrazovanie," *Prepodavanie istorii v shkole,* no. 4, pp. 7–30.

Kudriavtsev, V.N. (1992). "Gumanitarnie obshchestvennie nauki: sostoianie i perspektivi," *Novaia i noveishaia istoriia,* no. 4, pp. 46–54.

Kuptsov, V.I. (1991). *Vvedenie—problemi razvitiia obrazovaniia.* Moscow: Znanie.

Kuptsov, V.I. et al. (1991). "Programma kursa, 'chelovek i obshchestvo,' " *Prepodavanie istorii v shkole,* no. 5, pp. 126–38.

Lazebnikova, A.Iu. (1990). "Materialisticheskoe ponimanie obschestva i ego istorii," in *Programma Kursa "chelovek i obshchestro."* Moscow: USSR Academy of Pedagogical Science and the Scientific Research Institute for the Contents and Methods of Teaching, pp. 26–32.

—— (1992). *Osnovy sovremennoi tsivilizatsii, didakticheskie materiali k teme "razvitie znanii ob obshchestve."* Moscow: Nauchno-metodicheskoe ob''edinenie "Tvorcheskaia pedagogika": "Novaia shkola."

Levit, M. (1992). "Chto govoril Nestor," *Uchitel'skaia gazeta,* no. 7, pp. 6–7.

Meshcheriakov, B.G. (1990). "Primernaia programma kursa, 'chelovek i obshchesvo,' chast' I: chelovek," in *Proekt varianti tipovikh programm po kursy, "chelovek i obshchestvo."* Moscow: Gosudarstvennii komitet SSSR po narodnomu obrazovaniiu, glavnoe upravlenie prepodavaniia obshchestvennikh nauk, pp. 1–12.

Muckle, J. (1988). *A Guide to the Soviet Curriculum: What the Russian Child is Taught in School.* Beckenham, Kent: Croom Helm.

Muromtseva, L.P., V.A. Neveshin, and V.B. Perzhavko (1991). "Sredi knig: Problemi istorii SSSR na stranitsakh massovikh periodicheskikh izdanii v 1990 gody," *Prepodavanie istorii v shkole,* no. 1, pp. 148–57.

Nikiforova (1990). "Vi-Vlast', deistvuete," *Uchitel'skaia gazeta,* no. 47, p. 2.

"Obsuzhdenie shkol'nogo uchebnika po istorii SSSR" (1990). *Voprosi istorii,* no. 1, pp. 188–91.

Ostrovskii, V.P., V.I. Startsev, B.A. Starkov, and G.M. Smirnov (1990). *Istoriia SSSR, 11 klass.* Moscow: Prosveshchenie.

Ovchinnikova, I. (1992). "I dorogie uchebniki kupit' nevozmozhno," Interview with D.D. Zuev, director of Prosveshchenie Press, *Izvestiia,* no. 100, p. 3.

Panteleev, M.M. and N.A. Shepetov (1991). "Programma kursa 'sovremennii mir,' " *Uchitel'skaia gazeta,* no. 28, p. 5.

Prokhorov, A.P. (1989). "Obsuzhdenie proekta perestroiki prepodavaniia obshchestvennikh nauk," *Prepodavanie istorii v shkole,* no. 2, pp. 6–8.

——— (1991). "Vsesoiuznoi soveshchanie obshchestvovedov," *Prepodavanie istorii v shkole,* no. 1, pp. 3–10.

Punskii, V.O. (1991). "Prepodavanie istorii v pervie godi perestroiki," *Prepodavanie istorii v shkole,* no. 1, pp. 129–133.

Radzikhovskii, L. (1988a). "Stalinskaia pedagogika," *Uchitel'skaia gazeta,* July 14.

——— (1988b). "Brezhnevskaia pedagogika," *Uchitel'skaia gazeta,* August 30, p. 3.

Shchagin, E.M., et al. (1990). *Kniga dlia chteniia po istorii SSSR, 1917-konets 1930-x gg.* Moscow: Prosveshchenie.

Sherdakov, V.N. (1991). *Obshchestvo i nravstvennost'.* Moscow: Znanie.

Smirnitskii, I. (1991). Letter to the editor, *Ogonek,* no. 23, pp. 4–5.

Smirnov, S.B. and D.V. Bobkov (1991). *Istoriia chelovechestva, programma kursa.* St. Petersburg: Herzen Pedagogical University and Obrazovanie Press.

Sokolov, A.B. (1991). Letter to the editor, *Voprosi istorii,* no. 9–10, pp. 250–52.

Stepanov, S.A. (1990). "O perestroike prepodavaniia obshchestvennikh nauk v srednikh uchebnikh zavedeniiakh," *Prepodavanie istorii v shkole,* no. 3, pp. 118–24.

——— (1991). "Rekomendatsii vsesoiuznoi nauchno-prakticheskoi konferentsii po metodologicheksim methodicheskim problemam kursa, 'chelovek i obshchestvo' v srednikh uchebnikh zavedeniiakh," *Prepodavanie istorii v shkole,* no. 2, pp. 3–5.

Trushin, A. (1992). "Ne ochen' 'Happy English,' " *Uchitel'skaia gazeta,* no. 32, p. 2.

USSR State Committee for Education (1990). *The State Basic Curriculum.* Moscow: USSR State Committee for Public Education.

Vaillant, Janet G. (1992). "Inside Soviet Schools: History Classes," *Newsletter of the Institute for the Study of Soviet Education,* Indiana University, vol. 1, no. 2, pp. 25–29.

Viazemskii, E.E. (1992). "O programmakh i uchebnikakh po istorii obshchestvoznaniia v shkolakh," *Novaia i noveishaia istoriia,* no. 2, pp. 203–5.

Yagodin, G.A. (1989). "Ob ekzamenakh po istorii SSSR i drugim obshchestvennim distsiplinam v srednikh uchebnikh zavedeniiakh," Gosudarstvennii komitet SSSR po narodnomu obrazovaniiu, Prikaz no. 571 (December 30, 1988), *Prepodavanie istorii v shkole,* no. 2, pp. 3–5.

———— (1990). "Prikaz, O perestroike prepodavaniia obshchestvennikh distsiplin v srednikh uchebnikh zavedeniiakh," *Prepodavanie istorii v shkole*, no. 4, pp. 3–6.

Zharova, L.N. and I.A. Mishina (1992). *Istoriia otechestva, 1900–1940, uchebnaia kniga dlia starshikh klassov srednikh uchebnikh zavedenii*. Moscow: Prosveshchenie.

Zinchenko, V.P. (1992). "Ot khama sovetikus k khomo sapiens cherez ochelovechivanie obrazovaniia," no. 33–36, p. 11.

Zubkov, M.F. (1989). "Materiali, 'Kruglyi stol': aktual'nie problemi prepodavaniia novoii noveishei istorii v srednei shkole," *Novaia i noveishaia istoriia*, no. 2, pp. 180–85.

PROFESSIONAL EDUCATION

8

Education for Management in a New Economy

SHEILA M. PUFFER

Business education is big business in Russia these days. In the past couple of years in Moscow alone, more than a thousand business schools and training centers (Veselov 1992a) have sprung up like mushrooms after a rainfall. Yet, like the Russians' voracious appetite for mushrooms, their appetite for business education cannot readily be satisfied. The new business schools haven't begun to meet the huge demand, estimated at fifty times the supply, and 1.5 million managers and professionals need training in market-oriented management methods (Veselov 1992c). The training and retraining of such a massive number of people is a daunting task in any country under any circumstances. The task is infinitely more challenging in the Russia of the 1990s in light of the cataclysmic changes that the country is undergoing on virtually every dimension of the political, economic, and social landscapes.

The focus of this chapter is the way management education is evolving in Russia. We begin with an overview of the management education system that existed during the Communist period. This is followed by a discussion of how political, social, and economic changes have influenced management education since 1988. The latest developments in management education are presented next, including the types of business schools that have been created; the characteristics of the faculty, programs and curricula, and teaching methods; and a profile of four important types of clientele for business education. The chapter concludes with a discussion of the future of management education, presenting both a pessimistic and an optimistic scenario of the potential impact of management education on the economy, politics, and society in the New Russia.

Management Education During the Communist Period

During the Communist period, a vast network of educational institutions was created to provide initial training as well as upgrading and refresher courses (*programmy povysheniia kvalifikatsii*) for managers and administrators at all hierarchical levels and in all sectors of the economy. At that time, the Russian concept of management was different from that in the West, where management is considered a profession and is offered as a field of study at both the undergraduate and graduate levels. In contrast, people in Russia studied management after they had first completed their basic education. For example, many people who aspired to managerial positions completed the standard five-year institute or university program in a discipline, typically engineering or economics.[1] They would later be sponsored by their enterprise to attend management programs. Like many in the labor force, managers were required by government legislation to attend training programs on a regular cycle, generally every three to five years, depending on the place of their enterprise in the economic sector and their own level in the hierarchy.[2]

In the mid-1980s, just before perestroika was introduced, management education was directed by two powerful institutions that reported directly to the USSR Council of Ministers.[3] The Academy of Social Sciences oversaw management training for Communist Party officials, while the Academy of the National Economy oversaw programs for training managers of industrial enterprises and other sectors of the economy. The USSR State Committee for Public Education controlled and coordinated curricular issues and standards for all management training programs. It was also responsible for the financing and general administration of management institutes other than those that were funded and administered by sectorial ministries and large enterprises. For example, the small number of universities and institutes that offered five-year academic programs in management came under the jurisdiction of the USSR State Committee for Public Education. The system of management education was comprised of several levels of institutions and programs designed to meet the needs of managers ranging from heads of large enterprises to first-level supervisors. A typical program for senior enterprise managers during that period was the three-month management development program at the Plekhanov Institute of the National Economy in Moscow that I graduated from in 1980. The curriculum is presented in Table 8.1.

Table 8.1

Management Development Curriculum for Production Managers in 1980

General Management
 Methodological foundations of management
 Economic mechanism of the socialist economy
 Personnel management
 Sociopsychological aspects of management
 Foreign management experience

Industrial Issues
 Organization of industrial enterprises
 Economics of needs and consumption
 Economics of industry
 Economics and organization of labor
 Analysis of the administrative activity of industrial enterprises
 Problems of the rational use of the environment
 Automated management systems
 Statistics in the management of the economy
 Finance and credit in industrial enterprises
 Soviet law

Politics and Planning
 Economic policy of the Communist Party of the Soviet Union in the current stage
  of development
 Planning of the national economy
 Foreign policy of the Communist Party of the Soviet Union and the ideological
  struggle in the modern world
 Civil defense

Source: S.M. Puffer (1981). "Inside a Soviet Management Institute," *California Management Review,* vol. 24, no. 1, pp. 90–96.
Note: Curriculum of the three-month management development program for industrial managers at the Plekhanov Institute of the National Economy, Moscow, 1980.

Political Changes That Revolutionized Management Education

Three major pieces of legislation introduced in the late 1980s by President Mikhail Gorbachev as part of his policy of perestroika, or restructuring of the economy, had a significant impact on management education. These laws were the 1988 General Educational Reform, the 1987 Law on Soviet State Enterprises, and the 1988 Law on Cooperatives.

One of the major political factors that created significant changes in management education was the 1988 general reform of the Soviet educational system. The government targeted management education as an important means toward improving the country's abysmal economic performance. One of the changes was to make managers' career advancement and compensation contingent, in part, on professional certification and participation in continuing management education. The extensive list of requirements included attendance at monthly seminars on current production and managerial issues, all the way to lengthy, intensive management training at least once every six years. The effect of this policy was evident in several ways. First, it increased public awareness of the importance that government policy makers gave to management education. Second, by tying education to rewards, the policy gave managers an incentive to take training seriously. Third, it increased the demand for management education throughout the country.

The 1988 educational reform also resulted in a change in the funding for undergraduate students enrolled in five-year management programs at institutes and universities. Tuition and living expenses, which had been previously funded from the state budget, were now to be paid by sponsor enterprises that would hire students upon graduation. The purpose of this policy was twofold: It reduced state expenses, and it gave state educational institutions the opportunity to set tuition levels that might provide revenue for upgrading their plants and equipment.

The second major political factor affecting management education was the Law on State Enterprises of 1987. This legislation marked the beginning of the government's efforts to introduce elements of a market-based economy and make enterprises more independent and accountable for their financial performance. Decision-making authority over a number of important issues was decentralized from the planning and industrial ministries to the enterprise level. In particular, enterprises were required to be self-financing. Rather than receiving their budgets from the state, they had to finance their operations through the sale of their products and services. They also were required to compete with other enterprises and were granted the right to negotiate directly with foreign suppliers and customers rather than through the Ministry of Foreign Trade. In order to effectively exercise these new powers and responsibilities, managers needed to learn the principles of a market economy. Hence, the Law on State Enterprises created a large demand for new training programs in business and management.

The third political development that shaped management education in the late 1980s was the 1988 Law on Cooperatives.[4] This legislation opened the gates for the development of private enterprise by legalizing private businesses and granting them the same legitimacy in the economy as state enterprises. The 1988 law supplanted the 1986 Law on Individual Labor Activity which had permitted private enterprise on a small and highly restricted scale. The new law affected management education in two major ways. First, like the Law on State Enterprises, it created a demand for courses on conducting business in a market economy. Second, it permitted the creation of private business schools. Enterprising individuals quickly seized the opportunity to satisfy the demand for management training, and business schools and training programs began to proliferate. They were "almost as easy to set up . . . as shish kebab stands at busy intersections" (Vikhanskii 1992, p. 34).

In summary, three important pieces of legislation passed in the late 1980s had a major impact on management education. The laws greatly increased the importance of training managers about the market economy and created a huge demand for such training; they legalized the establishment of private business schools and made state-run business schools become more financially accountable and independent. These developments intensified after the breakup of the Soviet Union in 1991 and became particularly strong in the newly independent Russian Federation.

Social Factors Affecting Management Education

In contrast to the swift political changes that led to the proliferation of new business schools, social factors acted as a brake on their acceptance as legitimate institutions. The main obstacle was that most people understandably could not immediately reject the notion that capitalism was bad. Over the centuries, capitalism and entrepreneurship had never really taken root in Russia, and seventy years of Communism reinforced the belief that private enterprise was antithetical to a just socialist society (McCarthy et al. 1993). Social justice had been defined as the condition of everyone needing and being entitled to essentially the same things (Connor 1991, p. 139). Much energy was spent on envying others, with the prevailing attitude that more successful people should be brought down to one's own level, and not that one should improve one's own condition. The traditional idea of social justice also placed a greater value on the collective than on the individual. Individualism as a value was traditionally shunned as a threat to collectivism, to respect for authority, and to public discipline (Hollander 1991).

Business schools became a target of considerable public scorn as the proponents and propagators of new social values. By championing private enterprise, they were seen as promoting individualism and legitimating inequality arising from the rewards of individual initiative and hard work. The image of business schools was further tarnished when some people began associating them with the sharp increase in crime and corruption in business dealings in the freewheeling economy.

Economic Factors Affecting Management Education

The major economic factors that shaped the business schools founded after 1988 were competition and scarce resources. Business schools and training centers competed with one another for students from among the managers of state-owned and private enterprises that would pay large sums for training their personnel in market-based management. Schools billed "big name" speakers, both domestic and foreign, to attract participants, and vied for the few instructors who were skilled in market-economy subjects. State schools lost many of their best faculty members to private schools that offered markedly higher salaries. Training of new faculty was greatly constrained by a lack of funding. Programs for undergraduate and graduate students were given low priority because they were not financially self-supporting. Schools scrambled for classroom facilities, dormitory and office space, and entered into partnerships with foreign business schools and corporations in search of funding and technical expertise.

Management Education in the New Russia

Beginning in 1988, and as a direct result of the extraordinary political changes implemented in the USSR under Gorbachev, the uniformity that had characterized management education for decades under the Communist regime was quickly replaced by a dizzying array of business schools and management training programs that varied on virtually every dimension imaginable, including size, ownership structure, financing, faculty, programs and curricula, methodology, and clientele. With the fall of the Communist Party and the dissolution of the Soviet Union at the end of 1991, the proliferation of new business schools in Russia accelerated.

Types of Management Education Institutions

There are three basic types of organizations engaged in management education in Russia today: state business schools, private business schools, and private consulting firms. The extent to which business schools are state-owned or private is blurred in a number of cases where new business schools have been founded within existing state institutions. The scope and quality of management programs vary greatly (Veselov 1992a). Some schools are striving to develop high-quality, pedagogically sound programs, while others, primarily private consulting firms, offer lectures at high prices with more entertainment value than educational benefit. The characteristics of the top fifteen business schools in Russia as rated by a panel of experts at the newspaper *Finansovye izvestiia* in the fall of 1992 are listed in Table 8.2 (*"Finansovye izvestiia"* 1992).

State business schools are housed in universities and technical and economic institutes, as well as in training institutes affiliated with industries or large enterprises. A state business school typically has the legal status of a state enterprise. Each is self-financing and operates as a profit center, but receives buildings and some funds from the government. State-subsidized management training institutions were part of the highly developed management education network that existed during the Communist era. State institutions tend to be quite large, with tens of thousands of students, but the management schools housed in state institutions are in the fledgling stage and so far each has accepted an average of a few hundred students and has fewer than two dozen faculty. Many business schools began operations by offering management training for managers of state and private enterprises. Ranging from short one-day seminars to programs of several months, these programs set tuition high in response to heavy demand. A number of schools later began to develop five-year undergraduate business degree programs and one- or two-year graduate degree programs.

Among the private business schools are former state schools that had been privatized, as well as new schools that were created after private ownership was legalized. These vary in size, but most are still quite small due to their infancy. They typically have several hundred students enrolled and only a handful of full-time faculty supplemented by instructors hired on short-term contracts. The long-term strategies of a number of private business schools aim at making them permanent players in the delivery of management education and able to compete with state institutions.

Private consulting firms typically target working managers, and offer short seminars and training programs rather than full-time undergraduate or graduate education. One such company is Neuman Business School and Trade, founded in St. Petersburg by a Swedish academician and entrepreneur, whose firm also formed a joint venture with a Russian company in Iaroslavl that offers business training cruises, restores buildings, and trades a variety of goods (Okhotnikova 1992).

Table 8.2

The Top Fifteen Russian Business Schools in 1992

Rank	Name	Location	Number of Programs	Number of Students Trained Annually	Number of Faculty
1	International Business School (MGIMO)	Moscow	10	1,200	24
2	Graduate School of International Business, Academy of the National Economy	Moscow	8	600	16
3	International Management Institute (IMISP)	St. Petersburg	3	500	16
4	Higher Commercial School (MVES)	Moscow	6	450	12
5	Moscow International Financial-Banking School	Moscow	5	300	20
6	Lovanium International School of Management (LETI)	St. Petersburg	1	50	14
7	Center for Managers' Training, Plekhanov Institute of the National Economy	Moscow	4	250	6
8	Moscow International Business School (MIRBIS)	Moscow	6	350	6

	Name	City			
9	Russian Academy of Management	Moscow	n.a.[a]	n.a.	n.a.
10	Management Center, Ordzhonikidze University	Moscow	n.a.	n.a.	n.a.
11	Kaliningrad School of International Business	Kaliningrad	n.a.	n.a.	n.a.
12	Nizhegorodskii Institute of International Business	Nizhnii Novgorod	n.a.	n.a.	n.a.
13	Voronezh School of Entrepreneurs	Voronezh	n.a.	n.a.	n.a.
14	Moscow International School of Business for Industry and Science (MISBIS)	Moscow	4	120	6
15	International Center of Business Administration, Russian Diplomatic Academy	Moscow	4	250	10

Sources: "*Finansovye izvestiia* nazyvaiut piatnadtsat' luchshikh shkol biznesa" (1992). *Finansovye izvestiia*, no. 7 (10–16 December); "IBS MGIMO Survey on Business Schools in Russia (under contract with ILO." (1992). Unpublished report. Information collected by IBS MGIMO from official materials and conversations with deans and directors of business schools and training centers.

[a]n.a. = not available.

Financing

Sources of financing for business schools vary.[5] For example, Moscow State University School of Business Administration, which considers itself a state enterprise with the status of a profit center, receives half its funding from the government and half from its training program revenues. In contrast, the Graduate Business School for Foreign Tourism, which also calls itself a state enterprise, receives no state financing. The Moscow International School of Business for Industry and Science (MISBIS) was founded in 1992 as part of a joint stock company. Sixty percent of its funding comes from its training programs, and forty percent from the joint stock company MOST. The Russian Academy of Entrepreneurs, a private organization, depends on training program revenues for ninety percent of its income, with sponsors providing the remaining ten percent.

In finding ways to survive and grow, business schools became entrepreneurial, branching out into various business activities. For example, state schools leased classroom facilities to private management training firms at handsome rates. Some schools set up management consulting centers. Other schools, both state and private, created joint ventures with foreign partners who provide funding and technical expertise and share in the revenues from their management training programs. For example, The LETI-Lovanium International School of Management is a joint venture between St. Petersburg Electro-Technical Institute and Louvain University in Belgium. Similarly, the International Management Institute (IMISP) is a joint venture between St. Petersburg State University and Bocconi University in Milan, Italy. The Graduate School of International Business (MIRBIS) was created as a joint venture between the Plekhanov Institute of the National Economy (now the Russian Economic Academy) and the Economic Research Institute (NOMISMA) of Bologna, Italy, and has partnerships with a half-dozen European banks. These three business schools rank among the best in the country, according to a recent survey (see Table 8.2).

Faculty

The talent of its faculty is the primary resource of any educational institution. Business schools in Russia are faced with a twofold challenge here: the necessity to train their faculty in market-based management subjects and to offer them sufficient, competitive salaries so that they will not leave for more lucrative teaching and consulting opportunities.

Faculty members in state business schools are predominantly individuals who were hired prior to the political and educational reforms. Most were tenured and had job security, but were trained in disciplines such as Marxist economics and central planning systems that are unrelated to market-oriented management. Most of their expertise is in the theoretical aspects of economics and planning, and few have had practical experience in industrial or other enterprises. One Russian critic charged that many state business schools were "academically parochial and unable to develop a 'tough' culture of demanding excellence" (Panevin et al. 1992, p. 7). This situation resulted from "a system of easy tenure, automatic salary increases, unfinished Ph.D.s, and undemanding academic norms" (Panevin et al. 1992, p. 7). Other causes include low salaries and few rewards for excellent performance.

Private business schools face the same problem of finding faculty with expertise in market-based management, although they are not encumbered by instructors unwilling or unable to be retrained. Their strategy is to attract talented and qualified individuals, primarily from state schools, to work on contract. Both state and private business schools also hire experts and well-known individuals to teach as adjuncts in their management training programs at hourly rates that often exceed the monthly salary of full-time state-employed faculty.

Faculty Training

Since state business schools are required to retain existing faculty, various methods are being used to retrain them, including in-house training programs and study abroad. In 1990, for instance, six instructors at Moscow State University's School of Management were sent abroad for training: three to the United States, two to the IBM corporate training center in Brussels, Belgium, and one to the Institute for Management Development (IMD) in Lausanne, Switzerland (Vikhanskii 1992).

Some efforts to retrain faculty members have been undertaken with Western assistance. In 1991, the European Community spent more than fifty million ECUs in training faculty members in the republics of the former Soviet Union (Veselov 1992c), and U.S. government agencies such as the United States Information Agency have funded travel for Russian and American faculty to collaborate on course development.

U.S. participation in the retraining of Russian faculty includes an ambitious program sponsored by a consortium of five leading U.S. business schools. In 1991, Harvard University, Massachusetts Institute of Technology, Northwestern University, Stanford University, and the Wharton School at the University of Pennsylvania collaborated to create the Central and Eastern European Teachers Program, a two-year course designed to train a hundred faculty members, including several Russians from the Academy of the National Economy ("Central and Eastern European" 1991). After preliminary study of management topics in their home countries, the participants spent seven weeks in a general management program for faculty at Harvard Business School in the summer of 1992. Back in their home countries for the next year, they engaged in teaching, field research, case writing, and course development. In the summer of 1993, they returned to one of the five universities for a six-week program in a management specialization (e.g., strategic management or organizational behavior). The program was designed to "give a little topspin" (Sasser 1992) to retraining initiatives in the participants' home countries, with the idea that the greatest part of the effort and responsibility rested with the individuals themselves. Those who went through the program were described as "raw intellectual horsepower and spongelike in their desire to learn everything."[6] However, many of them admitted that it would be a challenge to change their teaching styles from lecturing to the interactive case discussion method they were exposed to in the program.

Training of faculty is a costly and time-consuming endeavor. The most successful programs are, of course, quite expensive. For example, the Central and Eastern European Teachers Program cost $25,000 per participant for tuition, room and board, and other expenses. The consortium of U.S. universities provided funding for the initial $3.5 million cost and hoped to raise additional funds from external sources to continue the program (Bradley 1992). Nonetheless, it is more cost-effective to train faculty abroad than managers, because each faculty member can subsequently teach dozens of managers and students.[7] The speed with which faculty can be trained in market-based management heavily depends on the funding available, as well as the willingness of foreign business schools to devote the time and effort to training their Russian counterparts.

Faculty Salaries

There is a wide disparity between faculty salaries in state and private business schools. Salaries in state business schools are set at such a low level that holding onto the best faculty is a critical problem. By contrast, private business schools and private management training firms are free to hire anyone at any salary. These schools have only a few full-time faculty members and rely heavily on part-time instructors. Many of these part-time teachers also have full-time appointments at state schools or training organizations in enterprises or industrial ministries and command premium rates as lecturers in private training programs. Affiliation with a prominent business school can provide access to lucrative consulting opportunities. For instance, in mid-1992 the prestigious state business school, the Academy of the National Economy, was restricted to paying its faculty members 3,000 rubles *a month*, not much more than the average national monthly wage then. Yet some of these faculty members also earned 1,500 rubles *an hour* as consultants for a large enterprise.[8]

Programs and Curricula

Most business schools, public and private, began their operations by offering management training to working managers. Programs ranged from general or single-subject seminars lasting a few hours to courses covering a variety of subjects and lasting several weeks or months. These programs commanded a high price and were profitable as long as a steady stream of managers could be attracted to them. Some schools offered programs in general management, while others catered to more specialized groups. IMISP in St. Petersburg offered several business programs in 1992: foreign trade in the market economy (four weeks, twenty students); management (two weeks, twenty students); and strategic management and marketing (two weeks, twenty students). Specialized business schools include the Graduate School of International Tourism in Moscow, which in 1992 offered courses in management in international tourism (five weeks, twenty students), accounting (four weeks, fifteen students), business law (four weeks, twenty students), and international finance (two weeks, twenty students), as well as a guide and translators program (four weeks, thirty students). Another specialized school is the Graduate School of Marketing (VNIIKS) in Moscow. In 1992, it offered a four-week program, called Marketing in Russia, to twenty participants.

An innovative program to train entrepreneurs has been developed by Professor Iurii Ekaterinoslavskii of the Russian Academy of Entrepreneurship (Ekaterinoslavskii 1992). His three-step program has the goals of developing the complete individual and promoting "civilized" entrepreneurship. In the first step, participants are given a battery of psychological tests. This is followed by a course designed to root out stereotyping and dysfunctional behavior through exercises, business games, and role-playing. In the third step, participants learn the skills and attitudes required to be an entrepreneur, and are also given instruction in physical fitness and stress management.

Another innovative program was initiated by the Russian Foreign Economic School in 1992. In addition to its regular curriculum, the school began to offer a distance learning program. Every two weeks, it broadcasts a series of business modules over the Youth radio station throughout the former Soviet Union. Modules have been developed on negotiations, human resource management, information management, financial management, and sales and service. Each module is accompanied by audiocassettes, workbooks, and readings. Certificates and diplomas are awarded upon successful completion of one or several modules.

By 1990, a number of business schools had begun to establish degree programs, including five-year undergraduate and one- and two-year graduate programs. Most were modeled after similar programs in the United States and Europe. In 1992, the Moscow Commercial University, under the Committee of Higher Education of Russia, offered four different five-year programs—management, trade, finance, and foreign economic relations—each having twenty to thirty students. Similarly, Moscow State University School of Management and the International Business School (MGIMO) both initiated five-year undergraduate programs in 1993. The ten modules comprising the undergraduate program of MGIMO, the top-ranked business school in Russia, are listed in Table 8.3.

Other degree programs have been launched in collaboration with foreign business schools. The Moscow Institute of Electronic Technology in Zelinograd, Moscow's equivalent of Boston's "Route 128" region of high-technology industry and educational institutions, established an undergraduate management program in collaboration with the University of Tulsa and welcomed an entering class of forty-seven in the fall of 1992. An MBA program was planned for 1993. The Academy of the National Economy in Moscow developed a one-year MBA program modeled after the Sloan Fellows Program at the Massachusetts Institute of Technology. Moscow State University's School of Management also plans to develop a one-year MBA program. In 1992, with funding from the United States Information Agency, the University of Pittsburgh collaborated with St. Petersburg State University to establish undergraduate and graduate programs. A number of other U.S. and European business schools are engaged in similar partnerships.

Typical courses include marketing, accounting, finance, organizational behavior, economics, management, and international business. Yet faculty

Table 8.3

Curriculum of a Four-Year Undergraduate Management Program in 1993 (Ten modules)

1. Management
   Includes principles of management and human resources management

2. Marketing
   Includes marketing research, environmental analysis, and corporate international marketing policy

3. Finance and Accounting
   Includes corporate investment strategy

4. Macroeconomics and Microeconomics
   Includes general rules of market development and behavior of individual players in the market

5. Business law
   Includes Russian law and international law

6. Management Information Systems, Mathematics, and Statistics
   Applied focus, includes processing economic information, mathematical analysis and forecasting, and training in the use of personal computers

7. Psychology

8. Sociology

9. Philosophy

10. English

Source: A. Manukovskii (1992). Dean, International Business School, MGIMO, interviewed by I. Chekinev, "Menedzher dlia novoi Rossii," *Vremia Moskovskoe*, pp. 14–16. Curriculum of the four-year undergraduate program at the International Business School (MGIMO), Moscow.

members have experienced difficulty in grasping some of these new concepts because they lack familiarity with market-based management. At the Harvard Business School faculty training program in 1992, the "conditioning of living in a planned economy" (Piper 1992) was evident in the logic that Russian participants used in a discussion of how prices would be affected as an industry reached full production capacity. In free markets, prices increase because of constraints on supply; but some participants reasoned that prices would drop because fixed costs could be spread over a larger volume. Cultural and economic differences also created bewilderment about the attention devoted in some U.S. business courses to seemingly irrelevant or trivial issues. For example, a Russian enrolled in Northeastern University's MBA program in Boston was amazed that his marketing class spent two hours discussing whether to sell deodorized socks in packages of two or four. He could not imagine such a discussion taking place in the shortage-plagued Russian economy (Shekshnia 1992). Russian executives, too, have been surprised at the differences they have observed in the managerial role of their Western counterparts. One Siberian company president who studied in Germany in 1989 was impressed by the extent to which senior executives in the West delegated responsibility for many important short-term operational matters in order to devote more of their time to strategic, long-term business issues (Kaniskin 1992).

Methodology

Russian educators have condemned the educational system that functioned during the Soviet regime as "a school of emasculation of creativity" (Korkhov 1991, p. 87). Traditionally, the lecture format was the predominant pedagogical method, and subject matter was taught from a theoretical and abstract perspective. Classroom protocol demanded that instructors prevent their authority from being challenged, that they maintain a formal distance from students, and that they present students with definitive answers.

Along with Western-style curricula, the new Russian business schools have adopted new teaching methods. A number of faculty have begun developing new materials and using the case discussion method, role-playing and experiential exercises, and computerized business simulations. Building a set of market-oriented management materials adapted to the Russian context is a slow and difficult process. A small number of Western business textbooks have been translated into Russian, but this is not a permanent solution for business and pedagogical reasons. From a business perspective, it is not currently feasible for Western publishers to target the Russian market because profits cannot easily be realized in hard currency. Some books, such as a Russian translation of an accounting text published by Houghton Mifflin Company, were subsidized by international agencies such as the United Nations and the United States Agency for International Development. From a pedagogical perspective, it is more expedient if Russian management educators prepare new material by adapting market-based business techniques and cases to Russian conditions. The European Foundation for Entrepreneurship Research (EFER) is one organization that has provided funding to Russian management faculty to develop case materials. In addition, some Russian management faculty are writing books to fill the need. For example, Professors Oleg Vikhanskii and Aleksandr Naumov from the School of Management at Moscow State University have written a management textbook that adapts Western management theory and practice to the Russian context.

Although many case studies, experiential exercises, and business simulations in Russian schools are now being patterned on Western practice, an indigenous form of such activities has been in existence since the late 1970s. Newly developed business games appear regularly in educational journals (e.g., *Kentavr* and *Professional*). The open game, for example, is a uniquely Russian technique used to solve complex, weakly structured problems that have no ready solutions, such as the problem posed by a polluting factory that is the primary employer in a town (Dudchenko 1990; Zhezhko 1992; Walck 1993). Open games are conducted by skilled facilitators in isolated settings and can last from several days to several weeks. Game participants represent different groups with different views of the issue. The goal of the game is to bring about deep personal, organizational, and social transformation by having participants question their values and show self-determination, responsibility, and openness in solving the problem.

Other games and simulations have been developed by Russian management consultants to bring about change in organizations (Prigozhin 1992; Rapoport 1992). Goals include increasing the involvement in decision making by employees at all levels and encouraging cross-functional collaboration in problem solving. Other experiential exercises and role plays have been developed for use in management training programs and management assessment centers. Innovative techniques include "paratheater," a sophisticated role play in which the manager plays the roles of scriptwriter, director, and manager. "Dueling" is an exercise in which participants take turns being the boss and exercising power (Tarasov 1992).

Some faculty have expressed reluctance to use more interactive methods due to their own inexperience, and an anticipated resistance from students who have been accustomed to a passive learning environment (Hemp 1992; Manukovskii 1992). Yet many of those who have personally participated in interactive learning have found it to be a highly effective way to develop an understanding of a subject. For example, senior executives from the Russian Ministry of the Aviation Industry competed in a computerized marketing strategy game, BRANDMAPS, during their training program at California State University at Hayward in 1989 (Wiley et al. 1992). The simulation gave them the opportunity to see the results of their decisions in a concrete demonstration of the workings of the market economy. Such hands-on learning experiences are crucial for accelerating the accumulation of knowledge about the market economy. Having lived exclusively in a centrally planned economy, most Russians lack free-market experience and a concomitant intuition for market transactions, the foundations upon which business education in the West builds.[9]

There are signs, however, that the game movement may be losing popularity in some circles. Some people have predicted that recent attempts to formalize and institutionalize the open game movement will lead to its demise, since open games depend on spontaneity for their survival (Zhezhko 1992). Others believe that the time for games and simulations has ended. Such games, they contend, are no longer necessary under the new political and economic conditions in which people are free to experiment directly in real-life situations where there are many serious economic and managerial problems that need immediate attention.[10]

Clientele for Business Education

Four important kinds of clientele that have special needs for business education are managers of state enterprises, entrepreneurs, women, and young people.

Managers of State Enterprises

Managers of state enterprises were the first customers for market-based management education. Training programs were quickly developed for them after the passage of the 1988 Law on Soviet State Enterprises. These managers wanted to learn how to exercise their increased decision-making authority (Ivancevich et al. 1992; McCarthy and Puffer 1992) in order to make their enterprises profitable either as state-owned or privatized organizations. Before the economy disintegrated into chaos in 1992, many enterprises were able to afford the high prices charged for management training, and business schools derived high revenues from training working enterprise managers. Demand decreased in 1992 as many enterprises faced financial crises and insolvency when prices were freed and inflation became rampant.

Entrepreneurs

The growing ranks of entrepreneurs were also prime customers for training in market-based management. By the end of 1991, there were 110,000 privately owned companies in the former USSR (*Pravitel'stvennyi* 1992). Further, one-quarter of respondents in a 1991 survey said they would "try to start an individual economic activity" if they lost their job in the state sector (Chernina 1991). In 1992, more than 46,000 enterprises were wholly or partially privatized in Russia, half of them in the last quarter of the year, suggesting that the pace would accelerate. Most of the privatized enterprises at that time were small businesses, and 80 percent were involved in retail trade and services. However, by the end of 1992, the number of privatized enterprises comprised only 6 percent of all Russian industry.

Founders of private companies tended to be younger, better educated, and more inclined toward risk and change than state managers were (McCarthy et al. 1993; Shama 1993). They were willing to pay high tuition for business training in anticipation of increasing their profits by applying their newly acquired knowledge in their businesses. However, the 1992 economic crisis prevented or discouraged some entrepreneurs from taking the new courses.

Women

The special needs of women in business education have political, economic, and social origins (Puffer 1994). Politically, women have not been well represented in the power structures of organizations. This has resulted in a low rate of sponsorship by enterprises of women employees in management training programs. The desperate economic conditions in the country have had particularly dire consequences for women. They have been hit hard with unemployment. As many as 80 percent of the unemployed in 1992 were women, who had occupied most of the administrative support positions in organizations that were downsized or eliminated. Women also suffer greatly from inflation because their wages are considerably lower than men's.

Social factors have hampered women's careers in business and management. There is great social pressure for women to stay home and take care of their families; career women suffer from discrimination and the effects of unflattering stereotypes. Although a small number of women have succeeded in enrolling in business schools, others have turned to newly founded organizations such as *Gil'diia* (Guild), that provide training for women who want to start their own businesses (Levine 1991/1992).

Young People

Young people of college age were the last group to be targeted for management education. The major reason was economic. This group could not afford to pay the high tuition charged by private business schools. State schools, too, had become self-financing, and needed to focus their efforts on training working managers in order to build up revenues. As described earlier, business education became available for more college-age students in 1992 and 1993 when a number of state and private business schools began offering full-time undergraduate and graduate programs. Unfortunately, tuition for these was costly. For instance, annual tuition at MGIMO was $2,000 (not rubles), making the program accessible only to a select few (Manukovskii 1992). Applicants were expected to find themselves corporate sponsors to finance their education. Ideally, the school would like to find its own sponsor who would finance its budget and enable it to offer free tuition to all. Another option pursued by a fortunate few students is to study in the West. For example, since 1990 Northeastern University in Boston has provided full scholarships for four students from Moscow State University to get an MBA degree.

Social as well as economic realities have dampened the interest of some young people in business education. While high-quality business schools have had little trouble recruiting academically oriented students, other young people would rather start doing business immediately than going to school. Some have been hired by foreign joint ventures such as McDonald's Restaurant and Pizza Hut, and received intensive and systematic on-the-job training in Western business practices (Vikhanskii and Steeves 1992). Other enterprising teenagers have discovered ways of making money with little or no capital by washing cars and delivering fast food, or by working for private firms that value their initiative and hard work (Auerbach 1993). Some have earned income far in excess of their parents and have begun supporting them. This situation has arisen even in families where the parents were talented academics and professionals employed in state institutions. These young self-made businesspeople may turn to more formal management education in the future, either to help them manage their growing businesses or to enable them to pursue careers in other organizations.

Efforts have also been directed toward teaching young children about business. Initiatives include visits from members of "Business Kids," an American organization that promotes entrepreneurship and business education for children. Additionally, individuals at Moscow State University organized a children's business newspaper, and a woman in Syktivkar founded an after-school program to teach children about entrepreneurship. These efforts are in sharp contrast to the child-rearing practices of the Communist period, when parents wanted their children to enjoy a carefree childhood and did not encourage them to be independent or to do chores to earn spending money. Many Russians have predicted that it will take at least a generation for Russian society to develop a more positive attitude about private enterprise and a market-based economy. Business education targeted at young children is a promising, long-term way of achieving such a social change.

The Future of Management Education

A Critical Time of Competition and Collaboration

Management education in Russia is at a critical point. The proliferation of business schools of all shapes and sizes over the past several years has given management education a high profile in Russian society. Not surprisingly, it has also become a highly controversial issue. As much as the new business schools have been hailed by market-oriented liberals as a solution for Russia's economic ills, so have they been condemned by conservatives as a threat to the stability that had been provided by central planning and communism.

Management education has entered a new phase. The start-up phase has drawn to a close and a shake-out has begun. Purveyors of management education must both compete and collaborate to survive as long-term players. Schools must compete among themselves to meet the needs of students. As consumers of business education become more discerning, they will support schools that have a reputation for high-quality programs that provide practical tools to conduct business in a market economy. Schools that fail to develop a sound strategic plan and secure the resources necessary to provide high-quality education will not survive over the long term.

Business schools must also collaborate with each other to define the field of management education, to establish procedures, and to set academic and institutional standards. The first major step toward collaboration took the form of a Moscow conference organized in October 1992 by MGIMO in cooperation with the Russian International Association of Schools of Business, the Russian Union of Industrialists and Entrepreneurs, the European Fund for Management Development, and the American Assembly of Collegiate Schools of Business. More than two hundred and twenty representatives from a hundred business schools in the former USSR, as well as fifty management educators from twelve other countries, discussed such issues as business school accreditation procedures, the role of the state in regulating and supporting business education, support from other countries, and ways of driving out programs of low quality (Mikhal'chuk 1992; Veselov 1992b and 1992c).

Potential Impacts on the Economy, Politics, and Society

Depending on the form it takes, management education has the potential to make a significant positive or negative impact on the economic, political, and social landscape.

A pessimistic scenario holds that business schools may come to be viewed in a negative light and have a negative impact if they fail to develop ethical standards for their own conduct and for that of their graduates; or if they fail to train managers well enough and quickly enough to make a measurable difference in the economic performance of the country. If "wild capitalism" *(dikii kapitalizm)* overtakes the country, some individuals could accumulate wealth at the expense of the average citizen, creating wide economic disparities and upsetting the norms of social justice that value collectivism (and "equal poverty for all") over individualism. Public resentment has already been directed toward the *nouveaux-riches*, and the crime and corruption which Russians associate with the accumulation of wealth have exacerbated negative public sentiment.

Business schools could bring about additional social imbalances with exclusionary admissions policies, creating an elite group skilled in the mechanisms of the market economy. In turn, business schools could become the scapegoat upon which the government could lay the blame for a failed transition to a market economy, for growing social inequality, or for the infiltration of the country by unsavory foreign influences. The government could appease those factions who want to return to central planning and socialism by shutting down business schools and punishing those who had the greatest visibility and involvement.

More optimistically, business schools in Russia have the potential to create a new economic infrastructure by teaching people how to privatize state organizations, start their own businesses, and design reward and control systems that foster productive work behavior and a healthy economy.

Business schools could also affect decision making in the political arena. Schools could form consortia to lobby the government to improve business education by providing financial aid to students and grants to support business schools, as well as by giving tax incentives to enterprises that support business education. Business school alumni could also form interest groups to influence government policy on the promotion and funding of business education.

Finally, business schools could play a central role in the transformation of social attitudes toward the market economy and capitalism. A number of schools market their programs as "civilized" entrepreneurship (Ekaterinoslavskii 1992) and "civilized" management (Manukovskii 1992) to assure the public of their honorable intentions and their dissociation from the negative connotations of business. Also on the positive side was a conference on business ethics organized in June 1993 by six leading business schools and associations and spearheaded by the Academy of the National Economy. Other steps that schools could take include engaging in public service campaigns to educate the general population about the positive aspects of ambition, individualism, and initiative. In addition, respected faculty members and graduates of business schools could lead by example with volunteer work to help solve serious social problems such as drug abuse and homelessness.

Conclusion

It is easy to be pessimistic about market-based management education in Russia. Too many people need to be trained, including both those who cannot easily let go of the old ways and those who want to do new things immediately without taking the time to learn the appropriate ways. Too few faculty are qualified to teach market-based management. Too few resources, including books, buildings, and computers, are available. And there is too much social and political resistance to a market economy to make for the easy delivery and ready acceptance of management education.

Yet, as this chapter has shown, there are reasons for optimism. A large number of initiatives have been undertaken in an astonishingly short time. Business schools have found enough funding to get started; training of faculty members has begun; new curricula and teaching methods have been developed; and there is a large demand for management training. Successful development of market-based management education in Russia will depend on allocation of the requisite resources to faculty, administrators, and students who are both talented and dedicated to high-quality market-based management education.

Notes

I would like to express my appreciation to Professors Oleg Vikhanskii and Aleksandr Naumov of Moscow State University's School of Business Administration for their advice and support, and to Tatiana Kozlova for the research assistance she provided in the preparation of this chapter.

1. In 1985 the percentage of managers with degrees from five-year programs in institutes and universities was as follows: managers and deputy managers of enterprises, institutions, and organizations—69 percent; managers of service and other facilities—39 percent; managers of departments and bureaus—70 percent; chief specialists—69 percent; head bookkeepers—23 percent; chiefs of shops, shifts, farm sections—28 percent; foremen—24 percent; work superintendents—38 percent (*Sbornik statisticheskikh materialov*, 1987).

2. For a description of a typical management development program for middle-level managers in the early 1980s, see Puffer (1981).

3. For a description of management training at various types of institutes in the educational hierarchy, see Zhuplev (1992), and McNulty and Katkov (1992).

4. The term, cooperative (*kooperativ*), adopted by the Soviet government to denote private enterprises, is no longer in use. It was meant to make private economic activity compatible with socialist ideology by suggesting that such activity did not exploit labor. For a comprehensive discussion of the cooperative movement, see Jones and Moskoff (1991).

5. Tatiana Kozlova and I obtained this information on funding sources directly from the business schools in a survey we conducted in November 1992.

6. B. Shapiro, Professor of Marketing, Harvard Business School, Boston, Massachusetts. Personal communication, 20 October 1992.

7. It cost between $7,000 and $8,000 to train each senior executive from the former Soviet Union who attended the one-month Fuqua School of Business program at Duke University in Durham, North Carolina (Puffer 1992). A number of industrial ministries and enterprises paid in hard currency to send some of their managers abroad for training. For example, in 1989 the Ministry of the Aviation Industry sent three groups of managers for four months to three universities: Northeastern University (McCarthy 1991), California State University at Hayward (Wiley et al. 1992), and Oklahoma City University.

8. E. Lobanova, Professor of Management, Academy of the National Economy, Moscow. Personal communication, August 1992.

9. B. Shapiro, Professor of Marketing, Harvard Business School, Boston, Massachusetts. Personal communication, 20 October 1992.

10. C. Walck, Associate Professor of Management, Michigan Technical University, Houghton, Michigan. Personal communication, 8 December 1992.

References

Auerbach, J. (1993). "Coming of Age in Capitalistic Russia," *The Boston Sunday Globe*. 4 January, pp. 20, 21.

Bradley, D. (1992). "Studying the Language of Capitalism," *Harvard University Gazette*, 24 July, pp. 3, 13.

"Central and Eastern European Teachers Program" (1991). Unpublished document. Boston, MA: Harvard Business School, September.

Chernina, N. (1991). "Micro and Macro Socioeconomic Changes in the USSR," *The International Executive*, vol. 33, no. 3, pp. 12–17.

Connor, W.D. (1991). "Equality of Opportunity." In A. Jones, W.D. Connor, and D.E. Powell, eds., *Soviet Social Problems*. Boulder, CO: Westview, pp. 137–53.

Dudchenko, V.S. (1990). "Igrovye metody v sotsiologii" (Game Methods in Sociology), *Sotsiologicheskie issledovaniia*, vol. 12. pp. 103–12.

Economic Newsletter (1993). Cambridge, MA: Russian Research Center, Harvard University. vol. 16, no. 6 (20 February).

Ekaterinoslavskii, I. (1992). "Diagnosis, Destruction, and Creation: A New Conception of Training Managers for the Market Economy." In S.M. Puffer, ed., *The Russian Management Revolution: Preparing Managers for the Market Economy.* Armonk, NY: M.E. Sharpe, pp. 149–57.

"*Finansovye izvestiia* nazyvaiut piatnadtsat' luchikh Rossiiskikh shkol biznesa" *(Financial News* Names the Fifteen Top Russian Business Schools) (1992). *Finansovye izvestiia*. vol. 7, 10 December.

Hemp, P. (1992). "Readying for Market Economy," *The Boston Globe*, 9 July, pp. 29, 30.

Hollander, P. (1991). "Politics and Social Problems." In A. Jones et al. *Soviet Social Problems*, pp. 9–23.

Ivancevich, J.M., DeFrank, R.S., and Gregory, P.R. (1992). "The Soviet Enterprise Director: An Important Resource Before and After the Coup," *The Academy of Management Executive*, vol. 6, no. 1, pp. 42–55.

Jones, A. and Moskoff, W. (1991). *Ko-ops: The Rebirth of Entrepreneurship in the Soviet Union*. Bloomington: Indiana University Press.

Kaniskin, N. (1992). "The Western Executive and the Soviet Executive." In S.M. Puffer, ed., *Russian Management Revolution*, pp. 41–51.

Korkhov, I. (1991). Cited in V. Krasnov, *Russia Beyond Communism*. Boulder, CO: Westview Press, p. 87.

Levine, J. (1991/1992). "Enterprising Woman," *Moscow Magazine*. December 1991/January 1992, p. 7.

Manukovskii, A. (1992). Interviewed by I. Chekinev in "Menedzher dlia Novoi Rossii" (Managers for the New Russia), *Vremia Moskovskoe*, pp. 14–16.

McCarthy, D.J. (1991). "Developing a Programme for Soviet Managers," *Journal of Management Development*, vol. 10, no. 5, pp. 26–31.

McCarthy, D.J., and Puffer, S.M. (1992). "Perestroika at the Plant Level: Managers' Job Attitudes and Views of Decision Making in the Former USSR," *Columbia Journal of World Business*, vol. 27, no. 1, pp. 86–99.

McCarthy, D.J., Puffer, S.M., and Shekshnia, S.V. (1993). "The Resurgence of an Entrepreneurial Class in Russia," *Journal of Management Inquiry*, vol. 2, no. 2, pp. 125–37.

McNulty, N.G., and Katkov, A. (1992). "Management Education in Eastern Europe: 'Fore and After," *Academy of Management Executive*, vol. 6, no. 4, pp. 78–87.

Mikhal'chuk, A. (1992). "*Kontseptsii net, no vse dovol'ny*" (No Concepts, but Everybody's Happy), *Kommersant*, vol. 7, 14 October.

Okhotnikova, V. (1992). "Swedish Firm to Train Russian Business People," *Business World*, 1 December, p. 3.

Panevin, Y.L., Rinefort, F.C., and Payne, S.L. (1992). "East-West Cooperation on Russian Management Development: Russian Views and a U.S. Response," *Journal of Business Affairs*, vol. 18, no. 2. pp. 5–9.

Piper, T. (1992). Cited in P. Hemp (1992).

Pravitel'stvennyi vestnik (Government Review). (1992). 22 January.

Prigozhin, A.I. (1992). "Game Methods of Collective Decision Making in Management Consulting." In S.M. Puffer, ed., *Russian Management Revolution*, pp. 100–120.

Puffer, S.M. (1981). "Inside a Soviet Management Institute," *California Management Review*, vol. 24, no. 1, pp. 90–96.

———. (1992). "The Fuqua School of Business Program for Soviet Executives." In S.M. Puffer, ed., *Russian Management Revolution*, pp. 227–33.

———. (1994). "Women Managers in the Former USSR: A Case of 'Too Much Equality'?" In N.J. Adler and D.N. Izraeli, eds., *Competitive Frontiers: Women Managers in a Global Economy*. Cambridge, MA: Blackwell, pp. 263–85.

Rapoport, V.S. (1992). "Managerial Diagnosis: Practical Experience and Recommendations." In S.M. Puffer, ed., *Russian Management Revolution*, pp. 83–99.

Sasser, E. (1992). Cited in P. Hemp, (1992).

Sbornik statisticheskikh materialov (Statistical Handbook) (1987). Moscow: Finansy i statistika, p. 50.

Shama, A. (1993). "Management Under Fire: The Transformation of Managers in the Soviet Union and Eastern Europe," *The Academy of Management Executive*, vol. 7, no. 1, pp. 22–35.

Shekshnia, S. (1992). "The American MBA Program: A Russian Student's View." In S.M. Puffer, ed., *Russian Management Revolution*, pp. 178–85.

Tarasov, V.K. (1992). "Personnel-Technology: The Selection and Training of Managers." In ibid., pp. 121–48.

Veselov, S. (1992a). "Shkoly biznesa: Kuda poiti uchit'sia?" (Business Schools: Where to Study?) *Biznes MN (Moskovskie novosti)*, vol. 14, April.

———. (1992b). "Vedushchie biznes-shkoly namereny postavit' zaslon khalture" (Leading Business Schools Intend to Drive Out Bad Quality) *Biznes MN (Moskovskie novosti)*, vol. 35, 23 September.

———. (1992c). "Biznes-obrazovanie v Rossii: Spros v 50 raz bol'she predlozheniia" (Business Education in Russia: Demand is Fifty Times Greater Than Supply), *Biznes MN (Moskovskie novosti)*, vol. 40, 28 October, p. 15.

Vikhanskii, O.S. (1992). "Let's Train Managers for the Market Economy." In S.M. Puffer, ed., *Russian Management Revolution*, pp. 33–40.

Vikhanskii, O.S. and Steeves, G. (1992). "'Doing It All For You' At Moscow McDonald's." In ibid., pp. 274–81.

Walck, C.L. (1993). "Organization Development in the USSR: An Overview and a Case Example," *Journal of Managerial Psychology*, vol. 8, no. 2.

Wiley, D.L., Kamath, S.J., and MacNab, B. (1992). " 'Sedpro': Three Soviet Executive Development Programs at California State University at Hayward." In S.M. Puffer, ed., *Russian Management Revolution*, pp. 201–20.

Zhezhko, I.V. (1992). "Open Games as a Method of Personal Transformation and Motivation." In ibid., pp. 158–77.

Zhuplev, A.V. (1992). "Management Education in a Time of Change." In ibid., pp. 11–26.

9

Reforming Medical Education in Russia

JULIE V. BROWN AND NINA L. RUSINOVA

The training of modern medical practitioners is a complex, time consuming, and inherently expensive endeavor. Societies have chosen to organize the process in a variety of ways; however, the nature and importance of the task are such that commonalities exist in spite of differences in socio-cultural, economic, and political environments. Medical training entails not only mastery of theoretical knowledge but of technical and interpersonal skills as well. Medical techniques are often difficult to learn, and they can change with startling rapidity. Even more significant, most skills can be attained only through hands-on experience, which at some point necessarily involves practicing on living human beings. Thus the education of medical practitioners raises a host of ethical concerns in addition to its other complexities.

Our goal in this chapter is to examine some aspects of medical education in contemporary Russia, focusing on recent efforts to reform the system of medical education and some of the obstacles to their realization. The Russian health-care system, like others, employs a variety of practitioners, each of whom undergoes some type of formal training. Our analysis is limited almost exclusively to the undergraduate training of physicians.

While the overall structure of undergraduate (and graduate) medical education in Russia has remained fundamentally unaltered for the past century and a half, during the Soviet period there were changes in both the length and the content of the training as well as in the numbers of students receiving medical education. Recurring dissatisfaction with the quality of physicians has periodically generated proposals for reforming the process of selecting, training, and evaluating students. Some of these concerns, as well as the proposed solutions, are more or less specific to the Soviet and Russian contexts; others reflect recurring dilemmas in the education of modern medical personnel, which are evident both throughout Russian and Soviet history and in medical education in other societies as well.

The Context of Medical Education Reform in Russia

Since the mid-1980s, discussions of the need to change the system of medical education have taken place within the larger context of the shortcomings of the health-care system as a whole. Most recently, the discussions have also reflected the budget crisis in post-Soviet Russia and the anticipated transition from a centrally organized and funded system of state medicine to a system based on medical insurance, changes which will undoubtedly affect the providers as well as the consumers of health care.

The first comprehensive proposals for reform of the Soviet health-care system were placed on the table during the late 1980s. These efforts were spearheaded by E.I. Chazov, a cardiologist who was minister of health for several years during the Gorbachev era. Chazov was not the first minister of health to suggest that change was necessary; however, it was during his tenure that the initial phases of a broad-based perestroika of the health care system were undertaken. Focusing on the effects of declining resources and an incentive system which stressed quantity over quality, Chazov's widely publicized critique of the Soviet health-care system was scathing. In a series of interviews in 1987 he drew the nation's attention to its shortcomings and promised systematic efforts at reform.

Compared with other industrialized nations, Chazov pointed out, the Soviet Union was spending a very small percentage of its national budget on health care. Even more significant, the percentage had been declining: from 4.1 percent in 1970 to 4 percent in 1987. Before the end of the decade, the percentage was expected to fall even lower.[1] The consequences of inadequate funding, he maintained, were evident throughout the system, including in programs of medical education.

Chazov also stressed the negative repercussions of an incentive system, which allocated rewards on the basis of size rather than quality of output. In an interview in *Literaturnaia gazeta* in April 1987, he cited numerous examples to illustrate the scope of the problem (Galaeva 1987). According to the minister, the system encouraged the addition of hospital beds with little regard for whether or not they were needed, or for medical and sanitary norms. It also resulted in a disproportionate expenditure on bricks and mortar for construction instead of essential modern medical equipment. Polyclinic budgets were based on the number of patient visits without regard for the quality of care they provided, and medical research institutes, many of them unproductive, continued to proliferate. In the case of medical education, Chazov contended, the results were similar: a greater emphasis was placed on the number of graduating students rather than on the level of their competence. Chazov's negative assessment of the existing state of medical education was part and parcel of the larger concerns about Soviet medical care as a whole, and many of its shortcomings were attributed to problems inherent to the system itself.

In the fall of 1987, the Central Committee of the Communist Party and the Council of Ministers approved a broadly based plan to restructure the Soviet health-care system. Entitled "Basic guidelines for developing protection of the population's health and for restructuring the USSR's health service during the twelfth five-year plan and for the period up to the year 2000," the document included a number of measures designed to upgrade the training of medical personnel (*Osnovnie napravleniia* 1987). Unionwide discussions of the proposed changes revealed widespread dissatisfaction with the existing state of affairs and in particular with medical personnel. According to one summary report in *Pravda*, almost one-third of the letters the newspaper received on the subject expressed concern about the qualifications of medical workers (Shchepin 1987).

The initial intent was to phase in several of the changes in medical education immediately, with the beginning of the 1988–89 academic year. In the short run, however, inertia prevailed, and little change occurred. In the years since the Soviet plan was first approved, the context within which the Russian health-care system functions has changed dramatically. The break-up of the USSR has altered the operation of what was formerly a Unionwide system. The consequences have been far-reaching, affecting even medical students, many of whom were enrolled in medical institutes outside of their native republics. Even more significant, the effects of the general budget crisis and concomitant transition toward more decentralized decision making and market-based economic structures have resonated throughout the health-care system. The system of medical education has been no more immune to these events than any other sector of the health-care system, nor indeed of the society as a whole. As we shall see, the momentous transformation which Russian society is currently experiencing has brought some unanticipated changes to medical education, while the persistence of organizational structures and entrenched interests has retarded the implementation of many preexisting plans for reform.

Problem Areas and Proposals for Reform of Medical Education

Student Recruitment

Medicine has never been the elite profession in Russia that it is in many other societies. The relatively modest social origins of prerevolutionary physicians by comparison with those of other professional groups has been well documented by social historians (Frieden 1981; Leikina-Svirskaia 1971). Perhaps the most significant change in the Soviet period was the dramatic increase in the number of women entering the medical profession, a result on the one hand of women's greater access to medical education and on the other of an occupational reward structure which encouraged men to enter other fields (Field 1957; 1967; Fitzpatrick 1979).

In recent years, however, those involved in the training of medical cadres have been greatly concerned over the level of commitment among the young people who become students in Russian medical institutes. Interest in this problem predates the Gorbachev-era proposals for medical perestroika. Michael Ryan (1990, p. 49), for example, has cited studies from the 1970s which indicated that as many as 30 percent of students enrolled in medical institutes at that time were uninterested in careers in medicine. One group of critics in the early 1980s asserted that this lack of motivation could be explained at least in part by the fact that entrance exams for medical institutes were held later in the summer than were those for many other institutes of higher learning. As a result, some students who did not gain admission to the institution and academic program of their first choice subsequently took and passed the entrance exams for medical institutes, rather than waiting a year to try again for admission to the program of their first choice (Ibid., p. 50). That such "by-default" medical students would be less than enthusiastic about their new studies is hardly surprising.

A variety of strategies have been suggested in recent years to deal with the problem of low student motivation. They include proposals that would both discourage individuals from selecting medical training without adequate reflection and stimulate interest among those who might already be inclined toward medicine. In the early 1980s, it was proposed that each aspiring physician be required to work for a year as an orderly in a hospital or polyclinic prior to admission to formal medical training (Ibid., pp.

50–51). In the reformers' view, this approach would both deter the un-committed as well as provide the added benefit of helping to staff medical institutions on evenings and weekends.

The 1987 proposals for medical perestroika also included changes in recruitment procedures. As was true of previous measures, greater empha-sis was placed on the importance of practical experience before medi-cal training. Individuals who had worked in the health-care system were to be given priority in admissions to medical institutes, and special provisions were to be made for their training. There were even limits placed upon the number of students who could be accepted into medical institutes directly upon their graduation from general secondary schools. In the words of Chazov:

> [P]ride of place is given to young men and women who have done at least two years' practical work in medical institutions. This period is enough to enable a young person, having chosen medicine as his vocation, to see if he has the stamina and compassion it requires (Chazov 1988, p. 29).

Chazov simultaneously announced plans for medically oriented secondary schools, which were to be established in Moscow and other major cities. The goals of these schools, according to the minister, were to give chil-dren the opportunity to develop practical medical experience by taking care of real patients and to help identify young people who demonstrated interest in, and talent for, medical careers.

Structure and Priorities in Medical Education

The basic structure of physician training in Russia has changed little since 1838. Regulations put into effect that year established a five-year se-quence of training at medical institutions throughout the Russian Empire (Frieden 1981, p. 30). The curriculum consisted of two years of study of the basic sciences (anatomy, physiology, pathology, etc.) followed by three years of training in the various clinical disciplines. While the content of the curriculum has changed significantly in response to advances in medical knowledge, the basic structure of medical training has not.

As is true in some West European countries, the training of physicians in Russia follows graduation from secondary school, and general educa-tion courses are included in the curriculum along with more narrowly focused training in scientific medical theory and practice. During the So-viet era, the period of training was lengthened from five to six years, with the final year being devoted to an internship (*internatura*) in a clinical setting. In recent decades, reformers have frequently discussed the advisability of adding yet another year to the curriculum in order to allow more time for in-depth study. The 1987 reform plan, in fact, dictated just such a change.

The pattern of separating theoretical and clinical training in undergraduate medical education is not unique to Russia, nor is uncertainty about its merits as a pedagogical approach. In the United States, for example, the rigid separation of medical education into preclinical and clinical years has provoked more efforts at reform over a longer period of time than any other single aspect of U.S. medical training (Kendall and Reader 1988).

In Russia, controversy has raged not only around the perceived consequences of the temporal separation of the two types of training, but also around the relative priority given to each. Critics have repeatedly maintained that too much time is devoted to general education and theoretical medical training, leaving students too little opportunity to master the technical skills that are fundamental to the practice of medicine. For example, Chazov reported in 1987 that recent testing of 350,000 physicians had demonstrated that many were incompetent. Based on the examinations, the minister declared, thirty thousand (or almost 10 percent) were put on probation and one thousand were completely denied the right to practice medicine. In discussing these results, Chazov stressed the inability of many newly graduated physicians to administer such common medical procedures as cardiograms and X rays and intimated that large numbers of them were also unable to perform even simple operations or to deliver babies (Galaeva 1987).

Possible explanations for these shortcomings have been widely discussed. Some critics (not surprisingly, clinical faculty members prominent among them) complain that too little time is dedicated to clinical experience and that the format of the curriculum does little to help students understand the links between theoretical study and the arts of diagnosis and treatment of real patients. Students' first direct contact with patients occurs only in the third year. While official descriptions of the medical training program indicate that 25 percent of students' time during the clinical years is supposed to be dedicated to practical training in polyclinics and emergency medicine, in reality it is often much less (Chazov 1987, p. 165). At least in some institutions, fourth-year students, for example, currently spend only four weeks (two each in the fall and in the spring) interacting with patients.[2]

This problem is aggravated by the sheer numbers of medical students throughout the country, which is a reflection of the long-standing priority given to quantity of output throughout all aspects of the health-care system. Medical institutes have been evaluated on the basis of how many graduates they produced rather than how well those graduates were trained. Institute budgets have been enrollment-driven, creating incentives for administrators and instructors both to expand the size of student bodies and to retain marginal students when at all possible. One of the results has been that class sizes tend to be quite large, certainly much larger than in a number of other societies. As one might expect, opportunities for hands-on experience in the classroom decrease in proportion to the number of students enrolled in a particular course.

Given the relative lack of opportunities which students have to practice essential procedures, their ability to observe and to assist experienced clinicians assumes particular importance. In this sphere as well, critics have complained that Russian medical education currently falls short. Far too often, they assert, the experiences available to students are remote from the types of medical problems that the average practitioner can be expected to have to handle. Rather, the emphasis tends to be upon more technologically complex and/or scientifically more interesting types of problems. Thus, for example, students may be provided the chance to observe or assist in a kidney or heart transplant operation but never have the experience of participating in a routine appendectomy (*Vrach* 1992, p. 42).

While the dilemmas posed by large class sizes may be peculiarly Soviet and Russian, many of the other problems are not. U.S. medical students also complain that they are required to devote too much time to what they consider esoterica (Wilson et al. 1992). Similarly, complaints that medical curricula overemphasize theoretical training are not only common in other societies, but they have a long history in Russia. At the turn of the century one of Russian medicine's earliest and most trenchant critics, the physician–novelist, V.V. Veresaev, wrote a caustic commentary on medical practice and the system of medical education in late imperial Russia. Presented in the form of an admittedly semi-autobiographical novel, Veresaev described an educational system which left students totally unprepared to deal with the problems of real patients. The narrator of his *Notes of a Physician* vividly describes his feelings of inadequacy as he departed his alma mater with his new diploma in hand:

> That which I had begun to understand in my final year of training now struck me full force: I possessed some fragmentary, completely unmastered and undigested knowledge. Accustomed only to watch and listen (but certainly not to act) and not knowing how to deal with patients, I was now a physician to whom patients would begin to turn for help (Veresaev 1903, p. 196).

Such feelings of inadequacy are doubtless endemic in the medical profession. Similar literature in other societies (including the United States) suggests that most new physicians feel overwhelmed by the awesome responsibilities suddenly thrust upon them when they must practice independently for the first time. Nonetheless, critics of Russian medical education are clearly convinced that the problem is particularly acute in their society. They seem less certain of how to solve it. The 1987 plan stressed the need for curricular reforms that would give students earlier and more frequent contact with patients and would more thoroughly integrate theoretical and practical training (*Osnovnie napravleniia* 1987). Achieving these goals would almost inevitably require a restructuring of much of the curriculum, yet the reform proposals have been notoriously short on details.

The same can be said for another change which was proposed in the 1987 plans for medical perestroika: a redirection of energy and resources into primary health-care. The reformers contended that primary care was the weakest sector in the nation's health-care system. As one means of alleviating this problem, they proposed the development of new programs within medical institutes to train family practitioners. However, these proposals were not accompanied by promises of increased funding. Rather, the implication was that the changes were to be accomplished through shifts in the allocation of existing resources.

Another curricular controversy in Russian medical education has centered on the role of general education courses, in particular those which in recent years have been referred to as the social sciences. Throughout the Soviet period, ideological instruction was as prominent a part of medical school curricula as it was of the curricula of most other educational institutions.[3] Mark Field (1967, p. 33) reported that approximately 250 hours of medical training were devoted to study of the principles of Marxism-Leninism. That was in the mid-1960s, and there was little change during the rest of the Soviet period. The stated intent of this coursework was to create physicians with a highly developed understanding and appreciation of their role in Soviet society and an ideologically correct perception of the nature of medical practice. Anecdotal evidence has long indicated that many (if not most) medical students barely tolerated this aspect of their education, regarding their political studies as an annoying waste of time and devoting as little energy to them as possible. Official concern with the quality of the instruction was evident as well in the Gorbachev era. The 1987 proposals included a reference to the need to "increase the professionalism of social science instruction in medical institutions" (*Osnovnie napravleniia* 1987). As in the case of other proposed curricular reforms, the plan lacked specifics.

Assessing Competence

The unsatisfactory skill level of many practicing physicians in the Soviet Union and post-Soviet Russia has been linked not only to weaknesses in the organization of the curriculum and to low student motivation but also to serious flaws in the system by which physician competence is assessed. Critics assert that the problem begins during medical training but continues long after the student years. Some of the most concrete proposals for reform of medical education have focused on assessing competence.

Medical students in Russia have traditionally been evaluated on the basis of examinations and written reports. During the preclinical years, they take examinations in each individual subject area; however, there are no general examinations to assess the extent to which students are able to integrate their knowledge and apply it to the problems of medical practice. Critics charge that this examination structure exacerbates the already difficult transition for students from theoretical to clinical work. During the clinical years, students' performance in most areas is assessed by a combination of oral examinations and written reports. Most medical educators have placed little emphasis on evaluating the practical clinical skills of their students, either through observing their interactions with real patients or, as is the practice in many Western societies, using models of clinical situations. Incomplete as this examination format is, in the view of many critics, its effectiveness is undermined still further by the unwillingness of medical educators to apply strict standards of performance. Chazov harshly criticized medical institutes for their paternalistic treatment of students:

> [Medical] students are adults. Many of them already have families when they graduate. But how do we treat them? We deny them autonomy. We coddle them: heaven forbid that students who receive a low grade [*dvoika*] should fail to graduate! Instead, we carry them on from course to course. Then we pass them over to the system of public health: "Here you are," we say, "do with them whatever you want!" (Galaeva 1987, p. 11).

As Chazov implies, the existing examination system has enabled the most marginal of students to complete medical degrees and be licensed to practice. Furthermore, new graduates have been assigned to workplaces without regard for the quality of their performance during their medical training (*Vrach* 1992, p. 42). These new physicians have not infrequently found themselves assigned to work in a field of specialization for which they have no special training. Developing the necessary competence at that point depends upon the initiative of the individual. Not only does the system of medical training poorly prepare new doctors for this task, but the incentive system operating in medical employment does nothing to encourage such extra effort. Salary and promotion have been linked neither to job performance nor to participation in continuing medical education.

The 1987 reform included several measures designed to strengthen the system of competence assessment. First, the plan called for the immediate introduction (effective with the 1988–89 academic year) of a system of compulsory state examinations to be administered at the end of the second and the fifth years of medical training. Second, the reformers were insistent that students who were not serious about their studies should be forced to leave medical institutes in the early, preclinical years. Finally, Chazov and his fellow reformers announced their intention to institute a set of prerequisites for a medical license. No longer would it be sufficient for a student merely to complete the required years of instruction in order to earn the right to practice medicine. Students must also be able to demonstrate their mastery of essential skills.

> [They] must not only pass exams in theory but also demonstrate their practical abilities. They will receive their diplomas only after they prove their ability to deliver a baby and perform an operation and their mastery of electrocardiograms and X rays (Galaeva 1987, p. 11).

According to the formal proposals, a student failing these examinations would be awarded only a temporary license to practice as a medical paraprofessional (*fel'dsher*). After one year, they would be entitled to retake the exams to receive their physician's degree (Chesanova 1987).

Continuity and Change in Russian Medical Education

As we have seen in the foregoing discussion, for a number of years there has been serious concern both within and outside the medical community in Russia over the perceived level of qualifications of medical personnel.[4] This concern has generated a number of proposals for changes in the content and structure of medical education, many of them from the highest levels of government. For reasons we will now examine, these ambitious plans have produced few concrete results. The failures of reform efforts notwithstanding, Russian medical education is currently undergoing a transformation; however, change is occurring less in response to planned initiatives than as a result of changing socioeconomic and political realities.

Internal Obstacles to Reform

A clinical faculty member from a provincial medical institute recently offered this explanation as to why the comprehensive reforms of medical education proposed in 1987 had not been implemented: "Nobody needs them" (*ni komu eto ne nuzhno*). His comment succinctly describes the essence of the problem faced by reformers. All but the most superficial reforms would involve fundamental structural modifications in the bureaucratic organizations within which medical training is carried out. Carrying out such changes would, at minimum, demand great expenditures of time and energy on the part of medical educators. More significant, perhaps, they threaten existing structures of power and authority in those organizations. These obstacles to reform, of course, are unique neither to medical education nor to Russia itself. A recent study of medical education reform in the United States, for example, argues persuasively that the changes which have occurred in American medical education over the last several decades have amounted to little more than "window dressing for the social organization" (Bloom 1988, p. 301).

In Russian medical education one of the clearest examples of new "window dressing" is to be found in the teaching of the social sciences. In most medical institutions, the departments responsible for ideological instruction have long been bastions of power. Evidence of the persistence of their influence in post-Soviet Russia is provided by the fact that the number of hours devoted to social science instruction remains fundamentally unchanged. Instead of courses in Marxism–Leninism, however, those departments now offer an array of courses in such topics as local history and popular health studies.

In other areas, even cosmetic changes appear to be the exception rather than the rule. The reorientations of curriculum that would be required to integrate theoretical and clinical instruction have not occurred; nor have examination procedures been revised to put a greater emphasis on the demonstration of competence in practical skills. On the contrary, most faculty continue to use familiar formats to teach their students. While some critics have attributed this passivity to a lack of professionalism among medical school faculty, it also seems clear that changing this aspect of medical education is not only intrinsically complex but also has the potential to increase the influence of clinical faculty significantly and at the expense of those involved in theoretical instruction. While power relationships among faculty in Russian medical institutions have not been studied systematically, anecdotal evidence as well as research on analogous situations in the United States offer support for the hypothesis that those departments responsible for preclinical instruction in the basic sciences tend to be quite powerful and more than willing to defend their professional turf (Bloom 1988). In such a case, inaction would appear to be the most effective defense.

A few medical institutes, including the First Medical Institute in Moscow, have created departments of family medicine (Smirnov 1992). However, in most cases administrative reform has been extremely slow. Furthermore, while lip service continues to be paid to the importance of primary care, social rewards are still disproportionately greater for medical specialists, a situation which reduces incentives for either faculty or students to commit themselves to general medicine.

Similarly, despite the loud protestations about the need to deter uncommitted students and eliminate underachievers, admissions procedures still favor regular secondary-school graduates over those with practical experience, and the timing of admissions examinations remains unaltered. Nor is there any evidence that larger numbers of students are being failed. This is hardly surprising, given that medical institute budgets continue to be enrollment-driven. Thus, the structure of incentives still encourages the admission and retention of large numbers of students.

External Sources of Change

While bureaucratic inflexibility and powerful interest groups have impeded reform of Russian medical education, current economic and political changes in the larger society are simultaneously having a significant impact upon it. Some of the most visible effects have been consequences of the fiscal difficulties the country is now experiencing. Faculty report that reduced medical institute budgets are affecting the educational process in a variety of ways. Because there is no longer enough money to pay for faculty members' travel expenses, for example, advanced students have lost the opportunity to gain valuable practical experience working under close supervision in diverse clinical settings during the summer months.

Changes in salary structures are reducing the incentives for clinical practitioners to teach at all. In the past, there were economic rewards for those who participated in clinical instruction. This is no longer the case.

As of August 1992, the salary for the head of a clinical department in a medical institute was approximately 4,000 rubles per month. This figure represented total reimbursement for the combined responsibilities of teaching, research, and clinical practice. That amount is about the same as the salary of an ordinary physician and approximately one-half the salary of the head of a hospital medical department with no teaching responsibilities.

The same economic forces that are markedly lowering the incentive of experienced clinicians to teach are apparently also deterring some potential physicians from entering the profession in the first place. Although official reports indicate that the overall number of first-year medical students was about the same in 1992 as it had been in previous years, applications to some medical institutes are down significantly, and faculty members express concern about the caliber of recent students ("V dobri chas!" 1992). That physician salaries remain so low and that there is great uncertainty about the shape the health-care system will take in the future mean that choosing this career at this time involves taking some risks.

On the other hand, medical institutes (like other institutions of higher education) now offer admission to paying students. This seems to be a strategy to supplement meager budgets; at the present time, however, most of these individuals are foreign students, that is, they are students from other republics of the former Soviet Union, many of whom were already enrolled in programs in the Russian Republic at the time of the Union's breakup. There clearly is concern on the part of many throughout Russia that higher education will soon be available only to those who can pay for it (Gurevich 1992). It is too early to predict whether active recruitment of paying students will become a common feature of Russian medical education. It seems unlikely, however, that medical education will be a popular choice for students if the cost of it cannot be expected to be offset by adequate earnings after graduation.

Anticipated changes to the Russian health-care system are also beginning to affect new and aspiring physicians. After decades of being guaranteed employment after graduation, students are now being warned that a number of them will face the real possibility of unemployment. Those students who graduated in 1992, unlike their predecessors, were not automatically assigned to jobs. Many were left to find employment for themselves. The effects of this dramatic change in policy have yet to be carefully examined. There is some indication, however, that young physicians who cannot find employment to their liking are leaving the field of medicine altogether. They seem especially likely to leave the field if their only possibilities for medical employment are in rural areas. Historically, rural clinics have been staffed by new medical-school graduates who were assigned to them for three years of required service after graduation. Staffing these clinics has always been problematic. At least in the short run, the elimination of the system of job assignments has the potential to exacerbate existing geographical inequities in the health-care system (Craumer and Cromley 1990).

Just as new and aspiring physicians are trying to adjust to changing realities, so too are a number of medical institutes. Now that they have far greater autonomy than in earlier years, some are eagerly experimenting with new programs and new pedagogical approaches. The Saratov Medical Institute, for example, has chosen to lengthen its training program by two years. The medical institute in Samara is experimenting with a new program of individualized instruction. The tuition is 200,000 rubles per year for Russian students (even more for foreigners), but the program offers great flexibility for students and the institute guarantees that those who complete the program will have jobs when they graduate (Samarin 1992). Specialized short-term training programs for undergraduate medical students and practicing physicians are being offered by a wide array of institutions and organizations on a remarkably diverse range of topics (from homeopathy and acupressure to clinical immunology and mineral therapies). Even Moscow State University has reentered the field of medical education after divorcing its medical faculty in 1929. The new program created at Russia's premier university is designed to train medical scientists, not practitioners, and administrators report that they have been inundated with requests for information from interested students (Paniushin 1992).

In conclusion, examination of the status of medical education in contemporary Russia reveals a number of continuities as well as some noteworthy innovations. In the short run, it seems likely that the increased pluralism characteristic of the health-care system as a whole will continue to be reflected in the diversification of medical training programs. In the longer run, one can predict that the proliferation of disparate educational programs will generate pressures for standardization. One would be hard pressed to find a modern society which does not exercise some control over the training and licensing of medical practitioners. More difficult to assess at this point is the most likely source of such pressure. Past experience suggests that regulation might well be generated from within the governmental bureaucracy. On the other hand, pressure from activists within the medical profession itself is another possibility. That strategy has been a common feature of medical professionalization in Western societies.

Finally, any speculation about the future direction of Russian medical education must take into account the role that will likely be played by a new but potentially very powerful actor in the health-care system, the medical insurance industry. As Russia moves—albeit slowly—in the direction of insurance-funded medicine, those who control the purse strings are likely to have a growing influence on the shape of the system as a whole, including the process by which its practitioners are produced.

Notes

1. The level of funding has since fallen even lower and is currently approximately 3.9 percent.
2. This charge was made by a clinical faculty member at a medical institute in St. Petersburg in late summer of 1992.
3. In the prerevolutionary era, the medical school curriculum in Russia included coursework in basic theology (Frieden 1981, p. 326).
4. Data collected by the authors in St. Petersburg in early summer of 1992 indicate that doubts about the adequacy of physician training persist among the general population. When asked to rank defects in the health-care system, respondents ranked inadequate preparation of physicians and poor quality of medical equipment at the top of their lists.

References

Bloom, S. (1988). "Structure and Ideology in Medical Education: An Analysis of Resistance to Change," *Journal of Health and Social Behavior*, 29:294–306.
Chazov, E.I., ed. (1987). *70 let sovetskogo zdravookhraneniia*. Moscow: Meditsina.
Chazov, E.I. (1988). *Restructuring Affects the Whole Health Service*. Moscow: Novosti Press.
Chesanova, T. (1987). "Na perelome: o perestroike sistemy meditsinskogo obsluzhivaniia v Leningrade rasskazyvaet nashemu korrespondentu ministr zdravookhraneniia SSSR akademik E.I. Chazov," *Leningradskaia pravda*, 24 April.
Craumer, P.R. and E.K. Cromley (1990). "The Changing Geography of Higher Medical Education in the USSR, 1917–1985," *Soviet Geography*, 31:555–72.
Field, M.G. (1957). *Doctor and Patient in Soviet Russia*. Cambridge, MA: Harvard University Press.
———. (1967). *Soviet Socialized Medicine*. New York: The Free Press.
Fitzpatrick, S. (1979). *Education and Social Mobility in the Soviet Union, 1921–1934*. New York: Cambridge University Press.
Frieden, N. (1981). *Russian Physicians in an Era of Reform and Revolution, 1856–1905*. Princeton, NJ: Princeton University Press.
Galaeva, A. (1987). "Vrach na poroge III tysiacheletiia," *Literaturnaia gazeta*, 29 April, p. 11.

Gurevich, V. (1992). "Vysshee obrazovanie mozhet stat' dlia bol'shinstva nedostupnym," *Izvestiia*, 30 May, p. 7.

Kendall, Patricia L. and George G. Reader (1988). "Innovations in Medical Education of the 1950s Contrasted with Those of the 1970s and 1980s," *Journal of Health and Social Behavior*, 29:279–93.

Leikina-Svirskaia, V.R. (1971). *Intelligentsia v Rossii vo vtoroi polovine XIX veka*. Moscow.

"Osnovnye napravleniia razvitiia okhrany zdorov'ia naseleniia i perestroiki zdravookhraneniia SSSR v dvenadtsatoi piatiletke i na period do 2000 goda" (1987). *Pravda*, 27 November.

Paniushin, R. (1992). "Vrachei gotoviat . . . v MGU," *Meditsinskaia gazeta*, 28 August, p. 3.

Ryan, M. (1990). *Doctors and the State in the Soviet Union*. New York: St. Martin's Press.

Samarin, G. (1992). "Million za diplom. I ne dorogo . . ., " *Meditsinskaia gazeta*, 21 October, p. 5.

Shchepin, O. (1987). "Zdorov'e: Bank idei." *Pravda*, 8 December, p. 3.

Smirnov, F. (1992). "Saburovskii eksperiment," *Meditsinskaia gazeta*, 4 September, p. 4.

"V dobryi chas!"(1992). *Meditsinskaia gazeta*, 4 September, p. 1.

Veresaev, V. (V.V. Smidovich) (1903). *Zapiski vracha*. St. Petersburg: A.E. Kolpinskii.

Vrach (1992). No. 3, p. 42.

Wilson, B.S., D.J. Pratto and J.K. Skipper, Jr. (1992). "Students' Perceptions of Teaching Innovations in Medical School: Are Things Changing?" *Sociological Spectrum*, 12:53–72.

10

Educating Russia for a Free Press

Nicholas Daniloff

With Mikhail Gorbachev's rise to power, the Russian media experienced a brief period of great popular respect. Between 1985 and 1991, strictures restraining the press were removed one by one. For the first time in seventy years, the ills of society—well known to Russians but little talked about publicly—were described by newspapers, magazines, and television in shocking detail.

The glory days of the media reached a crescendo between 1988, the year of the Eighteenth Party Conference, and 1990, the year of multiparty national elections. Everything was fair game and no one seemed to be above criticism. Blame was poured on the Communist leadership, dead or alive, including Lenin, Stalin, and Brezhnev; on the KGB security police; and on the bureaucracy. Not even Raisa Gorbachev, wife of the sitting general secretary, was above reproach.

In more recent days, the Russian media have fallen from the heights. With freedom of expression have come abuses which trouble the population. The press has libeled some individuals; on occasion, it has circulated distorted and unreliable information; it has divulged classified secrets; it has indulged in an explosion of erotica, pornography, and obscenity. During 1992, a number of events highlighted the growing dissatisfaction of various elements of society. For example, in June 1992, communist and nationalist opponents of President Boris Yeltsin's administration staged an extended and illegal demonstration outside the Ostankino headquarters of Russian State Television. They set up a tent city in defiance of city directives and harassed television employees, occasionally threatening violence. Their demand? Give the "red-brown" opposition a regular voice on television. Management at the station received a delegation of demonstrators and promised some air time but doubted that the arrangement would prove satisfactory in the long term.[1]

Then, in July 1992, Ruslan Khasbulatov, speaker of the Russian parliament, began an aggressive campaign to deprive *Izvestiia* of its independent status and to force it to become once again the organ of the Russian legislature. *Izvestiia* resisted, and its leadership vowed to fight to the end for independence. In October 1992, speaker Khasbulatov dispatched his parliamentary police force (which few people even knew existed) to the newspaper's building on Pushkin Square to seize physical control. When President Yeltsin countermanded Khasbulatov's order, the speaker was infuriated and promised to continue the struggle to subdue *Izvestiia*, and after that to put a halter on state television.

Finally, in October 1992, members of the nationalistic Pamiat' Society invaded the newspaper offices of *Moskovskii komsomolets* and disrupted the morning editorial meeting. Society members, garbed in black uniforms and jackboots, made threatening demands of the editors. One of their number, a father named Oleg, called on the management to stop publishing erotica, and to apologize to the Russian people for past insults.[2]

These incidents suggest that Russian society has not yet become accustomed to an independent media, nor has it acquired the tolerances required in a democracy. The observation of U.S. Supreme Court Justice Oliver Wendell Holmes, that freedom of the press requires freedom for opinions "we hate and believe to be fraught with death," remains deeply foreign to most Russians. Evidently, a long learning period will be required if Russia is to accept the principles of a free press.

Educating the Establishment

Under tsar and commissar, the Russian instinct has been to pursue press control, not press liberty. Thus it is hardly surprising that contemporary Russia is obliged to discover why unregulated media are needed in a democracy, and how to live with independent newspapers and broadcasting.

The roots of suppression in Russia go back a long way. In the seventeenth century, when England and other European nations were throwing off prepublication censorship, Russia was tightening controls over publishing. Nicholas I imposed particularly severe censorship after the Decembrist rebellion of 1825 sought to depose him and exterminate his family. By the turn of the century, restrictions were loosened by his son, Alexander II and his great grandson Nicholas II (Ostrow 1990, pp. 12–42).

By 1906, the Russian press was relatively free and well informed. But the pluralism of views which it reflected did not survive the Bolshevik Revolution of 1917. Vladimir I. Lenin, despite early claims of respect for a free press, began a ruthless campaign of subjugating the media once he came to power. His successors created one of the most rigid systems of press control the world has ever known. It was based on criminal sanctions against the denigration of the state and the communist system; on fear promoted by the KGB police; on a policy of tolerating no dissent from the Party line; on loyalty over competence; and on a formal censorship agency (Glavlit), created in 1922.

This artillery of regulation encouraged most writers and editors to practice self-censorship out of a concern for self-preservation. The bolder or more secure negotiated with the censors, making compromise deletions or additions glorifying Marx and Lenin. Others might trick the gatekeepers by writing in Aesopian language. Still others smuggled their works abroad. Some authors allowed their writings to be reproduced with typewriters or cameras. The more timorous penned "for the drawer," hoping for a fairer day (Dewhirst and Farrell 1973).

By the mid-1980s, the Soviet government was no longer able to continue tightening the screws of regulation. Six months before Gorbachev became general secretary, he had declared himself in favor of more honest public discussion (Gorbachev 1984). The people, he said, were mature enough to accept the truth. Once Gorbachev became Party leader, he advertised the more open style in a series of "walkabouts" in Leningrad, Minsk, and Kiev. His frankness was reminiscent of Nikita S. Khrushchev's.

Almost simultaneously, Party authorities began considering a detailed law on the press. Debates on this legislation raged in Party and journalistic circles between 1985 and 1990. The issues, of course, were: How much freedom? How much control? What protections for the Communist Party? What propaganda considerations? How much liberty for journalists (Ostrow 1990)?

In the end, conservatives yielded to reformers. The 1990 Soviet Law on the Press, drafted largely by Iu.M. Baturin, M.A. Fedotov, and V.L. Entin, took the remarkable step of banning prepublication censorship. This law was superseded in February 1992 when the Russian parliament passed its Law on the Press. While the Russian law maintained the ban on censorship, it also made some concessions to the conservatives by detailing a number of impermissible topics and requiring registration with the authorities.

Given this continuing conservative-liberal struggle, it was not surprising that one of the first decrees promulgated by the coup plotters of August 1991 was a ban on the critical press. They had no love for philosophical concepts of freedom. Their goal was power. To their astonishment, independent journalists violated the press ban from the start and continued collecting and distributing uncensored information by whatever means available.

When Boris Yeltsin emerged victorious from the failed coup, he also exhibited the repressive instincts of the Communist school in which he grew up. He immediately banned the Communist and opposition press. However, pressure from Communists and democratic journalists forced him to rescind the prohibition within a month (Tolz 1992). Thus, Boris Yeltsin learned a fundamental lesson: In a democracy, the opposition must be heard.

But to what extent must it be heard? How loudly may the opposition shout? And how far in a democracy may officials go to turn down the volume of its opponents' voices? These are questions which every democracy must struggle with, and not surprisingly in Russia, the line between freedom of expression and control of opposition is being drawn more restrictively than in America. The government of Boris Yeltsin has found a number of levers by which to manage the media. Basing itself on the Brezhnev-era constitution and the RFSFR Law of the Press, the government has resorted to warnings, lawsuits, dismissals, and arrests to intimidate critics. Some examples:

- On March 23, 1993, conservative TV host Aleksandr Nevzorov was prevented from going on the air for a two-week period in St. Petersburg for overstepping "all permissible bounds." Authorities objected to his attacks against Yeltsin.
- In 1993, the Moscow prosecutor's office brought charges against *Moskovskii komsomolets* and *Chastnaia zhizn'* for publishing advertisements for sexual services. The advertisements offered a salary of 100,000 rubles a month to men and women "without complexes."
- During 1992, the Ministry of Information issued warnings to the conservative newspaper *Den'* and the liberal newspapers *Komsomol'skaia pravda* and *Nezavisimaia gazeta* for publishing stories of which it did not approve. In St. Petersburg, the editor Aleksei Andreev was arrested for printing articles of an allegedly neo-Nazi and anti-Semitic nature in his newspaper *Narodnoe delo*.
- The year 1992 ended with Yeltsin dismissing Egor Iakovlev, one of the leading editors of the glasnost period, as head of Russian State Television, apparently because he was too independent and would

not follow presidential orders. Iakovlev went on to found a new independent newspaper called *Obshchaia gazeta*.

Such incidents obviously created a chill among editors and journalists. The situation was not dissimilar from the self-censorship mentality of the Glavlit period. Yet from Yeltsin's point of view, these restrictive actions were relatively minor. The far greater issue was the struggle to influence popular attitudes through control of state television.

"How can you rule if you don't control television?" French President Charles de Gaulle is reported to have asked President John F. Kennedy. Undoubtedly the same question troubles Yeltsin and his advisors. They know that on any given night as many as 200 million people in the former Soviet Union may be listening and watching the evening news show "Novosti." The Yeltsin government exercises major influence over television programs through Iakovlev's replacement, Viacheslav Bragin, and through frequent telephone calls from the president's office. Interference has been so intense that Igor Malashenko, first deputy director, resigned in protest at the beginning of 1993.

A case in point was the television coverage of the death of Yeltsin's mother in March 1993, at a time when the president was involved in a serious contest with the speaker of the Russian parliament. In an obvious attempt to win sympathy for him, state television gave extended coverage to Yeltsin attending his mother's funeral. After twenty minutes of graveside reportage, there was a brief and unflattering report on Speaker Khasbulatov. Similarly, in its coverage of the May 1, 1993 demonstration, state television sought to leave the impression that Communist hardliners were to blame for injuries and death.

Such slanted coverage was deeply resented by Yeltsin's opponents in the Communist-dominated parliament. Not surprisingly, they attempted to wrest control of television from the president. On March 29, 1993, the Ninth Congress of People's Deputies voted to create a federal monitoring panel "to guarantee freedom of speech" on state television. Minister of Information Mikhail Fedotov (one of the authors of the Law on the Press) denounced the measure as a return to the Brezhnev-era censorship. A group of liberal deputies appealed to the Constitutional Court to judge whether the resolution was constitutional or not. These liberals asserted that the parliamentary resolution violated the separation of powers. But on May 28, 1993, the Constitutional Court ruled in favor of parliament and against the government. It was far from clear, however, whether the government would respect the court's judgment.

Russia's incipient democratic leanings will be put to test as the country struggles to bring into existence a new constitution. What have leaders learned about free expression and freedom of the press? Will they adopt the American model of a cryptic description of press freedom guaranteed by judicial review? Will they seek to spell out all the perils and possibilities as attempted in the controversial Law on the Press? Or will they find their own middle ground—one that bans censorship yet makes clear that media may be legally suppressed through court procedures? This latter possibility seems all too likely.

Educating the Editors

The biggest lesson that Russian newspaper editors learned at the start of Boris Yeltsin's administration was not that freedom of expression is essential in a democracy, but that an independent press must be financially viable. As Yeltsin moved aggressively toward a market economy in the beginning of 1992, editors found the ground shifting under their feet: no more financial subsidies; no more inexpensive newsprint; no more simple distribution through the mail or the Union press agency Soiuz Pechat'.

By February 1992, Russian publishing was in a state of crisis. Runaway inflation threatened newspaper operations. Rising prices, falling readership, and escalating costs doomed even the most well-established newspapers. The cost of newsprint, for example, rose from 33 rubles a ton in 1991 to 240 rubles a ton by the start of 1992. By mid-1992, a ton of newsprint cost 21,000 rubles.[3]

The first reaction of editors was to raise newspaper prices. In the Brezhnev years, newspapers cost a few kopeks an issue. But even the income generated at a ruble an issue was insufficient to cover spiraling costs. By March 1992, central newspapers were forced to conduct a resubscription campaign. Prices for six-month subscriptions were raised from twenty to fifty rubles, then to ten times that much. *Nezavisimaia gazeta* began asking 500 rubles for a six-month subscription; *Izvestiia*, 360 rubles; *Komsomol'skaia pravda*, 300 rubles; and *Trud*, 300 rubles. *Literaturnaia gazeta* and *Moscow News*, which come out only once a week, set their subscription rates at, respectively, 182 rubles and 250 rubles.

These hikes depressed readership and, consequently, circulation dropped dramatically. At this time, the average monthly wage was approximately 2,400 rubles a month, and the poverty line hovered around 1,500. *Izvestiia*, which had enjoyed a circulation of some thirteen million, now found it could sell only three million copies an issue. The circulation of *Pravda*, which had been in the millions of copies, dropped to hundreds of thousands.

If the free press was not to go out of business at the very start of the democratic era, emergency measures were urgently needed. In February 1992, editors appealed to the Yeltsin government to reinstate direct subsidies, at least temporarily. Yeltsin responded positively and ordered the Ministry of Information to render assistance. It was an opportunity for the Yeltsin administration to extend generous aid to supportive newspapers and to deny assistance to the opposition press. Had Yeltsin really learned the lesson that democracy requires pluralism?

To its credit, the Yeltsin team decided in favor of diversity. Yeltsin's advisors argued that a broad spectrum of ideas, including those of the political opposition, should be represented in the press. An official of the Ministry of Information explained: "The minister sees his job as the destruction of the old system which did not allow free expression or the free collection of information. Criticism of the government is an indispensable subject in order to sell newspapers. Even under the period of stagnation, there were publications which criticized. So we have been getting used to this psychologically. In time, everything will fall into place."[4]

Subsidies amounting to 12 billion rubles a year (out of a total national budget of six trillion rubles) were designated for the press. Assistance was intended only to cover the gap caused by inflation. Subsidies were tailored to individual newspapers on the basis of their financial reports which were filed with the ministry. There were other criteria as well, which one ministry official explained: First, priority was given to social, cultural, and educational publications, especially those aimed at children and young people. Second, government organs, such as state television or the newspaper of the Russian parliament, *Rossiskaia gazeta*, would not receive subsidies because they are already financed from the state budget. Third, no assistance was offered to erotic or pornographic publications. Fourth, account would be taken of a number of other factors: the newspaper's traditional niche, the size of its circulation (especially if it is circulated in the states of the CIS), and how often it comes out. Thus, well-established newspapers such as *Pravda*, *Sovetskaia Rossiia*, and *Den'* receive help just as do the democratic newspapers *Izvestiia*, *Komsomol'skaia pravda*, and *Moskovskii komsomolets*.[5]

Another problem that newspaper editors faced in 1992 was distribution. Soviet newspapers depended on Soiuz Pechat' to handle sales and to distribute in cooperation with the postal authorities. However, the cost of distribution climbed precipitously as the successor agency to Soiuz

Pechat´, Rospechat´, increased its fees to absorb the rise in transportation costs.

Newspaper editors tried a number of stop-gap measures. One approach, used by *Komsomol'skaia pravda* and several other Moscow-based newspapers, was to print "*tsena svobodna*" ("price open to negotiation") on the front page. They then invited private entrepreneurs to haul and distribute newspapers for whatever price they could get. "However," reports Dmitrii Babich of *Komsomol'skaia pravda*, "this system amounted to only a drop in the bucket."[6]

Editors complained, too, that Moscow kiosks, which formerly sold newspapers on the sidewalks, were no longer helpful. Privatization forced the new kiosk owners to concentrate on profit-making items like women's lingerie and foreign goods. Newspapers proved to be more trouble than they were worth: they brought little profit and were capable of alienating buyers who objected to their political bias or their sensationalism.

The economic crisis obliged newspaper editors to learn about management in a free-market environment. They began casting about for new ways to sustain operations and welcomed the suggestions of colleagues in the West. Moscow editors explained to this writer that they were adopting a range of new ideas, such as attempting to sell inside information to Moscow-based foreign correspondents and newspapers abroad for foreign currency (the resulting battle of confidential newsletters quickly became fratricidal, with one sheet killing off another); restructuring office headquarters to provide rental space to third parties, often business operations not connected with journalism; eliminating costly foreign bureaus, and relying on "firemen" journalists to rush to crises abroad as needed; reducing the frequency of publication and the size of circulation, and raising prices; and seeking Western partners and sponsors. (*Izvestiia* entered into cooperation with Turkish investors; *Pravda* found a Greek benefactor; *Komsomol'skaia pravda* developed a relationship with the *Providence Journal*; and *Nezavisimaia gazeta* found an American partner for an English-language edition.)

Russian State Television has learned a lesson of a different sort, one involving objectivity and ethics. The management has been trying to maintain what it called "a common television space" covering the territory of the former Soviet Union. However, difficulties have arisen: first, each new republic wanted to create its own domestic television service, but Russian State Television demanded payments for air time which exceeded local television budgets. Second, the republics felt that Russian State Television's news coverage had a pro-Russian bias. Even its "neutral" news coverage was considered by one or another ethnic group to be biased against it.

Television managers were forced to consider the issue of journalistic behavior. Was objectivity possible and desirable? Should Russian journalists agree on a universal code of ethics? Should each individual organization have its own code? Should there be some mechanism like a national press council for resolving disputes? These questions were recognized as important by most editors. But Russian life was so chaotic by 1992 and 1993, that ethical considerations were constantly being pushed into the background. "I wanted to create an ethical code for *Nezavisimaia gazeta*," Chief Editor Vitalii Tretiakov said in an interview, "but I keep getting distracted. Competition continually interferes."[7]

Igor Golembiovskii, chief editor of *Izvestiia*, has been a strong supporter of a code of ethics for journalists and has succeeded in not getting distracted from this issue. On January 29, 1993, *Izvestiia* adopted and published its own code of ethics which it said had been developed by studying the ethical codes of newspapers in numerous countries. Chief among the standards which the newspaper adopted were accuracy, a self-imposed ban on check-book journalism, protection for confidential sources, avoidance of hidden means for securing information except in extraordinary cases, the right of organizations and individuals to respond to articles about them, and respect for privacy.

"We base ourselves on the idea that our duty to protect the freedom of the press in the interests of society and to struggle against all types of censorship will receive strong support if readers are certain about the ethics of journalists' conduct," *Izvestiia* stated. Additionally, the paper appointed a prominent Moscow defense lawyer, Boris A. Zolotukhin as ombudsman.[8]

Educating Journalists

The changes that erupted in Russian society have required major changes in education. Russians have put aside the familiar demands of a command economy as they have learned about market forces. Similarly, independent journalism began making different demands on state-controlled newspapers and broadcasting. How quickly could new approaches be learned? How would veteran professors, steeped in Marxism-Leninism, adapt to new conditions? How expeditiously could new textbooks be prepared? How successfully could Western help be arranged?

In Russia as in the United States, about half the practicing journalists have been educated through university programs. The other half are employees who began their careers on the bottom rungs of provincial newspapers and worked their way up, occasionally achieving responsible positions in Moscow and St. Petersburg.

Journalism education in Russia has been evolving since the 1917 Revolution. The Old Bolsheviks counted among their ranks a fair number of writers and pamphleteers. Lenin, a prolific writer, occasionally signed himself "Literator." Their appreciation of the power of the printed word was great, and in the years after the Revolution, they set up institutes which offered practicing journalists short courses in Marxism–Leninism. Gradually, as the new regime established itself, journalism studies at these institutions were expanded to include beginners and combined the teaching of practical skills with propagation of the Party line.[9]

The first formal school of journalism was created at the Belorussian State University. Then in 1952, the Department of Journalism was established at Moscow State University. By 1992, the Commonwealth of Independent States could claim twenty-seven universities with journalism departments. Fourteen were located in Russia—at Moscow, St. Petersburg, Ekaterinburg, Vladivostok, Irkutsk, Krasnoiarsk, Tomsk, Rostov, Kazan, Voronezh, Saransk, Ufa, Makhachkala, and Vladikavkaz.

The journalism department of Moscow State University is generally regarded as Russia's premier journalism school. It is headed by Dr. Iasen N. Zassurskii, a specialist in American literature. Appointed dean three decades ago at the age of twenty-nine, he has been regarded as a flexible centrist, a man of loyalty to authority yet seriously interested in the outside world, especially the United States. As conditions changed, he began revamping his department and sharing his experience with the other twenty-six schools. The schools meet annually as an association to exchange views and develop goals.

One of the first challenges that Zassurskii had to face down was an effort by Khasbulatov to take away the eighteenth-century buildings of Moscow University opposite the Kremlin where the journalism department is located. With the help of the department's numerous alumni, many of whom hold prominent media jobs in Moscow, he was able to deflect this challenge.

The Moscow journalism program runs for the usual five-year course leading to a first university degree or diploma. The academic year is divided into two semesters. Students take ten to twelve courses each semester, many of which meet only once or twice a week. Able-bodied male students are required to take military instruction. Both men and women are able to make contacts in the Moscow media world which may lead to firm job offers. The Moscow school lists more than a hundred professors, instructors, and researchers and some 2,374 students in daytime, evening, and correspondence courses (interview 1992).

Courses are largely theoretical, although some skills such as the principles of reporting and editing are also taught. Complaints have been raised that journalism education is not changing rapidly enough to meet the new conditions of a free-market economy and democracy ("Professiia—reporter?" 1990). But at Moscow, at least, some important first steps have been taken. Some of the most important changes have been a de-emphasis on the teaching of Marxism–Leninism, a more honest approach to Soviet history, access to the West through exchange programs, and a new emphasis on independent thinking. Zassurskii's department, even in the Brezhnev years, enjoyed something of a reputation for being "liberal." While the school was officially turning out loyal Communist journalists, Zassurskii quietly opened avenues to a broader education. Vitalii Tretiakov, editor of *Nezavisimaia gazeta*, credits the dean with introducing him to the Greek and Roman classics as well as to modern Western political thought.

A lack of appropriate textbooks has been a continuing problem in recent Russian journalism education. "No real textbooks are available yet," Zassurskii told this writer in 1992. "We read Stephen Cohen's book on Bukharin. We use newspaper articles and memoirs. Obviously, lectures here are very important." Another innovation of Moscow State University's journalism program involves religion. Dean Zassurskii has persuaded Metropolitan Pitirim, formerly chief of the publications department of the Moscow Patriarchy, to teach a course on journalism and the Russian Orthodox Church. Other courses, on journalism and Judaism, have been offered by a Moscow rabbi. Attention was also paid to environmental journalism. The Center for Foreign Journalists in McLean, Virginia, and the Freedom Forum of Arlington, Virginia, have lent assistance to this program.

As financial independence of newspapers became more important, the Moscow school sought help in advertising and public relations. The American Advertising Federation opened a branch at Moscow State University, and a representative of the American Newspaper Advertising Bureau lectured there on public relations during the 1992–93 academic year.

Finally, the subject of ethics came in for a new look. Ethics is a subject notable for its absence in post-Communist Russia as avaricious entrepreneurs set out to reap excessive profits. In journalism, as already noted, editors have been seized with the issue. The Moscow school has traditionally offered a course in journalistic ethics by Professor D.S. Avraamov, but it was developed during the Communist period and is reportedly in need of updating.

Ties with the outside world have been extremely important in bringing Russian journalism education in line with the West. The Moscow State University's School of Journalism, among other schools, developed exchanges with a number of American institutions of higher learning, including the American University, Belmont University, Columbia University, the University of California at Berkeley and at San Diego, Emerson College, Northeastern University, and Wesleyan University. About twenty-five Russian students have been going abroad every year during the last few years; Moscow State University has sent students to Germany, France, Holland, Poland, and the United States.

Dean Zassurskii believes students have much to learn from American journalism, which strives for objectivity grounded in verifiable fact, as distinct from the tendency toward heavy partisanship in Russian journalism. He also believes that a greater respect for facts in Russia would be a healthy development: "If we don't lose our analytical approach, it would be very significant for us to acquire more facts." But he added, "American journalism is quite different from European, and in that sense European journalism is closer to ours."[10]

Just as Russian newspapers are seeking foreign financial sponsors, so Moscow State University and other schools have reached out to the West. Sometimes help comes from unusual sources. The Church of Scientology, for example, refurbished the Moscow school's reading room. The hall was renamed the Ron Hubbard Reading Room and has various works of the church founder displayed on the shelves. Similarly, the Reverend Sun Myung Moon of the Unification Church brought a dozen Moscow State University students to America in the fall of 1991. Meanwhile, a full-length statue of Lenin, the demon of press control, still graces the second floor of the school.

Educating the People

Press control was supposed to bolster popular support for the Soviet regime and promote the march toward "the bright future." But the unintended happened: Heavy-handed control eroded media credibility and turned the press into a popular laughingstock. In the later Communist years, few believed without reservation what was written in the press;

reading between the lines became a daily exercise. The Russians' view of the press was summed up by a joke from the 1960s: *Pravda* has the difficult job of reporting a competition between an American Ford and a Soviet Pobeda in which the Ford won in every single category. The next day, *Pravda* reported, "The results of the motor-car competition were not surprising. Our Pobeda placed second. The American Ford automobile ended in the last place but one."

No wonder that the move away from controls in 1986 was greeted by many Russians as a long overdue step. At first, ordinary readers turned to their daily newspapers and broadcasts with unbounded enthusiasm. Publications that had been deadly dull, such as *Moscow News*, *Ogonek*, and *Argumenty i fakty*, now led the way under courageous editors in making dramatic disclosures. For a while, there seemed too much to read. The mood of readers was reflected in a poll carried out by *Moscow News* at the end of 1988. In September of that year, the newspaper questioned 547 Muscovites, asking them to grade various institutions using the traditional five-point grading system. Eighty-six percent of the respondents gave the print press an "A," and 77 percent gave radio and television the same top mark. Sixty percent gave the Communist Party Central Committee high marks, but only 42 percent did the same for the KGB security police. In a follow-up poll in February 1989, the press received an "A" from 87 percent of 700 respondents, while radio and TV were given this rating by 80 percent. The media were clearly doing very well! (Tretiakov, 1989)

After the first flush of excitement, however, disenchantment began to set in. By 1990, many Russians were beginning to grow tired of the negative picture of society to which they were now relentlessly exposed: gang violence, teenage pregnancies, serial killers, nuclear accidents, drug addiction, police brutality, corruption at all levels of government, leaders' peccadilloes, and details of the blood purges. Then came the attempted coup.

The Freedom Forum of Arlington, Virginia, had planned to hold a meeting on the free press at Moscow State University on August 19, 1991, the first day of the coup. Moscow State University faculty members later reported to this writer that they had noticed leaflets calling for resistance as they were walking to the meeting. This was the first sign that journalists, who had now breathed the fresh air of free expression, were not going to abandon the press without a fight. At the meeting, Dean Zassurskii predicted that the coup would fail, and, in a long-distance telephone conversation with Northeastern University officials in Boston the same day, he repeated his conviction.

Since those anxious days, the Russian public has gone back to being unhappy with the press. A number of phenomena explain why.

1. Hate-mongering and anti-Semitism. Anti-Semitism has always been just below the surface in Russia. Now two small newspapers, *Russkoe voskresen'e* and *Pul's tushina*, have earned a disreputable reputation for constantly harping on the "Jewish-Masonic" conspiracy as the root of all Russia's troubles.
2. Pornography. This exploded in the late 1980s, and has continued to grow as an industry. Soft-core broadsheets such as *Venera* and *On i ona* flood hawkers' stands in Moscow's subway stations. A homosexual newspaper, *Tema*, has also made its appearance. Foreign hard-core pornography has been invading the Russian market as barriers have come down, and it has served as a model for domestic producers. The pornography issue pits conservatives against liberals, with the former wanting complete suppression and the latter urging "civilized" methods of control.[11]
3. Unauthorized disclosures. The opposition newspaper *Den'* prided itself on its ability to wheedle classified information out of the bureaucracy. In its issue for January 17–30, 1993, the newspaper published excerpts from the classified transcript of President Boris Yeltsin's meeting with President George Bush in Moscow on January 3, 1993, with Boris Yeltsin. Six months before, in its issue for the week of July 26-August 1, 1993, the newspaper published classified correspondence between Foreign Minister Andrei Kozyrev and U.S. Secretary of State James Baker. In these "Dear Andrei" letters, Baker urged the foreign minister to join UN sanctions against Serbia. The letters made it appear that Kozyrev was willing to forsake Russia's traditional ally to do Washington's bidding. The apparent motive for the publication was to undermine the position of the liberal-minded Kozyrev.
4. Libel. A failure to check the facts or to quote correctly can result in libel suits, or the threat of them. *Den'* lost one such suit when it was found guilty of plagiarism and treason. It was ordered by the court to pay a penalty of 150,000 rubles.
5. Lack of professional standards and sensationalism. The Russian media have traditionally been more opinionated and less fact-based than their American counterparts. This is probably as much a result of the historical lack of access in a closed society as it is a part of the more general European tradition of partisan journalism. Under the democrats, access to official sources has not notably improved—on the contrary, journalists frequently complain of having difficulty contacting knowledgeable sources. Falling readership has pushed editors to become more sensa-

tionalistic, occasionally in the style of England's and America's tabloid press. *Vechernaia Moskva,* for example, opened its pages to faith healer Alan Chumak, who claimed that anyone reading the issue with his article would experience an improvement in well-being. Similarly, state television has given major air time to astrologers and quacks.

6. Corruption and outside pressures. Hard economic times make individual journalists vulnerable to bribery by special interests. Several leading journalists were suspected of operating with KGB backing. One American journalist who worked for a short time on *Kommersant* reported that several reporters on that business newspaper were "on the take" from a number of commercial enterprises. When confronted, the reporters passed off their outside activities as "small business," which they said the government wished to encourage. The low salaries of many journalists explain why many reporters can be bought. At *Nezavismaia gazeta,* many journalists were earning 6,000 rubles a month when the subsistence level had risen to 8,000 rubles a month. Journalists were tempted, and some succumbed, to writing advertising, disguised as news stories, for a fee. Dean Zassurskii reported that a Russian businessman offered to help finance Moscow State University's independent radio station, Ekho Moskvy, if broadcasts would repeatedly advertise his products, and only his products.[12]

7. "Unfair" criticism of leaders. President Yeltsin has been described as "the American occupation government" since his return from the United States in June 1992. The opposition newspaper *Chto delat'* (circulation 20,000) has been leading a crusade to oust him. Gavriil Popov resigned as Mayor of Moscow after a series of attacks on him in March 1992 by *Komsomol'skaia pravda, Literaturnaia gazeta,* and Russian State Television for allegedly having illegally leased prime Moscow property to a French concern at bargain-basement prices. Media critics say these attacks were not properly documented.

The people's current attitude toward the media can be judged by a poll conducted by *Izvestiia* in July 1992. Only 40 percent of those questioned believed that the Russian media were objective, while 44 percent said they thought newspapers and broadcasting were biased. Another 49 percent said they believed that government interference in the media was greater in 1992 than it had been under Gorbachev (Tolz 1992). In another poll, conducted by Mnenie (Opinion) Service, 37.3 percent of the 1,500 people questioned throughout Russia thought that the media were not critical enough of government leaders, while 11.1 percent thought the criticisms were too harsh, and 20.2 percent thought that coverage was about right; 31.4 percent, however, had no opinion on this matter (*Mnenie* 1992). The results of another poll asking identical questions, conducted by the (VTsIOM) survey organization, produced figures of 35 percent, 21 percent, 29 percent, and 15 percent, respectively (Ibid.).

Conclusion

Despite these disappointments, neither the public nor the leaders are likely to demand a return to the heavy controls of the past. One indication comes from an independent poll of 1,706 Muscovites in August 1992, which showed that 60 percent of those questioned supported an independent *Izvestiia* in its struggle against the speaker of the Russian parliament (Levinson 1992).

In the future, the Russian press may suffer some new regulations, but history is against a wholesale return to censorship. For one thing, Russia's depressed economy will force any government—even a very conservative or military one—to reach out to the West for help. The West will, in all probability, insist on verifying how that assistance is used. It will insist, too, on access to Russian resources and information. Western help will be an influence for openness.

Second, the pervasive presence of foreign media in Russia will keep political and economic developments in the spotlight. Radio Liberty, financed by the United States and broadcast from Munich, Germany, has set a very high standard for all of the new Russian journalism to emulate. Furthermore, the proliferation of new communications technologies—fax machines, e-mail, satellite telephones, modem-assisted computer transmissions, among others—will make it impossible to return to the arbitrary intimidation of the Stalin era, a major element of the old censorship system which cannot be reimposed.

Finally, the Russian people have learned with horror of Stalin's crimes. They have seen that one-party rule leads to catastrophic mistakes. They have recognized that an opposition is essential for testing and correcting policy errors. In short, they have begun to learn a difficult lesson of democracy: an independent press is a prickly porcupine but no democracy can live without it.

Lev Novozhenov, deputy editor of *Moskovskii komsomolets*, summed up the situation this way at the end of October 1992: "I need freedom of the press. I don't know if Russia needs it. The Russians are a complicated people. They always want what they don't have. When there isn't freedom, they want freedom. When there is freedom, they want law and order. But I think there must be some norms with which man can live, rather like norms of permissible radiation."[13]

Notes

1. Recorded interview with Ministry of Information officials, Moscow, August 5, 1992.
2. Recorded interview with Lev Zh. Novozhenov, Moscow, October 28, 1992.
3. Recorded interview with Ministry of Information officials, Moscow, August 5, 1992.
4. Recorded interview with Igor Golembevskii, Moscow, August 5, 1992.
5. Ibid.
6. Recorded interview with Dmitrii Babich, Boston, MA., July 14, 1992.
7. Recorded interview with Vitalii Tretiakov, Moscow, August 4, 1992.
8. Recorded interview with Igor Golembevskii, Moscow, August 5, 1992.
9. Recorded interview with Dmitrii Babich, Boston, MA., July 14, 1992.
10. Recorded interview with Iasen N. Zassurskii, Moscow, July 31, 1992 and August 10, 1992.
11. Interview with Zinovii Iuriev, Sept. 19, 1992, Andover, VT, September 19, 1992.
12. Recorded interview with Iasen N. Zassurskii, Moscow, July 31, 1992 and August 10, 1992.
13. Recorded interview with Lev Zh. Novozhenov, Moscow, October 28, 1992.

References

Dewhirst, M. and Farrell, R. (1973). *The Soviet Censorship*. Metuchen, NJ: Scarecrow Press.

Gorbachev, Mikhail S. (1984). "Zhivoe tvorchestvo naroda—doklad tovarishcha M.S. Gorbacheva," *Pravda*, no. 346 (December 11), pp. 2–3.

Interview with G. Lazutina and K. Litvinov (1990). "Professiia—reporter?" *Vestnik vysshei shkoly*, September, pp. 35–41.

Levinson, Aleksandr (1992). "Nam nuzhny nezavisimye *Izvestiia*," *Izvestiia*, no. 176 (August 5), p. 2.

Moskovskii, Gosudarstvennyi universitet imeni M.V. Lomonosov fakul'tet zhurnalistiki (1992). *Otchet o deiatel'nosti fakul'teta za 1991 god*. Moscow, pp. 1213.

Ostrow, Joel, M. (1990). *Legal Reform in the Soviet Union and the Law on the Press: Sources, Process, Prospects* (unpublished Masters Degree thesis), Massachusetts Institute of Technology.

Sluzhba "Mnenie" (1992). Rossiiskie oprosy (Russian Poll), R/05/92. Moscow, p. 4.

Tolz, Vera (1992). *After Glasnost*. RFE/RL Research Report, vol. 1, no. 39 (October 2), pp. 4–9.

Tretiakov, Vitalii (1989). "Few Straight-A Students As Yet," *Moscow News*, no. 19 (May 14–21), p. 13.

Winick, Charles and Grisha Dotzenko (1964). *USSR Humor*. Mount Vernon, NY: The Peter Pauper Press.

11

Issues in Teacher Education

STEPHEN WEBBER AND TATIANA WEBBER

The importance of teacher-education reform for educational and societal change can be seen through a comparison of the present situation in Russia with two precedents—one that achieved its aims, and one that did not—and by examining what the consequences were for the societies concerned. For an example of successful teacher-education reform, we can look to the France of the Third Republic. Jules Ferry, the minister of education, founded *Ecoles Normales* in which to train the *Instituteurs* who would lay the foundations of the Republic throughout France.

> The role of the *Instituteur* in building the republican sentiment of the Third Republic cannot be overestimated. . . . One only has to think how, between 1880 and 1914, the *Instituteurs* went out from the *Ecoles Normales* to every village in the land to disseminate the principles and beliefs of the Republic (Neather 1993, pp. 39–40).

Ferry's initiative in teacher education provided a foundation for the Third Republic, and in the long term exerted an influence on the development of French society well into the twentieth century.

An example of unsuccessful reform, on the other hand, can be taken from Russia's own past, during the period immediately following the October Revolution. The education authorities (Narkompros) under Anatolii V. Lunacharskii vigorously advocated the introduction of the unified labor school, which was to be founded upon principles of humanistic, child-centered education, breaking the authoritarian, content-based traditions of the tsarist school system. Although such plans received enthusiastic recognition from radical educators around the world, not enough attention was given to the task of preparing teachers to carry out the reforms. Some of the teachers who were left from tsarist times would have opposed the reforms through political conscience or through inertia—the teaching profession worldwide, after all, has a reputation of conservatism. Others, however, were willing to adapt and implement reform—but their needs for retraining were on the whole ignored, leaving them confused by the demands being made on them to "humanize" the school, confusion which very easily led to disillusionment and a decision to carry on as before. Those young teachers who went through training after the Revolution were left to reform the school largely by enthusiasm alone; there was a lack of educators sufficiently qualified and able to train teachers in the ways of the "new school." Although the school experiment was finally laid to rest by the advent of Stalin and the return of the prerevolutionary pattern of rigid subject-oriented school life, its fate has already been sealed long before through Narkompros's failure to address teacher education reform.

> The conception of a new school drawn up by Lunacharskii's group could not be implemented, and not only because a totalitarian regime snuffed out the humanitarian school, but also because a contingent of teachers versed in the new conception of the school had not been produced (Bolotov 1991, p. 4).

Following the collapse of the "humanized" school, the authoritarian model was reintroduced and was to remain the backbone of Soviet education for more than sixty years. The experience of the 1920s serves as an ominous precedent for today's reformers in Russia: then, as now, the intention was to build a society fundamentally different from its predecessor; reforms were supposed to break the mold of an authoritarian, subject-oriented school in favor of a "humanized" establishment. In the current situation, as then, society is in crisis (albeit not to such an extent as in the postrevolutionary years); there is a risk that the teaching force in the 1990s, as in the 1920s, may be left confused and bitter at calls for reform from above if insufficient attention is granted to their training needs.

The lesson to be learned from the 1920s is that teacher-education reform should come before general educational reform. Yet the educational authorities in Russia today have had to accept the fact that, by the time they assumed responsibility for the direction of education in Russia following the demise of the Soviet Union, the impulse for change in education had already passed to the grassroots with the emergence of increasing numbers of "alternative" schools the most notable consequence. Teacher-education reform must now strive to catch up with the movement for change and attempt to guide its future development. Together with integrating teacher-education reform with that of education as a whole, it will also be necessary to confront a range of issues within the teacher-education system that influenced the nature of the training provided during the Soviet era. An indication of the scale of the task facing the reformers is provided by the results of surveys of attitudes among teachers, such as one study conducted in 1989 in which 83.6 percent of those questioned expressed dissatisfaction with the initial teacher training which they had received (Gershunskii and Pullin 1990, p. 311), a figure echoed by a more recent survey of Moscow teachers in which 85 percent of young teachers complained that their training did not reflect advances in pedagogical theories and did not prepare them for working in a system undergoing ever-growing diversification ("Kafedra: Statfakt" 1992, p. 22). With regard to in-service training, the statistic is even more alarming: 93.6 percent of teachers in an official survey were not content with the training provided (Dneprov, Lazarev, and Sobkin 1991, p. 122).

In this chapter, we shall examine the cause of such discontent with the present system and then go on to look at the proposals for reform, assessing their prospects both for solving the inherent problems of the teacher-education system and for providing an adequate foundation of training from which successful reform of education as a whole can take place.

A Review of the Teacher-Education System

Structure and Organization

The structure of the Soviet teacher-training system changed little from the 1930s to the end of the Soviet era in 1991. The most important link in the chain was the pedagogical institute (*pedinstitut*), which was classified as a higher educational establishment (VUZ), and which trained the majority of the country's teachers for the senior grades of the Soviet secondary school. University courses also included a compulsory element of pedagogical training, and a good number of university graduates found themselves allocated to school teaching posts under the distribution system,[1] although such recruits were outnumbered nine to one by graduates from the *pedinstitut*. In the pedagogical school (*peduchilishche*) students received secondary specialized education and were prepared for teaching at kindergarten and primary levels. The other components of the teacher-education network were the pedagogical classes that had been founded in the senior forms of secondary schools in more recent years and the institutes for in-service training (IUUy).[2]

The most striking aspect of the Soviet teacher-education system was its rigid uniformity: the same pattern was followed across the entire country, with no diversity permitted in areas with definite regional and national characteristics. Curricula, finances, appointments of rectors (presidents)—all such decisions came from the center, the educational authorities in Moscow. Although such centralization suited the purposes of the Soviet authorities in their desire to forge unity in their disparate empire, the consequence for the running of individual establishments was a stifling lack of independence which made it difficult, for example, to adapt quickly enough to changing conditions or to respond to regionally specific issues.

The system was also marked by a lack of differentiation in course provision: for example, *peduchilishche* graduates who wished to requalify as secondary school teachers had no option but to follow a complete five-year course in a *pedinstitut*. This was despite the fact that they had already covered a good deal of the material when they had studied for their present qualification. Those with higher education who wished to train as teachers were granted a concession allowing them to pass through the course in three years.

During the perestroika era (1985–1991), some attempts were made to grant a degree of independence to the higher educational establishments. The reform-minded chairman of the State Committee on Education Gennadii A. Yagodin declared:

> Inside the walls of the institute they know much more than those in the ministry's *apparat* about the many practical questions which are linked with the training of young specialists. This is why we have given the VUZy the right to solve independently any problems which arise. Don't wait for step-by-step directions. The time of directives and instructions has passed (Rostovtsev 1988, p. 6).

Institutes were to be given some leeway in the content of the curriculum, for example, and, in accordance with the policy of democratization, rectors were to be elected by institute collectives. However, early optimism that these initiatives represented a newfound independence soon faded; as with so many reforms under perestroika, these moves did not prove effective. With regard to changes in the curriculum, for example, institutes were limited to alterations totaling no more than 15 percent of the whole timetable, and all modifications had in any case to be ratified by the ministry, which was not prepared to allow much in the way of radical innovation. The "election" of rectors more often than not saw the incumbents retain their posts.

In financial terms, the entire education system suffered from being funded under the "leftover" principle, which allocated to education whatever was left after other sectors of the economy that were deemed more important (such as the military) had received their share. Within the education system itself, teacher education was not seen as a priority issue, and traditionally occupied the position of the poor relative. Pedagogical institutes lacked the prestigious status of universities and the material support offered by industrial sponsors to many technical institutes. The *pedinstitut's* clients—the schools—were in no position to offer any such support. Consequently, the teacher-education system was unable to equip its establishments adequately, a situation which changed little since this observation in the 1960s: "No proposals for improving the work of the pedagogical institutes will have a chance of success unless we stop looking on them as second-rate institutions, for whose work blackboards and chalk are enough" (Mikhalev 1965).

Apart from the consequences for teaching resources, lack of funds took a toll on all areas of an institute's life. Only 25 percent of pedagogical institutes in 1991, for example, were considered to possess suitable premises for their purposes, and they were only able to employ half the necessary service staff. Some 40 percent of students were found to suffer from chronic illnesses because of lack of space and poor conditions in their badly maintained hostels, as well as from poor food and a lack of efficient health care (Dneprov, Lazarev, and Sobkin 1991, p. 125). With regard to the provision of places in hostels, there was a shortfall of 25 percent (*Sistema obrazovaniia* 1992, p. 12).

Attempts to alleviate the problem were initiated under perestroika, when self-management of finances was encouraged. Yet even if institutes managed to pass through the bureaucratic red tape involved in transferring to self-management, the freedom it gave was limited because of restrictions on the extent an institute could freely use the money at its disposal.

A practice of buying off graduates was also introduced, under which interested parties—usually commercial organizations—paid an agreed amount to an institute, often in kind, for example, with computer equipment. Although such practice contravened the distribution system, an institute more interested in the prospect of material gain would turn a blind eye to the rules in such cases. However, the scheme failed to bring about a substantial improvement in the material position of the institutes, as there was a limit to the number of students who would be "adopted" by interested parties. While foreign-language specialists may have attracted companies looking for interpreters, for instance, students from other disciplines were less marketable. The problem of finances was left unresolved.

The Content of Teacher Education

The pedagogical institute curriculum was badly overloaded. Students received almost nine thousand hours of instruction over the five-year course, amounting to an average of thirty-six hours per week in an academic year that lasted an average of thirty-one weeks. In addition to their studies students had to engage in compulsory extracurricular activities, such as involvement in the *Komsomol*. During summer vacation (and sometimes during the academic year itself), they could be called upon to work in the fields or in a factory for up to two months.

With regard to the content of training, an examination of the allocation of hours to the different subject groups reveals a heavy imbalance toward the specialized subject program (the subjects that the teacher would teach in school). These subjects comprised between 60 and 70 percent of the whole curriculum. The pedagogical cycle, with between 9 and 13 percent of the curriculum, was given fewer hours overall than the social sciences (ideological subjects), and fewer even than the combined total of subsidiary subjects which included physical education, nursing (for female students), and military training (for male students). For example, students in a five-year course would spend 668 hours on physical education lessons compared to 400 hours in the study of pedagogy. This state of affairs is somewhat surprising, to say the least, when one remembers that the course was ostensibly a teacher-training program. Why was the curriculum structured in this way?

First, one can note the lack of development in the curriculum over the years.

> The fundamental model of the curriculum of a higher pedagogical educational institution took shape in the 1920s and subsequently underwent very minor changes. . . .In half a century life has changed beyond all recognition, requirements imposed upon the schools and the teachers have increased greatly, yet the curriculum in the higher educational institution remains just what it was half a century ago (Men'shikov 1991, p. 39).

As time passed, the position of the pedagogical cycle, which once was given a major share of the curriculum, was eroded, and more class hours were allocated to the social sciences, specialized subjects, and subsidiary courses.

The position of the social-science cycle, which included such subjects as scientific communism, Marxist–Leninist philosophy, political economy, and the history of the CPSU, was guaranteed in all higher educational establishments. The stress laid on these subjects by the authorities was in accordance with the teacher's role in the vanguard of bringing the Communist faith to the rising generations:

> The Soviet teacher is first and foremost an ideological educator, responsible for developing among young people a scientific, social, political and civic outlook. To be equal to this task, the teacher, in addition to receiving a thorough specialized and professional training, should acquire a broad philosophical and socio-political outlook (Tomiak 1972, p. 111).

During the early years of perestroika, the emphasis on ideological education increased, although the influence of these subjects waned toward the end of the Soviet period as opposition to the Communist faith grew in the country. However, the subjects were never removed from the curriculum once and for all.

Although the specialized subject programs were heavily oriented toward theoretical aspects, they were nevertheless thorough courses that often matched those offered by the universities in scope and overall quality. Yet while there was a course within the specialist cycle on teaching methods, students and staff complained that it gave little in the way of practical training and was divorced to a large extent from the reality of the school classroom. The specialized subjects owed their dominant position in the curriculum to the nature of the Soviet school curriculum, which placed comparatively little emphasis on the development of pupils' cognitive skills but rather required them to memorize the material given to them and reproduce it during examinations. The teacher was seen as a "subject-teacher" who would act mainly as a purveyor of specialized knowledge.

The pedagogical courses that were provided were heavily oriented toward theory and gave little in the way of practical knowledge that could be applied in the classroom. Students were not sufficiently well trained in classroom management and child psychology, for example. Soviet pedagogy was further handicapped by ideological constraints, which limited theory to views acceptable to Communist doctrine, and thus denied students access to the experience of other educational systems. Soviet student teachers were led to expect that their classes in school would be full of enthusiastic, motivated pupils, all equally able to comprehend the work presented to them. As a result, they were not prepared to deal with mixed-ability groups comprised of children with particular educational needs.

Although the amount of time devoted to the practice-teaching component of the teacher-education course can perhaps be considered adequate (fourteen weeks in the five-year course), its success or failure was often left to the conscience of individual supervising teachers. Sometimes, especially in the case of shortage-ridden village schools, student teachers would be given a full timetable and used as replacement teachers for the duration of their practice teaching, with little attention paid to their own needs. The result of neglecting the pedagogical training of prospective teachers was predictable:

> Nine percent of the time is allotted to this cycle [pedagogical-psychological]. The same amount is allotted to medical training. But surely no one is going to claim that the pedagogical institute is turning out qualified medical personnel. The professional qualifications of [*pedinstitut*] nurses is such that they don't even know how to give injections. And, alas, just about the same thing characterizes educators' psychological qualifications. This is all built into the curriculum: we are consciously programming ignorance (Men'shikov 1991, pp. 39–40).

Such was the pedagogical training undergone by the majority of Soviet teachers. There were exceptions to this norm, such as that to be found in the so-called innovator-institutes, notably the *pedinstitut* in Poltava. These institutes were permitted to develop experimental curricula, for example, in which pedagogical training was often given a substantially higher profile than it had in the standard curriculum. The Poltavian experiment produced a successful course entitled "The Foundations of Pedagogical Mastery," which gave much emphasis to practical work and proved popular among students, who praised it for the preparation it gave them for working in the classroom (Ziaziun 1988).

In addition to these institutes, which enjoyed the tolerance of the authorities, there was also the work of individual teacher-innovators, such as Amonashvili, Shatalov, Il'in, and others, who gained an increasing amount of popular support in the country during the 1980s after widespread coverage of their methods by the media. They pooled their ideas to create the concept of a pedagogy of cooperation (*pedagogika sotrudnichestva*) aimed at humanizing the process of school education. In the later years of perestroika, the innovators and their followers began to organize courses for teachers who wanted to learn of their methods.

Yet the fruits of such innovative work took years to filter through to teacher-training establishments in the country at large, and even when they did, their influence was often muted. In 1990, for instance, a pedagogical masters course was introduced in the curriculum of pedagogical institutes, inspired by the work in Poltava. Although this was seen as a progressive move in the field of pedagogical education, the academic staff who were assigned to teach the course often were not sufficiently familiar with its content, with due consequences for the quality of the course's delivery. The same fate befell many such attempts to bring the ideas of the teacher-innovators to students in training. This typifies the approach taken to the reform of teacher education in the perestroika years. In 1990, for instance, the USSR State Committee on Public Education published a concept of pedagogical education, which included a great many high-sounding phrases—such as the statement that the graduate of a pedagogical establishment should have "a love of children, the desire and ability to give them his/her heart"—but which, as Dneprov, Lazarev, and Sobkin point out, failed to give concrete proposals for the direction of reform in practice (Dneprov, Lazarev, and Sobkin 1991, p. 122).

The above refers specifically to the pedagogical training given in the *pedinstitut*. What of the courses provided in the *peduchilishche* and the university? In universities, pedagogical training was much more limited in scope than that in the *pedinstitut*, both with regard to theoretical instruction and teaching practice. Since the *peduchilishche* was not a higher educational establishment, its curriculum had much less emphasis on the study of social science than that in the *pedinstitut*. It also gave less time to the study of specialized subjects. Consequently, more time could be devoted to the study of pedagogy. Although the theoretical aspects of the course suffered from the same drawbacks as the *pedinstitut* course, many of the *peduchilshche* lecturers had themselves taught in school and thus were able to draw on their own experience to enhance the practical side of the program. By contrast many *pedinstitut* lecturers had spent most, if not all, of their career in higher education.

In-Service Training

It was sometimes suggested that shortcomings in initial training were compensated for by the in-service training system, in which teachers received training once every five years at the IUU. However, this notion is contradicted by such statements as the following:

> No teacher commented spontaneously on the usefulness of the entitlement to one term's in-service training every five years. We did not gain a sense of this period of training out of school as assisting teachers with their immediate problems in school (Poppleton et al. 1990, p. 95).

The reference to their "immediate problems in school" echoes the complaints of many teachers, who felt that courses placed too much emphasis on theory and failed to give the help required in providing access to new developments in education. Although the pedagogy of cooperation, for example, was widely promoted in the educational press and elsewhere during the late 1980s, teachers were often unable to become familiar with its methods because of a lack of effective in-service course provision. This situation was reflected in the results of a survey of teachers:

> They [teachers] complained that the in-service providers were still dealing in outmoded concepts and methods from the past. The teacher training and in-service institutes have themselves not yet formulated ideas and materials to match the new concepts of individualized, humanized, interdisciplinary and differentiated teaching. This is causing Soviet teachers frustration and stress (Gershunskii and Pullin 1990, p. 314).

The grievances of teachers who formed the discontented 93.6 percent of those questioned included the criticism that in-service training courses did not take into account one's previous training and did not make use of the results of educational research and the experience of Soviet and foreign educators. Teachers also complained that there were no financial incentives to attend in-service training courses. Further, the various establishments involved in the teacher-education system were criticized for their lack of cooperation with regard to in-service training (Dneprov, Lazarev, and Sobkin 1991, p. 122).

The concept of retraining only once in five years was also felt by many teachers to be too restrictive. There was a lack of short courses designed to deal with specific issues. Absent too was a program of support for new entrants into the teaching profession; for the most part, new teachers were left to fend for themselves in the schools after graduation.

Academic Staff

A point often made in current proposals for reform is the need to humanize the learning process in pedagogical training, with regard to staff-student relations and teaching methods. Relations between staff and students in Soviet VUZy have traditionally been much more formal on the whole than they are in, say, Great Britain or the United States (a formality, however, that may not have been so unusual for a student from France, for example). Linked with this has been the tendency of lecturers to employ a teacher-centered style, with students making a comparatively limited contribution to lessons. As a result, VUZ lecturers are now being urged to adopt a more student-centered approach, making greater use of discussion work and simulation exercises, for instance.

The employment of such traditional methods by the academic staff may be better understood, however, if one examines the crippling teaching load endured by *pedinstitut* lecturers. This ranged from 750 to 850 hours per academic year for a full professor or a *dotsent* (a senior academic) to between 950 and 1050 hours for senior and assistant lecturers (Dneprov, Lazarev, and Sobkin 1991, p. 123). Given the extent of this workload, lecturers could perhaps be forgiven for adopting approaches which were less demanding on them. The overloaded nature of the lecturers' work also provides some explanation in answer to criticisms that the staff of pedagogical establishments were less well qualified in comparison with staff of other types of VUZy, in particular with those of the universities. The figures above refer only to teaching duties and do not include time given to administrative and research activities. Not surprisingly, *pedinstitut* lecturers found it difficult to find the time required for postgraduate study.

This situation was compounded by the rigidity of the postgraduate system in the USSR. The first stage of postgraduate studies lasted for three years of full-time study, while *doktorantura* courses could last for many years. On average, the defense of a *kandidat*'s degree (equivalent to a Ph.D.) in a humanities subject came when the student was thirty-six to thirty-eight years old, with the corresponding age for defense of a doctorate being fifty-four. The average age of professors in pedagogical institutes was over sixty, and across the Soviet Union there was usually only one, perhaps two professors per institute, while in thirty out of the two hundred pedagogical institutes there was no professor at all. Because only professors had the right to supervise postgraduate students, this had obvious consequences for the numbers of postgraduates in the institutes (Kruglov 1991, pp. 91–92). The late defense of postgraduate dissertations can thus be blamed partly upon the scarcity of potential supervisors—hopeful postgraduates could wait for years even to be admitted to a course and often had to travel away from their post to study for the postgraduate degree.

Lecturers also had to come to terms with the low status of their profession and its low level of material reward. The status of a *pedinstitut* lecturer, for example, was lower than that of a university lecturer, while a *dotsent* was likely to earn approximately the same amount as a bus driver. Such conditions deterred many from beginning a career as a lecturer, and a good number of those who did enter the profession sought to leave after awhile: in 1992 the shortage of lecturers amounted to some 20 percent

(*Sistema obrazovaniia* 1992, p. 12). Male lecturers were a particular casualty, their absence leading to the "feminization" of the staff, with the male–female ratio standing at 17.3 to 82.7. (It must be noted that, despite such figures, most rectors are in fact male.) In addition, owing to the difficulty of attracting younger candidates to the profession, the average age of academic staff was quite high, with the number of lecturers over sixty years of age having doubled over the last thirty years (Dneprov, Lazarev, and Sobkin 1991, p. 123).

Educational Research

Apart from the difficulties faced by lecturers in conducting research, the organization of educational research from the highest to the lowest levels was beset by shortcomings. Research was overseen by the Academy of Pedagogical Sciences, an aloof, ivory tower–like institution, which was too distant from the school and the teachers it was supposed to support. Postgraduate research students faced problems similar to those encountered by lecturers, with school teachers often finding their time commitment too great a burden to consider starting a research degree. Research work of a more private nature was occasionally performed at a grassroots level but without official support. The teacher-innovators, for example, had to endure severe criticism and censure from the powers that be. Finally, pedagogical institutes were often criticized for not paying attention to research work at the undergraduate level: whereas other types of VUZy required students to write a dissertation as part of their final examinations, for example, in the *pedinstitut* there was no such obligation.

There has been a lack of research into the practice of education, with due consequences for the development of the Russian school. The learning process, as a highly complex, constantly evolving phenomenon, requires a solid theoretical base from which to produce methodologies to be applied in practice. Such a basis of theory is now needed more than ever in Russian education, given the fundamental nature of the change through which the school is passing, and careful attention must therefore be paid to the question of educational research to ensure that the necessary foundation for the school and the teachers is provided.

Students

The most hotly debated issue concerning students revolved around their professional orientation toward teaching, namely the reluctance shown by many *pedinstitut* graduates to teach in the schools. In 1990, for instance, the chairman of the State Committee for Education lamented the fact that only one in two graduates from pedagogical institutes went into teaching (Pleshakov 1990, p. 2), while a good number of those who did subsequently left for careers elsewhere. Traditionally, the blame for such a situation was placed first on the students, for failing to perform their social "duty," but also on the pedagogical VUZy entrance procedure, which took little if any account of a student's aptitude to teaching. As a result, a great deal of energy was expended on schemes to attract the "right" sort of entrants, that is, students who would be sure to devote themselves to teaching careers.

It was felt that the problem could be solved by directing "suitable" candidates toward teaching from an early age, so pedagogical classes (*pedklassy*) were introduced into the senior grades of some ordinary secondary schools. *Pedklassy* aimed to select children who displayed an inclination toward teaching and, while they completed their secondary schooling, prepare them for a teaching career. The pupils received instruction in pedagogical subjects and in psychology and conducted teaching practice of a limited duration. On graduating from a *pedklass*, the pupils were entitled to work in a kindergarten or could proceed to further pedagogical training.

The problem of attracting people to teaching was felt most acutely in rural areas, owing to the much poorer living conditions found there. The distribution system attempted to supply the villages with teachers by assigning graduates to work there for three years, but such recruits often did all they could to escape such a fate. Even students who hailed from the country often strove to find a way to stay in the town, by finding a job or by marrying a town-dweller. Incentives in the form of housing and slightly better pay also failed to solve the problem. It was therefore decided in the 1970s to adopt a new approach to staffing village schools, by offering entrants from rural areas noncompetitive entrance to pedagogical establishments on the condition that they return to their homes after graduating and work in the local schools.

In general, the standard of education offered in village schools is lower than that found in the towns and, as a result, a lower percentage of village youth has continued onto higher education. The opportunity to enter a VUZ with much reduced requirements was therefore accepted gladly by many, and the pedagogical institutes saw an influx of rural youth. In 1985, for example, between 50 and 66 percent of *pedinstitut* students were being admitted on a preferential basis (Golovin 1985, p. 21). Problems arose as a result of the academic weakness of many such students in comparison with their peers from the towns, and a significantly high percentage of them dropped out of their courses. One *pedinstitut* rector, lamenting what he saw as falling academic standards among students, identified the non-competitive entrance system as the major cause for this decline.[3] Another critic was more blunt, accusing the system of creating "a vicious circle . . . when inferior graduates from the pedagogical institutes become poor teachers who prepare poor school-leavers who are the future candidates for admission to the same institutes on a non-competitive basis" (Shturman 1988, p. 289). She also notes:

> This measure is ineffective, as in most cases the weak students scrape through the institutes, are awarded the same degrees as everyone else and find jobs in places which they prefer and not in the outlying regions or in the villages, or in a different profession altogether (Ibid., p. 285).

In fact, many students, whether from town or country, had no intention of making teaching their career from the moment they entered the institute. Why, then, did they opt to study in a pedagogical establishment? As Filippov noted in 1969, "Many young people strive to get into a VUZ not because they are attracted to a given concrete profession, but because they strive for higher education as such" (Higgins 1976, pp. 157–58). In fulfilling this desire they may have had little choice as to the type of establishment they entered: "The percentage of pedagogical higher education institutions is unconscionably high; therefore a considerable percentage of youth are compelled to attend these institutions, although they know beforehand that they will not work as teachers" (Dzhilavian 1981, p. 96). Students who wished to study a particular subject, for example, may have had to opt for pedagogical training, if that course was not available in other VUZy in that area.

The problem of professional orientation, however, lay not so much with the attitudes of the students as it did with the nature of the teaching profession in the Soviet Union. Despite official propaganda to the contrary, teaching traditionally suffered from a lack of status. As one teacher put it, "In the past, teachers were regarded somewhat differently, they were the people who brought enlightenment to the people about forty years ago. But now the teacher commands no authority. Just as education and upbringing itself commands no particular degree of respect" (Poppleton et al. 1990, p. 96).

In comparison with those in other graduate professions, not to mention blue-collar workers, teachers were badly paid and received fewer benefits.

This fact alone could be enough to deter even an enthusiastic prospective teacher. To attract young people to teaching required above all a massive commitment on the part of the state to improving the teacher's material position. The authorities, however, chose to ignore this simple truth and continued to blame the situation on the attitudes of students.

Meanwhile, the schools suffered from a shortage of motivated, well-qualified staff. While there were, without doubt, talented, enthusiastic teachers to be found throughout the school system, the nature of the Soviet teacher-education program took its toll on the overall quality of the graduates it produced, as can be seen through such comments as: "School headteachers state that the graduates of pedagogical establishments are not ready for practical work with children" (Kruglov 1991, p. 88); and, "The education received in the pedagogical establishment for the majority of graduates is not sufficiently 'pedagogical,' and many of them cannot, in the first years of working in school, solve independently professional tasks, and as a consequence leave education" (Belozertsev 1992, p. 61).

Measures for Reform

It will have become obvious from the preceding discussion that there is a range of problems which affect the teacher-education system in Russia, issues which must be tackled if the quality of teachers (and of the education system itself) is to improve. In addition, teacher education is called upon to integrate its reforms with the reform of education as a whole, and to provide the teaching force that will bring about these reforms in the school. We will now examine the extent to which these issues are being addressed.

Organization

According to the Russian Ministry of Education, decentralization and regionalization are priorities, the aim being to break the rigidity and uniformity of the highly centralized Soviet system. In accordance with these goals, much administrative, financial, and curricular control is expected to be devolved to individual establishments and regional authorities. Institutes, for example, are already able to devise their own teaching programs. The central authorities intend to monitor the situation by means of a system of standards for pedagogical education, for which an assessment procedure has been devised.

The role of the ministry in financing pedagogical establishments will henceforth be limited to supplying salaries and student stipends. (Owing to the severity of the present crisis, however, the ministry is finding even this task difficult, and many lecturers have experienced delays of months before receiving their salaries.) Pedagogical establishments are to self-manage their finances and are being encouraged with great vigor to seek alternative means of raising capital. For instance, it has been proposed that municipal colleges be set up within the framework of institutes and colleges, which would offer a variety of paid courses in academic and vocational subjects, together with other services, to the public and to industry. Yet, as has been the case before, the potential of pedagogical establishments to make money in that way may be limited by comparison with that of other institutions which are more commercially oriented.

A further attempt to raise capital has been provided by the "contract" system (*dogovornaia sistema*) which has superseded the buying-off scheme described earlier. A school, commercial organization, or other institution agrees to pay for a particular student's education in return for a contract binding that student to work with that institution upon graduation. Such deals involve substantial sums of money, thus bringing a welcome source of finance for the pedagogical institute concerned. The scheme made a relatively slow start in its first year of operation (1992), with the total number of students entering under contracts standing at just 6 percent in VUZy across the Russian Federation (Prelovskaia 1992, p. 3). There are signs that the number of students entering under contracts will increase in the years to come, but it remains to be seen whether this scheme will provide a solution to the financial requirements of the teacher-education establishments, particularly in the short term, during the current period of severe economic difficulties in Russia. Despite its intentions, the ministry may well be forced to take a more active role in financing teacher education than it would wish.

Structure

To break away from the rigidity of the existing system, pedagogical education is to be restructured to allow for the provision of differentiated courses for students of various educational backgrounds. Short-duration postgraduate training programs are being developed for students with non-pedagogical higher education who can proceed to such programs either directly upon graduating or in order to retrain from other professions. This represents recognition of the fact that the days of distribution—of compelling graduates to fulfill their social duty—are over, and that from now on market forces are to dictate employment trends in Russia. With the growth of the commercial sector, there is a greater choice of professions, and teaching will have to compete hard to attract students; it is hoped that a differentiated course structure will help toward this aim.

The concept of a teacher-education continuum (*nepreryvnoe pedagogicheskoe obrazovanie*) is being stressed in the proposals for reform. Institutes and schools are to be grouped in complexes which will support and complement each other in terms of course content, providing a smooth progression from school-based pedagogical training to in-service provision and educational research. This concept came into favor during the perestroika years, and experimental complexes have been operating for some time. In the Belgorod *peduchilishche-pedinstitut* complex, for example, both the institute and the school benefited from combining the more practical approach of the *peduchilishche* with the experience of the *pedinstitut* in specialized subject provision (Reshetnikov 1991, pp. 93–96). In the Poltavian experiment the *pedinstitut* formed the nucleus of a "teaching-scientific-pedagogical complex" (UNPK), which in addition encompassed several local schools. UNPK coordinated such activities as professional orientation among teenagers, teaching practice, and research projects, and duly helped to foster closer links between school and institute (Ziaziun 1988).

Existing types of pedagogical establishment are to continue to function, adapting to new requirements. For instance, special faculties are to be set up in the pedagogical institutes to conduct the retraining courses described above. Alongside the traditional institutions, however, a number of new types of pedagogical establishments are to be created.

The Pedagogical Lycée and Gymnasium

These will perform a similar function to *pedklassy*, taking pupils from the eighth or ninth grades (fifteen-year-olds), and providing elementary pedagogical training in addition to ordinary secondary education. One interesting early example is the Male Pedagogical Lycée in Volgograd, which has as its aim the promotion of the teaching profession among boys in an attempt to offset the female-male imbalance in schools (Il'menev 1991). Those who matriculate from pedagogical lycées and gymnasia will be able to work as teachers in kindergartens or in the primary sections of secondary schools, and, if they wish, to have direct entry to a higher education establishment *hors de concours*.

The Pedagogical College

Pedagogical colleges are being formed mainly on the basis of existing *peduchilishche*. Judging by the model of those colleges already functioning, these establishments will differ from the traditional *uchilishche* in the length of the course (three years instead of two for secondary-school graduates), and in the provision of additional subjects such as special educational needs and a foreign language. It is intended that pedagogical colleges assume the status of establishments of the first stage of higher education.

The Pedagogical University

Pedagogical institutes may apply for accreditation as pedagogical universities, a title that was first granted to the prestigious Lenin and Herzen Institutes in Moscow and Leningrad. The number of pedagogical universities is now growing, with more institutes eager to follow, lured by the greater status which it is hoped the university title will bestow. To be allowed to rename itself a university, an institute undergoes a process of assessment in order to ascertain whether its curricular provision and research activities merit the title. The assessment is conducted by a committee appointed by the education ministry in Moscow.

This process of renaming pedagogical establishments accompanies a larger trend in Russia, which has seen a good number of establishments with political, economic, and social functions renamed with titles that, on the surface, appear to reflect the transition from Communist state to democracy. However, it is often the case that a change in name is not matched by significant modifications in the actual character of an establishment, which continues to operate much as it did before. Such a phenomenon can also be noticed in certain pedagogical establishments that have been renamed. Yet this is to be expected—change cannot occur overnight, and some time will pass before real differences can be seen. The policy of renaming can in fact play a part in the aim to raise the status of pedagogical education and of the teaching profession as a whole for, as has proved the case in other countries, the title "university" appears to bring with it a greater prestige than "institute."

The Regional Pedagogical University

The next link in the teacher-education continuum is another product of the policy of decentralization. It is the intention that regional pedagogical universities will be founded on the base of successful provincial pedagogical institutes. Among other things, they will be responsible for coordination of research projects, in-service training, and the management of resources in their regions, allowing regionally specific issues to be dealt with more effectively.

The University of Pedagogical Mastery (UPM)

UPMs are being set up principally on the basis of existing in-service training institutes (IUU), which are to be reorganized into "service and innovation centers." These centers will function, as IUUy did before, as centers for in-service training and are intended to provide courses of a more practical nature than those previously available. At present, the state guarantees retraining for each teacher every five years; teachers can attend courses in the interim, but are usually required to pay a fee.

UPMs are also to provide support for newly qualified teachers and have been given the tasks of conducting educational research and organizing short-duration (probably one- or two-year) courses for students who already have higher-education qualifications to retrain as teachers.

Postgraduate Teacher Training

The provision of postgraduate training courses is a necessary step in the reform process. Owing to the greater choice in professions now available in Russia, it will be difficult enough to attract students to the teaching profession, but the task will be harder if teacher training is obtainable only through five-year undergraduate courses. Short-term postgraduate courses such as those now planned make teacher training accessible to a much wider range of potential students, including those who come to teaching after some time in other professions. Programs are already running, for example, to retrain former military officers. Such courses will also allow the authorities to respond more rapidly to staffing requirements in the school system. As mentioned above, re-training faculties are also to be established in pedagogical institutes, thus broadening the basis of the initiative.

Another possible course of action is on-the-job training for would-be teachers (similar to the British licensed teacher scheme and the alternative certification program in the United States), a course of action that has been proposed by the Russian Ministry of Education (Dneprov, Lazarev, and Sobkin 1991, pp. 185–86). Although it would perhaps be unwise to rely upon such on-the-job training as a major source of teacher supply, this could provide a quick solution to staff shortages.

If such a measure were introduced, the role of part-time teacher education may be enhanced; students could study for their teaching qualifications concurrently with working in school. For this to be achieved, flexible courses of reasonably short duration would have to be devised. The part-time element of teacher education has traditionally played a major part in the functioning of the system as a whole, with 45 percent of teachers entering the profession via this route. However, part-time departments had to tolerate underfunding and a lack of material and human resources, and courses suffered from inflexibility in content and length (Kruglov 1991, pp. 90–91). The authorities would do well now to devote attention to part-time education with regard not only to training programs, but also to the availability of postgraduate taught and research courses, to encourage teachers to participate in educational research alongside their full-time job.

In-Service Training

The restructuring of refresher courses to give adequate and efficient training for the existing cadre of teachers must surely be seen as a priority. While it is hoped that initial training will produce graduates ready to work in a reformed school system, it will be the more experienced teachers who will have to lead the way.

The task of convincing experienced teachers of the need to revise their approach to teaching, to change the practice they have followed for ten, twenty, or thirty years, is a difficult one indeed. The teaching profession throughout the world is notoriously conservative, a fact that has hampered and even defeated initiatives in the education systems of many countries. Much effort will be needed in Russia to win the support of an already demoralized profession.

In-service training should be thorough and ongoing, available to all teachers, and consist of training that can be put to immediate practical use in the classroom. What must be avoided is the practice of the past—a constant stream of high-sounding directives that leave the teacher confused and alienated. It is hoped that the recently introduced system of categories will help to attract teachers to in-service programs and postgraduate research, as such activities will influence the awarding of categories and, consequently, of salary scales ("Ofitsioz—Tul'skii pedsovet" 1992, p. 21).

The question with which one is confronted, of course, is who will conduct this retraining. Because the advisers are still unsure how to proceed themselves, it is not uncommon at present for IUUy to direct teachers in need of further training to other schools in their areas that already have experience in the new approaches. There is a particularly pressing need to retrain teachers of the social sciences, an area which has obviously been seriously affected by changes in society. The authorities must act quickly to form groups of advisers who are well acquainted with (and supportive of) the changes in direction that are required of the Russian school, as well as the means of bringing them to life in the classroom.

A Two-Tier Structure

In addition to the creation of pedagogical education complexes and the emergence of new types of pedagogical establishment the teacher-education system will also have to prepare itself for the reorganization of Russian higher education into a Western-style two-tier system offering a *bakalavr* (bachelor) degree after three to four years and a *magistr* (master) degree after one to two further years. Such was the intention laid down in a directive from the Russian Ministry of Education in June 1992. The directive went on to state that a number of pedagogical institutes were to experiment with the new system beginning in September 1992, with other establishments joining them in increasing numbers. By 1995, at least 50 percent of pedagogical institutes and universities are to be operating under a two-tier structure ("O mnogourovnevoi" 1992).

According to intentions published thus far, persons holding a *bakalavr* in pedagogical education will be able either to teach two subjects up to the ninth grade of school, or one subject to the eleventh grade, while the degree of *magistr* will entitle one to work in any secondary, specialized secondary, or higher educational establishment, and will also bring them the right to enter postgraduate courses (*aspirantura*).

Courses to be offered will vary according to the individual establishment, although they will have to comply with the standards in pedagogical education referred to above. In establishments that have begun to introduce the two-tier approach, a greater emphasis appears to be placed on the role of student research at the *magistr* level and to some extent at the *bakalavr* stage. This coincides with other initiatives to revise the provision of research courses and postgraduate studies in general. In the Herzen Pedagogical University in St. Petersburg, for instance, *magistr* courses are being offered in a range of subjects, including pedagogy, and a two-year paid course in Waldorfian methods is also to be run. There is a definite need for such one- and two-year courses to exist alongside longer re-search-based programs, in order to make postgraduate study more accessible for schoolteachers. It is also essential that there be widespread school-based research into the progress of the implementation of the reform program, in order for any shortcomings to be assessed and rectified at an early stage. It is hoped that such initiatives will go some way toward redressing the lack of practical research in education.

Merging Institutions

A logical step to accompany the introduction of a two-tier system is that of merging pedagogical establishments and other professional VUZy with universities, to form large complexes under a unified administration. Such a move would appear to make financial and academic sense: administration costs would be reduced, making such universities more capable of withstanding material difficulties; and academic resources could be pooled, with departments from the various VUZy joining forces to offer a much more flexible range of courses. Indeed, those lecturers and students with whom the authors have discussed the idea are, on the whole, in favor of merging.

In undertaking such a policy, Russia would be following the example of education systems of other countries in which teacher education has moved closer to the universities over the last hundred years. This transition has not been smooth in many cases, with pedagogical establishments eager to preserve their identity and universities often adopting a rather superior attitude to the invasion of academia by such a "practical" subject as teaching. Another potential obstacle arises from the fact that mergers will almost certainly result in great reductions in the administrative and academic staff, with those in senior positions in the smaller establishments displaced by more highly qualified colleagues from the larger institutions. Not surprisingly, such a policy is certain to encounter a hostile response and opposition from its potential victims. As a result, it is likely that the process of merging institutions, if it is to be carried out, will take some considerable time.

The Content of Teacher Education

As one lecturer put it, "The inertia of the academic staff and a desire to continue to work in the old way is not helping to change for the better in the case of the curriculum."[4] The older average age of lecturers will play a part in this, as many will undoubtedly find change difficult even if they do support the aims of reform. One must also take into account the possibility of opposition on political grounds, from lecturers who may well lament the passing of the now discarded ideology of Communism.

Despite these problems, however, modifications of a substantial nature have been introduced in a good number of establishments. In one case, for example, the timetable for the pedagogical-psychological cycle has been increased to 33 percent of the total, a significant improvement, with the specialized-subject cycle reduced to between 25 and 30 percent. Yet merely increasing or decreasing the number of timetable hours with a stroke of a pen will not solve the problem. As has been mentioned above, lecturers need to be retrained to equip them for the new demands being made on them. However, the question of such training is causing practical problems for many institutions which are finding, for example, that the increased costs of sending lecturers on courses in other towns are too great for their budgets. If a course is run, suitably qualified staff must be found to lead it. Given these factors it is clear that change in the teacher-training curriculum will not take place overnight.

Attempts to reduce the overload on students are also being made, but again are subject to "teething" problems. In place of the thirty-six-hour week, for instance, a twenty-eight-hour week was introduced. However, the total amount of hours in the overall curriculum was not reduced, which has led departments to prepare two timetables: one with twenty-eight hours for the inspection of the establishment authorities, and one with from forty to forty-eight hours for actual use. Since free attendance at lectures is now permitted, the students themselves are regulating their own workload, with attendance at lectures, in the words of one lecturer, "not exceeding" 35 to 50 percent.[5]

Despite the downfall of the Communist ideology and instructions from the ministry to depoliticize education, the social sciences have more or less retained their position in the curriculum, with the same numbers of staff continuing to teach virtually the same material as before, only under such new course titles as "Politology" instead of "Scientific Communism." It is surely only a matter of time, however, before these subjects fall victim to the new conditions of the market and financial self-management, for they will find it quite difficult to attract financial support. It is intended that social sciences be retained in the curriculum, because it is deemed important for the future teacher to be politically and economically aware. It is also suggested that the cycle be more related to work in school, with, for example, courses on educational management.

In the long term, the content of courses will depend upon the development of the two-tier system and the merging of educational establishments. The effect of mergers may lead Russian higher education away from professionally oriented courses and see the *bakalavr* stage assume a more general character, thus allowing students to delay decisions about choice of profession until a later date than has thus far been allowed. In this system, the experience of pedagogical institutes in specialized subject provision will be a great asset, and these departments could therefore find a new role in a larger university context.

Whatever form pedagogical studies assume in the future, one thing is certain—the content of pedagogical disciplines should be thoroughly revised in accordance with changing approaches to teaching in the Russian school itself. Schools are to move away from rote learning to become much more pupil-centered, with an increased emphasis on group work, problem solving, and the general development of cognitive skills. The task of the teacher-education system is to replace the "subject-teacher" with "pedagogues," who in addition to having a thorough knowledge of their subjects, are competent teachers, capable of stimulating their pupils and catering to their all-around educational needs. The training of such pedagogues should expose them to a wide variety of educational theories and give them ample opportunity to apply these theories to practice, both in simulations inside the training establishments and in live classroom situations through well-structured and ongoing teaching practice.

Giving Russian educators access to the experience of foreign education systems is being encouraged as a priority issue. To complement exchanges and joint research projects, for instance, international pedagogical universities are to be founded to bring together educators from across the world, to offset the long decades of isolation during the Soviet era. The first such establishment is the Pacific University in Magadan, which involves institutions from Russia, the United States, and Japan.

Staff

As mentioned above, the reform process is being slowed by the difficulty of retraining existing lecturers. The logical solution, of course, is to introduce new blood into the teacher-education establishments, thus providing an academic staff that will be better able to implement reform. Given the greater emphasis on the pedagogical disciplines in the curriculum, this recruitment drive could target suitably qualified candidates with school-teaching experience in order to bring teacher-training establishments closer to the school. Such a goal may well be facilitated by the spread of complexes where the different phases of teacher education will be brought into closer contact with each other. However, the successful recruitment of academic staff requires that a number of practical problems be faced.

Apart from the time it takes to train new replacements, the task is complicated by the material position of lecturers, which is currently forcing increasing numbers to leave the profession altogether and seek employment in the more profitable commercial sector. Lecturers, lacking the economic muscle of certain other professionals, are in no position to demand higher salaries and benefits. They can only hope that the ministry and the government will keep its vow to make education a priority. In the 1992 education law of the Russian Federation, it is stated that the salary of lecturers in higher education should be twice that of the average salary paid to industrial workers in Russia ("Zakon Rossiiskoi Federatsii" 1992, p. 15). This intention may prove difficult to realize in the present economic climate, but in the long run, if young academics are to be attracted to the profession, such promises will have to be kept.

Students

At present, issues concerning students are also linked to the current economic situation in Russia. First, there is the recent lack of interest in higher education among Russia's young people. Why study, they ask, when they can now find a good-paying job in the commercial sector that does not require a higher education *diplom*? Some potential students are also having to forgo entrance into a VUZ because economic hardship has forced them to find full-time employment in order to earn enough money for themselves and their families. Many students have to supplement their stipends with earnings from one or more jobs in their spare time.

Such problems are likely to fade as the economic situation improves. In the long term, higher education will again become attractive to young people as professional life settles down. However, the authorities will have to realize that from now on, with the abandonment of the old distribution system and with pedagogical establishments free to regulate their own intake without any obligations to the state planning committee, the number of students attracted to teacher training will reflect market forces. There now exists a much wider range of possible professions for graduates, many of which will offer better pay and conditions than teaching. Some students, who are given to teaching, may still be relied upon to enroll, and others may be attracted by new opportunities opened up by the diversification of the school system, but one can assume that some persuasion will be required to convince the majority of potential students that teaching can offer an adequate material reward. Teaching must be made an attractive option.

Conclusion

The program for the reform of teacher education that is being pursued in Russia is certainly ambitious and wide ranging. The reforms are also pervaded with a pragmatism that sets them apart from those of the Soviet years, bound as the latter were by ideological restraints and a desire to preserve the overall status quo. The current proposals may well provide long-term solutions to the problems afflicting the teacher-education system and education in general, by providing a more flexible system of teacher training that is better suited to the needs of teachers and schools and is supported by a more effective system of in-service training and educational research.

If the reformers are to create the foundation for such long-term change, they will have to address a number of issues upon which the movement for reform may otherwise founder. The first concerns the pace and scope of change. Instead of approaching the reforms one step at a time, the ministry appears to be trying to achieve too much, too soon. As well as changes in the content of teacher education, there are fundamental changes to be made in its structure and organization such as the introduction of the two-tier system and the possible merger of establishments. Most of these changes are scheduled for completion by 1994 ("Ofitsioz—Tul'skii pedsovet" 1992, p. 20). The desire to achieve rapid results is understandable, given the Russian context: the reformers are trying to throw off the legacy of the past, appease the demands of a crisis-weary population, and silence the attacks of a considerable array of opponents. But while such an approach might be advocated in, say, the economic sphere, education would surely benefit from a more measured policy; otherwise, there is a real danger that the reforms may collapse.

The education ministry may also be well advised to take a more cautious approach to the question of regionalization and diversification of pedagogical education. While these aims are important for the long-term strategy, the rush to implement them could well prove counterproductive. There is a risk that the reforms may be misinterpreted or may encounter opposition and disruption. Federation-wide standards for pedagogical education do not fully compensate for the loss of control over the direction of change. Precedents in educational reform indicate that fundamental change in the nature of a country's education system, such as that being pursued in Russia today, is more effectively introduced under centralized control. Jules Ferry's success with the *Ecoles Normales* lay to a great extent in the uniform nature of their implementation throughout France. A further example is provided by comparing two more recent attempts at educational reform in Britain. Implementation of the 1965 policy to replace the selective secondary-modern/grammar-school system with a unified comprehensive school model was resisted by some Local Education Authorities (LEAs) for many years. By contrast, the 1988 Education Act in Great Britain achieved its aim of introducing a national curriculum by adopting a far more centralized approach than had ever before been the case, thus overriding the powers of the LEAs. While the Russian education ministry may feel it is safe to leave regionally specific issues to be resolved at the local level, until it can be sure that the broader aims of reform are universally accepted across the land it would surely be prudent, in view of the turbulent atmosphere in Russia at present, to keep a tighter hold on the reins in order to ensure that reform follows its prescribed path.

Perhaps the most important observation to be made concerns the actual course of the reform process: much of the program for change, in education and in society, is of a remedial character, seeking to correct what are perceived as the causes of the present crisis. But building a new society involves more than mere rejection of the past and a reliance upon the vague notions of democracy and the market. To implement change of the type envisaged in Russia will require a fundamental modification of the philosophical framework of that society. Ferry and his contemporaries had a vision of the France they wanted to create with the help of the *Instituteurs*. If Russia's teachers are to understand the role they are to play in the country's education system, they must be sure of the identity of the new Russia they are to create.

Notes

1. The distribution system was a measure by which the state economic planning organ, Gosplan, aimed to ensure the effective distribution of qualified personnel throughout the economy. Upon graduation, young specialists would be assigned to a post for up to three years. Only on completion of their assignment would they be free to find employment elsewhere. Young teachers were often sent to rural areas that suffered from shortages of staff. Since the conditions of village life were considerably lower than those in the towns—adding to the inconvenience of being taken away from their homes—the distribution system was not popular among students. A good number

sought to escape the system, either through legitimate means such as marriage or simply by not reporting for duty, the latter course of action entailing the risk of legal proceedings. In recent years, the distribution system proved to be more and more difficult to enforce, and it has now been abandoned.

2. In 1992, there were ninety-seven pedagogical institutes in the Russian Federation, with 458,000 students. Of these institutes, four (with 44,000 students) had been given the status of pedagogical university. In addition, there were 353 pedagogical schools, with 295,000 students. With regard to in-service training, there were eighty-nine IUUy, which trained 60,000 teachers every year (*Sistema obrazovaniia* 1992, pp. 11–12).

3. Conversation with the authors, December 1990.

4. Correspondence with the authors, 1992.

5. Ibid.

References

Belozertsev, E.P. (1992). "Pedagogicheskoe obrazovanie: Realii i perspektivy." *Pedagogika*, nos. 1–2, pp. 61–65.

Bolotov, V.A. (1991). "Reforming Teacher Training in Russia." *Institute for the Study of Soviet Education Newsletter*, Indiana University, vol. 1, no. 1, pp. 3–7.

Dneprov, E.D., V.S. Lazarev, and V.S. Sobkin (1991). *Rossiskoe obrazovanie v perekhodnyi period: Programma stabilizatsii i razvitiia*. Moscow: Ministerstvo obrazovaniia Rossiiskoi Federatsii.

Dunstan, N.J. (1985). "Soviet Education Beyond 1984." *Compare*, vol. 15, no. 2, pp. 176–87.

Dzhilavian, L.Kh. (1981). "The Professional Attitude of Teacher Training Graduates in the Armenian SSR Toward Their Profession." *Soviet Education*, vol. 23, no. 6 (April), pp. 92–96 (translated from *Sotsiologicheskie issledovaniia*, 1978, no. 4, pp. 141–43).

Gershunskii, B.S., and R.T. Pullin (1990). "Current Dilemmas for Soviet Secondary Education: An Anglo-Soviet Analysis." *Comparative Education*, vol. 26, nos. 2/3, pp. 307–18.

Golovin, V. (1985). "Non-Competitive Admission." *Current Digest of the Soviet Press*, vol. 37, no. 31, p. 21 (translated from *Izvestiia*, 6 August 1985, p. 3).

Higgins, J.M.D. (1976). "Problems of the Selection and Professional Orientation of Soviet Pedagogical Students." *Comparative Education*, vol. 12, no. 2, pp. 157–62.

Il'menev, Iu. (1991). "Litsei pedagogicheskii, muzhskoi." *Narodnoe obrazovanie*, no. 8, pp. 54–60.

"Kafedra: Statfakt" (1992). *Uchitel'skaia gazeta*, 8 September, p. 22.

Kruglov, Iu.G. (1991). "Podgotovka uchitelei: Problemy, problemy. . . ." *Sovetskaia pedagogika*, no. 4, pp. 87–92.

Men'shikov, V. (1991). "Are We Teaching Any Old Thing, Any Old Way?" *Soviet Education*, vol. 33, no. 3 (March), pp. 37–50 (translated from *Narodnoe obrazovanie*, 1989, no. 11, pp. 39–44).

Mikhalev, G.M. (1965). "Sovershenstvovat' podgotovku uchitel'skikh kadrov." *Sovetskaia pedagogika*, no. 6, pp. 104–9. In Grant, N. (1972). "Teacher Education in the USSR and Eastern Europe." *Comparative Education*, vol. 8, no. 1, pp. 7–29.

Neather, E.J. (1993). "Teacher Education and the Role of the University: European Perspectives." *Research Papers in Education*, vol. 8, no. 1, pp. 33–46.

Nikitin, E.M. (1992). *Finansovo-khoziaistvennaia deiatel'nost' v usloviakh perekhoda na novyi khoziaistvennyi mekhanizm.* Moscow: Ministerstvo obrazovaniia Rossiiskoi Federatsii.

O deiatel'nosti ministerstva obrazovaniia Rossii v 1991–1992 godu (1992). Moscow: Ministerstvo obrazovaniia Rossiiskoi Federatsii.

"O mnogourovnevoi strukture pedagogicheskogo obrazovaniia" (1992). Prikaz no. 355, Ministerstvo obrazovaniia Rossiiskoi Federatsii, 15 June.

"Ofitsioz—Tul'skii pedsovet" (1992). *Uchitel'skaia gazeta,* 11 August, pp. 20–21.

Pionova, R.S. (1991). "Pedagogicheskoe obrazovanie: Strategiia na budushchee." *Sovetskaia pedagogika,* no. 8, pp. 71–75.

Pleshakov, L. (1990). "Vek zhivi, vek uchis'." *Ogonek,* no. 36 (1 September), pp. 1–2, 31.

Poppleton, P., N. Bolton, R.T. Pullin, and G. Riseborough (1990). "Perestroika and the Soviet Teachers." *New Era in Education,* vol. 71, no. 3, pp. 92–97.

Prelovskaia, I. (1992). "Po kontraktam nachnut uchit'sia lish' 6–7 studentov iz 100." *Izvestiia,* no. 172 (29 July), p. 3.

Reshetnikov, P.E. (1991). "Podgotovka uchitelei v komplekse 'peduchilishche-pedinstitut'." *Sovetskaia pedagogika,* no. 5, pp. 93–96.

Rostovtsev, Iu. (1988). "Demokratizatsiia. Glasnost'. Samostoiatel'nost'." *Studencheskii meridian,* no. 3, pp. 4–7.

Shturman, D. (1988). *The Soviet Secondary School.* London: Routledge.

Sistema obrazovaniia Rossiiskoi Federatsii (1992). Moscow: Ministerstvo obrazovaniia Rossiiskoi Federatsii.

Tomiak, J.J. (1972). *The Soviet Union.* Newton Abbot, UK: David and Charles.

"Zakon Rossiiskoi federatsii ob obrazovanii" (1992). *Uchitel'skaia gazeta,* 4 August, pp. 10–15.

Ziaziun, I.A., ed. (1988). *Uchitel', kotorogo zhdut.* Moscow: Pedagogika.

EDUCATION AND SOCIAL ISSUES

12

Confronting Sexuality in School and Society

LYNNE ATTWOOD

Describing life in the postcapitalist future, the German socialist August Bebel predicted: "The satisfaction of the sexual instinct [will be] as much a private concern as the satisfaction of any other natural instinct" (Bebel 1917, p. 343). The Bolsheviks clearly did not agree. After the Russian Revolution, sex became more of a social issue than it had been before and remained so throughout the country's history. By the end of the 1920s, a single model of sexuality had been defined, to which all Soviet citizens had to adhere: heterosexual, monogamous, confined to marriage, and committed to procreation. The less information people had about sex, the less likely they were to wander from this path. Accordingly, there was a virtual silence on the subject, save for a few dire warnings about the physical calamities brought on by masturbation or the psychological turmoil wrought by premarital sex.

This has all changed, and the silence of the past has now been replaced with a cacophony of sexual imagery. Pornographic or "erotic" publications are hawked on almost every street corner in Russia's cities. Sex, of the angry and aggressive type, is a staple of Russian cinema. Even serious current-affairs journals decorate their pages with pictures of nudes. Nothing that could be genuinely described as sex education has yet appeared in the school curriculum, though there is much discussion about the prospect. In the meantime, "erotica" has stepped in to do the job, and Igor Kon (1991, p. 7), the acclaimed sociologist and sexologist, has suggested that publications such as *Eros* and *Spid-info* (both of which would be described as "soft porn" in the West) can serve a valuable pedagogical function.

This chapter explores the links between past attitudes toward sex and

263

the situation which now exists in post-Soviet Russian society. We will begin by discussing the evolution of the official Soviet view on sex and looking at how this shaped the information that citizens were given on sexual matters. We will look at the pedagogical debates that have emerged from time to time on the advisability of introducing sex education into Soviet schools and at the watered-down version of sex education which actually entered the school curriculum under the name of "sex upbringing" (*polovoe vospitanie*). We will then make some suggestions as to why the Soviet state felt such a strong need to keep control over the sexual behavior of its people. Against this background, we will turn to the current situation, looking at the mass of sexual information and images that flourish in post-Soviet Russia and at their possible consequences for male and female relations.

The upheavals of the Revolution and the Civil War resulted in a maelstrom of sexual anarchy into which large numbers of people, particularly the young, flung themselves. The country's new leaders responded to this so-called new morality with concern, debating the meaning of "free love," how much of it was a good thing, and whether more information and education about sex would serve to encourage or control it. Lenin took a particularly conservative stance on such matters. He complained to Klara Zetkin that the false notion had come into being that "in communist society satisfying sexual desire and the craving for love is as simple and trivial as 'drinking a glass of water,' " and that this had been taken up with a vengeance by the young. He conceded that: "Thirst has to be quenched. But would a normal person normally lie down in the gutter and drink from a puddle? Or even from a glass whose edge has been greased by many lips?" (Zetkin 1965, p. 106). He clearly dismissed the idea that giving young people more information about sexual matters might produce more responsible behavior. When he heard that socialist women in Germany were organizing study groups to discuss the future of relations between the sexes, he exploded: "I could not believe my ears. . . . The first state of proletarian dictatorship is battling with the counter-revolutionaries of the whole world. . . . But active Communist women are busy discussing sex problems and the forms of marriage—'past, present and future.' They consider it their most important task to enlighten working women on these questions" (Ibid., p. 101). Still more alarming to Lenin was that "sex problems are a favorite subject in your youth organizations, too, and that there are hardly enough lecturers on this subject. This nonsense is especially dangerous and damaging to the youth movement. It can easily lead to sexual excesses, to overstimulation of sex life and to wasted health and strength of young people" (Ibid., p. 102). It would appear from this that Lenin saw no clear distinction between discussions on gender relations and discussions about sex, a confusion which was to continue throughout Soviet history.

It has been argued that the ferocity of Lenin's views on sexuality and sex education reflect a strong personal asceticism. (His own extramarital affair with Inessa Armand might challenge this view; but as R.C. Elwood makes clear in his biography of Armand, there has never been any real evidence for the affair, and there are a number of reasons to doubt it [Elwood 1992, ch. 8].) Lenin's own explanation for his impatience with the subject was that sex distracted people from more pressing concerns. A preoccupation with sex should be left to the idle and decadent bourgeoisie, since young workers had more important things to do: "Healthy sports, such as gymnastics, swimming, hiking, physical exercises of every description and a wide range of intellectual interests is what they need, as well as learning, study and research, and as far as possible collectively. This will be far more useful to young people than endless lectures and discussions on sex problems. . . . There must be no weakening, no waste and no dissipation of energy" (Zetkin 1965, pp. 108–9). In other words, sexual urges should be sublimated into other activities more useful to the new society.

Aleksandra Kollontai, the primary Bolshevik theoretician on gender issues, was more aware of the political significance of personal relations. She argued that a socialist society intent on radically transforming people's lives could not ignore the question of what form male and female relations would take. The old bourgeois family was dead; it had been based on women's economic dependence on men and could not survive the abolition of private property. It was important, then, to decide what would take its place. Kollontai did not see the sexual profligacy of the early 1920s as a model for the future and expressed her disapproval of what she called the "wingless Eros," affairs based on nothing but instant sexual gratification. Instead she favored the "winged Eros," sexual liaisons founded on mutual attraction and respect. These might not be permanent: women would no longer be economically dependent on men and so were free to leave a relationship if they found it no longer suited them. They would, however, be meaningful and sincere while they lasted (Kollontai 1919; 1977).

What of the offspring produced by short-term relationships? Kollontai did not see this as a problem; indeed, she welcomed new citizens from whatever sources. To the present-day Western reader, her staunch pronatal stance comes as a shock. Her concept of "the new Soviet woman" was indivisibly linked to the concept of motherhood, and she saw reproduction as the driving force and inevitable result of all sexual relations. "The healthy instinct of reproduction is at the heart of conjugal relations," she wrote, "whether they be painted in the enchanting colors of young love, in the ardent tones of passion, in the soft shades of spiritual harmony and accord, or in the bright blaze of physical attraction, which is soon burned out" (Kollontai 1921, p. 22). The young couple's pleasure need not be disturbed by fears about how they would support their offspring since child care would become a social function, with the state shouldering all financial responsibilities.

Such an approach was rather utopian, however, in the impoverished circumstances in which the fledgling Soviet state found itself. Despite Kollontai's proclamations to the contrary, provision for children remained largely an individual matter. When relationships disintegrated, women were, as always, the ones left "holding the baby," and often with little support from the father. In the sexual climate of the day, he was likely to have fathered a series of families and was in no better position than the state to finance them. The magazine *Rabotnitsa* became a forum for abandoned women, and distraught letters frequently appeared in its pages throughout the 1920s: "I am separated from my husband. He left me with two children, five and seven, and lives himself now with another, and already has a child from her. He does not help my children at all, and it is very hard for me"("Pochtovyiashchik" 1923, p. 32).

Kollontai's approach to sexuality was unacceptable to her colleagues for a number of reasons. Free love was seen as potentially destabilizing, wasteful of vital energies that could be put to better uses, and financially impractical. There were simply not the means to "support the offspring of unregulated sexuality" (Clements 1979, p. 235). A more conservative approach had crystallized into the official Bolshevik position by the end of the 1920s. Abortion remained legal from 1920 to 1936, but not in order to give women control over their own fertility; along with contraception, it was seen as a temporary but necessary evil until the state was in a stronger financial position ("Ob abortakh" 1925, p. 32). It might be the Soviet woman's ultimate duty to produce a stream of future workers for the state, but only when the state had the means to support them until they became workers.

Accordingly, the information that people were given on sex and personal relations was for the most part highly conservative. Komsomol discussions were dominated by "middle-aged men from the party elite, many of whom were physicians, [who] took on the task of hammering out a sexual code for young communists" (Clements 1992, p. 49). *Rabotnitsa* included some articles on sexual matters—information on sexual diseases, for example, as well as on abortion and contraception. In some cases, however, this seems to have had other, more covert purposes; for example, one article on syphilis uses the disease as part of its antireligious propaganda, informing readers that religious rituals help spread it because the healthy and the infected drink from the same cup and kiss the same icon ("Voprosy zdorov'ia" 1926, p. 21).

With Stalin in power, Kollontai's vision of new socialist forms of personal relationships was firmly laid to rest. The lifelong monogamous family was reinstated in the center of Soviet life, and was now called on to increase its reproductive capacity. The introduction of a massive program of industrialization, and the Revolution's failure to spread to other countries, meant that an expanded army of workers and soldiers was required both to build and defend the new society. Abortion was outlawed in 1936. In an ironic echo of Kollontai's views, women were now told that sex would lead inevitably and unquestionably to childbirth.

Rabotnitsa gives us some examples of what passed for sex education in the Stalin era: "The sex life of a woman is connected with pregnancy, birth and the feeding of the child" begins one article, insisting again a few lines later that "the normal sex life of normal people is inevitably connected with pregnancy." It goes on to tell women not to start their sex lives before the age of 18 or after 30, because a first pregnancy should occur only between these ages. Childbirth, they were told, not only satisfies a woman's desire for motherhood, but is also essential for her psychological and physical well-being, because her body achieves its full development only after she has had a child. Aborting a pregnancy is very harmful, and it is entirely in women's own interests that the government has banned it. Contraceptive devices are also problematic, and should only be used on the advice (and under the supervision) of a doctor. Onanism is a dangerous habit, which must be fought against decisively. (It is surely no coincidence that in this pronatal climate the Biblical term "onanism" was used for masturbation, since Onan achieved his notoriety for unproductively squandering his seed.) Finally, the author insists that the woman turn "not to a neighbor, nor to a friend, and not even to her mother" for advice on sexual matters, but only to the medical authorities (Dr. "N-ik" 1940, p. 19). Persuading women to shun all sources of advice other than the official medical services was presumably a way of breaking down personal loyalties and support systems and establishing tighter state control over even this most intimate aspect of life.

There is not one mention of a male partner in this article, despite his obvious importance in the reproductive process. Perhaps his role is minimized because he functioned only as a surrogate; the "real" father of the nation's children, and the symbolic husband of every Russian mother, was Stalin. This idea is clearly reinforced in the cinema of the day. In Dziga Vertov's 1937 film *Lullaby*, a succession of mothers appears on screen cradling their infants, functioning as a collective symbol of the motherland (*Rodina-mat'*). No fathers are depicted; when the mothers and children march together in a Red Square parade, it is Stalin, the Father of the People (*otets naroda*), who proudly watches over them, and later gathers the children into his paternal embrace. In Mikhail Chiaureli's 1949 film *The Fall of Berlin*, Stalin is the symbolic lover of the young heroine, argues critic Liliia Mamatova (1991, p. 115); when she gives a speech at the Palace of Culture she pays no attention to her real boyfriend in the audience but gazes instead at a huge portrait of Stalin, turning her speech into a declaration of love for him.

The Communist Party's message in the Stalin era was, then, that the masses should divert their sexual urges into love for the leader and confine any real-life sex to procreation. Yet the Party was not entirely successful in bringing the sex lives of its citizens under control. The incidence of underground abortion and even infanticide makes it clear that not everyone accepted an indivisible link between sex and childbirth. *Rabotnitsa* carried frequent articles denouncing the perpetrators of these crimes, attempting to shame readers into compliance by insisting that it was not material difficulties, lack of living space, or family conflicts that prompted women to abort their babies, but "simply the lack of desire, which should be normal in a healthy woman, to give birth to a child." Soviet women who sought to get rid of their babies were portrayed as either freaks of nature or as antisocial elements from the past who had somehow survived in the new society (Piatkova 1941, p. 19).

In the more relaxed ideological climate following Stalin's death, there was covert acknowledgement that the old approach to sexuality had not achieved its aims. Articles began appearing in the pedagogical press expressing concern about the sexual license of some people, particularly the young, and its unfortunate consequence, teenage pregnancy. It was admitted that onanism continued to be rampant, with one report revealing that the majority of boys and almost one in two girls indulged in it by the time they reached adulthood (Gudkovich and Kondratov 1977, p. 51). As one concerned commentator put it: "Undesirable habits of sexual life are especially difficult to uproot, since they are very deeply embedded.

Individuals' intimate feelings, thoughts, and actions are not easily detected, and because of this they are hard to control" (Atarov 1964, p. 54). The Party still wanted control over sexuality, then, but it was now argued that different methods might be more successful at achieving it.

Some educational theorists began to wonder aloud if the absence of sex education in the past had been such a good thing. Giving young people more information about sex might, instead of overstimulating sexual activity, help to regulate it (Kolbanovskii 1964). Conservatives reacted to this idea with an anger reminiscent of Lenin's tirade against Klara Zetkin. In an article entitled "Filth," P. Lynev (1966, p. 4) denounced a lecture delivered to medical students as "pornographic nonsense" dressed up in pseudoscientific language, aimed at the "mass seduction of minors." He was equally suspicious of books on "female hygiene." T.S. Atarov (1964, p. 56) claimed to approve of sex education, but what he meant was that parents and teachers should "divert children's and adolescents' attention [away] from questions related to intimacies of life." N. Dolina (1964, p. 2) summed up the conservatives' attitude with her outraged exclamation, "There are no forbidden subjects! Nothing is shameful or secret!"

The conservatives won the battle, and sex education was judged to be a matter for parents and not teachers. Over the next two decades, however, a growing literature appeared to help them with the task. The authors of this material began by expressing their opposition to the view that sexuality existed in childhood (dismissing Freud's views as a "slander of the innocent infant" [Kolbanovskii 1964, p. 9]), but their advice to parents consisted of warnings about the need for constant vigilance and strict hygiene to prevent the premature awakening of this supposedly nonexistent sexuality (Ibid., pp. 9–10; Gudkovich and Kondratov 1977; Atarov 1964, pp. 60–63; Gyne 1960; Piradova 1965; Khripkova 1969; 1970a, p. 29; 1970b, pp. 99–101; Khripkova and Kolesov 1981; 1982; Imelinskii 1972; Musina 1979, pp. 116–19; and Obozova and Shtil'bans 1984, pp. 18–19).

Cleanliness was said to be of prime importance. Babies should be washed and have their diapers changed with frequency, since otherwise they might start to itch and, subsequently, to scratch, hence stimulating the genitals. Parents should be careful not to touch or irritate the genitals when washing babies, and should avoid stroking, patting, and fondling their lips, buttocks, and nipples. Not even very small children should be washed together, lest they develop a curiosity about each others' bodies. Older children should be made to wash their hands in cold water at night and should be trained to sleep with their hands above the covers.

Perpetual supervision was of equal importance: Children should not be allowed to lie awake in bed for extended periods, or be left alone for long on the toilet. They should not be allowed to play together unsupervised, lest older and more informed children introduce a sexual element into normally innocuous games such as "fathers and mothers."

Any activities which might stimulate sexual awakening should be discouraged: Children should not be allowed to slide down banisters, because it was not the process of sliding which they enjoyed but the "rubbing and warming of their genitals, which . . . is accompanied by erotic sensations" (Kolbanovskii 1964, p. 10). Girls should be taught to ride a bicycle "in such a way that the edge of the saddle should not protrude between the vaginal lips" (Atarov 1964, p. 62). Clothes should always be loose, and children's trousers should not have pockets. When teenagers were dancing together, they should be discouraged from having any physical contact, and there definitely should be no kissing or embracing. Children should not be exposed to literature, films, or television programs of an erotic nature, and listening to Western pop music should be avoided since this was just "a short step from . . . imitating the sexual morality of a world that is alien to us" (Kolbanovskii 1964, p. 8). They should be encouraged instead to study, play sport, and be actively involved in Young Pioneers and Komsomol, which would serve to divert surplus energy away from sexual matters.

Sleeping arrangements were important: Children should never share a bed, with either their parents or other children, as "the closeness to another body may cause irritation, giving rise to erotic sensations" (Khripkova 1969, p. 54). From the age of six, boys and girls should sleep in separate rooms (although how this could be managed in the cramped conditions of Soviet life was not explained).

Certain types of food should be avoided, especially those which might overstimulate children and keep them awake—coffee, alcohol, anything greasy or sharp. Too much food was harmful because it produced a flow of blood to the pelvis and hence to the sex organs. Boys were also to avoid drinking too much liquid as an overfull bladder put strain on the penis.

The first sign of trouble was masturbation. Although it was not denied that girls masturbated, male masturbation received far more attention. It was said to lead to a range of physical and psychological problems: It put pressure on the nervous system, causing premature exhaustion; it led to inflammation of the sexual organs, which in extreme cases could impair adult sex life; and it resulted in acute depression, because masturbators felt so ashamed of their weakness of will, and, as time went on, "they get deeper into the experience and begin to avoid people. They shun the collective, become withdrawn, and fall easily into despondency and pessi-mism" (Khripkova 1970a, p. 25). Premature sex was, of course, still worse: It exhausted the young body and led to a sense of shame and humiliation. It also encouraged boys to have a negative attitude toward women, because they were too young to appreciate the spiritual qualities of their partners and hence would see them only as sex objects, a condi-tion known as "psychosexual degradation of the personality" (Khripkova and Kolesov 1982, p. 46).

The existence of homosexuality among adolescents receives no men-tion in such texts; it was clearly not even conceivable to Soviet sexologists at this time that Soviet youngsters could develop such a vice. A medical doctor, I. Gyne (1960, p. 37), refers to adult homosexuality, but clearly sees it as synonymous with pedophilia: "Homosexuals try by any possible method to win the sympathy of young boys; they buy them sweets and cigarettes and cinema tickets, they give them money, help them with their homework, and generally pretend that they selflessly love young people. But after such preparations, they sooner or later proceed to action. Don't allow them to touch you! Don't be shy of your parents and teachers, tell them immediately about any such attempts with yourself or with other boys! And parents and teachers will quickly and willingly help you. Ho-mosexuality is a punishable crime, and homosexuals well know this; therefore being saved from them presents no problem." This tough stance on homosexuality was later the cause for much back-patting on the part of the Soviet medical profession when the AIDS virus was discovered. The virologist P.N. Burgasov (1986, p. 15), for example, with an optimism which was to be short-lived, explained, "In our country the conditions for the mass spread of the illness are absent. Homosexuality constitutes a grave sexual perversion and is against the law."

By the mid-1970s, another spate of articles in the press made it clear that parents were still failing to turn their offspring into paragons of moral virtue. The existence of "sexual hooliganism" and teenage pregnancy was acknowledged. The high divorce rate was placed under scrutiny, and some writers suggested a link between young people's ignorance of the realities of conjugal life and the subsequent failure of their own marriages (Vedeneva 1981; "Kak pomoch' Ol'ge" 1981; Postol 1983; Voinov 1984). In an attempt to deal with these problems, sex education was put back on the agenda. Advocates argued that if children did not get information from a reliable source, they would get it in an unsavory and distorted form from wherever they could. Vladimir Vasil'ev (1982, p. 130) made an ironic illusion to Lenin's denunciation of the "glass of water" comparison: "Who will drink from a dirty puddle," he asked, "if there is a pure spring nearby?"

A group of pedagogical experts led by A.G. Khripkova was dispatched to Sweden to learn about the sex education program that had been introduced there. They were not impressed. In a series of interviews with the press on her return, Khripkova described her embarrassment, "even as a professor of physiology," at having to report her observations to the Ministry of Education. "I came back from this trip very much 'more right wing,' " she said. "While before I had argued for a more intensive program of sex education in our schools, the experience of Sweden forced me to reconsider my views" (Khripkova 1979b, p. 3). The Swedish experiment was prompted by the best motives, she conceded, but the absence of a ban on pornography meant that "depraved material" made its appearance inside schools in the guise of educational texts. As a consequence, instead of strengthening the family and reducing the incidence of venereal disease, sex education had resulted in a heightened interest in pornography, a collapse in morals, and "so-called group families: a group of young people share a house, a 'house without partitions,' and children are born without anyone knowing who their fathers are" (Khripkova 1979a, p. 14). The Soviet Union, Khripkova said, had no need of sex education if this was the result. Instead, she promoted a program of "sex upbringing" (*polovoe vospitanie*): "moral upbringing with regard to one's membership of one or the other sex" (Khripkova 1979b, p. 3). This was hardly a program of sex education, but of sex-role socialization, aimed at training boys and girls into more traditional gender roles.

It was no coincidence that "sex upbringing" was promoted against the background of intense concern over the so-called demographic crisis. The new Soviet woman, thrust into industry by Stalin's five-year plans, had come to prioritize work over family, with the result that family size had contracted in Russia and the other European republics to an alarming degree. This had led to a sharp imbalance in birth rates between this part of the country and the Central Asian republics, where the traditional large family prevailed. The prospect of the military, and eventually even the country, being dominated by Asians was the cause of much concern, and meant that the balance in women's lives in the European republics had to be changed (see Attwood 1990, pp. 4–6). As G. Belskaia argued in *Literaturnaia gazeta*, "Our schools are to be praised for their success in bringing up girls to be good citizens, but it is time we paid more attention to making them more feminine and housewifely, more kindly, neat and gentle" (Belskaia 1977, p. 12).

After a trial run in selected schools in the European and Baltic republics, "sex upbringing" formally entered the school curriculum in the 1984–85 academic year. Pupils in the last two years of secondary school received two hours of instruction per week on "The Ethics and Psychology of Family Life." For eighth-grade pupils, there was one hour of instruction per week on "The Hygienic and Sex Upbringing of Pupils." Neither contained anything which could genuinely be called sex education. What little there was on this in the course outline was often ignored by embarrassed teachers (Kon 1991a, p. 343). A. Egides (1988, p. 30) has argued that "The Ethics and Psychology of Family Life" taught nothing that children would actually want to know, and consisted of little more than a set of slogans along the lines of, "the family is the basic cell of Soviet society." T.I. Iufereva (1985) made it clear that its main purpose was to rekindle traditional ideas about masculinity and femininity and a stronger sense of family responsibility, with girls seeing their main adult function as having children rather than professions. "Up to now, school children's ideas about the psychological differences between men and women have been formed by chance. With the introduction of the new school subject, teachers will be directed toward the upbringing of children according to the laws of personality development connected with sex" (Ibid., p. 84).

Why did such resistance to sex education, as distinct from sex-role socialization, prevail for such a long time, and in the face of strong evidence that ignorance about sex was counterproductive? There are a number of possible reasons. To some extent, the Soviet approach can be seen simply as an inheritance from the prerevolutionary past. The Orthodox Church had a powerful influence on social attitudes before the Revolution, and, as Kon (1993, ch. 5) has noted, it was among the most conservative of Christian churches, shunning images of the naked body in its art and elevating chastity into a golden virtue in its followers. Such an attitude formed the background against which the revolutionaries had been reared, and, despite their active rejection of religion, it is likely that something of it entered into their own Weltanschauung. With Stalin in power, there was a clear attempt to deify the Bolshevik leadership and turn Marxism–Leninism into a new faith (Michelson 1992), and this led to an increased flow of religious dogma into Bolshevik ideology. In such conditions, Orthodox attitudes toward sexuality would be expected to find a strong foothold.

Even if such ideas began as a legacy from the past, they clearly suited the new society. Work replaced prayer as the primary act of devotion, and the energy which was needed to fuel work could not be squandered on something as frivolous as sex. It had to be brought under rein and confined to its one permissible purpose, the production of new citizens. With the population depleted by the Terror of the 1930s and World War II, the nation needed more children; "multiple motherhood" became a patriotic duty and, from 1944, was even rewarded with military-style medals. Production and reproduction were the dual foundations on which Soviet communism was to be built. In this society based on plans, neither could be left to chance.

Kon (1991b) argues that totalitarian politics[1] also demanded the suppression of sexuality for ideological reasons. Sex is a personal experience, and thus inappropriate in a society which seeks to make everything communal. It is a private act, and so threatens the leadership's control over the population's behavior. Thwarted sexual urges could also be usefully employed in other ways: they could be sublimated into work, into love for the leader, and into a passion for communism. Reference to the sublimation of sexual desire into other activities appears repeatedly in Soviet texts, from those of Lenin onward. In his diatribe against Freud, the only good thing Kolbanovskii can find to say about him is that he accords sublimation a prominent role. However, he refuses to allow Freud the credit even for this, arguing that "diverting the adolescent to different, diverse forms of activity in order to distract his attention from his sexual feelings was justified by pedagogical practice long before Freud" (Kolbanovskii 1964, p. 12).

In short, satisfying the sexual instinct could not be allowed to remain a private concern, as Bebel had once declared it to be. Sex became an issue between the state and its citizens. This was underscored by the guidelines for teachers of the school courses on sex upbringing. As Kolesov (1980, p. 10) put it, children should be brought up with "the conviction that a person is not independent of society even in the sphere of the most intimate relations between members of the opposite sex."

In late- and post-Soviet Russia, sex has remained an issue, but of a rather different type. When glasnost uncapped journalists' pens, they began to reveal a state of sexual anarchy in Russia far greater than that which had confronted Lenin at the time of the Revolution. Gorbachev continued to speak about family matters in the language of his predecessors, stressing the need to strengthen the family, reduce the divorce rate, and "make it possible for women to return to their purely womanly mission" (Gorbachev 1987, p. 117). In reality, however, the state had lost control of the sexual lives of its citizens. Increasing demands for pluralism in political life were mirrored by growing pluralism in sexual relations. Prostitution flourished and was accorded a peculiarly high status: many journalists writing on the subject could scarcely conceal their respect for these so-called independent business women who had found a means to enjoy the kinds of lifestyles normally reserved for the country's political elite ("Eshche. . ." 1990, p. 7), while surveys apparently showed that Russian girls saw it as one of the most prestigious occupations to which they could aspire (Shlapentokh 1992, p. 175). Teenagers have invented a new game, "Daisy," in which the girls lie naked on the floor with their heads together and their legs radiating out like petals while the boys go from one to another like honey bees. The boys in youth gangs are said to keep a stock of "general girls" whom they pass around among them, either for individual or group sex (Eremin 1990). Rape and sexual violence is reportedly on the increase (Ibid.; Musina 1992; Svetlova 1992).

It is hard to know how much of this kind of behavior is new, and how much had already existed behind the idealized image of the Soviet Union. Certainly a frequent visitor to the Soviet Union would have been aware that the real sex lives of young Soviets did not match the picture portrayed in official writings. Perhaps some level of sexual rebellion is inevitable in a society that attempts to keep such tight control over people's sexuality. The refusal to submit to such control becomes a form of dissent; sex becomes an act of subversion.

Yet if sexual license did not begin with Gorbachev's reforms, it does appear to have increased in the years since then. This might be a temporary gorging after the imposed starvation of the past, combined with the desire to replace the past absurdities of Soviet life with the supposed normality of life as lived in the West. It has been suggested that post-Soviet youth has "interpreted 'modernity' and 'Westernism' as being permeated with amoralism and cynicism" (Shlapentokh 1992, p. 175), and, in the desire to be like Western teenagers, they have embraced these qualities with a vengeance.

The response from the authorities has been mixed. On the one hand, a strong conservative element either refuses to acknowledge what is happening (many of the recent articles on male and female relations in the more conservative educational journals have the same style and content of those appearing a decade ago), or proposes to deal with it by reasserting the old controls. On the other hand, there is a strong liberal voice that calls for greater tolerance of sexual behavior which may be considered deviant but which does no one else any harm. It is argued on this side that the state is justified in imposing legal controls on people's personal lives only in order to protect other people from coercion, exploitation, and disease (Kon 1991a, p. 247).

The excesses of teenage sexual behavior are causing concern among both conservatives and liberals, however, particularly in light of the AIDS threat. Many see ignorance about sexual matters as one of the main reasons for sexual irresponsibility, and the question of sex education is once again on the social agenda. A 1990 survey conducted by the magazine *Ogonek* found that the majority of the population supported some form of sex education, though there were differences of opinion about how best it should be carried out. The establishment of special courses in schools and colleges was favored by 45.6 percent of respondents, and 42.5 percent supported the development of a popular literature on the subject. Only 3 percent felt that young people needed no instruction on sexual matters (Ibid., pp. 342–43).

Despite the strong popular support for sex education, it has still not entered the school curriculum. Some commentators see this only as a matter of time, however, and a number of the former Soviet republics (Russia, Ukraine, and Belarus) have declared their intention to introduce sex education into schools as part of a family-planning program (Kon 1993, ch. 5). There is still no consensus on what sex education actually means, however, and what form it should take. Kon, echoing the Polish educational sociologist Mikolai Kozakevich, suggests that there are three possible approaches to the subject. The first is characterized by an emphatic "no"—giving teenagers information about sex just encourages them to do it, so the less information they have the better. The second approach declares an enthusiastic "yes"—sex education will wipe away all sexual problems and perversions, and will do away with rape and marital disharmony alike. The third is a more cautious "yes, but," based on neither irrational fears nor overoptimistic hopes, and promoting not an unregulated mass of information but as much as is necessary. He acknowledges that this last approach is also not without its problems; it presupposes that teachers know exactly what and how much information is necessary, whereas in fact this is a rather slippery concept which varies between cultures, eras, and generations (Kon 1991a, pp. 349–52). There is also a strong likelihood that teachers who claim to support this approach have quite different ideas about what the "but" actually means; and that some, relying on the confusion between the concepts of sex and gender relations, will continue to teach sex upbringing in the place of sex education.

Khripkova, one of the principal exponents of "sex upbringing" in the 1970s, places herself firmly in the "no" camp. In a personal interview, she told this writer that she has abandoned her work in this field because there is no longer any interest in sex upbringing, and she wants no part in a program of sex education. She continues to hold the view that sex education only leads to the corruption of young people, and recalls her horror at discovering that the sex education program in Sweden involved teaching children how to use condoms. Her views are not entirely consistent, however; asked if she did not think that the onset of AIDS had made some information about safe sex necessary, she conceded that this was the case. The Russian Academy of Education's Laboratory of Biology, of which she is a member, is currently producing a series of booklets to be used in a new school course called "The Human Being" (*Chelovek*), which will address a variety of social problems, including AIDS. It will include some information about condoms, but she admitted that the problem of availability in Russia would invalidate much of what was said. The most important thing, in her view, was to emphasize the danger of homosexual contact, particularly in view of its recent legalization, of which she strongly disapproved.[2]

Some educational theorists who claim to support a more genuine program of sex education argue that the old course on sex upbringing—"Ethics and Psychology of Family Life"—could continue to form the basis of such a program. Since the academic year beginning in 1991, however, this course has ceased to be compulsory, and few schools now teach it. Many had already abandoned it before they had official permission to do so; the presentation of a single model of family life, endorsed by repeated reference to the views of old Bolsheviks (Kollontai excepted) and by the constant evocation of the ill-defined but sanctified concept of "socialist morality," had become inappropriate even in the early years of the Gorbachev reforms.

Luiza Kovin'ko, of the Russian Academy of Education (formerly the Academy of Pedagogical Sciences), is still an unrepentant supporter of the course, and argues that it could form the basis of a more frank sex education program. She insists that even in its earlier form it included some sex education, covering such topics as male and female anatomy and family planning. This was incorporated into a broader program of moral upbringing, however; sexual relations were shown to be just part of the network of male and female social roles and obligations. Kovin'ko links the demise of the course to the drop in the cultural level in present-day Russia, in its broadest sense. Schools no longer see it as their duty to teach young people about family life; as a result the divorce rate continues to rise alarmingly, having reached, she said, 80 percent in Moscow in 1990. In despair at the state of education in existing schools, Kovin'ko's personal solution is to take her course and her convictions into the newly burgeoning private sector. She is joining the staff of a new experimental school, where she intends to resurrect "The Ethics and Psychology of Family Life," first as an option and then, if it goes well, as a compulsory subject. She has also been working on a new text for the course, though as yet it is only in manuscript form. In the meantime, she will use existing course materials which, she insists, contain much that is still relevant and can easily be adapted to current conditions, with teachers simply leaving out the parts that refer to defunct ideas and institutions.[3]

The only text currently available for pupils of the course, however—*Sem'ia*, by Tamara Afanas'eva—seems so permeated with the ideas and moral judgments of the past that it surely has nothing to offer the contemporary Russian teenager. The second and most recent edition was published in 1988, three years after the onset of Gorbachev's "new thinking" and against a background of much improved relations with the West. Yet one of its most prevalent themes is still the contrast between the socialist morality in Russia and the moral anarchy of the West. This is particularly clear in the one chapter which tackles the subject of sex. Afanas'eva expresses her strong disapproval of the "sexual revolution" in capitalist countries, and links it to two main factors. The first is that capitalism has fostered a consumer culture which has spread into sexual relations; human beings are seen as commodities like any other, to be used and discarded. "The fetish of change as a basic indication of an individual's or family's prosperity now determines the style and morality of the behavior of many representatives of well-to-do circles in bourgeois society. The rejection of constancy as a symbol of conservatism and backwardness of opinions has become for people of a certain type a sign of 'modernity.' " The second factor she puts forward, which now takes on a particularly ironic ring given the collapse of Marxism–Leninism in Eastern Europe, is that the capitalist countries are experiencing a severe moral crisis brought on by the weakening of religious influence, and that, unlike the socialist countries, they have no alternative set of moral ideals which enable people to regulate their own behavior. Even before the West's current crisis, Afanas'eva continues, it had a dangerous understanding of "free love" which stood in sharp contrast to that of the Soviet Union's; as Lenin observed, in the West it was identified as the freedom to commit adultery, to bear no responsibility toward one's partner, and to shirk the duty of having children, while in the Soviet Union it meant the ability to form relationships which were not based on economic need. AIDS is the price now paid by adherents of the West's understanding of free love, striking down the "lovers of 'forbidden fruit' "—prostitutes, homosexuals, and simply those who adopt too flippant an attitude toward sex. (Afanas'eva 1988, pp. 101–3).

Afanas'eva does not promote more information about safe sex as a way of controlling the spread of AIDS. To her, as to Khripkova, sex education is a vile corrupter of youth. She points to the experience of the West, where "propagandizing the 'technology of sex' has led to a situation in which 'enlightened' youth have begun to display an inclination for all kinds of perversion, and the number of psychological problems has grown sharply in this fertile soil, to say nothing of the rapid growth in venereal disease. A greater and greater number of boys and girls do not want and are not able to develop normal family relations" (Ibid., p. 100). She contrasts this with the "communist position": "neither fleeting passion, nor vulgar and dirty marriage without love, but citizenly marriage with love" (Ibid., p. 103).

Despite the fact that men are far from immune to AIDS, Afanas'eva shows more concern about preserving the moral purity of women than of men. She justifies what she refers to as "moral inequality" between the sexes on the grounds that a mother's behavior has a much greater influence on her children and so needs to be placed under tighter regulation. In her view, the woman is the moral custodian of society, "and if she refuses to be firm and correct [in her behavior], then we say goodbye to [society's] moral foundations." The feminist movement has much to answer for; in challenging the "moral inequality" between men and women, it has played a large role in the erosion of the West's moral foundations and has also led to a contraction in the birthrate. There should be a strict dichotomy of male and female roles, with men being strong, decisive, firm, and fearless, and women diffident, modest, and faithful (Ibid., p. 99).

It is difficult to imagine the current generation of Russian school children reacting with anything but scorn to such an outdated, sanctimonious text. A rather different approach is advocated by Igor Kon. Although to Khripkova he is a dangerous figure dedicated to extending the rights of sexual minorities,[4] Kon, like Kovin'ko, places himself in the moderate camp, favoring the "yes, but" approach to sex education. His understanding of this middle path is clearly very different from hers, however. Like Khripkova and Afanas'eva, he refers to the West's experience of sex education, but not as an incitement to moral license; rather, he sees it as convincing evidence of the need for and benefits of sex education. This has been proved to have no effect on the age at which young people begin their sexual lives, he argues, but it can sharply reduce the incidence of teenage pregnancy by providing people with information about how to avoid it. It does not standardize sexual behavior and stamp out "perversions," but it promotes more understanding and tolerance of other people's behavior. It cannot solve all sexual problems and bring harmony to all conjugal relations, but it does help people to come to terms with their problems and to resolve the conflicts arising from them. In giving young people more knowledge about sex, it also gives them more responsibility over their personal lives. Kon sees the government's neglect of this subject as a crime, and not one which can be attributed to ignorance "since we have the experience of other countries" (Kon 1991a, p. 349–52). As we shall see in due course, this enthusiastic appraisal of the West's experience of sex education could be seen as somewhat overoptimistic.

In view of the continuing conservatism of much of the educational establishment, as well as the increasing privatization and decentralization of education, the immediate future of sex education in post-Soviet schools remains uncertain. In the meantime, a number of other steps have been taken to provide people with information on sexual matters. Preparations are underway to establish a course on sexual problems for medical students. Clinics providing advice on sexual matters have been set up in a number of cities (Kon 1993, ch. 5). There is also a growing literature on the subject. A few Western sex manuals are now available in translation, such as Alex Comfort's *The Joy of Sex* which appeared in Russian in 1991. A number of mainstream Russian magazines and journals— even the more conservative ones such as *Vospitanie shkol'nikov* and *Sem'ia i shkola*—also offer regular insights into "intimate life," though the information they provide is sometimes dubious and often still painted with a heavy coloring of moral judgment.

In a typical piece in *Vospitanie shkol'nikov*, S. Agarkov makes it clear that he is providing young people with information about sex solely in order to help them create more successful marriages (Agarkov 1991). We find only one acknowledgment that sex and marriage do not always go together when the author notes, uncritically, that even a relatively lenient society will censure "sexual 'freedom' " in a girl more than in a boy because "the main burden of bringing up an illegitimate child lies on the woman" (Ibid., p. 61). In some ways, however, this article is a marked improvement on what passed for sex education in the past. Masturbation is presented as something normal, which almost all boys and many girls engage in; it has none of the dire consequences outlined by earlier Soviet writers. There is also a coy hint at female pleasure, when Agarkov suggests, "In a harmonious intimate relationship, the woman finds a way of delicately directing her husband's caresses" (Ibid.). He fails to give female readers any advice as to where they might direct these caresses, but it is a start.

In an article on contraception in *Rabotnitsa*, Iakov G. Zhukovskii also makes it clear that sex should remain firmly bound to marriage and provides some rather dubious information about different methods of contraception. He suggests, for example, that barrier methods are difficult for the inexperienced to use and so it is better to start out with oral contraceptives; however, in the interests of the woman's health, these should be used only for three to four months at a time. There is no suggestion that young people could be taught how to use barrier methods, no mention that oral contraception does not guarantee protection for the first month, and no advice as to what couples can use when the woman is resting from the pill. He then tells readers that the best advice he can give them is still to refrain from sex completely until they are married (Zhukovskii 1990).

A sex therapist who writes regularly for *Rabotnitsa* takes a similar stance. In one article, he seeks to reassure troubled readers about the wide parameters of sexual "normality" in the behavior of husbands and wives (Grishin 1991). In another, on sexual perversion, he makes it clear that what counts as acceptable behavior is extremely narrow if it takes place outside of marriage. His list of sexual perversions includes fetishism, exhibitionism, narcissism, voyeurism, and homosexuality, all of which are portrayed as severe problems requiring immediate medical attention. Yet the example he gives of narcissism is simply that of a pubescent boy whose mother catches him exploring his genitals in front of a mirror; this is surely nothing more than masturbation, or even simple curiosity about his changing body. Readers are assured that all of these perversions can be treated, including homosexuality; sufferers should take comfort that they will not be arrested for the offense if they apply voluntarily for treatment (Grishin 1990).

The most comprehensive Russian book on sex, Igor Kon's *Vkus zapretnogo ploda* (Taste of the Forbidden Fruit), published in 1991, has a rather different tone. Aimed at a broad popular readership, Kon covers virtually every aspect of his subject. He begins with a historical outline of research on sexual issues and goes on to explore sexual attraction, sexual orientation, legislation relating to sex, sex crimes, prostitution, pornography, sex techniques, "sexual hygiene," contraception, sexual diseases, sexual deviations, and so on. The book is packed with illustrations, many of which would induce apoplexy in the more conservative educational writers: as well as photographs of transvestites and transsexuals, it includes reproductions of erotic sketches and paintings from different countries throughout the centuries depicting people exploring the joys of masturbation, group sex, homosexuality, and even bestiality. The aim is not to titillate readers, however. The message is that human sexual activity knows no bounds, and never has; the Soviet Union's past asceticism was a deviation from the norm, and what it insisted were recently invented bourgeois perversions have in fact existed in all cultures and at all times. Kon has inherited some of the old Soviet reliance on "experts," promoting "professional psychological help" for people in a variety of groupings which would do better to organize support networks of their own, such as rape victims and gay teenagers. However, on the whole his text is a calm, dispassionate challenge to past orthodoxies. This is particularly clear in his treatment of homosexuality. To Kon, homosexuality is not a crime, a perversion, or an illness, but simply a fact of life. He acknowledges that there is no clear consensus on its cause but because it is not a disease, there is no point in attempting to "cure" it. In any case, he says, it is a problem only because society treats it as such. Tolerance toward sexual minorities, he urges, is the "only social policy which corresponds to the spirit of a democratic society" (Kon 1991a, p. 242).

Despite Kon's professed adherence to a relatively cautious approach to sex education, in some respects he seems to subscribe more to the "yes" model: the more information about sex, the better. He has put his name to two soft-porn publications: he is chief editor of the glossy magazine *Eros* and editorial advisor on the tabloid *Spid-info* (AIDS info). Kon claims that these are not pornography but erotica, and that erotica is a positive development in post-Soviet society. In the past, a "barracks attitude" toward sex had developed from a combination of factors: the official view that it was dirty and shameful if carried out for any other reason than procreation; the difficulty of experiencing it as anything else in the overcrowded hostels and communal apartments in which most people lived; and the ignorance bred by the absence of information. This "barracks attitude," which reduced sex to a purely functional coupling, was, to Kon, far coarser and more primitive than the worst examples of Western pornography (though he is surely unaware of the depths to which Western pornography has now sunk). Against this background, he says, erotica is cause for celebration. It represents a liberation from the old strictures of Soviet society; it is an essential part of the process of democratization; it will provide people with a richer understanding of history and art; it will enable them to lead more fulfilling sex lives; and it will help fight the spread of AIDS. Erotica, then, helps to make up for the lack of sex education (Ibid.).

Spid-info declares its educational stance both in its name and its front cover caption—"for those who, possessing knowledge, live calmly and happily!" The name is misleading, since there is very little information on AIDS or how to avoid it, but amid the gossip on Western film and rock stars, there is advice and information on sexual matters given by a variety of "experts." Some of this passes amusing judgment on the teachings of the past. For example, a sex therapist commenting on the case of a young woman who can only reach orgasm when she pretends she is being watched by a crowd of men explains that this is a reaction to her strict upbringing, which included being made—by a mother clearly influenced by the texts we discussed earlier—to sleep with her hands above the bed covers "so that, God forbid, I would not explore 'down there'!" (Tumanovskii 1992) For the most part, however, the information is contradictory, inaccurate, and trivialized by the accompanying illustrations.

Even according to Kon's own definitions of the terms, the photographs in *Spid-info* would have to be described as pornographic and not erotic. For Kon, erotica presents the person as a whole being, in the full richness of his (sic) experience, whereas pornography focuses only on the sexual aspects and reduces the person to a sex object. Erotica is concerned with the humanity of its subjects and hence is highly moral, whereas pornography defies the humanity of its subjects and humiliates them. This is particularly the case with women, he adds: pornography "strengthens the traditional ideology of male supremacy, of sexism" (Kon 1991a, p. 7).

Yet it is difficult to see how the illustrations in *Spid-info* could be said to respect the richness of their subjects' experience, or refrain from humiliating them, or challenge the sexism inherent in pornography. An article on female orgasm, for example, entitled "A Partner Is Not a Mechanic, A Woman Is Not An Automobile," is accompanied by a photograph of a clothed man with a spanner in his hand lying under the torso of a naked woman (Podkolognyi 1992, p. 16). A discussion of a phenomenon new to Russia, phone-in sex, is illustrated by a naked woman posing as a phone, a dial resting across her legs while she holds aloft an outsized receiver (Nevskii 1992). Alongside an article on fetishism is a photograph of two naked women ecstatically draping themselves in items of male clothing (Aleksandrov 1992). A supposedly concerned look at the growing number of teenage prostitutes is accompanied by a series of photographs of naked teenage girls posing in a bathhouse; while their bodies are fully exposed, their eyes are discreetly hidden by black bars! ("Deshevka–2," 1992, p. 6). Women's bodies adorn the covers of every issue. The cover of *Spid-info* no. 7 bears a particularly curious photograph of disembodied female legs sitting on a chair, while a pair of male eyes appears in the right-hand corner. The message is that men look, women are looked at. This is reinforced by the fact that a number of pictures have naked women posing alongside clothed men. These are particularly disturbing images in view of *Spid-info*'s professed educational mission. The message young people are most likely to get is that women are vulnerable, passive, and ever-available, and that they exist primarily for men's sexual pleasure. This does not bode well for the development of women's roles, social or sexual, in the future.

Eros, aimed at an older readership, is only a little better. A naked, huge-breasted blonde pouts seductively on the front cover of the first issue; inside, two more naked women gambol together against various natural backdrops, reinforcing a traditional link between women and nature. The high-brow claims of the journal are emphasized by the reproduction of paintings, or in most cases, details from these paintings, which depict breasts or buttocks. It would seem, then, that the members of one sex are being turned into objects of consumption for the other. It is difficult to see how this is liberating for the population as a whole. A number of Russian scholars have suggested that past ignorance about sexual matters has left people of the former Soviet Union unable to discriminate among the different forms of sexual information and imagery now on offer, resulting in an awkward confusion over the boundaries between pornography, erotica, and sex education.[5] Apparently, not even eminent scholars like Kon are immune to this confusion.

How can we summarize the difference in attitude toward sex and sex education in Soviet and post-Soviet society? Although we do not find a consensus on the subject, there is a trend away from a uniform view of sexual relations and toward acceptance of pluralism in sexual behavior. It is now argued that an attempt at strict control over people's sexual behavior was an inevitable feature of authoritarian rule, part of the government's desire for control over all facets of its citizens' lives, with doctors and teachers acting as its proxies. In the words of B. Kochubei and N. Semenova (1991, p. 48), Soviet people got used "to think[ing] that above them stood someone who 'knows how it should be'; he might be called Doctor, Teacher, or Leader, but absolutely with a capital letter." Old habits die hard, however, and the phenomenon of "experts" telling people how to live their lives still continues to haunt the pages of the Russian press. Kochubei and Semenova compare recent articles in *Newsweek* and *Moskovskii komsomolets* on teenage sexuality, and find that in *Newsweek* the word "must" appears only once, and not in the words of the authors themselves but in a quotation from a parent; in contrast, in the first five

paragraphs of the *Moskovskii komsomolets* article "there are seven asser-
tions of necessity: the word 'must' appears three times, 'it is time' (to do
something) twice, 'it is essential' once, 'without fail' once" (Ibid.).

Giving people more information about sex and enabling them to use it
freely allows them to take greater responsibility for their personal lives.
Hence, advocates see sex education as an important step on the path to
democratization. Tolerating different sexual preferences, and accepting
that there is not one model of sexual behavior which everyone must follow, is part of the broader concept of pluralism.

Accepting that sex education is necessary, however, is a long way from
knowing how to go about it. There is no clear idea as yet of what form sex
education will take in Russia, only vague references to the "experience of
the West." This change in perception of the West, from dark imperialist to
shining example, has clearly blinded many Russians to the problems that
continue to exist in the West, in the realm of sex education no less than in
market economics. Jane Mills's discussion of the confusions and dilemmas confronting British teachers is almost certainly applicable to other
Western countries, and gives us an idea of some of the problems that will
confront Russian educators when they do embark on their own sex education program (Mills 1992). Mills describes a state of awkwardness and
confusion as teachers try to determine what and how much they can say to
pupils without offending parents, a confusion compounded in multicultural schools. Most teachers play it safe and pitch their classes at the most
conservative level. As it seems less contentious to discuss sex in purely
biological terms, the tendency is to concentrate "on the protection angle—
how not to get pregnant, how not to catch a sexually transmitted disease,
how not to be sexually abused or raped. The female body is perceived as a
site of passive vulnerability exposed to the danger of rampant male hyper-
sexuality" (Ibid., p. 202). AIDS has inevitably made sex education a more
pressing concern, but has not made it any easier to teach. In view of the
government directive that there should be no propagandizing of homosexuality in schools, many teachers are scared to mention it at all, which
leaves an obvious gap in any teaching about AIDS (Ibid., p. 207). Because
teachers feel uncomfortable discussing different forms of sexual activity
with their pupils, advice on safe sex is limited to little more than how to
use a condom. In the words of one teacher, " . . . all this talk about
condoms means one thing—vaginas are only there for penises to go into
them" (Ibid., p. 207). Female sexuality is portrayed, then, as something
entirely passive. Few teachers dare to suggest that sex can be pleasurable
for women as well as for men.

The end result is that sex is portrayed, as in the Soviet Union of the past, "as something that happens within the context of a morally responsible relationship, i.e., marriage. [Teachers are] not allowed to address teenagers directly and talk about what you 'do' with someone you fancy. So sex education is sterile and remote—unconnected with what young people want to know" (Ibid., p. 211). This is a curious echo of Egides' remark about the course, "Ethics and Psychology of Family Life." The fact that sex education in British schools shares surprising similarities with the Soviet Union's "sex upbringing" courses, despite the different ideologies of the two countries and the different attitudes of the teachers, suggests that there are inevitable difficulties in the teaching of such a sensitive subject. When sex education finally gets off to a start in post-Soviet Russia, it may find that its problems are just beginning.

Notes

1. While Western scholars have long debated the applicability of the term "totalitarian" to anything but the Stalin era of Soviet history, Russian scholars have now embraced it to describe the full seven decades of Soviet power.
2. Personal interview with the author, November 1992, Moscow.
3. Personal interview with the author, November 1992, Moscow.
4. Personal interview with the author, 1992, Moscow.
5. This view was expressed in a personal conversation with the film critic Elena Stishova, and echoed by a number of other scholars I spoke to in Moscow in July–August 1992.

References

Afanas'eva, T.M. (1988). *Sem 'ia*. Moscow.
Agarkov, S. (1991). "O sekretakh intimnoi zhizni," *Vospitanie shkol'nikov*, no. 6, pp. 59–62.
Aleksandrov, Aleksandr (1992). "V sekte neprikasaemykh," *Spid-info*, no. 12, pp. 16–18.
Atarov, T.S. (1964). "Sex Education," in Helen B. Redl, ed., *Soviet Educators on Soviet Education*. London: Glencoe Press, pp. 53–77.
Attwood, Lynne (1990). *The New Soviet Man and Woman: Sex-Role Socialization in the USSR*. London: Macmillan; Bloomington, IN: Indiana University Press.
Bebel, August (1917). *Woman Under Socialism*. New York: New York Labor News.
Belskaia, G. (1977)."Otkuda berutsia plokhie zheny" (1977). *Literaturnaia gazeta* 7 September, p. 12.
Burgasov, P.N. (1986). "SPID: Vosprosov bol'she, chem otvetov," *Literaturnaia gazeta*, 7 May, p. 15.
Clements, Barbara Evans (1979). *Bolshevik Feminist: The Life of Aleksandra Kollontai*. Bloomington, IN. and London: Indiana University Press.
———. (1992). "The Utopianism of the Zhenotdel," *Slavic Review*, fall, pp. 485–96.

"Deshevka–2" (1992). *Spid-info*, no. 7, July, pp. 5–7.

Dolina, N. (1964). "Ne pri vsekh," *Komsomol'skaia pravda*, 15 December, p. 2.

Dr. "N-ik" (1940). "Gigiena polovoi zhizni zhenshchina," *Rabotnitsa*, no. 27, p. 19.

Egides, A. (1988). "Sovet i podderzhka" (interview by T. Ostroverskaia), *Sem'ia i shkola*, no. 12, pp. 28–31.

Elwood, R.C. (1992). *Inessa Armand: Revolutionary and Feminist*. Cambridge: Cambridge University Press.

Eremin, V. (1990). "Seksual'naia vsedozvolennost' pronikaet v podrostkovuiu sredu," *Vospitanie shkol'nikov*, no. 6, pp. 25–28 .

"Eshche odna zakritnaia tema" (1990). *Argumenty i fakty*, no. 16, p. 7.

Gorbachev, M.S. (1987). *Perestroika*. London: Collins.

Grishin, A. (1990). "Izgoi," *Rabotnitsa*, no. 11, p. 26–27.

——— (1991). "Doktor, Ia bolen?" *Rabotnitsa*, no. 9, p. 37.

Gudkovich, L.N. and A.M. Kondratov (1977). *O tebe i obo mne*. Stavropol'.

Gyne, I. (1960). *Iunosha prevrashchaetsia v muzhchinu*. Moscow.

Imelinskii, K. (1972). *Psikhogigiena polovoi zhizni*. Moscow.

Itkina, Anna (1982). "Narkom. Aleksandra Kollontai," in *Zhenshchiny russkoi revoliutsii*. Moscow, pp. 189–200.

Iufereva, T.I. (1985). "Obrazy muzhchin i zhenshchin v soznanii podrostkov," *Voprosy psikhologii*, no. 3, pp. 84–90.

"Kak pomoch' Ol'ge?" (1981). *Komsomol'skaia pravda*, 20 September, p. 2.

Khripkova, A.G. (1969). *Voprosy polovogo vospitaniia*. Rostov-on-Don.

———. (1970a). *Razgavor na trudnuiu temu*. Moscow.

———. (1970b). "Voprosy polovogo vospitaniia," *Sovetskaia pedagogika*, no. 3, pp. 95–106.

———. (1979a). "A kakov vzgliad pedagogika?" *Rabotnitsa*, no. 9, pp. 13–14.

———. (1979b). "Neobkhodima mudrost'-polovoe vospitanie-grani problemy," *Sovetskaia Rossiia*, 16 Dec, p. 3.

Khripkova, A.G. and D.V. Kolesov. (1981). *Devochka-podrostok-devushka*. Moscow.

———. (1982). *Mal'chik-podrostok-iunost*. Moscow.

Kochubei, B. and N. Semenova. (1991). "Chto zhe takoe seks i kak s nim bortsia?" *Sem'ia i shkola*, no. 10, pp. 47–49.

Kolbanovskii, V.N. (1964). "The Sex Upbringing of the Rising Generation," *Soviet Education*, vol. 1, pp. 3–13.

Kolesov, D.B. (1980). *Besedy o polovom vospitanii*. Moscow, p. 107.

Kollontai, Aleksandr (1919). *Novaia moral i rabochii klass*. Moscow.

———. (1921). *Prostitutsiia i mery bor'by s nei*. Moscow.

———. (1923). "Revoliutsiia byta," in *Trud zhenshchiny v evoliutsii khoziaistvo*. Moscow.

Kollontai, Alexandra (1977). "Make Way for Winged Eros: A Letter to Working Youth," in *Selected Writings*. London: Allison and Busby.

Kon, Igor (1991a). *Vkus zapretnogo ploda*. Moscow.

———. (1991b). "Erotika—eto khorosho ili plokho?" *Eros*, no. 1, pp. 5–7.

———. (1993). "Sexuality and Culture," in James Riordan and Igor Kon, *Sex and Russian Society*. London: Pluto; Bloomington, IN.: Indiana University Press.

Lynev, P. (1966). "Griaz'," *Komsomol'skaia pravda*, 24 September, p. 4.

Mamatova, Liliia (1991). "Mashen'ka i zombi: Mifologiia sovetskoi zhenshiny," *Iskusstvo kino*, no. 6, pp. 110–18.

Michelson, Annette (1992). "The Kinetic Icon and the Work of Mourning: Prolegomena to the Analysis of a Textual System," in Anna Lawton, ed., *The Red Screen*. London: Routledge, pp. 113–31.

Mills, Jane (1992). "Classroom Conundrums: Sex Education and Censorship," in Lynne Segal and Mary McIntosh, eds., *Sex Exposed*. London: Virago, pp. 200–15.

Musina, I.M. (1979). "Nekotorye voprosy polovogo vospitaniia v sem´e i shkole," in *Sanitarno-gigienicheskoe vospitanie shkol´nikov*. Minsk, pp. 116–19.

Musina, Mariia (1992). "Zhenskie Strakhi," *Rabotnitsa*, no. 3–4, pp. 24–25.

Nevskii, Aleksandr (1992). "Zhenshchina vashei mechty," *Spid-info*, no. 8, August, p. 26.

"Ob abortakh" (1925). *Rabotnitsa,*, no. 2, p. 32.

Obozova, A.N. and V.I. Shtil´bans (1984). "Buduschchie muzh´ia, buduschchie zheny," *Zdorov´e*, no. 3, pp. 18–19.

Piatkova, E. (1941). "Podpol´nye abortarii," *Rabotnitsa*, no. 17, p. 19.

Piradova, M.D. (1965). *Iunosha i devushka*. Moscow.

"Pochtovyi iashchik" (1923). *Rabotnitsa*, no. 2, p. 32.

Podkolognyi, Fedor (1992). "Partner—ne mekhanik, dama—ne avtomobil´," *Spid-info*, no. 8, August, pp. 16–17.

Postol, M. (1983)."Trusting One Another," *Current Digest of the Soviet Press* (*CDSP*), vol. 35, no. 6, p. 18.

Shlapentokh, Dmitry (1992). "Lovemaking in the Time of Perestroika: Sex in the Context of Political Culture," *Studies in Comparative Communism*, vol. 25, no. 2, June, pp. 151–76.

Svetlova, Elena (1992). "Sindrom zhertvyi," *Sovershenno sekretno*, no. 2, pp. 16–17.

Tumanovskii, Konstantin (1992). "Vse myi rodom iz detstva . . . ," *Spid-info*, no. 11, pp. 13–14.

Vasil´ev, Vladimir (1982). *Muzhskoi razgovor*. Moscow.

Vedeneva, I. (1981). "Dochki-materi," *Komsomol´skaia pravda*, 16 August, p. 4.

Voinov, L. (1984). "The Teenager, the Law and Us: A Losing Game," *CDSP*, vol. 36, no. 40, p. 11.

"Voprosy zdorov´ia" (1926). *Rabotnitsa*, no. 16, pp. 21–22.

Zetkin, Klara (1965). "My Recollections of Lenin," Appendix to *Lenin on the Emancipation of Women*. Moscow.

Zhukovskii, Ia.G. (1990)."Neskol´ko interv´iu po voprosam kontratseptsii," *Rabotnitsa*, no. 20, pp. 30–31.

13

After Graduation, What?

The Value of an Education in the New Order

DEBORAH ADELMAN

> *I'm living through a very complicated time period. Terrible. I'm unlucky. Because before, everything was simple and clear. In the forties and fifties . . . it was clear: if somebody was your enemy, he was your enemy. Now everybody's your enemy, but everybody says they're your friend. It's hard to figure things out.*
> —Alexei, twenty-one-year-old vocational-school graduate,
> co-owner of small optical cooperative

Alexei's mood is fairly typical among the young adults I interviewed during a three-week visit to post-Soviet Moscow in the summer of 1992— young adults I had met as teenagers on a longer research trip to Moscow in 1989.[1] The three years that had passed since I last spoke with them had brought momentous changes to their country. In 1989, the sense of excitement and hope for change that was prevalent in all of Soviet society during the period of glasnost shaped much of what they said. By 1992, the doubt and disorder that characterize life in post-Soviet Russia had become the dominant influence.

"Nobody could be satisfied with what is going on here now," Alexei says. "I don't think there are people who are really optimistic, who believe that something is going to come of all this. Because things are going to get even worse." Alexei's pessimism about the prospects for his country is shared by many young people who, for better or worse, belong to a generation beginning its adult life at a particularly uncertain and unstable moment in Russia's history.

In a short period, the world these young adults grew up in has been turned upside down. Russia is in turmoil; the Soviet political and economic order is being dismantled, but the transition to a market economy is seriously hampered by unresolved major issues, such as securing the right to own land and the privatization of state-owned enterprises. The economic and political breakdown has brought great social problems, evidenced by increasing violence and crime. Price increases and high inflation have eliminated hard-earned savings and resulted in the impoverishment of great numbers of people in a society that previously offered its citizens a fairly stable, albeit modest, standard of living. While some people are attracted by new opportunities to open up private businesses, much of the commercial activity is speculative in nature and does not produce any goods.

Many Russians feel deep resentment toward the types of commercial ventures that have given a small sector of the population the opportunity to make large amounts of money and have further increased the gap between the wealthy and the average citizens. At the same time, however, particularly among the young, making large amounts of money is now considered prestigious. *Delat' den'gi* (Making money) has become a common expression in Russian, one I have heard repeated in many conversations. This reflects the general preoccupation for economic survival and a shift in people's values in a society where previously the prestige of one's career was probably just as (if not more) important as the salary one brought home.

These changes force students to regard their education in a new light and reconsider plans for work and careers. This is particularly true for people the age of those whom I interviewed—recent secondary-school graduates who had received most of their education under the old regime. They have been prepared under one economic and social order, only to find themselves, upon graduation, facing a completely new set of expectations about what lies ahead. This conjunction of the old and the new leaves them with educational, career, and lifestyle choices inherited from the Soviet system while at the same time they must cope with the rather different questions and uncertainties of the current moment.

In the last few years, there has been a marked devaluation of the prestige of higher education, in part as a consequence of the intense criticism of the Soviet educational system during the period of glasnost. But changing economic circumstances have also played a major role in changing students' attitudes toward education: a higher education no longer holds much promise of a job or a successful career. In the Soviet system, a higher education was considered an important step for success and for integration into official society. With the breakdown of the old official ideology, "official society" is no longer of great relevance. More important, a higher education is no longer necessary or even useful for gaining access to the most lucrative types of activity, particularly the buying and reselling in which so many people now engage. New profitable business opportunities are more attractive to many young people than studies, even though most of these businesses as part of the transition to a market economy are uncertain, face significant obstacles, and frequently fail quickly.

The need to earn a substantial amount of money affects even those who still make the choice to get a higher education. A journalism student at Moscow State University observes that increasing financial need has forced students to find new ways to earn money to supplement student stipends which, in the face of high inflation, do not even begin to meet the minimum requirements for room and board. And for many, these new types of income-producing activities have taken precedence over studies.

> The banal forms of student jobs for earning a little money, like unloading freight cars, have long ago gone into oblivion or become jokes. Only one of my friends, Tolik, uses his physical or intellectual capabilities in order to earn money. He worked as a night watchman in Mandelshtam Park, then he started giving lessons, and three times a week he sings with an accordion in the underground street crossings. The singing turned out to be the most profitable of all (1,200 a month), so soon he's going to give up on the lessons. But Tolik is an exception. The rest make money in different ways—buying and selling. . . . I think the majority of my comrades would answer the question 'What is most important for them' by saying simply 'business' " (Pankratov 1992, p. 3).

Graduates prepare to move into the labor market in the midst of these changes, which have affected their whole society, including their own families. The move from a planned economy to a market economy has changed the prospects of vast numbers of people in the former Soviet Union. It has been particularly hard on the more vulnerable sectors of the labor market, especially women, who are bearing the brunt of layoffs and unemployment and who are having more difficulties than men in entering the private sphere: an estimated 70 percent of the newly unemployed in Moscow are women (vanden Heuvel 1992, p. 32). The public sector is shrinking, leaving many people in precarious working situations. The employment guarantees of the past are gone.

These problems—the preoccupation with money and a lowered standard of living, the questionable importance of education, and the threat of unemployment—all have had a significant impact upon the young adults in Moscow who related their experiences of the last three years to me. In the face of changes none of them could have predicted, they look at their past decisions about education and career and wonder if their choices still have any relevance today or will be at all useful in the future. The examples that follow represent the experiences of only a few, but they reveal important aspects of the ways average young adults view their own possibilities within the emerging order in Russia today.

Alexei: Starting a Business

Alexei graduated from a vocational secondary school[2] in 1989 with training in carpentry. Since his graduation, he has, in his own words, lived "at least four lives." He worked at a two-year job assigned to him by his vocational school but left it after only two months. He spent a brief period on another school-related carpentry assignment at Gorbachev's *dacha*. His work experience is already diverse—in addition to his brief stint as a carpenter, he has worked as a fireman, a ditch digger, a street vendor and has started his own small optical cooperative which has closed and reopened twice, due to intrigue and in-fighting. During this short period, he has also managed to get a medical exemption from military service, although he has no actual health problems, and has turned down various offers to start up or join other small businesses.

Alexei's scattered entry into the world of work over the last three years, his interest in business, and his avoidance of military service are good examples of how the uncertainty of the postperestroika period manifests itself in the lives of young adults. When I first met Alexei, before the breakup of the Soviet Union, he was finishing his last year of vocational school and had begun to consider plans for the future. As a vocational-school graduate, he was supposed to begin working immediately for two years on a carpentry job,[3] wherever his school assigned him, and he was quite unhappy about this prospect. Observing friends who had completed general academic high school and were free to seek a higher education, Alexei—the son of university-educated parents—wondered if his choice to enter a vocational school and become a worker had been a mistake. But he accepted the job assignment, and his description of it suggests one reason why Russian vocational schools have had little success in assuring that graduates would stay in the trades they had studied.

> They sent me to work at a construction site, with another friend of mine, Misha ... to a state farm where they grow a lot of greens, tomatoes,

vegetables. We were supposed to work on a building there. But they didn't give us work in our profession. Instead, they sent us out into the fields, into the heat. They said to us, "Guys, we want you to go out there, somewhere within a kilometer there is a telephone cable. We'd like you to go out and look for it. Dig for it. Find it." So we asked, "How are we going to find it? Where is it?" And they said, "We don't know. Go and look for it. If you find it, you do, if you don't, you don't. But we know it's there. A secret cable, a military cable. They forgot about it a long time ago and that's why we don't know where it is. Go ahead and dig for it. Let us know if you find it." So we dug, for about two months. Of course I can't say we did a lot of digging. It was hot, and we were too lazy to dig, we'd keep going off and eating cucumbers and tomatoes, but really we had no choice but to go out and dig at least a bit. . . . Of course we didn't find it.

Many vocational school students do not even make the attempt that Alexei did: at least one-fifth of all vocational school graduates do not begin their work life in the field for which they had trained ("The Country's Public Education" 1989). And those who do are not retained: within five years of vocational-school graduation, virtually no former students are found in their original workplace ("Who Is Boss" 1992, p. 17).

In 1989, Alexei was planning to get a higher education at some point in the future—not because any particular career attracted him, but simply because most members of his family were college-educated, and he viewed a higher education as a symbol of true passage into adulthood:

Studying is good; it just hasn't worked out yet. . . . I want to [continue studying] but I can't. I want to go to college, but I don't have the knowledge of math I need. My whole family—my sister, my sister's husband, and all my relatives—are engineers, members of the intelligentsia. Of course I will be too. But I have to understand what work is in order to be an intellectual. To go to college, I have to study first, master some trade first. I'm not mature enough now. When I feel like studying, when I'm drawn into my math books, I'll know I'm mature enough. . . . I'd sooner work for a while and then go on to study because it's never too late, and I don't feel like it just yet. I'm still thinking about what profession to choose from the ones you can study for.

In 1992, after three years of unrelated jobs and activities, Alexei no longer had plans to continue studying, learn another profession, or to practice the trade he had studied in vocational school. Reminded that three years earlier he had had plans to go to college and learn a profession, he reflects: "I thought that when I grew up I might want to go on to an institute of higher education. Well, I've grown up now, and I see that I don't want to!" He would like to continue running his optical cooperative: he finds the work interesting and, more important, he emphasizes, quite profitable.

Alexei's cooperative consists of a small booth in a metro station in the heart of downtown Moscow where he and two co-owners accept prescriptions for eyeglasses. Through a network of special contacts, they locate and purchase the lenses and frames—items in chronic short supply. Since none of them have any optical training, they pay a professional optician to grind and fit the lenses. Like so many new businesses in Russia, their cooperative does not produce anything, but essentially buys and resells at a high profit, "not just 15 percent a day," Alexei notes, "but 800 percent! Just for one order."

Despite Alexei's enthusiasm for this work, however, he is not certain that his cooperative will survive. There have been problems from the beginning: the two friends who had initially invited him to become a co-owner eventually asked him to leave the business, but they allowed him to keep a small share of their stock of eyeglasses. Alexei sold these as a street vendor in the middle of winter and with the profits was able to reopen his own version of the same cooperative, specializing in hard-to-find lenses he was able to obtain through "good connections." Some of these lenses included the last stock from a shipment of humanitarian aid from West Germany to the former Soviet Union—a shipment which, Alexei noted, was not supposed to have been sold for a profit and which had been stockpiled and hoarded and kept from the public for which it was intended for several years.

Now, two other friends whom Alexei invited to reopen the cooperative with him have taken over much of the business. Alexei feels they are trying to push him out of it, since now that he has shared his entire network of connections with them, they no longer need him. One week before our conversation, Alexei had entrusted the document establishing the business in his name to his friends in order to secure a new lease on the booth. At the time we last spoke, they had not returned it to him. He noted wistfully that people had warned him not to invite friends into a business venture.

On the verge of losing a business to people he had considered friends, Alexei feels deceived and frustrated. Three years after graduation, after various attempts to find engaging and lucrative activities, he is troubled and confused about what he will do next. Not surprisingly, however, to the extent that he can envision his future, he continues to picture it connected to some type of business endeavor.

> To tell you the truth, I don't imagine my future anymore. Or maybe I
> imagine it this way: I'll sign some kind of agreement with somebody in

Poland, I'll get selling rights to things that have gone out of fashion, that already aren't in demand anymore. Things that stores haven't been selling for two, three years. . . . Our fashion is about five years behind. In Poland, those things have already gotten very cheap because they're not in demand. And so I can make good money off of them!

Alexei's forays into business make him one of what many are calling the new generation of Russian youth. Faced with a situation in which the old economic order is collapsing and a new one is not yet defined, he and many young people like him are trying to find a way to survive economic hard times and make sense out of a world that has changed dramatically. For Alexei, as for so many people struggling in Russia today, excitement about political and economic change has given way to the primary preoccupation, survival, which, in the current inflationary period means finding ways to make more money—often through speculative activities.

The change in attitude toward money is one frequently cited by people discussing the current generation of young Russians. Commenting on how this new generation has broken with the past, a former school teacher, who herself has left the public sphere to work as an interpreter for an American firm in Moscow, observes:

In our old life, to count money . . . for example, Americans, they pay you a salary and never put it in an envelope. For me it was an insult to get money like this. We were above money. We were above materialism. And our kids are quite the opposite. For them to ask 'how much' is quite easy. They have no complexes (Gladstone 1992).

Alexei is experiencing this economic upheaval and the change in attitudes within his own immediate family: his mother has been laid off from two jobs in succession, his father earns a minimal salary as a researcher in a government institution, and the kindergarten his sister's two small children were attending has been shut down for lack of funding, leaving his sister, a working mother, in an extremely precarious position. As an entrepreneur, Alexei is the only one in his family making a significant amount of money, no small concern in the current inflationary period. And Alexei's parents, former members of the Communist Party who had been privileged enough under the old system to spend years working abroad on government teaching assignments, have come to approve of Alexei's business activities, although they had been very much opposed at first.

While it is true that new and diverse opportunities are available to him that would not have been possible in preperestroika Soviet society, Alexei thinks that the chances for young people to find meaningful careers and activities have not improved for most. Contemplating his own experiences and that of his friends, his assessment of the situation of young people in Russia today is bleak.

> Things certainly haven't gotten any better for young people in the sense of having things to do. People have just gotten involved with crime. Crime has grown more than anything else around here. And speculation. That's what young people are getting involved with. Like my friends. More than half of my [former] schoolmates drink. They're alcoholics. One has gotten involved with karate. Another stayed in the army and became an officer. One is working with me at the optical cooperative. One went to the university. One is working. Another one has been in prison for four years and he's going to be there for a long time. He killed someone.

The rapidly increasing cost of living and general economic decline have changed Alexei's plans for the future. Indeed, to talk of "plans for the future" seems almost contradictory to him, given the breakdown of the old order and radical changes in Russia today. The shape of Russian society even within the next year or two is uncertain—and such uncertainty is simply not conducive to planning for the future. Yet choices must be made. Despite the problems his cooperative has encountered, Alexei has made a clear decision to join the private sector and is determined to find his niche in it. Given the right circumstances, he says, he is sure that he could make vast sums of money.

Alexei now feels that a higher education would do nothing to help him obtain basic economic security, and he is no longer interested in pursuing one. Without an adequate income, he would not be able to help his family, which is lacking in resources, nor, he adds, would he even consider marrying his girlfriend since a wedding and the expenses of having and supporting a child have risen so much in the last year. But Alexei still holds education in some esteem—he would, after all, prefer the greater honor of having a diploma from an academic high school over the one he has from a vocational school. In this sense, his attitude remains rooted in the past: in Soviet society, even though the economy required far more manual workers than professionals, a higher education was valued and sought by many. Approximately 40 percent of the working class had some type of diploma in higher education (Mandel 1989, p. x). But although Alexei is a vocational school graduate, the fate of becoming a worker no longer threatens him—private enterprise has changed that. His plans are to remain involved in profitable commercial ventures. He has no interest in practicing the trade he learned.

Lyosha: Becoming a Farmer

Lyosha, a friend of Alexei, also twenty-one, is another former vocational-school student trying his hand at private enterprise. When I first met him in 1989, close to graduation, he wanted to continue his studies and get a higher education, as did most of the vocational school students I met then. There was no particular area in which he wanted to specialize; he was simply attracted by the prestige of a higher education. Even in 1992, he still regretted his decision to study in a vocational school because he felt that it had prevented him from continuing his education: "I think that if I had kept going in [general academic] school and finished it, I probably would have gone on to an institute," he said. "If you finish tenth grade, more than half of those people go on to an institute. They go right after school, they don't just go right to work."

But as a vocational-school graduate Lyosha was forced to enter the difficult and confusing world of adult life more quickly than those students who had been accepted at a university or institute and who, at least for the duration of their studies, would not yet have to find a trade or occupation or define a career. Trying to decide between old and new options—either practicing the trade he had learned in vocational school or getting involved in a private business—Lyosha had spent the three years since graduation from vocational school in much the same scattered way as his friend Aleksei: after graduation, at the age of eighteen, he was drafted into the army. He did not want to serve, but reported for duty and went through three months of basic training. Determined not to serve his full two years, he went to great lengths to receive an early medical dismissal:

> I told the [military] doctors I was having severe back pains, like I had kidney problems. I poked my finger and put blood in the urine samples. That makes it seem as if there is some protein in the urine. And that indicates that the kidneys are not working. The hard part was doing those things in such a way that the doctors wouldn't notice what I was up to. [The doctors] know that a lot of guys are just faking it, and a lot of guys don't pull it off, but I got lucky. They believed me. I complained a lot about serious pain.

Once free from the army, Lyosha returned to Moscow, trying to decide what to do next:

> I went home for three months and just took it easy, resting at home. After that I went to work at a factory, in my profession, assembling radios. A

place near where I live, but it was really an unhealthy place and I didn't
want to keep working there. You work with micropieces and there's a lot of
smoke and it's bad for your eyes. I worked there for a month but I couldn't
take it so I left. I don't like that profession, that's clear.

Eventually, Lyosha was invited to participate in an agricultural project
designed to interest young people in becoming independent farmers,
through a new private youth center in Moscow that works primarily with
vocational-school students. As part of the program he went to Canada for
three months to live with a farm family and learn about the life of the
independent small farmer. The experience convinced him that he wanted
to continue the project and become a farmer. Upon his return, he took
classes for two months at an agricultural institute in Moscow, where he
learned about various aspects of farming, from learning to drive a tractor
to planting and preparing a crop. After a long delay, the youth center, with
the financial backing of a wealthy Soviet emigre sponsor,[4] was able to
lease land from a state farm near Moscow.[5]

Lyosha considers farming extremely important and worthy work, particularly in view of the urgent need to increase agricultural production in
Russia. But despite training and enthusiasm for the project, he and the
other youths involved in it are experiencing great difficulties in its implementation. These problems illustrate the complex situation of small
private farmers in the face of the unresolved issue of land tenure and the
resistance from the state and collective farms which still account for and
control the majority of agricultural production in Russia.

> When the state farm gave the land, the director promised to help, to give us
> tractors, all kinds of promises to help, but so far there hasn't been any real
> help. They're tricking us. The [youth] center gave the state farm half a
> million [rubles] credit for the land, but the farm isn't fulfilling their part of
> it. The director of the state farm promised to give us a tractor, and we asked
> him about this every morning. We would go to him and ask about the
> tractor and every day he just kept saying, "Tomorrow, tomorrow, tomor-
> row." For two weeks in a row he kept saying "tomorrow." But now a month
> has gone by and nothing has been plowed! ... They just don't let people
> get down to work. I know a lot of farmers, and they all have problems. [The
> state farms] give them land, so they buy cattle, and they promise to give
> them hay, promise them they'll help them with everything, but they don't
> do it.

Lyosha is personally disappointed and frustrated by the difficulties his
project is encountering, but explains them as part of what he sees as the
major problem that the transition to a market economy faces: breaking
down entrenched power structures that inhibit private initiative. He points

out that the agricultural sector has been particularly difficult to restructure, and accounts for his own difficulties within this broader context:

> The directors of these state farms just don't want to lose their power. You see, if a farmer is well-organized, he will do two times as much as the director of the state farm can get done, even though the state farm may have six times as much land. But if a farmer works well, he will be much more productive and get much better harvests than the state farm, and the directors get jealous of that. And they want control because they've gotten used to it already, for sixty years, they've been the important ones. So I think they do a lot of these things on purpose, to keep farmers from being successful. Of course that system is going to break down, but I think it will be a long time yet before that happens.

But Lyosha cannot wait long for the obstacles small farmers face to be removed: he is receiving only a small stipend from the youth center, and it does not even begin to cover his basic monthly expenses. He still lives at home with his parents and is able to manage for now, dependent on them. But he does not like this dependence, and in any case the family needs more money since his mother has had to stop working due to serious health problems. He needs to earn enough money to help support the whole family.

When I met with Lyosha at the beginning of my three-week stay in Moscow, he was excited about his project. But by the time I was preparing to leave, he was full of worry and anxiety over its fate: he had lost almost three weeks of planting time because the tractor and plow were still not available. He was almost certain that he would not be able to get a large crop into the ground this year. He had plowed as much as he could with a spade, but expected to harvest from that only enough for his own personal needs. Without the crop, he faced a year without any income or activities from the farm. In our last conversation, he told me that he was almost certain he would be leaving the farm project even though he considered it more socially worthwhile than the buying-and-selling activities with which he had previously experimented. But the need to increase his earnings will probably take him away from farming, to look for work as a salesman in a private store where salaries are relatively high, even though he is not very interested in this work.

Olya: "A Young Pioneer Girl from a Vocational School"

When I met her in 1989, Olya was finishing her last year of a vocational school that trained students to print such items as transportation passes.

She was unhappily preparing to begin working. She and her classmates were expected to work their two-year assignment at the polygraphics factory affiliated with her vocational school—the same factory where they had already completed their practicum. The daughter of workers, Olya was about to become a worker herself. But she didn't like the polygraphics factory. The work was dirty, boring and regimented, and led nowhere; as a young woman concerned about her looks, her health, and fashion, she found the constant contact with oil, grease, ink, and other chemicals highly undesirable.

She did not intend to remain a worker, certainly not in the polygraphics factory. She lamented having entered a vocational school, a decision she had made at the age of fifteen in order to learn a trade and begin working immediately; she wanted to help her mother, who, in the process of divorce, faced the burden of supporting two children by herself. Olya told me that if she had finished general academic school she would have been free to pursue a higher education or go on to a technical college. She believed that people should continue studying, and in 1989 she herself intended to do so, as soon as she finished her two-year work assignment at the factory.

When she entered the vocational school, Olya had no particular interest in the trade she would learn there. Once she had begun her practicum at the factory affiliated with the school, she realized she didn't like her chosen trade at all. She began to hate the factory at the same time that she was preparing to begin there as a full-time worker. In 1989, at seventeen, Olya felt she had already given up part of her youth and freedom.

> On June 1 we start working. We'll already be the working class. Grown people. Big changes are ahead. I think it is going to be really hard—getting up early, not having any time. When you're studying, you have more free time. When you're working, you have more responsibility, you have to answer for your work, you grow up. Your childhood ends. . . . They told us from the first year [in the vocational school] that we are the working class, that we have a trade, that we have work responsibilities, unlike tenth-graders,[6] and we are more mature than they are . . . they told us that we are better prepared than school kids are; they don't have a profession, and they still have the institute ahead of them. But going straight to work means giving up a part of your freedom. Everybody says that it is easier to study than to work. I'm not a free person—work binds you, and if you work, you're not a free person.

In the world Olya inhabited in 1989, a higher education had seemed to provide a guarantee to the future. She felt that she had denied herself that guarantee by enrolling in a vocational school at age fifteen, a decision she deeply regretted:

If I could turn back time, I would decide to finish tenth grade, and get my certificate. But there's no going back now. . . . It's a difficult moment in my life, but what am I going to do? We pay for our own mistakes.

Ultimately, Olya avoided working in the factory by getting a false medical exemption at the suggestion of one of the young women in her graduating class, who also did not want to work in the factory. In fact, Olya notes that most of her graduating class did not want to work in the factory, and most were able to find some way to avoid it:

> Nobody wanted to go there to work, especially the girls. But we were supposed to work there for two years, so we started to talk about how we could get out of it. It was easier for the boys because they were on their way to the army. But there were five of us girls who were supposed to stay there to work. So one of my girlfriends said to me, "Look, Olya, my vision is bad, I'm going to get a medical certificate that says I can't work there for health reasons." And she was able to get one easily because the truth is that they really were about to do an operation on her at the Feodorov eye clinic. So she got her medical certificate, and it wasn't a trick. A second girl got married and so she went off on maternity leave—of course she wasn't planning on working there! There were three girls left. Another girl who I had gotten to know said to me, "Look, Olya, I have an acquaintance who is a doctor; let's get a medical certificate that says we can't work there." And so I got a medical certificate that said I couldn't work there, couldn't work at any polygraphic factory, that said I was allergic to some of the chemicals they use there. I got out of it.

Freed from working at the polygraphic factory, Olya had no need for the skills she learned in vocational school and no interest in looking for work that might require them. Next, she and a friend attempted to become airline stewardesses, but were disappointed by the "training" they underwent there—working in the kitchen of Vnukovo Airport.

> We wanted to become stewardesses, but we started to work there in the kitchen for awhile. Flying is one thing, that sounds romantic, the pilots and all, but of course cleaning potatoes and that kind of work is another thing! We had to work in that kitchen because the people who are in charge there are really idiots. They think that if a girl wants to work on a plane, she needs to go through some sort of preparatory phase. So a person who wants to work flights has to go through that kitchen work at the airport. But I don't think their practice has anything to do with the work! I think that they just sent people to wherever they needed somebody to fill jobs at the airport, wherever they are short of hands; they send people there as if it were a practicum.

Olya's practicum was short-lived—ten days. She continued to look for a job, determined not to work in a factory, and eventually found a clerical position in a transportation agency that processes and delivers railway freight shipments to and from the Moscow region. In 1992, she had been at the agency for a year and a half. She said she was satisfied with her job and liked her coworkers. And she was happy to have avoided the dirt and regimented schedule of the factory.

Her search for work may have ended. "I like working there," she says, "and I have no intention of leaving, as long as they don't end up closing down the place on us. I'll probably stay there until it's time to go on pension." But her salary is low and she cannot meet her own expenses—she still lives at home and many of her needs are paid by her mother. "To get a better job," she adds, "a person needs a wiser head than the one I've got, and more knowledge than I have, more experience."

But Olya doesn't expect to get more knowledge. Adamant three years before that she would somehow find a way to continue her education, by 1992 she had no interest at all in a higher education:

> I don't want to study anymore. Absolutely not. Why should I continue studying? Let's suppose that I went to an institute or to a technical school, where am I going to work after that? In production again? Work for the government? Why do I need to do that? Of course not! Study? Definitely not, not for anything! No. Who needs those studies nowadays? Who needs that diploma? Nobody! Right now people are working without having a diploma, making money. The most important thing now is making money, and that diploma is just a piece of paper. Maybe that diploma can help you get a good job, someplace, but only in rare cases. . . . Right now at work, the girls I work with, practically all of them have a higher education. One trained as a lawyer, another has a degree in mechanical engineering. A third one also has some kind of higher education in computers. All of them have a higher education, except for me! And there we are, working together, doing the same work, getting the same salary!

Olya has indeed managed to avoid working in either industrial production or a government enterprise: the transportation agency is a cooperative venture. But her position in it is as a low-paid clerical worker. Her coworkers are all women. The director is a man. Although she knows that she does not want to cast her lot with the state sector, she feels she has no access to the private sector's more profitable side because she is a woman and comes from a family with few resources.

> You need some sort of a foundation [to get involved in business]. Connections. Some kind of experience so you have some idea what you're doing. And how are you supposed to do that? Get it from your friends, your parents? Suppose a little Young Pioneer girl comes straight from the vocational school and takes it into her head to get into business. Well, that's great. They'll say to her, what in the world do you think you're doing? . . . If

you don't have anything to begin with, it's just a joke to try to get into business.

Olya's doubt about her access to the private sector is well-founded. In the new Russia, women are not only becoming unemployed in greater numbers than men, they also face greater obstacles in gaining access to the credit and resources that would allow them to set up their own businesses (Babak 1992, p. 24). A senior researcher at the Institute for the Study of Public Opinion, commenting on the prejudices and stereotypes that contribute to limiting women's access to private enterprise, says, "Public awareness has formed an image of 'women's professions' which, because of their nature, are in no way connected to risk or enterprise. And business is always risk" (Ibid.). But Olya, for now, is happy that she has found employment that is relatively secure and has saved her from the years of factory work she had faced after her graduation from vocational school.

Tanya: Teachers—the Poorest, the Most Miserable

Tanya was a sixteen-year-old ninth-grader when I first met her in 1989, one year away from secondary-school graduation. She was determined to enter a pedagogical institute after finishing school and then to become a school teacher. The daughter of working-class parents, Tanya viewed becoming a teacher as a significant step that would take her across the class boundary into the intelligentsia, a step she would make with pride if she succeeded.

> I'm from a working-class family. But I'm going to be an intellectual—a teacher. They say here, "Where are you headed? To the intelligentsia! Then your level has to be higher!" But I think basically anybody can become an intellectual. Depending upon the way he has been raised, even a worker can become an intellectual in the way he relates to his work, to the people around him, even though officially he is not an intellectual. But in terms of how he thinks, he can be a very educated and cultured person.

But Tanya was far from certain that she would succeed: about to graduate from an ordinary neighborhood school, she was worried that her academic preparation was insufficient to enable her to pass the competitive entrance exams into the pedagogical institute where she wanted to study. Nevertheless, her plans and hopes centered on a satisfying career working with children.

Three years later, Tanya has completed two years of a three-year teacher-training program in a new, experimental teachers college. Although she has been disappointed by the level of instruction at her college and questions whether or not the program is really innovative or experimental, she had remained committed to the idea of becoming a primary-school teacher. But even so, her view of her choice of career has changed markedly: rather than a prestigious stepping stone into the intelligentsia, Tanya now views her future as a teacher as one of poverty and economic uncertainty. As a new teacher, she will most likely work in a public school and, as an employee in the state sector, she will face all the insecurity of those who depend on a system that shows signs of a serious crisis. Even if Tanya finds a teaching position, which in the current circumstances is no longer guaranteed, she will be paid by a government that is having a difficult time paying salaries that already are inadequate in the face of high and increasing inflation. Tanya fears that her decision to become a teacher does not bode well for her future:

> As a teacher . . . I depend entirely on government money. Our work doesn't pay for itself because we don't produce anything, and that's why whatever the government is able to pay us, that's what they pay us. But what about when they don't want to anymore, or can't? And we get less than everybody. Medical workers, cultural workers, and teachers. The poorest. The most miserable. Working for the public sector means having a life of financial problems. . . . Teachers, doctors, anybody who works for the public sector is not going to have an easy time in life and I know I am creating problems for myself by making the choice that I am making.

For Tanya, the biggest obstacle three years before, had been getting accepted into an institute of higher education. Now, just one year short of achieving her long-standing goal of becoming a teacher, she remains committed to her profession but aware of the fact that circumstances were quite different than they had been when she had first decided on her career. Although teachers have always received a low salary, the rise of a private sector where some people make vast sums of money through commercial activity has made the salary of a teacher even lower in comparison and the career less desirable. In fact, many teachers—particularly those with skills that are in high demand, such as foreign languages—are leaving the schools to find work that brings in more money—either teaching in new, private schools that are opening up, or leaving teaching for other types of work in private companies. Several teachers I knew had started working long evening hours with private students, tutoring to supplement an income that no longer allowed them to feed their families. Viewing this, Tanya has resigned herself to what she expected will be a lifetime of low wages and relative poverty.

In 1989, Tanya had felt there was a great distinction between those with a higher education and those without, between the working class and the intelligentsia. But, as she pointed out in 1992, there is another, more important distinction now: the difference between those who work for the shrinking and troubled state sector, and those who work independently in the private sector where large profits can be made. She has already begun to experience the difficulties of remaining in a public-sector occupation: She and some of her classmates had been scheduled to work as counselors at a summer camp for a month in July. By the beginning of June, Tanya had already prepared activities for her charges and was looking forward to the responsibility and learning experience of taking care of a group of children. But less than two weeks before she was to go, the practice was canceled. The price of a full thirty-five-day session at the camp had gone up to 15,000 rubles[7] and trade union subsidies had disappeared, so it was too expensive for many parents to send their children. Because the camp would have fewer children than originally planned, there was no need for the college students to work as counselors. Further, the camp simply had no money to pay them. The college resolved the situation by sending Tanya and her classmates to work as volunteers at day camps in and near Moscow. This assignment was far less interesting to Tanya, and working as an unpaid volunteer forced her to become completely dependent on her parents for the rest of the summer.

Tanya would eventually like to work in a private school, where she believes there are possibilities for innovative teaching and where the wages are higher, but the competition for positions in private schools is considerable. She believes that as an inexperienced young teacher, she would find it almost impossible to get employment in one of them. And although she has accomplished what she set out to do, changing circumstances have dampened her enthusiasm and her feelings of accomplishment. "My optimism has also really fallen. I wouldn't say it's disappeared, but it's fallen quite a bit," she says. But she feels that young adults of her age group are caught in a particularly difficult situation, and the current group of secondary-school students about to graduate probably will do better than she and her peers:

> I remember how people used to go around saying about us, "Oh, those young people. They don't care about anything." But that wasn't the truth. We did care! But now the [secondary school] students . . . of course you can't say that they're bad, but they've all gone off in only one direction—into commerce! Of course those students who are going into commerce are more optimistic than I am! When you've got some change in your pockets,

it's easier to be optimistic! So maybe something will come of those students after all.

Adding to Tanya's concerns about the future is the fact that she has fallen in love with and decided to marry a man who is training in a military academy to become a border guard, a "second poor choice in terms of my well-being," she says, laughing at herself. Once considered desirable, a military career no longer brings prestige or security. Cutbacks in the ranks, changing and volatile borders, and the general criticism of anything connected with the old regime have all eroded the advantages a lifetime in the military once had.

> I joke around to Seryozha, "There's no incentive for me to marry you!" But of course I'm marrying for love. Because before it was the case that these military schools were popular. There were always a lot of girls hanging around them. It was considered prestigious to marry a soldier or border guard. Now one could only marry a soldier for love because there are no advantages whatsoever. A sensible girl wouldn't go after a military man at all!

Tanya adds that her fiance, Seryozha, could do what many graduates of military schools are now doing—using skills learned in the military to organize their own businesses as security and bodyguards. "That's certainly something they know how to do well," Tanya says, but adds that Seryozha is not interested in that option. He does not want to risk his health and his life to protect someone else's possessions. Instead, he will pursue his military career, despite the insecurity. And Tanya is resigned to a life of financial difficulties in which she and Seryozha will continue to need support from their parents:

> When you work for the state sector now, like we are going to, it means you will never become self-sufficient. It forces you to be dependent. The only people who are independent are the few people who also manage to get involved in business.

Tanya is caught between the old and the new. She expresses impatience with her parents' way of thinking, noting that her father in particular likes to talk about how, under Communism, basic necessities were very cheap. "He remembers how a half-liter bottle of vodka used to cost 24 rubles, and now it costs 100, 150, a crazy price," she observes. "So he thinks that all we have to do is change our prices back to those pennies and that's it, we'll have Communism." But despite her disagreements with her father, Tanya herself is just as critical of the changes that have taken over her society. "People are too tired now. What is this already, the fifth year of change?" And nobody wants to work anymore. They all want to go into commerce!" Interestingly, Tanya's father has actually benefited from the very changes that he criticizes. An electrician by trade, he and ten other coworkers have opened up a small enterprise and work on jobs obtained through private contracts. He has increased his earnings considerably, earning from 3,500 to 4,500 rubles a month. She compares this salary to the 1,300, 1,200 and "sometimes only 900 rubles" a month that teachers earn—the salary range that awaits her if she finds work in her profession.

Overview

The experiences of Alexei, Lyosha, Olya, and Tanya illustrate how developments in Russian society leave young people with a variety of choices, many of them new, most of them uncertain. The change in their attitudes toward education is easy to understand: there is little reason for a young person concerned with economic security to count on a higher education to provide it. At the same time, the experiences of Alexei and Lyosha illustrate how ventures into the private sector are equally insecure.

Vocational-school graduates face the world of work earlier than their counterparts in academic high schools who continue studying to get a higher education. College and university students, even if they take jobs to earn money, can postpone commitment to a profession or career during the years of their studies. Because vocational students face decisions about incorporating themselves into adult life earlier, they seem more willing or have greater need to experiment with current business possibilities—many of them speculative, such as Alexei's. And the emergence of a private sector provides them with opportunities to avoid the stigmatized blue-collar work for which they have been trained. Alternatively, they can earn more money by doing that work in a private venture, although in the case of Alexei, Lyosha, and Olya, the skills they learned in vocational school have turned out to be completely irrelevant to their lives today.

Given the developments within Russian society today, the future of a student attending the prestigious Moscow State University probably does not seem any more secure than does the future of an Alexei or a Lyosha. The major factor that distinguishes people now, as Tanya suggests, is no longer whether or not they have a higher education, but whether or not they become part of the private sector. In this sense, Alexei's future may very well be more prosperous than Tanya's, despite her move into a professional position. And given the increasing exclusion of women from the private sector, it is probable that gender will become an increasingly important factor in determining career success in the new Russia. Proposed legislation that would in effect limit women's access to the best jobs in the private sector has considerable parliamentary support (vanden Heuvel 1992, p. 32); and general attitudes discourage young women like Olya even to contemplate a business venture, whereas young men like Alexei and Lyosha have already made several forays into business. "The tragedy is that our system of education and upbringing of girls and young women is geared toward having them take the kind of work where they are carrying out somebody else's decisions and directives," asserts a lecturer from the St. Petersburg Institute of Political Sciences, "which is why women do not have the reserves of self-confidence without which there is no way to become involved in entrepreneurship" (Babak 1992, p. 24).

It is still early to assess the consequences of these changes for education in Russia. At the same that time education has become much less valuable in the eyes of many young people, there are new experimental schools with innovative curricula and new college programs to improve teacher training. Perhaps fewer students will choose to pursue a higher education—certainly there will be less work for university graduates as the scientific and research institutes that employ many of them make drastic reductions in staff. Out of necessity, students may simply devote less and less time to studies and more time to making money. Others may get a degree without any intention of working in that profession. "Only five of my classmates are planning to practice the profession they're studying after they graduate and are working regularly with newspapers and television," notes a journalism student at Moscow State University. "The majority figured out a long time ago how risky the newspaper business is and the only thing they thirst for is the diploma that corresponds to their studies" (Pankratov 1992, p. 3).

But in these times of economic hardship, there are students like Tanya whose choice of profession and whose commitment to studies have not changed even given the probability that it will lead to a life of financial insecurity and dependence. Yelena, a nineteen-year-old, told me that she wants to get as broad a liberal arts education as she can, without regard to what type of work she can find afterward. She has taken entrance exams twice but has not yet been accepted at university. Currently preparing for her third try at the exams, she explains her determination to achieve something that many of her friends tell her will bring her very little:

In these times, you have a choice: you either think about ways you can make money, get into business, or you think about spiritual, educational, not material things. One or the other. If you get 900 rubles a month for your work, you just decide you're going to live without a dacha and without a car. Period.

Notes

1. Much of the material in this chapter is taken from a series of in-depth interviews I conducted with eleven Moscow teenagers of diverse backgrounds. These interviews took place in 1989 and in 1992. All statements by Alexei, Lyosha, Olya, Tanya, and Yelena are taken either from the 1989 interviews published in *The Children of Perestroika* (M.E. Sharpe, 1991), or from *The "Children of Perestroika" Come of Age* (M.E. Sharpe, 1994).

2. In the Soviet/Russian educational system students must choose an academic, technical, or vocational track. The choice, made upon completing the eighth grade, is an important one that has significant long-term ramifications for students. Academic-track graduates generally prepare to enter an institute of higher education upon completing the eleventh grade. Technical-vocational school students train three years for white- and blue-collar occupations while simultaneously completing the universal secondary curriculum; they are expected to enter the workforce upon graduation. Vocational education, which is mandated to produce low-skilled blue-collar workers, is an extremely stigmatized type of education: students often end up in vocational schools as a result of disciplinary or social problems, rather than out of a commitment to a particular trade, and they have the reputation of being unmotivated and low achievers. The choice between educational tracks has been a significant factor in reproducing class structure, and it is unusual to find children of university-educated parents such as Alexei enrolled in vocational schools.

3. Upon graduation, all vocational-school graduates are supposed to receive a two-year work assignment in their trade. Vocational schools cost the government significantly more than general academic high schools, and students receive the two-year assignment in order to pay back some of what the state has invested in their education. All the vocational students I met were unhappy about this work assignment which eliminated other more desirable options for work and study upon graduation.

4. A wealthy Soviet emigré living in Europe provided the center with initial funds to start the agricultural project. Many new entrepreneurial projects depend upon private sponsors. The concept has become so widespread in Russian that the English word "sponsor" has been incorporated into the Russian language.

5. Most people attempting small-scale independent farming projects lease land from the state and collective farms which still control much of the agricultural production in Russia.

6. Until recently, secondary school included first through tenth grade. The tracking decision was made after the eighth grade. But recent reforms have mandated that schools begin one year earlier, so secondary education now goes through the eleventh grade. The tracking decision is now made after ninth grade. To avoid confusion, this essay refers to the previous system of ten years, as the students I interviewed had all graduated before there was an eleventh grade.

7. This was an enormous sum in the summer of 1992 when I spoke with Tanya. Since then, prices have continued to rise rapidly.

References

Babak, E. (1992). "Zhenshchina i rynok," *Ekonomika i zhizn'*, May, p. 24.

"The Country's Public Education on the Eve of Radical Changes" (1989). *Soviet Education*, vol. 31, no. 7 (July), pp. 35–43 (translated from *Vestnik statistiki*, 1988, no. 3).

Gladstone, Brooke, producer. (1992). "The New Generation in Russia," (Soundprint). National Public Radio Documentary Series.

Mandel, E. (1989). *Beyond Perestroika*. London: Verso Press.

Pankratov, A. (1992). "Lomonosov v Moskvu ne poedet," *Moskovskie novosti*, no. 23 (June 7), p. 3.

vanden Heuvel, K. (1992). "Women of Russia, Unite!" *New York Times*, September 12, p. 32.

"Who Is Boss in the 'Forge'?" (1992). Interview with Viktor Vasil'evich Shapkin, director of the All-Union Scientific Research Institute of Vocational-Technical Pedagogy, by M. Shanygina, *Russian Education and Society*, vol. 34, no. 6, pp. 14–28 (translated from *Molodoi kommunist*, 1990, no. 6).

14

The Labor Market and Education in the Post-Soviet Era

IGOR V. KITAEV

Developments in countries of the former USSR are attracting close attention due to their drama and unpredictability. In this regard, developments in the area of higher and postgraduate education in these societies and reaction to changes remain less explored, perhaps due to their previously passive subordination to official ideology and centrally planned economic functions. Even at present, with the drastically changed needs of society and the labor market, education in the former USSR is lagging behind events and is only beginning to be converted from a supply-driven to a demand-oriented system.

The qualitative mismatch between higher education and the labor market offsets the impressive quantitative figures of graduates and diploma specialists who have been the first victims of unemployment due to structural adjustment policies in the public sector. While enormous public resources are still being wasted to teach overspecialized disciplines never required after graduation, the students and would-be qualified personnel are totally defenseless in the face of a market economy. According to a recent public opinion poll, 54 percent of Russian students consider their financial situation "unsatisfactory" and another 34 percent— "partly unsatisfactory."[1]

Unless the former USSR's educational system becomes sensitive to market requirements, the economy will stagnate due to the tremendous degree of mismanagement and to the shortage of personnel capable of operating under market economy conditions. That the countries of the former USSR could well deteriorate is suggested by the IMF Assessment Project carried out by the Alexis de Tocqueville Institution of Arlington (in the United States). According to G. Fossedal, chairman, the IMF is most successful in countries with long-standing democratic and capitalist traditions and can hardly be the "bold, energetic catalyst" needed to re-build the former communist states.[2]

However, the traditions and practices of the informal sector and self-employment—so-called "black" and "gray" economies—are widely disseminated across countries of the former USSR. As described by G. Grossman, these informal activities "began with the October Revolution, with roots reaching deep into the Russian past."[3]

For countries of the former USSR, a prerequisite for faster transition to the market economy is personnel who have obtained a mixture of market economy competence and entrepreneurial mentality. As confirmed by the experience of Western companies in the former USSR, "to survive, enterprises in the former Soviet Union must acquire not only Western technology but Western know-how in management, marketing, and distribution."[4] The key question in the former USSR and Eastern European countries is "whether national populations will have the flexibility, the vision, and, above all, the commitment and the will to function effectively. If the human resource factor tests out, Eastern Europe will join Western Europe in the much-discussed European common house. If the populations are not motivated but apathetic, the newly liberalized economies of the continent's eastern half will end up hopelessly behind the integrated single market of its western half. Production structures would remain inefficient, factories and agriculture unproductive, and the state apparatus cumbersome."[5]

Students and Changing Patterns of
Labor Market Opportunities

For many decades, the whole life, social status, and professional career of an average Soviet citizen was largely programmed by graduation from the secondary or higher education level and was highly dependent on one's parents and education. During the Stalin and Khruschev years, manpower planning schemes based on rapid industrial development stimulated upward mobility, but under Brezhnev and thereafter, the number of highly qualified personnel exceeded demand by the labor market and denied career opportunities to large cohorts of overqualified graduates, in particular in the engineering and technical disciplines. The unjustified fragmentation of higher education specialties, and the increase in their number to 375 in recent years, have further widened the discrepancies between education and the labor market in the USSR.[6]

In Moscow at the present time, 95 percent of the registered unemployed have a higher education diploma, and according to the labor market forecasts for the next year, some 30 percent of new graduates of higher education institutions will become unemployed. In St. Petersburg, a mere one-half of 2,047 university graduates in 1992 were recruited in conformity with their diplomas, and among technical university graduates—only 20 percent. In Belarus, graduates of higher educational institutions constituted a majority among the 15,000 unemployed registered in April 1992, while the government projected the further shrinking of public-sector employment during this year by 25 to 30 percent. The least chances of finding employment corresponding to one's education are faced by graduates of electronic engineering and teacher training colleges; accountants and bookkeepers have the best chances.[7] To offset the increasing threat of graduate unemployment, the Russian educational authorities have recommended that free (totally financed from the government budget) admission to higher education be reduced by 30 percent in 1992.[8]

Young people are in an unfavorable position for competing with working adults for long-existing jobs, but have more chances of getting new jobs created in the private and informal sectors. A sampling of one of the newly emerged private Moscow banks showed that many senior positions are occupied by 20- to 30-year-olds who have no higher education or degree in other than their job disciplines.[9] The rationale behind this deliberate bank management policy was that investments in on-the-job training of young people was considered more cost-efficient and forward-looking than retraining orthodox old-timers.

An "upside-down" structure of the labor market in the countries of the former USSR with a deficit of low-skilled workers and an abundant number of highly qualified specialists has now led to a paradoxical phenomenon whereby janitors with a secondary education are offered salaries two to three times those of university professors or high-level researchers, whose qualifications are no longer valuable due to the changed labor market demand. For the last two years, salaries in the informal [private—A.J.] services sector have increased 30–50 times, in industry—10–30 times, in agriculture—10–15 times, whereas in the areas of public education, health care, science, and culture financed by the governments— only

3 times.[10] In this regard, Brodinsky stressed that *"perestroika* has not yet improved the condition and prestige of teachers. Miners in the Soviet Union still earn from three to four times as much as teachers."[11] Many students are proud that "after hours" they can earn more in the informal sector or self-employed than do their professors.

Without deep-rooted traditions of organized private entrepreneurship, labor flows of graduates, dropouts, and the unemployed from the former public sector are increasingly entering the informal sector and self-employment because these are areas that existed during the communist regime, have an easy access, and are familiar to all strata of the former USSR population. Informalization and small-scale privatization are rapidly developing mainly in services (shops, transportation, construction, repairs, hairdressers, etc.) and small-scale industrial and technological entrepreneurships.

While public employment is shrinking, a structured corporate private sector has not yet emerged in the countries of the former USSR and does not create the number of jobs commensurate with those cut in the public sector. The 1992 joint study on the former USSR by the IMF, the World Bank, the OECD, and the EBRD posed a question that remains unanswered: "How can property be privatized while the concept of ownership has not been clearly defined and property rights have not been fully guaranteed?"[12]

The self-sufficient public enterprises in heavy industry are being converted into the cooperative property of workers; those that are bankrupt are still being financed by governments frightened by social unrest. So far, large-scale entrepreneurs have to survive on their own in a hostile environment of high taxes and stiff competition with the public-sector enterprises, continuously subsidized and assisted by the governments. As asserted by K. Borovoi, president of the Russian Stock and Commodity Exchange, the governmental authorities continue to intervene in the grassroots economic activities and assist the bankrupt public enterprises, rather than building a system of incentives and stimulating private and informal entrepreneurships.[13] According to Frank, "Soviet *perestroika* and East European privatization are destroying old forms of economic organization before, and much faster than, they are replacing them with new ones. . . . Both the Soviet Union and especially Eastern Europe began by marketizing the industrial and commercial state monopolies and permitting them large measures of private monopoly power instead."[14]

One way to describe the process of reform currently going on in the former USSR is to say that private entrepreneurship is only "being legalized or tolerated or encouraged. This new toleration of market-like activity takes place in the context of a centrally planned economy, and one that is likely to remain centrally planned for a long time to come."[15] For instance, *The Economist* is rather skeptical about A. Vol'skii, who heads the Union of Industrialists and Entrepreneurs of Russia, which represents managers in factories that produce two-thirds of Russia's industrial output. "Despite the word 'entrepreneur' in their organizations' titles, none of these men represents the thousands of genuine Russian entrepreneurs who have started business in the past six months. They are leaders of the old guard, the bosses of giant state enterprises, especially defense plants."[16]

The Western presence in the former USSR economies is modest now but constantly increasing, "encouraged by many business managers in the republics who are soliciting Western help to salvage enterprises they cannot seem to operate successfully on their own."[17] The Western companies are normally forming joint ventures by acquiring a stake in enterprises still officially government-owned. For example, the U.S. Commerce Department records more than 2,000 deals between Americans and the former Soviet authorities, amounting to total investments of about 300 million U.S. dollars, but with only about 50 of these deals actually functioning so far. Covering a marginal proportion of the labor market, joint ventures and foreign businesses are, nonetheless, a priority attraction for former Soviet youth and a potential means to absorb graduates and other highly qualified unemployed.[18]

Mentality Barriers to Human Resources Development

The "value priorities" of the majority of the population were dismantled with the collapse of the communist regime and the USSR, and have not been adequately compensated for by relevant new ideas. Besides, "old" beliefs and complexes stick in the mentality and prevent the absorption of new ideas.

In general, despite strong trends to the market, public opinion in the former USSR still continues to cherish the "command" economy, and trusts and favors the public sector and its activities. From the point of view of an average middle-aged former Soviet citizen, the "command" economy was associated with a guaranteed minimal set of social benefits, stable and predictable for a well-to-do life today and tomorrow. On the contrary, according to the same conventional view, the market economy is linked to cuts in social welfare and a lower standard of living, inflation, the threat of unemployment, and an unstable and unpredictable future. As witnessed by a Russian man-

ager, "doctors of sciences become furious when they are offered employment in small-scale entrepreneurships or are recruited by their recently
junior colleague. . . . They still believe only in public-sector jobs."[19]

The older generation, particularly among teachers and parents, considers the private sector and its activities somewhat illegal, temporary, and
not a good prospect for a professional career for their children. This is due
to the fact that the former communist ideology always proclaimed the
dominance of the public sector in the economy and suppressed private-
sector activities by all means available—by military force in the twenties
and thirties to taxes in the fifties and sixties.

The optimal "communist" mode of behavior dictated a strict vertical
subordination from "top" to "bottom" so that orders and decisions should
be accomplished almost without any discussions, explanations, or initiatives. Despite the obvious deficiencies of that system of "command" management, its existence through many decades had a serious impact on
people's behavior, depriving them of incentive-building, initiative, and
decision making. However, for many it was a convenient way to escape
from their own failures and personal responsibilities, delegating them to
the decision makers at the top of the system. Needless to say, a substantial
share of former Soviet teachers and students was and is influenced by this
conservative mentality, in particular in the provinces and less-developed
republics of the former Soviet Union. As Grant has put it, "it need not be
assumed that commercial values of a particular kind will always commend
themselves to the former Soviet peoples, even as a set of organizational
nostrums, let alone as a social ideology. Many Russians and others are
already experiencing disenchantment with the new dispensation, and it
seems that the collectivist and egalitarian streak, in Russian society in
particular, is still strong, though it lacks focus at present."[20]

For many years the official propaganda favored the image of an "absolute" equality of man within a collective entity. That motto, indeed, guaranteed anyone in the former USSR a minimal amount of social benefits
and subsistence irrespective of real input. Perhaps the most visible implications of this ideologically biased policy were the following:

(1) People were losing the meaning and purpose of productive work.
Whether their work was of better or worse quality, whether it was productive or counterproductive, salaries were paid to everyone with only modest
differences depending on quality and effectiveness. The labor force experienced no direct correlation between the substance and effects of its work
and its ideology-biased remuneration, and there were no incentives for
higher efficiency and productivity. Psychologically, the labor intensity and

working discipline were considered useless at lower levels of management.

(2) "Hyper" equality imposed from the top blocked individual opportunities for the sake of collective interest. Being within a unified team and complying with "the rules of the game," one was not expected to become wealthier and more prosperous than one's colleagues by definition. Thus, in the view of public opinion, a higher-than-average level of welfare was a privilege either of a limited number of party and government authorities or of black-market operators. The conventional wisdom of Soviet citizens assumed that it was almost impossible to improve their standard of life significantly without a successful party or government career (which used to be a rare case) or violating the existing regulations and getting involved in illicit operations. The mentality of the former USSR population in general has difficulty in apprehending the motivations and incentives for business. Particularly in the provinces, many still prefer less remuneration in the routine public sector than much more profitable but risky private business.

But it could be wrong and dangerous to articulate extreme individualistic values as an alternative to extreme Soviet collectivism. An emphasis on personal achievement at the expense of counterparts or colleagues in the same company caused dramatic failures among the first postcommunist entrepreneurs. Their experience confirmed the need for an appropriate combination of individualistic values with due respect to human environment and abilities to organize and manage private collective activities. J. Attali, president of EBRD, observed that "the bulk of what needs to be done will rest on the shoulders of the citizens of these countries themselves, . . . on their ability to face challenging reappraisals. . . . Many have attempted to divide the world into individualistic and communitarian societies. In fact both tendencies exist in all societies, and, when misconstrued, each can become a grotesque caricature."[21]

As noted by the late F. Peregudov, deputy chairman of the USSR State Committee for Public Education, "we must acknowledge that our society has not yet learned how to view people's abilities, talents, and skills as a national treasure and do what is necessary to multiply and make effective use of them. Meanwhile, we have been shocked by massive incompetence and low professionalism."[22]

Attitudes of Youths toward a
Professional Career

An unusual phenomenon compared to other countries' experience is that, during profound social transformation in the   countries of the former

Table 14.1

"What actions are you likely to take if you are unemployed?"

	1990 %	1991 %
"Start receiving an unemployment allowance"	6	3
"Try to improve my qualifications and find a job corresponding to my education"	32	39
"Take any job, even a less-qualified one"	8	12
"Leave the city and become a farmer"	23	10
"Get involved in entrepreneurial activities"	18	14
"Search for work in other cities"	4	4
"Get involved in illicit operations"	7	9
"No comment"	2	9

Source: Poisk, 1992, no. 14.

USSR, the teenage and student community to a large extent is inactive and invisible in the political and social sphere, but is increasingly pragmatic and active in the informal sector and self-employment. Sandi explains this by saying that "during the first stages of post-totalitarianism, certain state structures are renewed, but only at the top, while underneath, bureaucracies are preserved. Political apathy is encouraged by the old structures and residual *nomenklatura*. The fight for everyday subsistence, added to low wages, inflation, and shortages, keeps people occupied mostly with the material aspects of life, sometimes with mere survival."[23] Regarding specifically former Soviet youth, G. Kutsev, one of the top-level officials in charge of education in the former USSR, noted that "with full justification we can call young people the bewildered generation; young people are disillusioned with the ideals of socialism, assuming that their elders are bureaucrats, Stalinists, and conservatives.... The complex socioeconomic and political situation in society is the context in which the new generation's character is being shaped. Mounting unemployment and the difficulties graduates encounter in finding jobs are having a terrible impact on young people. The people's moral level is going down, conscientious labor is losing its prestige, and conflicts in family and marital relations are worsening."[24]

In a public opinion poll in Moscow's higher education and vocational training institutions in 1990 and 1991, students were asked: "What actions are you likely to take if you are unemployed?"; the results are shown in Table 14.1 above.

Table 14.2

**Qualities and Skills Considered
Essential under a Market Economy**

	% of Respondents
Ability to establish business contacts	96
Economic competence	64
Entrepreneurial mind	59
Cunning and mean mind	27
Ability to be rational in spending	21
Honesty and reliability	13

With the strong shift toward a market economy, these responses may now seem ambiguous and should be adjusted for the controversial situation of 1990–91, when the drive toward the market economy was questioned by Soviet leaders. This explains the drop in interest in entrepreneurial activities by 4 percent and demonstrates the real difficulties facing those wishing to start their own private business from scratch in 1990–91, as well as the 7 percent of "no comment" responses. Still, the 3 percent decline in those satisfied with the prospect of relieving unemployment pay showed growing economic activism on the part of Moscow students. The 4 and 2 percent rises in readiness to take a less-qualified job and become involved in illicit operations indicate a loss of hope of being employed in the public sector and a growing popularity of the informal sector and self-employment, which were normally run on the periphery of the law in 1990–91. An impressive 13 percent decrease in those willing to become farmers manifests the growing opportunities in the urban informal sector.

Meanwhile, the substantial share and increase to 39 percent of those who are eager to improve their qualifications and find a job corresponding to their education evidently represents the majority of "wishful thinkers" protected from the changing realities by their parents.

The last observation is confirmed by another 1991 poll in Moscow. When asked "What would you do under desperate financial constraints?" 55 percent of students answered "turn to parents for help"; 18 percent— "start an illicit business"; and 4 percent—"try to find a job in the public sector." The rest preferred not to answer the question.[25]

Table 14.2 reflects a January 1991 survey in Kuzbass (a coal-mining region in Siberia) among 1,000 secondary school graduates who identified the human qualities and skills that they considered essential under a market economy.

Obviously, respondents underestimated the significance of economic competence and entrepreneurship as compared to the ability to establish business contacts. The survey confirmed that former Soviet youngsters consider "a cunning and mean mind" twice as important for business as "honesty and reliability." It is also worth noting that the same survey found 39 percent of youth in Kuzbass felt no need to prepare themselves for market relations.[26]

With no recent statistical data available, eyewitness evidence suggests that positive attitudes to the market economy among former Soviet students have increased in 1992, although heterogeneity persists.

Regarding the attitudes of youth toward education, the change is that success in life and "room at the top" no longer include higher education as a must for many teenagers, or, to be more precise, include only a limited number of higher education profiles (economics, finance, law, foreign languages). The 1991 survey of 15,300 secondary school students in Moscow and the Moscow region indicated that a growing number of former Soviet youth are willing to obtain jobs that require a minimal education but promise more "gray" income (tip-taking and the like)—waiter, hair stylist, taxi driver, etc.[27]

One should not underestimate an increasing desire among youth to try life abroad, as witnessed by the soaring figures of legal and illegal immigration to North America and Western Europe, and even more sweeping forecasts—6 to 20 million. "Usually, the inclination to migrate is highest in younger, independent adults with relatively high levels of education," warns Bernd Hamm with regard to former Soviet youth.[28]

The new attitudes of youth toward their future careers are summarized in Table 14.3.

The cumulative cause-and-effect reactions of former Soviet youth toward education and training in the period of transition to a market economy have been described by Peregudov as consisting of:

- an orientation toward secondary, rather than higher, professional levels;
- a decline in the prestige of knowledge and a diminished interest in education;
- a decline in the quality of learning and in the qualities of specialists being graduated;
- a belief that one does not need to learn much to acquire an occupation.[29]

Table 14.3

Career Expectations of Young People

Symptoms	Motivations
1. A desire for fast success in terms of personal wealth	—Unwillingness to "waste time" on any unproductive activities not bringing immediate revenues, including politics and higher education —Financial independence
2. A growing fascination with prospects in the informal sector and self-employment	—Lessening trust in public-sector employment —Higher earnings
3. Small-scale entrepreneurships composed only of students and/or youngsters	—Confidence in their own abilities —Disregard of parents' and other adults' experience
4. Readiness to take risks and get involved in illicit activities	—Disbelief in the legal means of upward mobility —More liberal, but still clumsy and controversial, legislation

The Present Role of Higher Education and the Teaching Profession

Higher education did not provide the spark to ignite changes toward democracy and the market economy, nor did it promote them. Through the decades, Soviet educators at large remained a reliable channel of official propaganda and resisted any attempts at improvisations and experiments. Even Soviet experts had to admit that in higher education, "the stress on extending contents resulted in students overworking, to the detriment of creative and individual development."[30] The need to introduce new content, methods, and structure into the former USSR systems of education was met not by the system itself, by professors and teachers, but penetrated it via the badly damaged social environment, i.e., as a side effect of the failure of communist ideology, the crisis of the centrally planned economy, and the political dismantlement of the USSR.

When the former totalitarian system was being eliminated in the late 1980s to early 1990s, the role of the educational system in the process was minimal and controversial. It provided only one important input—it emphasized the gap between the existing curriculum and the rigid bureaucratic organization of the school system, on one hand, and the facts of life and increasing democracy, on the other. Disillusioned young people indifferently observed the collapse of the regime and had no motivation or incentive to save the heritage of the past seven decades of wars, heroic deeds, and inflated expectations.

Substantive changes in the area of higher education in countries of the former USSR are progressing more slowly than might have been expected. The rectors normally represent the "old guard" and are reluctant to take initiatives, unless forced to by the market environment. The political and bureaucratic obstacles are still strong enough to break any indigenous initiative—for example, undertaking more objective sociological research.[31] To close or reform an institution or a department that does not correspond to the present needs of the labor market is still taboo. Many rectors have occupied their positions for fifteen or twenty years and consequently lack motivation and the spirit of reform. A minority of the "new wave" educators are facing the necessity for tradeoffs with the conservative majority. For economic reasons, the best teachers and graduates of teacher-training institutions are not drawn to school employment. The result is reduced quality, competence, and morale of the remaining teaching force, which is still imbued with the certainties and comfort of the totalitarian state.

Paradoxical as it may seem, the same legions of higher education lecturers who for many years were teaching the basics of Marxism and Leninism have now switched, without apparent difficulty, to teaching Westernized social sciences and anthropology. Moreover, a study published by *Sovetskaia pedagogika* in 1991 noted that 57 percent of higher education teachers were not professionally qualified to occupy their positions (i.e., were not competent in subjects they taught).[32] Kerr observes that "textbooks are being revised, but what is more difficult to change is the mindset of those who taught these courses under the old regime, and in many cases continue to teach them today. Even for the most willing new advocate of market principles, it is difficult suddenly to drop years of assumptions, ways of approaching a topic, examples, and methods of assessment."[33] Brodinsky summarizes the views shared with him by former Soviet educators of Nizhnii Novgorod (Volga region) in the following way: "Teachers are still timid, still conformist, still waiting for direction—even as they hear more and more about getting rid of central dictation [of materials and methods]. . . . There is a spirit of "Let's change! Let's become modern." But let's admit it, the corpus is slow in moving, and neither teachers nor higher authorities know where to go."[34]

The growing autonomy of higher education institutions in the countries of the former USSR, which was not backed up by relevant experience, brought confusion to their activities. Essential issues such as enrollment, costs and financing, admission and graduation requirements, standard curriculum design, regulation of student flows, examinations and certificates, etc., remain undetermined. Students are allowed a degree of choice among subjects. With no operational accreditation system in view, the higher educational institutions feel free to call themselves whatever they prefer—college, university, academy, etc.—and issue self-made certificates. They also have to experiment on their own with the length and organization of the school year, teaching materials and methods, management and administration. Tuition fees, still contradicting the valid constitution, are allowed for students enrolled above the quotas imposed by the governments. Open elections of rectors, deans, and other executives are becoming the norm in universities and other higher education institutions, but the role of the rank-and-file and student community in this respect is restricted. For example, elections of the rector at Moscow State University in early 1992 ended in the predictable promotion of the former vice-rector.

Perhaps one of the most evident shortcomings of school reform during the first years of perestroika is that "the rationale of democratization has been wide and unfocused. The old regime has been attacked without the coherent expression of a new philosophy, despite the reassertion by some educators of a progressive view of teaching."[35]

Failure of Soviet-made theory and practice and incompetence in market operations created a high demand for foreign curricula and teaching methods. A Western diploma or certificate is considered the best possible for employment or further education, and serves as an unofficial equivalent of quality of education. One of the consequences is a flow of Russian students to study abroad, another is a rise of cooperation with foreign educators. The first cooperation agreements started under Gorbachev at the government level, but growing demand forced the educational institutions to grasp the initiative and pursue the process on their own as a means of income generation. The majority of cooperation agreements concern higher and postgraduate education, mainly in the fields of economics and business administration, but they rarely cover full courses and normally envisage:

- lectures and seminars by invited foreign professors;
- exchanges of teachers and students;
- use of translated textbooks, tests, exercises, and examination requirements;
- study tours to foreign countries;
- certificates equal to those of a foreign partner, usually bachelor's and master's degrees of a school of business or faculty of economics.

Small private institutions are particularly active in this area and often simply copy all components of training without any cooperation agreements and issue their own certificates. Foreign companies, involved in joint ventures and other business in Russia, prefer to train and retrain their former Soviet personnel abroad.

Entrepreneurial Trends in Higher and Postgraduate Education

Despite the obvious obstacles, the spirit of change and entrepreneurship is penetrating the area of education like a "chain reaction" to the facts of life. As witnessed by V. Karakovskii, a prominent Russian expert in Soviet public education, "Money-exchange relations have come into the schools. Buying and selling has been going on for quite a while—from the most costly items . . . down to what would seem to be harmless trifles, like candy wrappers [*fantiki*, used in the game of forfeits]. Adults look at it and are touched: 'Ahhh, the children are playing *fantiki*.' But the teachers know that a candy wrapper is a form of currency, that it is equivalent to a certain amount of money, and that accounts are settled. We were not able to conquer *fantiki*."[36]

Only after heated and lengthy debates between the conservatives and reformists has the recent Russian legislation on education officially legalized the already existing entrepreneurial activities of educational institutions. These include:

- leasing of real estate, space, and equipment;
- sales of goods and equipment;
- consulting and marketing services;
- shareholding and stock exchange operations, etc.

Nevertheless, these entrepreneurial activities are tax-free only if reinvested in the educational institutions and can be stopped if considered counterproductive to their mandatory educational activities.[37]

At the present time, the vacuum in market competence and/or the correction of any of the deficiencies of past public education is being progressively filled with:

1. economics and business administration courses in public universities and other higher education institutions. Now almost every higher education institution provides such one- to four-year classes on payment of tuition fees. Often, however, these are former "socialist" curriculum subjects such as Marxist political economy with cosmetic adjustments, taught by the same staff. The cooperation agreements with foreign universities described above are more helpful, but are still rare;

2. mushrooming profit-oriented formal and informal private and para-
state institutions of all levels, providing a flexible variety of educational
services. They are able to compete with public education in specialized
postgraduate and/or advanced courses. The bulk of these services provide
continuing education through private, intensive, short-term courses with a
duration of two weeks to one year, designed as an addendum to public
secondary or higher education;

3. extramural education and self-learning methods via the textbooks
and monographs of Western authors, translated and published by both
private and public printshops; the intervention of the mass media, primarily educational TV broadcasting; and the development of correspondence
networks, including open universities.

In this regard, public training and retraining centers set up to promote
awareness of current economic realities among unemployed graduates are
not very effective at present, as they are designed to meet public-sector
employment opportunities.

There are also numerous examples of extracurricular entrepreneurship
initiatives coming "from the bottom" of the higher education institutions
as a means of generating income. For example, at Chuvash State University, an indigenous faculty of "applied commerce" is being established
whose purpose will be to stimulate and coordinate investments of the
students and staff, as well as extramural resources, into the designated
enterprises. The staff and students of Moscow State University decided to
set up their own commercial bank, the University Credit Union. Its primary purpose is to protect the savings of the university community from
inflation and to provide loans at low interest. The University of St. Petersburg is leasing its space to thirteen small-scale private businesses and is
participating in three joint ventures.[38]

Still, these changes and initiatives may not be compatible with the
outdated curriculum of the former USSR secondary and higher-education
institutions. As observed by V. Kinelev, chairman of the Russian State
Committee for Higher Education, "we are trying to make the education
system more dynamic so that it will be able to respond rapidly to all the
fluctuations of a market economy and labor needs. The vital question is to
change the content of the humanities curriculum, which used to contain
too much ideology. It is the most difficult problem for us."[39]

However, these intentions will require substantial efforts to change the
present picture. For instance, the 1990–91 poll among secondary-school
graduates showed that 28 percent are unaware of the term "cost-recovery,"
and 96 percent of the term "cost-effectiveness." In the course of the Janu-

ary 1991 survey in Kuzbass (the Siberian coal-mining region) 49 percent out of the 1,000 secondary school graduates interviewed could not explain the term "market."[40]

Another example explicitly demonstrates the deficiencies of the curriculum in economics in the former USSR. A recipient of a graduate degree in economic sciences from Moscow State University in 1986 reported that "he had had no exposure to the theory of the firm, industrial organization, public finance, game theory, public choice, or anything involving utility functions. Instead, the Soviet student received a thorough background in Marxism, the history of the Communist Party, and a curious hybrid of socialism and marginalism, known as the 'System of Optimal Functioning of the Socialist Economy.' . . . The result was that although this Soviet economist was trained as a professional, the profession in question was not economics—at least not as it is conceived of in the West."[41]

Besides, both the curriculum and teaching methods of present entrepreneurial education and practices are not well coordinated and organized within higher education institutions. In its decision of July 9, 1991, the Russian State Committee for Higher Education has recommended to the higher education institutions the establishment of posts for vice-rectors in charge of student and staff economic support and employment, and business activities.[42]

These activities and initiatives are not necessarily supported by the governmental and local authorities. For example, some decision-making educational authorities such as E. Dneprov, Russian minister of education, emphasized human personality development and subordinated entrepreneurial education to it: ". . . our policy is not driven by economics. We thought that it was important to make the child self-determining, self-finding. Of course, the human personality finds itself in the social and economic spheres. But it is only the free human who can find his place in society. This idea is number one, and notions regarding the transition to a market economy must follow this basic beginning."[43]

Until now, lectures in economics, management, marketing, and so on, have often been a quick remake of classical Western monographs and basics of economics traditionally taught in the USSR. They are at best relevant to a well-established private sector, and have little to do with the current "wild West" situation in the economies of the former USSR and the routine problems of the informal sector and self-employment. The Western mode of market economy competition has not yet been developed in these economies, and newly emerged entrepreneurs now either become monopolists in the local markets (for example, in services accorded by the informal sector and self-employment) or have to fight the state's red tape (at higher levels of organized entrepreneurial activities) as their first priority instead of engaging in market analysis or training their staff in economics. The same 1991 Kuzbass survey discovered that only about 5 percent of those interviewed acquire their knowledge in economics in school, compared to 8 percent from their parents, 31 percent from individual readings, and a tremendous 54 percent from the supportive environment.[44] V. Kadannikov, director-general of the giant "AvtoVaz" company producing "Lada" cars, passed advanced training courses for chief executive officers in the U.S. and then worked abroad. He draws a line between foreign experience and former Soviet realities: "I say to my colleagues most seriously—to train you according to foreign schemes means to spoil you. The practice is turning everything upside down. We live in a country where the red-tape system has already been terminated, but a market system is not yet operational."[45] Even more categorical is M. Khodorkovskii, 29-year-old chairman of the board of directors of MENATEP International Financial Corp., one of the leading financial and banking groups based in Moscow: "My chief executive officers are rarely professional bankers. Mainly they are people with intuition: chemists, road constructors, construction engineers. Either a person understands money making or he does not. Either one understands what will yield profit or one does not. And, what is most amazing, it is impossible to teach it. I can easily train a clerk or a cashier, but education is useless in training someone how to evaluate the prospects of a project."[46]

The explanations for these obvious underestimations of studies in economics on the part of former Soviet entrepreneurs can be:

- many former Soviet managers and entrepreneurs now operating have had no formal education or training in economics and business administration, like Khodorkovskii, a graduate of Moscow Chemical Technology Institute, but were successful in business;
- the links of higher-education institutions with local and national business, industry, and commerce in the area of economics and business administration are not well developed and are largely seen by the latter merely as charity activities;
- the quantitative lack of Soviet-trained, highly qualified specialists in market economics discourages newly emerged entrepreneurs from treating formal entrepreneurial education seriously;
- the actual shortage of resources and paramount opportunity costs fail to make private investments in formal education and training in economics cost-effective.

Moreover, even good Westernized courses develop competence in economics but not necessarily entrepreneurial skills and attitudes. Kerr notes that "perhaps most fundamental to the further development of a free market system is a clear sense of what it means to be an entrepreneur. There is much interest in making a profit (preferably quickly), but little awareness that such activity is accompanied by risk. Willingness to take a reasonable risk is more an attitude than a skill to be learned, but much may depend on the extent to which it can be cultivated among the new businesspeople of Eastern Europe and the NIS (New Independent States)."[47] The result is that such entrepreneurial skills as creativity, initiative taking, problem solving, decision making, leadership, management, team spirit, public relations, etc. are not being developed by the formal educational system but are being disseminated informally among former Soviet youth under the influence of worsened subsistence conditions, better opportunities for business, and Westernized images.

Conclusions

Structural adjustment in the countries of the former USSR is gradually forcing human resources to review their traditional approaches to the means of earning a living, to professional careers, and to the achievement of social status. The process is painful and controversial, particularly in the provinces, where it is often distorted by political turmoil and ethnic conflicts. Middle-aged and older teachers and parent communities in general are reluctant to change their behavior and continue to cherish socialist values and the "command" centrally planned economy. Being less faithful to Soviet values and more socially mobile, the younger generation is adapting better and faster to the new democratic and market environment. Though rather passive in the political sphere, they are increasingly active in grassroots businesses.

The traditions of small-scale entrepreneurship, the informal sector, and self-employment survived through the communist regime and now serve as a basis for the entrepreneurial activities of youth in the countries of the former USSR. They attract students and teenagers due to the obvious advantages of the informal sector in any country—easy access, no need for substantial startup capital outlays, no need for sophisticated technologies and equipment, and minimal requirements for education and training.

The larger-scale corporate private sector is yet to be set up in tough competition with public and cooperative enterprises that are still heavily subsidized by the governments. Employment is shrinking in the public sector and is not equally compensated for in the private sector, so that the unemployed, in particular youths and unemployed graduates, are channeled to the informal sector and to self-employment.

The student community in the countries of the former USSR is passing through a period of change in mentality: from one-way dependence on adults and public-sector employment to indigenous entrepreneurial activism, although many still do not feel the need to prepare for a market economy and rely on their parents.

The opportunity costs of teaching and studying in a large number of higher education institutions of engineering, and in overspecialized technical profiles that previously served the needs of the military-industrial complex, have skyrocketed in the transition to the market, and their prestige and quality have been damaged. Many students and staff now combine studies and lectures in higher education institutions with informal activities and self-employment. The entrepreneurial activities of students are mainly concentrated in the urban services and in the small-scale production sector.

With the end of the period of destruction of totalitarianism and of rigid central planning, and with the societies of the former USSR entering the postcommunist era, a paramount demand is for an increase in the constructive and creative skills to be delivered by higher education and training. Even the most conservative educators, faithful to the past regime, can no longer remain passive observers, as they were recently, and they are forced to react to the changed environment, at least superficially.

However, the public systems of higher and postgraduate education are only slowly making substantive and organizational changes. Many higher education institutions consider entrepreneurial education only as a means to improve their incomes. The lack of a competent and motivated staff and adequate training materials are complicating the situation even when the courses in economics and business administration are delivered for tuition fees.

So far, the private and quasi-state institutions were able to provide only short-term specialized alternatives to public education, first of all in postgraduate education. The potential of cooperation agreements with foreign universities is far from being utilized due to the mutual lack of information and contacts, particularly in the provinces.

The issues of preparing youth for a market economy have not yet been comprehensively addressed by the public and local educational authorities; they depend on the initiatives on behalf of educational institutions and students themselves. The links of higher education institutions with local and national private business, industry, and commerce are incidental, largely viewed as charity and not as a serious channel of communications and transfer of competence.

At present, formal entrepreneurial education in the former USSR higher and postgraduate education is largely aimed at classical economic theory and competence to manage a well-established private sector. It is rarely relevant to the initial stages of privatization underway in the former USSR economies and to daily informal sector and self-employment problems, and does not assist the growing number of unemployed graduates. At present, under former Soviet conditions, fighting red tape appears to be a higher priority for newly emerged entrepreneurs than a deeper knowledge of economics and business administration. The demand for the development of entrepreneurial skills—problem solving, initiative taking, creativity, etc.—is not being met.

The trend toward more and better human resources development in the countries of the former USSR, including entrepreneurial formal and nonformal education, is inevitable. The challenge is to promote, coordinate, and organize the process in appropriate forms according to the demands of democratic societies and labor markets, and youth aspirations.

The central and local education authorities in the countries of the former USSR are facing a necessity to collaborate with national and foreign higher education institutions, as well as industry and commerce, in dealing with such pressing issues of entrepreneurial education as:

1. a need for updated curricula and training materials in economics, management, and business administration for the different levels and types of education, training, and self-learning adjusted to contemporary conditions, i.e., with more emphasis on practicalities and externalities of the initial period of economic activities, including informal sector and self-employment operations;

2. designing in-service teacher training and retraining schemes to improve the competence of trainers and the quality of instruction in economics and business administration, together with qualitative, market-oriented changes in teacher-training institutions;

3. creating national networks of focal points for entrepreneurial education for coordination of activities and better dissemination of positive experience, under the auspices of educational institutions, industrial and commercial entities, mass media, etc.

Given the scale of the countries of the former USSR, these and other measures ought to be organized and coordinated within the framework of a series of countrywide projects and programs sponsored by the governments, educational authorities, and institutions, together with national and foreign industry and commerce.

Notes

1. *Poisk* [Search], 1992, no. 12.
2. *The Financial Times*, 13 July 1992.
3. G. Grossman, "Informal Personal Incomes and Outlays of the Soviet Urban Population." In *The Informal Economy: Studies in Advanced and Less Developed Countries*, eds. A. Portes et al. (Baltimore and London: The Johns Hopkins University Press, 1989), p. 164.
4. *The International Herald Tribune*, 28–29 December 1991.
5. E. Laszlo, "Changing Realities of Contemporary Leadership: New Opportunities for Eastern Europe," *Futures*, 1992, vol. 24, no. 2, p. 172.
6. *Poisk*, 1992, no. 17.
7. Ibid., 1992, no. 15.
8. *Stolitza* [Capital], 1992, no. 31.
9. *Pravda*, 4 August 1992.
10. *Poisk*, 1992, no. 13.
11. B. Brodinsky, "The Impact of *Perestroika* on Soviet Education," *Phi Delta Kappan*, 1992, vol. 73, no. 5, p. 385.
12. *The OECD Observer*, "Radical Reform for the Soviet Union," 1992, no. 169, p. 11.
13. *Moskvichka* [Muscovite], 29 May–4 June 1992.
14. A. G. Frank, "Economic Ironies in Europe: A World Economic Interpretation of East-West European Politics," *International Social Science Journal*, 1992, no. 131, p. 49.
15. J. M. Pogodzinski and C. Antes, "The Transition from Central Planning to a Market Economy: A Computable General Equilibrium Model," *Economics of Planning*, 1992, vol. 25, no. 2, p. 140.
16. *The Economist*, 20 June 1992, p. 77.
17. *The International Herald Tribune*, 28–29 December 1991.
18. Ibid.
19. *Birzhevye novosti* [Stock Exchange News], 1992, no. 14.
20. N. Grant, "Education in the Soviet Union: The Last Phase," *Compare: A Journal of Comparative Education*, 1992, vol. 22, no. 1, p. 78.
21. *The European*, 9–12 April 1992.
22. F. I. Peregudov, "Restructuring the Vocational School," *Russian Education and Society*, 1992, vol. 34, no. 7, p. 70.
23. A. M. Sandi, "Restoring Civil Societies in Central and Eastern Europe," *Futures*, 1992, vol. 24, no. 2, p. 110.
24. See "Youth and Society" in *Russian Education and Society* (July 1992), vol. 34, no. 7, p. 7.
25. *Poisk*, 1992, no. 12.
26. E. D. Novozhilov, "Vocational Training of Students in the Period of Economic Reform," *Sovetskaia pedagogika*, 1992, nos. 1–2, pp. 28–29.
27. Idem, "Graduates of Educational Institutions in Transition to Market," *Sovetskaia pedagogika*, 1991, no. 9, p. 13.
28. B. Hamm, "Europe—A Challenge to the Social Sciences," *International Social Science Journal*, 1992, no. 131, p. 13.

29. Peregudov, "Restructuring the Vocational School," p. 72.

30. A. Savelyev, "Reconstruction of Higher Education in the USSR," *Higher Education Policy*, 1989, vol. 2, no. 1, p. 35.

31. E. A. Weinberg, "*Perestroika* and Soviet Sociology," *The British Journal of Sociology*, 1992, vol. 43, no. 1, p. 5.

32. Novozhilov, "Graduates of Educational Institutions."

33. S. T. Kerr, "Democracy and the Free Market in the NIS and Eastern Europe," *Academy News*, 1992, vol. 15, no. 1, p. 2.

34. Brodinsky, "The Impact of *Perestroika*," p. 380.

35. M. McLean and N. Voskresenskaya, "Educational Revolution from Above: Thatcher's Britain and Gorbachev's Soviet Union," *Comparative Education Review*, 1992, vol. 36, no. 1, p. 86.

36. See "Youth and Society" in *Russian Education and Society*, vol. 34, no. 7 (July 1992), p. 21.

37. *Uchitel'skaia gazeta*, no. 28, 4 August 1992.

38. *Poisk*, 1992, no. 2.

39. *The Times Higher Education Supplement*, 27 March 1992.

40. *Sovetskaia pedagogika*, 1991, no. 9; Novozhilov, "Graduates of Educational Institutions."

41. Alexeev, M. et al. 1992. "Economics in the Former Soviet Union," *Journal of Economic Perspectives*, vol. 6, no. 2, p. 139.

42. *Poisk*, 1992, no. 31.

43. V. D. Rust, "School Reform in the Russian Republic. An Interview with Edward Dneprov," *Phi Delta Kappan*, 1992, vol. 73, no. 5, p. 376.

44. Novozhilov, "Graduates of Educational Institutions."

45. *Moskovskie novosti* [Moscow News], no. 32, 9 August 1992.

46. *Stolitza*, 1992, no. 32.

47. Kerr, "Democracy and the Free Market," p. 8.

Index

DATE DUE

			Printed in USA

HIGHSMITH #45230